A.

Why did you not
visit me in sunny
Moscow?

Love Ego.   4.5.01

FALTERING SPRING

Letters from Moscow

Ekkehard Schirrmacher

MINERVA PRESS
LONDON
MIAMI   DELHI   SYDNEY

ISBN 0 75410 955 0

First Published 2000 by
MINERVA PRESS
315–317 Regent Street
London W1R 7YB

Printed in Great Britain for Minerva Press

FALTERING SPRING
Letters from Moscow

A portrait of economic, political, social, religious
and cultural life in modern Russia in the late 1990s,
as seen through the eyes of an expatriate businessman
who lived, worked and travelled widely
among the diverse people of this vast land in transition.

*This collection of letters is dedicated, with love, to my wife,
Mary Ann and my daughters, Katherine, Laura and Gemma.
Without their constant support and understanding I would not
have been able to spend time in Moscow and wider Russia
to experience at first hand the trauma of the rebirth of a nation
in transition. While I was away, Mary kept the household
and family in perfect order, ready for my return.*

*It is also dedicated to the well-being of the Russian people,
who struggle through adversity and misunderstanding
to rebuild hope in their land and their historic future.
Their everlasting patience has been a revelation.*

'There is only one good – knowledge.
There is only one evil – ignorance.'

Diogenes

Acknowledgements for the Pictures, Maps and Cartoons

The sources for the pictures, maps and cartoons are:

- My wife, Mary Ann.
- Theresa McCurrich, my daughter Katherine's friend.
- My own, using Mary's camera in Uzbekistan.
- The cartoons are from The *Moscow Times* and *The eXile*. The artists are: Romon Papsuev of *The eXile* and Igor Shein, Konstantin Koukso, Viktor Balabas, Viktor Bogorad, Igar Revyakin of The *Moscow Times*. Both papers have kindly granted rights for reproduction.
- The reprints from *Zavtra* newspaper in Chapter VI have been allowed by their editorial department – my thanks also to them.

Map of Russia

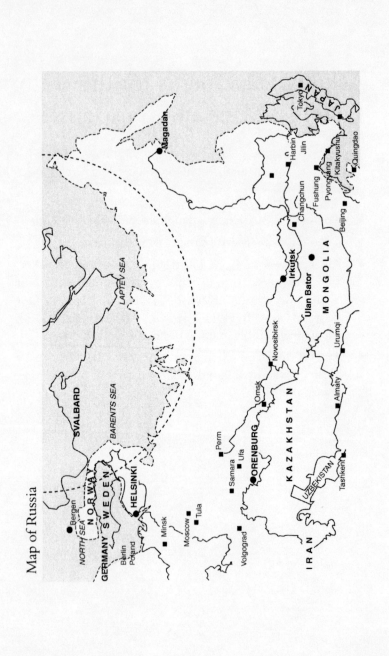

International Time Zones Map

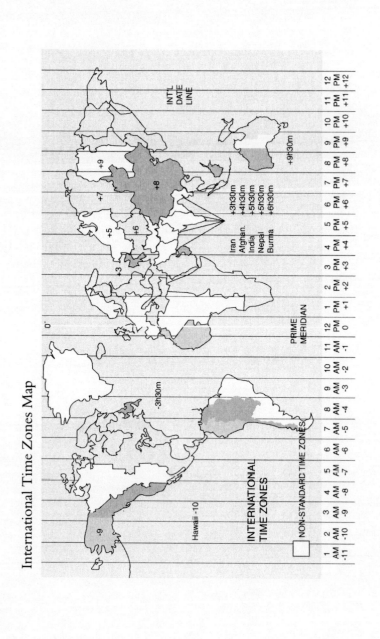

About the Author

Born in 1943 in former East Germany, Ekkehard Schirrmacher, now a British Citizen, has lived, worked and been educated in the UK since the age of five. After many years in senior commercial management, including two PLC directorships, and extensive international travel in the course of his work, he found his way to Russia between 1995 and 1999. He initially trained as an accountant and gained his MBA from Cranfield School of Management in 1969. This is his first book.

Introduction and Additional Author's Notes

Modern Russia is a fascinating, enigmatic, confusing, dangerous, frustrating, exciting, but fundamentally troubled land. A true mixture of enquiry and ambivalence with a healthy dose of scepticism is possibly the most appropriate approach to the local learning experience. Not all one sees or hears should be taken at face value in judging or understanding this country. There is much more than initially meets the eye simmering beneath an apparent changing exterior. Little about the place is ever simplistic. The Russian ability to make simple matters complicated is legion, particularly those that in our Western opinion are elementary and logical. We have to accept that Russian logic and ours in the West are on different planets. When a country such as the former Soviet Union is in such fundamental transition, we should throw away past preconceptions and look anew at their search for a national identity and reason for being. In truth, the former Tsarist Empire and the former Soviet Union were really only held together by central oppression. That unravelled in 1991 and continues within the Russia of today. We should accept that their way of doing things is not ours. It is not better or worse, just different. These pages try to explore those differences and endeavour to touch all sides of a complex equation.

These pages also attempt to delve into and explain some of the many myths and riddles surrounding the Western public perception of this land. Experiences gained, first hand, over some four years and compiled as 'letters home' is the medium chosen. To some that may mean an apparent superficial rather than an academic approach. This book is no attempt to be a work of scholarship. It is not a travel guide, nor is it an economic essay, or even a political history of modern times. Some say it does not easily fit onto the specialist segmented and category shelves of a book shop. Social anthropology is possibly the nearest generic description. Some who have read earlier drafts have encouraged me to rewrite the entire work to be more specific in its chapters, to fit a clearer target audience and identifiable place on the bookshelf. However, after much thought, I have left the basic style and structure as originally envisaged because the complexity of the subject requires a degree of spontaneity that only the medium of letters and personal observations can give.

Despite many searches on diverse bookshelves in Western shops, I have as yet not found another comprehensive portrayal of ordinary life in the Russia of today. I failed to find descriptions of daily toil near the end of the millennium for the average Russian trying to regain his self-respect. To fill that perceived gap, I believe the efforts and time to compile this work have been worthwhile. Others have told me that these pages have opened their eyes, but it would sell more and have been published earlier if I were a widely-known personality. However, I am an ordinary person describing ordinary life in a country full of ordinary people. The response to changing circumstances by these ordinary individuals is a fascinating story that needs to be told. Have patience with the text as it unfolds from the first days of arrival in June 1995 and through both periods of permanent life as an expatriate businessman over nearly four years. Each letter or chapter should be read in conjunction with the date it was completed. Each chapter tells a separate story. But the whole completes the wider picture. Only thus does the development of the experience make sense.

Potentially Russia is one of the world's richest countries, if the untapped natural mineral resources in the globe's largest single political surface area could be developed for the common good. The urgent goal of regeneration could thus be achieved, by a highly educated population, for the benefit of all the community. This, including the rebuilding of a grey and dehumanising Soviet infrastructure created by eighty and more years of totalitarian rule and neglect. That is the tantalising potential achievement of a currently dispirited and rudderless people. Yet there are those who have grasped the new capitalist realities as entrepreneurs, with similar characteristics reminiscent of the American continent in the past age of the 'Wild West' culture. Within a vacuum currently bereft of acceptable legal, political, economic or social structures, these individual Russians have truly created fortunes in the new 'Wild East' since the demise of Communism in 1991.

Many of them also lost their gains in the crash of 1998. History will show that the failed policies of Gaidar, and compounded by Yeltsin and Chernomyrdin, had their origins in the mad scramble for unregulated capitalism in the vacuum so evident in 1991. That bubble so abruptly unravelled with such serious consequences in 1998. Few commentators during those panic days of the August 1998 crash saw the origins of this further blow to ordinary folk in the failed privatisation policies of Chubais and his cronies within the 'oligarchy'. The media and the financial markets saw only the events 'of the day' and dramatised them with knee-jerk reactions. Having lived in Moscow during those dismal days, it made the difference between the daily struggle and a historical perspective understandably difficult. The following pages try to disentangle these and many other contradictions that are so evident in today's

Russia.

Some of the former Communist countries in what we now call central Europe have embraced the concepts of democracy and capitalism with both vigour as well as conviction. Unfortunately in Russia, the ideological systems we call Bolshevism and democracy as well as the concept of modern market capitalism are all still in conflict. Not only do the ideas themselves clash, but more importantly for Russia's transition, the methods used to implement democracy and capitalism are being managed by individuals still steeped in the failed Bolshevik politics of former days. Until a new generation has emerged that has no attendant baggage from past ideologies, it is hard to see that the Western-style concepts and methods required to develop local capitalism and democracy, as we know them, will have definitions that we understand, or more importantly take root here.

The sometimes benevolent dictatorship of Tsarist Russia, followed by stifling Communist oppression and now ruled by a so-called democratic government, has left a population, increasingly bewildered and disillusioned, but searching for a clear identity while living in a crumbling infrastructure. Their history has never allowed free and unfettered self-expression for all. Dare they take the bold steps into an unknown tomorrow with a clarity of vision? Or do they continue to fear their future based on their turbulent heritage? Invaded in the last 1,000 years from east, north, west and south by, among many others, Mongols, Swedes, French, Germans, and British, the successors to the ancient kingdom of Kiev Rus and the emerging state of Muscovy (ruled between 1263 and 1276 by Prince Daniel, generally regarded as the founder of the Moscow dynasty and the youngest offspring of one of Russia's greatest sons – Alexander Nevsky) are faced with fateful choices. The now ever-present tsarist double-headed eagle may represent both a longing for the 'comforting' past as well as a hope for a new democratic, economic and constitutional glory.

Faltering steps to create a modern democracy have begun, but based on no historical tradition of a voice for all or training on how to use it when at last achieved. Nor do they currently fully understand the individual and collective responsibilities that are part of that democratic process in our Western comprehension of such principles. Capitalism is rampant, but without the checks, balances and regulations we have introduced to protect the individual. To recreate in less than a decade a political, social, legal and economic structure, that took centuries in Western Europe, is a monumental and as yet undelivered task. Much has been achieved in the short years since 1991, although much has yet to be accomplished. At the same time, there is a danger that their current democratic and economic dream could tip back into a gloomy past. Sadly for them, the longer-term effects of the events following the 1998 economic crash are yet to be felt in full. The initial view would indicate that more steps were taken backwards than forwards. Hence the title to this book, which expresses hope but at the same time retains a large degree of caution. But then the rocky road to fame and fortune was never easy.

Russians regard 1991 as the date of their freedom from past totalitarian oppression. To achieve their goals they require ingenuity, vision, time, money, patience from the West and most importantly of all – leaders of stature and repute. Ingenuity is ever present, but the remainder are in increasingly short supply. To add to the problem of finding politicians of stature, is the murky divide between the interests of big business and that of the political elite.

Some would tell you that the business 'oligarchy' actually runs Russia. Thus the people are truly trapped at the crossroads of the pain of their violent past and their uncertain future.

Since 1991 they have had to come to terms with the loss of superpower status as well as realise that: they did not reside in the 'paradise' hailed by their former Communist masters; they live within an economic, social and security vacuum created by the destruction of one political system, while the fabric of another as yet eludes the imagination of their emerging democracy; and to cap it all, they have become one of the largest debtor nations in the world today. Their new-found inability to feed themselves from the harvest of their land is but a symptom of the loss of individual initiative of a highly-educated population searching for self-confidence and a clear identity on the world's new stage. We should not be surprised at the resultant continuing economic, social, political chaos and individual personal despair affecting the majority. Nor should we be surprised at the personal hurt that such a fall from past influence has left with some of the constituents of an ever-proud nation.

I have been granted the privilege to glimpse a little of the enigma that is Russia today over a four-year period. For nearly two years I lived in Moscow, in 1995 and 1996. Followed by regular visits in 1997 and a second spell of permanent life in Moscow in 1998 and early 1999. From that experience, the following is but a glance behind the curtain the Russian people have learnt, over many years, with which to surround their conscious national being. Today they remain a proud, but have also become a disillusioned, nation. Their apparent patience is legion. We in the West would not accept their problems as they do. They bear many troubles with equanimity, but are capable of intense emotional reaction. We should beware of the signals of their true distress. The reaction, when and if it comes, will be not from the ideological or political head, but from the 'gut' and the heart.

An initial occasional letter to family and friends in my home country, England, to inform them of my varied experiences, developed into a desire to record a fascination and frustration with this land of diverse ethnic peoples, politics, geography, and its challenges for future development. The letters, by the very nature of personal communication, contain my prejudices, ambivalence to the land and its people and often express my own opinion. You should therefore, not be surprised at the combination of wonder, doubt and conviction at the events experienced and described in these pages. Through the medium of using regular letters to communicate my thoughts, what follows is based on continuing experience of events in this land. It also tells a story, rather than being a work of academia. Some material is anecdotal, some is from public data and personal research, most is gleaned from personal experience.

Due to the nature of the land and the people, as well as their responses to change, over the four years in which these words have been in preparation, I have altered my position towards their future and the conclusions I draw. Such is the pace of change and speed of events that one can only watch in awe the reaction of the people to constant flux. Such singular encounters cannot easily be transmitted in one written attempt, thus the combination of letters represents recollections of my life among Russians in Moscow and some other parts of this vast land over successive months, then sent to my friends. They are now edited and collated as a whole and completely updated with new thoughts on current events. On occasions, repetitions occur in consecutive letters. Some, but not all, have been removed on editing, as it could detract from the message.

Yeltsin is no longer president of the Russian Federation. Maybe he is in name, but not in spirit or in deed. He has now become a national irrelevance at best, and a serious destabilising liability at worst. But his legacy will affect the future. His achievements as it turned out were few. His prolonged illness in 1996, recovery from heart surgery and then a further period of pneumonia created governmental intrigue and paralysis at the same time. History will not thank him for the additional price his people have paid while they waited for his recovery. His gathering irrationality and recurring medical state in 1998 gained no plaudits from friend or foe. His demise was ignominious for himself and his people. However, if he has a legacy, it may have been a six-year period of relative, in Russian terms, stability from the confusion of the years between 1989 and 1993, while the population came to terms with the challenges of new capitalist realities. But what will happen post his final demise is a chapter yet to be recorded. These pages describe more than the influence of one man. They are the totality of experience in the time I lived in Russia, and conclusions on what might happen in the future. The continued presidential existence, or not, of one man will, in the short term, have little effect on the solution of the multitudinous Russian problems. Having said that, there may have been some contrary good for the Russian people in the forcible removal from office of General Alexander Lebed in October 1996. He could turn out to be a true focus for the people's democratic opposition in the coming months or years, if the newly-reconstructed Communist Party does not take this constitutional role seriously. Others may believe their fate to be determined by Yuri Luzhkov (the enigmatic mayor of Moscow) as a future leader. Do not either rule out the potential of Primakov being a possible contender. History will tell us what will happen in 1999 and beyond. These pages try to find out why. The competence of Russians to create abundant intrigue is such that political alliances are made and broken for personal enrichment rather than national duty. I, for one, will be awaiting political events with more than a passing interest. The words that follow will not fade just because political personalities change. Because of the depth and complexity of modern Russia's challenges, the basic thoughts expressed in these pages will, in my opinion, remain true for many years to come.

The task the Russian people have in front of them is huge. There will be many failures on the way, before they again, one day in the future, participate as economic and political equals on the modern world stage among the 'greats'. In the meantime, they suffer the pangs of a nation in withdrawal. The previously hopeful glimpse of a national democratic and economic spring shows signs of faltering. The public sector of the economy is at best moribund, and at worst bankrupt. However, the growth and wealth of the emerging private sector, particularly in Moscow until 1998 was quite staggering. Since its creation in 1991 some estimated this new-found wealth to equal forty per cent of total GDP in 1997. In the twenty-eight years I have lived in the West Midlands, I can count two millionaires among my acquaintances. In my four-year association with Russia I can easily think of twenty-five friends or colleagues who have that status. But the split, between the rich centre – Moscow – and the regions, just as between the rich and poor population, grows ever wider by the day. The 1997 list of the world's richest people in *Forbes* magazine counted three Russians in the top fifty wealthiest on this earth. Quite whether these fortunes were made with the same requirements of honesty and integrity as is demanded by our Western legal and governmental authorities is of course open to debate. What is fact is that their gathered wealth is larger than many fortunes made in the Middle East of the late seventies and early eighties. It is also true that the turbulent environment of the mid-nineties allowed the few to gain at the expense of the many. The 'New Russians' display their winnings with alacrity. In 1997, some statistics will tell you that eleven per cent of world tourist spending emanates from this land. Yet multitudes across the land remain poor and dispossessed. Nor have they moved out of the area of their roots and seen another world. The resulting ambivalence about investment in the country by foreign companies is thus understandable given the apparent contradictions and uncertainties. Economic theory tells us that the untold potential wealth of the land gives rise to further optimism. Current economic management leads one to the conclusion that such thoughts are entirely misplaced. Had capital flight, non-payment of taxes or corruption not occurred at some estimated levels since 1991, then this alone, according to some, could have contributed an additional $600 billion to national wealth. Then the nature of this book would have been completely different. But that money never flowed for national regeneration. No default, no crash of 1998, no unpaid wages, no banking crisis could have been the prize. But then, 'This is Russia.' It just does not work in our apparent 'normality'.

There are many doubts if their current leaders, or even those who stand in the wings, are of the stature this moment in history demands for the development of national salvation. I share those concerns. As such we should not abandon the people in their hour of need. If we do, the proud Russian bear may once again become a potential isolationist threat to our own way of life. If I can assist in the process of mutual understanding, then I will have been of some minor use to the Russians in their thankless but historic task. In the course of these pages I have tried accurately to record my personal experiences, the views and thoughts expressed by the many Russians I have met and grown to respect and the Byzantine habits of their current rulers.

Comment is made in various chapters about the manner in which the Western press reports events in Russia today on many an occasion. But we all know that the media only reports what sells a story for today. Unfortunately we live in an age of five-minute 'sound bites' that apparently represent the truth. The overall impression of the country I had before I went, was broadly correct, the reasons behind the story were often not, or then misreported. And certainly little had prepared me for the reality of ordinary life. I see the trauma of this land from my entirely individual perspective, and stand by my right to view life here through my, and not their, journalistic licence.

Throughout the letters, I predominantly use two currencies. The US $ and the Rouble. The former is the unofficial alternative monetary exchange for Russians, although illegal to use for purchases. Where the Rouble will end up is anybody's guess. In recent times it has become dangerously unstable. When I first landed in Moscow in 1995 one could exchange $1 for Rbl.4,400. By December 1997 the Dollar/Rouble value had fallen to 5,960. The 1 January 1998 saw a re-denomination, which deleted the '000s'. The day before devaluation, on the 17 August 1998, there were Rbl.6.25 to $1. On the day of completion of the manuscript in early January 1999, Rbl.20.86 purchased $1 on the official exchange. It was about Rbl.22.5 to $1 in the street exchange booths. Thus over a four-year period, the Rouble's purchasing power had fallen by just under a factor of 5. Most of this occurring in just the last four months of 1998. We must expect more pain and decline to come. Some gloomy pundits tell us to expect Rbl.40 to $1 by the end of 1999.

As a naturalised Englishman of East German extraction, having lived in the UK for forty-nine of my fifty-six years, I learnt the hard lesson of acceptance as a boy after the war.

In Russia, even earnest foreign scholars of their way of life may not be taken to their complicated bosom after fifty or more years. They are adamant that they were the rightful victors of the Second World War and feel aggrieved that the Western allies still do not recognise their contribution to the full. They call it 'The Great Patriotic War'. Living among the Russians gives credence to their belief. The Russian absolute conviction in the different sanctity of their life and heritage is so inviolate that they believe only they have a sole right to local wisdom. Despite this I have tried, from a feeble Western perspective, to enter their world and record my impressions.

Some in Moscow have warned me that certain influential Russian apparatchik and 'New Russians' may not like my comments about them and their medieval methods. It has even been suggested that my security will be at risk if I publish. Others have said that I should be careful on any future visits. If these warnings be true, that only goes to show the depths these archaic individuals have fallen to try to make a point. If it happens, their point will have backfired. I will make mine in a civilised manner as befits a mature member of the modern human race. The ordinary Russians I have met and grown to admire require that response.

My family was split by the legacy of two dictators – Hitler and Stalin. My father protected my mother, brother and myself from the advancing Russian army after the war. But that split family and heritage. The scientific background to my family and life as a youth made contact with the reasons for those events many years ago more than difficult. Were my father still alive, I often wondered while writing these letters what he would have made of the decline of influence of Russia today.

Before editing and compiling this compendium of past letters, a number of Russian friends and acquaintances were asked to read all, or parts, of the manuscript and comment, to check any factual errors and to critique the descriptions of their national and individual psyche. I am therefore enormously grateful to, among others, Marina Belenkaya, Svetlana Abramova, Irina Gyreva, Victor Sokolov, Andrei Sokolik, Father Gennadi and Slav Gregoriov for taking the time to compare my thoughts to theirs. Their help, guidance and advice has been recognised during the editing process. Where relevant, changes have been made to the original letters as a result. The end product, however, remains my entirely personal view.

My sincere thanks also to the many unwitting contributors to the anecdotal evidence recalled in these pages. Where historical events have moved on since writing the original letters, footnotes have since been added or the words updated. For security reasons, I am unable to reveal some of my other varied sources of information in high places, but I respect their input and deep concern for the fate and future of their land. History will vouch to the veracity of their contribution to my completed composition. Most economic data mentioned has been gleaned from public sources in Moscow and the UK, and is accordingly annotated as to the source.

Ekkehard Schirrmacher
Moscow, January 1999

Both political cartoons, almost exactly two years apart (20/2/97 and 19/3/99) and both without a title, appeared in The *Moscow Times*. They encapsulate the mood of the time without any further comment being needed in the interpretation of the resurgent national emblem – the double-headed eagle...

Contents

Chapter I
Some Reasons for Adventure
June 1995

'Extracts from a Later Letter'

Like millions of others, my future life was totally changed by wartime events over fifty years ago. The subsequent meeting of the Russian and American armies in Torgau on the River Elbe just prior to armistice added further personal poignancy. This town of my birth had been home to my family for many generations. In 1948 the UK became my home and gave me a new chance in life. The family business, founded around 1630, was one of the few, even under Communist rule, after the war, that remained in the private hands of the family left behind. It continues so today. Who knows what might have been different for me, my brother and parents – 'if'? None of us can turn back the clock or change the course of history. Looking back is a distinctly negative pastime, although we surely are allowed to wonder – what if? What is evident, is that the former USSR and its successor – the Russian Federation – dominated the environment of those in my family who remained behind the 'curtain', and equally affected the few of us who 'escaped'. From 1945 till 1989 when the Iron Curtain finally came down, Communist ideology and Western counter-politics were dominant for them and for us. This ever-present political nonsense affected my knowledge and understanding of, and communication with, those left behind to live a then unknown life.

An inner desire had always nagged within to find out more of my past and what had shaped parental thought. What was this place and ideology that had split families, communities and nations, and held the rest of the world to ransom during the period of the Cold War? Unless and until full interchange occurred between the peoples of East and West, what lay behind the impenetrable barrier of Stalin's construction would not only remain a mystery to most of us, but continue to split mine and thousands of other families who had suffered a similar fate. Minor attempts to try to find out and seek to travel there had come to naught in my youth, and no commercial opportunities to do so had, as yet, come my way in later years.

Like most of us, I too was influenced by the media as to the apparent state of affairs east of Dresden, Leipzig and beyond into the lair of the 'Evil Empire' as former US President Ronald Reagan naïvely branded them. Without knowledge of our past, how can most of us examine the future with ease? If we cannot fully understand our yesterday or today, we cannot deal with tomorrow as complete individuals. History and its legacy surely mould not only nations, but individuals as well. The true symbols of my cultural heritage in central Europe were merely pages in a faded and almost forgotten book. They had never become part of my conscious adult being. I was missing something.

It was with joy and anticipation therefore that in 1989, just before the Berlin Wall finally collapsed, that I went back expectant, after forty-one years, to the land and town of my birth. The experience was both emotional and thought provoking. But... what events and people had produced: this crumbling infrastructure? This fear of us? True ignorance of our lifestyle, and ours of theirs? A people who lived in a time capsule and had lost the art of individual thought? Sixty-five years of tyranny under Hitler and his Communist successors had savagely disturbed their lives. I was clearly the one who had led a lucky life. I hardly knew them or their circumstances when the time came to revisit. The myth, built up by years of Western media indoctrination of an industrial and military power with the might to threaten our Western existence, began to crumble. However, East Germany, as it was then, was merely a satellite state of the ultimate paymaster – the USSR – now the Russian Federation.

In early 1995, after an unfortunate business experience had created more than enough free time, at last an opportunity to find out a little of the 'bigger picture' in Russia came my way. It was too good to miss. Here, at last, was the chance to place the final piece in the jigsaw of understanding fully what kind of people and policies had dominated the thoughts and actions of a disrupted family. Not only had the tentacles of Russian political thought and deeds created a particular individual and stilted perception of their domain for me, but it had affected the lives of every man, woman and child in the rest of the world. Western governmental foreign policy and spending on defence had been totally directed towards protection against an apparently all-powerful enemy and military machine. This, on the assumption that they might one day steamroller us as they had Poland, Hungary, Bulgaria, Czechoslovakia and many other lands in Eastern Europe in the past. The legacy of one madman – Hitler – had been compounded and replicated by another – Stalin. So it was with more than eager anticipation, accompanied with just a little trepidation, that I landed at Sheremetevo airport in Moscow on a hot, humid and sunny day in June 1995…

…In a free moment during their many talks, former President Gorbachev is alleged to have joked with Ronald Reagan. He said to the American president that he had both good and bad news. 'Well, Mikhail, tell me the good news.' The discourse continued with the disclosure that Lenin's mother had recently been found to be still alive in rural Siberia with a new world record for longevity.

'Oh that is interesting,' retorted Reagan.

'What then is the bad news?'

'She is pregnant,' came Gorby's reply...

...Please indulge me one last thought. ...What would this Russia? ...Their democratic, economic and social condition? ...Their true role in world events? ...Their relations with us in the West over the last fifty years? ...And my future life have been like ...if Churchill had succeeded in persuading the Americans and other wartime allies to turn the German army around and jointly face and conquer these Eastern lands in 1945? ...If? ...But as has been said before, looking back is a distinctly negative pastime.

Chapter II
Where is Reality?
April 1996

In 1918, a Red Army leaflet[1] explained to young recruits why the Red Star appeared on the Soviet Flag and on their uniforms. It said: 'There was apparently once a beautiful maiden called Pravda (truth) who had a burning red star on her forehead which lit up the whole world and brought it truth, justice and happiness. One day the red star was stolen by Krivda (falsehood) who wanted to bring darkness and evil to the world. Thus began the rule of Krivda. Meanwhile Pravda called on the people to retrieve her star and return the light of truth to the world. A good youth then apparently conquered Krivda and her forces and returned the red star to Pravda. Whereupon the evil forces ran away from the light, like owls and bats, and once again the people lived by truth.' The leaflet made the parable clear: the Red Army were the brave lads fighting Krivda and her evil supporters, and the red star became their symbol to protect the poor peasants and workers and lead them in their fight for truth. Somehow I feel that history shows that this particular tale was told the wrong way round by the Communist leaders of the time.

Some will also in similar vein associate the colour red with all the Communist regimes of the world. Those who believe that this comes from another post-revolutionary

---

[1] According to Orlando Figes in his book 'A Peoples' Tragedy'.

myth are incorrect. The Russian word for beautiful is *krasiva,* and that for red is *krasnoi.* In time they became mixed. Thus Red Square in Moscow should properly be called 'Beautiful Square' with no political connections and as the 1917 revolution was held by the Communists to be a beautiful event, the colour red thereafter symbolised the Communist Party that came to power. Hence the colour and star of the still current Russian Army, the past flag in the USSR and that in China today.

On the subject of the Communist Party, we often use the word 'Bolshy' in our language. The origin is Russian. In Russian, *Bolshoi* means big. *Bolshevik* means majority. In 1906 at a revolutionary meeting in St Petersburg, a vote on a minor political matter was taken. Lenin won the vote and Trotsky lost. Forever thereafter the terms *Bolshevik* (majority) and *Menshevik* (minority) have crept into worldwide usage as ideological labels based on a simple myth of language misuse. Another story tells us that the later tsars were fanatical about railways. Nicholas I developed the important line joining the major cities of St Petersburg and Moscow. He apparently took many ideas from the expansion of the British network. According to some[2] the Russian name for a railway station – *Voksal* – emanates from the story that when he and his family travelled in Britain they always appeared to alight at or pass through Vauxhall station.

Who knows the truth to any of these stories. What is true, is that over time one realises that nothing in this country should be taken at face value on first encounter. There is always a hidden meaning or explanation behind all that happens here. Over the years of developing the thoughts expressed on these pages, it became apparent that the process of change is so great in this emerging democ-

---

[2]Channel 4 TV News on 29 September 1997.

racy that it is better to say nothing if lack of knowledge or insufficient close contact prevents more detailed involvement. A pity that the media circus reporting on events in this land do not heed a similar lesson.

Other pieces of useless information come to mind but the above may give some flavour of the sort of myths and misunderstanding we have spun over years of mutual lack of contact. The title of this chapter poses a question many have tried to answer about this confusing country. Every state has associated myths, misconceptions and an abundance of historical legends. Russia appears to have more than its fair share of such anecdotes and hence resulting impressions are often garbled. I can only try to scratch the surface. Many of the rest of these pages endeavour to delve deeper. Whether the analysis is correct depends to a large extent on having asked the correct initial questions. Hopefully I have. What is certainly true, is, that Russia contains more myths and riddles, many as yet unknown to us Westerners, than many other nations on earth. Possibly in a country ruled by propaganda for so many years, affecting even ourselves, after time both they and we began to believe what often turns out through later events to be untrue.

Such myths continue today in the way we view much of what happens here. Since arriving here, it is clear from the Western press reports that I saw prior to my arrival and while living in Moscow that our media misreports many of the Russian problems and opportunities in a social, economic and political sense. They only see the negative. Much mutual misunderstanding results. Fear of Russia and its political intentions remains. But such is the media all over the world. What is superficially true is that this is a far more difficult place for the foreigner to live in than might be expected from a former superpower.[3] Eighty and more years of neglect and totalitarianism have taken their toll. It shows in the attitudes of the people and the infrastructure surrounding daily life. Logic is not a word to use about daily life. Many of the communication failures between East and West are a direct consequence of the Iron Curtain that separated understanding in either direction for so long. Our press unfortunately continues to exacerbate and encourage this divide. Even in these days of freedom of speech and instant communications, the divide of misconception remains.[4]

The *Financial Times* particularly ought to know better as they are reputed to have a stake in Financial *Isvestia*, the equally pink financial supplement appearing in the old *Isvestia* newspaper. They report, but late, and then it seems to me, in an incomplete manner. They, and others still report matters in a biased and often governmental sponsored way, or as they believe it suits the West. They hail 'reformers' in the mould of our Western ideal, without a thought of what might be good for Russia. The names of Gorbachev and Chubais come to mind as favourites in the West. An average Russian would vehemently disagree. But then correspondents here do the same as elsewhere – produce sound bites for mass appeal gleaned by hanging around the Foreign Ministry press centre near Park Kultury Metro Station. I am told that the beer there is cheaper than elsewhere. They rarely go to the regions or out to the heart of true Russian tradition where the real people live. The

---

[3]In 1995, Moscow was rated as Europe's worst city to live in. By 1996 it had dropped to fourth worst, behind Kiev, Tashkent and Sarajevo. The survey was published by the Geneva-based Corporate Resources Group (CRG).

[4]Western media reports of the economic and political collapse in August 1998 were an exception. The daily increase in the population's misery was recorded accurately.

local daily English press, The *Moscow Times*, appears not to be so influenced by political bias and most world or local news is reported fairly. Though some have told me that The *Moscow Times* was funded by the CIA through a Dutch parent company. I have no evidence that this comment is correct. If true, however, cheap continuing indoctrination, I suppose. Much of the local Russian press and electronic media is still currently under Yeltsin's, or his banker cronies' (the oligarchy), direct and indirect influence. It shows in the sort of reports you continue to receive over the period this book has been in preparation. While this letter is completed, the forthcoming presidential election is subject to such poor reporting.

Life is different in many ways to that we know and understand in the West. My flat is only two hundred metres from the Duma, (the lower house of parliament), where all the Western electronic media like to show the 'punch ups'. How civilised we are at home, only verbal fisticuffs from Denis Skinner. And less than ten minutes' walk from St Basil's, Red Square and the Kremlin. It is certainly an experience to record a few of the enormous changes (not all good) that have taken place here in the last few years.

I do not know any members of the Federal Government personally, but have access to foreign economic specialists to gain any introductions into the corridors of power our business might need. Some of them have been here for some time and most speak Russian fluently. One of them was previously an economic advisor to the former Gorbachev administration. I have had close business dealings with ministers in the Moscow City administration and have been introduced to their methods of moral conduct. Russians have, understandably, little experience as to the management of a mixed economy – and still trust few foreigners. If I said that Zuganov would fit into the right of centre of the Labour Party today, few would believe me but, if his policies are realised, it appears true. Such is the misunderstanding created by the word – Communist. Old habits die hard everywhere, and that label will remain for many years. Living here makes it totally understandable why the former Communist parties are apparently resurgent in many former East European countries. In simple terms the population is fed up with the crime, corruption, economic mismanagement and lack of real change for the personal good of all since the Iron Curtain fell. Expectations cannot unfortunately ever be met for all in such short timescales. Russians have always understood the rules of autocracy and find democracy difficult to understand or follow. And who in the West is helping them to cope? It would appear to be in Western governmental interest to keep Russia weak. We should also not forget that Yeltsin and his cronies were Communist apparatchik till a few years ago. They do not have the longer dissident pedigree of Havel in Prague or of the Polish electrician. Nor have they a history of close Western ties.

Let me try to give some impressions of the country resulting from trips to Rostov-on-Don, Naberezhnyye Chelny, Irkutsk, Vologda, Suzdal, Rybinsk, St Petersburg, Novosibirsk, Tutaev, Miass, Chelnyabinsk and Krasnadar among other cities.[5] The very nature of letters of this sort gives rise to only anecdotal and possibly, in some opinion, superficial comments. What follows is an account of my experiences, not only in Moscow and the privileged areas, fully reported in the West, but also of the regions that suffer in their unreported way with little hope of early resolution of their special problems. Superficial or not, the message is very real.

This is not one country, but an artificial collection of

---

[5]Six visits were later made to 'Asia' – that is east of the Urals or the River Don.

nearly one hundred and fifty ethnic groups thrown (or forced – by tsars and Stalin alike) together by a turbulent history. And that encompasses only the Russian Federation. The fifteen newly-independent republics which were part of the former USSR have many other ethnic groupings whose history and habits are not covered in these pages. How many have read *Hadji Murat* by Tolstoy? A story of the thirty-years war between the Russians and the Chechens in the mid-1800s, about the Imperial Russian quest to subdue the Caucasus. Like Northern Ireland, little changes. Their divided ethnic, social and religious history remains. But do we in the West know or understand the chronicle that created local thinking? No. But we try to judge through our jaundiced perspective. Just as we in our land object to misrepresentation by others, we should beware the reaction if we practise equal faults on others.

We judge, just as the Russian's do, by pigeonholing concepts and ideologies. At the same time assuming that the definitions and methods used to manage these concepts and ideologies are just the same here as in the West. They have an emerging democracy, they have capitalism of sorts. But not all participate in these processes. More importantly the management is in the hands of so-called 'reformers' who in truth are still closet Bolsheviks. Few of us can change the habits of a lifetime. Neither can the managers and politicians of Russia's unwieldy behemoth of a governmental system or industry. Their words may be modern and attune to Western thinking, but the methods used to create a new society are as Byzantine as ever.[6] In the past, Russia was dominated by power-seeking apparatchik. The same remains today, but we wrongly believe them to have

---

[6]The clash of three ideologies (Bolshevism, capitalism and democracy) is a developing and recurring theme in these pages. Have patience with the wider explanation of my thoughts.

changed their methods. Not so.

Here we have a country whose population were told under a former totalitarian regime that they lived in 'paradise' compared to us in the West. At that time they had no way of comparison. When the barriers came down, the disillusionment they began to live with included: loss of 'empire'; reduction in national pride; realisation that one apparently bad old system had not been replaced by a better alternative they were neither ready nor prepared for; and that it was not the 'paradise' they thought was universal. Their trauma was instant. The period of their rehabilitation will be long, tentative and uncertain. The protracted healing process of Britain's loss of world status after the Second World War lasted a generation. The resultant effect on individual attitudes to their own government and political leaders, to each other, and on their inner soul is debilitating and fully understandable.

It is hard to imagine past achievements in space exploration and other modern technology successes when one travels the land. The benefits we have come to expect for the common man were, and continue to be, raped. The resulting political and social vacuum created in 1989 (although for Russian purposes the key year of change was 1991), following the collapse of the old regime, caused a major crime wave. Mafia domination of economic life and corruption reached the highest places. A community emerged more split between 'have and have not' than anything Margaret Thatcher ever created. The resulting trauma shows in the way people think and act and its effects are felt in all sections of the community. They have little sense of diary in the Western business perception. They enjoy making a crisis out of nothing at the drop of a hat. All this is interspersed with bouts of drinking vodka, which, for them, make the world look better after the second glass. No one warned me that a spare liver was part of the survival kit.

Logic has nothing to do with the daily life we foreigners are obliged to live here. There is a two-tier pricing system, and we are on top. Moscow has become one of the world's most expensive places to live for Western businessmen. And certainly it is not a place to bring the pampered European family to try to enjoy a 'normal' Western life. We, the expatriates, have only one role in life – work. To be accepted by the Russians themselves requires time, ability to understand their circumstance and extreme patience. For all its apparent negatives, Russia is still a fascinating place to experience.

Because of Stalin's demands to create a powerful industrially-based economy equal to the West and capable of defending the motherland, fifty per cent of Russian manufacturing industry became historically geared to defence-related production. World events have now changed that. In the game of winners and losers, Russia has lost more than most as a result. I am reminded of a visit to the main repair facility of the Russian Army transport corps in Rostov-on-Don, near the Black Sea in the south. Unthinkable only a few years ago that a foreigner could visit such a place. It would have been regarded as an act of espionage. This plant formally employed five thousand people. Today it is idle, having had no orders for seven months. The army major in charge was the only person around and all we wanted was to see if we could use the facilities to create a local service facility for construction-related machinery which my company sold in Russia. He entertained us with tea and chocolates hoping we might be his economic salvation. I never did return to find out what happened to him. His story is not singular. Similar sites and stories are found increasingly across this land.

Then we have the civil aviation lottery. Aeroflot has now broken into a multitude of diverse pieces. Formerly with some sixteen hundred planes of which today less than six hundred are rated by some as reaching current Russian safety standards – never mind Western. Just look around at any airport. The multitude of planes on the ground with red engine covers are not thus only for the winter. Often they are just mothballed, being raided for spare parts to keep others aloft, or just do not work. I use the term Aeroflot loosely. The hasty privatisation process affecting all sections of former enterprise and all strata of society has led in the aviation sphere to nearly one hundred and eighty new aviation transport companies appearing across the Russian Federation. Some with maybe one plane only, and many totally unsafe. These planes were mostly built with the military in mind. All these defence-related plants have few outlets in the world of today. But what to do with the former employees? As yet no real solution or policy. In a sophisticated society that has spent years developing legal structures that work and a business-cum-financial framework, there would be solutions or reasonable flows of capital to hand. No doubt in time the skills will be retrained and the buildings reused. But here everything moves fast and stops dead at the same time. The trouble is that few of us know which gear we happen to be in, or in which direction the future lies. The government certainly has little idea. Well if they have, they show little sign of revealing their true intent.

Realising the size of the place is important as a background to understanding the social, economic and political pressures that exist today, as much as any other factor. Were you to fly non-stop from Tokyo to London you would enter Russian airspace after some thirty minutes. Nine hours later you cross the Baltic Republics, Estonia, Latvia, Lithuania, on your way to Western Europe. It is further to Irkutsk in the middle of Siberia (near Lake Baikal – which contains twenty per cent of the world's fresh water supply) from Moscow, than from London to New York.

Then you have only crossed two thirds of the country. Between London and Sydney some eleven time zones change our body clock. From London across Russia to the Bering Strait on the borders with Alaska, there are thirteen of which eleven cover the territory of the Russian Federation. A sixth of the world's land surface makes its presence felt.

With Russia as an autocracy for centuries, democratic principles as we judge and pigeonhole the world are a novelty. The disenfranchisement of the serfs only occurred in 1860. Some still belie this change today. Stalin really only followed an inbred acceptance of absolute rule that had been the way of life since the formation of the country. The difference being, that under the tsars, management of agriculture and the skills of a relationship with the soil were handed down from father to son. Under Stalin's pressure to create an industrial society and the deliberately created famines of 1933/34, in the drive to move the peasant from the land into the factories, this was lost. Agricultural collectivisation killed it completely. Today, only sixty per cent of the food consumed in Russia is home grown. In the Moscow of the mid-nineties it is as low as forty per cent.[7] Therein lies a major problem for the next few years. Unfortunately, that situation seems unlikely to change in the near future with current policies. In the short years since the 1991 coup, the country has lost its ability to feed itself. No real policies exist to rectify the situation. Yet at the same time they are one of the latent richest countries in the world in terms of natural and mineral resources. They, however, remain largely untapped. A sensible land ownership policy would assist and help solve both agriculture requirements and foreign-income flows from the sale of

---

[7]GOSKomstat. By 1998, imported food took at least a fifty per cent share of national consumption. Some say more.

mineral wealth. But as yet not to be, from either Yeltsin or Zuganov, and certainly not from Zhirinovsky. In time, such things will come to pass, but currently entrenched attitudes and powerful groupings, trying to ensure personal gain, slow such modernisation processes. The shadowy group known as the 'oligarchs' emerged to prominence during the privatisation process managed by Anatoly Chubais. Their power in both financial and political terms should never be underestimated.

With one hundred and fifty ethnic groups, it is unsurprising that there are social tensions, particularly with the Moslems in the southern part of the country, as shown in Chechnya and the other Caucasian republics. Many of those 'northern Russians' whom one meets, show themselves to be an extraordinarily racially-biased people. Their inherent dislike of ethnic minorities, including Moslems and Jews, is evident. It is little surprise to find that the fifteen former countries, now part of the so-called CIS, have begun to increase the policing of their mutual borders. Russians now need visas to go to many parts of their former empire. No free entry into the Baltic Republics etc. Yet in hindsight and with a closer knowledge of the people, one does have to wonder at the lack of bloodshed during the period of the break-up of the former USSR. Given the magnitude of the event this on reflection is a credit to their national patience. A trait to be more than wondered at. Few in the West would react with similar dignity. But then few in the West have their recent history.

We foreigners have to use separate terminals at the airports to be processed.[8] Interesting the first time round, but becomes rather wearisome after a while. Even the plumbing repairs in an Intourist hotel in Suzdal become a bore after paying $77 (twice the Russian rate) for a room

---

[8]Significantly eased since better terminal buildings have emerged.

that would cost $25 at home. That is if its lack of standards were allowed by the local authority. In Rostov-on-Don at its local Intourist hotel it was $100 per night and both times I stayed there was no hot water. The first visit was in the winter at minus 20°C outside. Not a pretty experience when not expecting such a morning wake-up.

Moscow and St Petersburg, together with some industrial areas of the Urals, are relatively privileged places to live. Particularly Moscow. Locals still have to have permits to reside there. One of my Russian staff even divorced his wife, so she could marry his best friend, who had a Moscow living permit. They then moved to Moscow from Kiev and reversed the marriage process. All this to live in the capital. Yet not all in the Moscow infrastructure works as in other major world cities. The lift in my block of flats, an old building from the 1930s, only works five days out of seven (built in 1935 and claims to be an Otis). And the security entry system on the main door to my block has broken three months after installation.[9] The drains in the city centre work poorly in heavy rain as I found out in a thunderstorm that had the water over the sills on my car a few months after first arriving here. But the locals think this is just a normal mode of life. Complaint only results in higher blood pressure. But it certainly adds to the experience of being here.

Moscow is a superficially modern city with most basic amenities. The further east one goes, the less financial support exists from central budgets and it shows. On the Trans-Siberian railway, a section of track was recently removed, enabling a food train to be hijacked by the local town council, as they had no tax receipts from the centre

---

[9] Both pieces of equipment continued to function in this manner all the time I lived in this particular flat. During the month of September 1996, the lift gave up the ghost for a complete month.

for three months. This eastern area of this vast country is one of the heartlands of the extreme nationalistic political factions – Zhirinovsky et al. When one goes there, dissatisfaction with central government performance is obvious. Little has been done for these people under any regime. Particularly now that they hear about market reforms – unfortunately they have hardly experienced them. Up to 6,000 miles from Moscow is a different world. Some thirty per cent of the total population who live in the remoter agricultural regions have seen or benefit little or nothing from the changes of the last six years. Indeed, their particular economic conditions have become distinctly worse in these last few years of apparent change. The same applies to many of the multitude of artificial towns created in the last seventy years (some large with up to half a million inhabitants) that are single industry locations. Many Muscovites I have met are happy to sacrifice a whole generation, particularly the pensioners, the dispossessed and the poor, to achieve their short-term material goals. But they have the opportunities in that city. Those in the regions sit on the untapped natural wealth, but do not have the power to act, or the wherewithal to develop their latent riches. These latter people ignore the centre to keep their sanity. They call it reality, I call it a sad waste of eighty years of human existence.

But the Metro in Moscow is impressive. Not only is it a major people-mover system, (fourteen million passengers per day), it is as beautiful as reported. Started by Stalin, each station is decorated differently. One suddenly finds stained glass, chandeliers and political statues among the crush of people. And a train usually comes every ninety seconds. It is also very easy to find one's way.

There has been much in the Western press about payment of back wages, or lack of it. This sad fact of Russian life today does not just apply to the coal miners who receive maximum publicity, but also to the police, the teachers, nurses, the army (including some of those in Chechnya) and most public-sector employees. The private sector is not excluded. Despite what has been reported, the problem will not be solved in the short term. It will certainly reoccur after the presidential election due to the parlous state of government finances. A teacher in a secondary school earns some Rbl.200,000 per month (nearly $42),[10] but a monthly pass on the Moscow Metro costs $12. The saddest sight of all is the pensioner in the street extracting a meagre living. Their lot is a heavy one. Below my flat is a soup kitchen. But how would you live on $11[11] per month as a pensioner? This was one sight I never could accept in all my time here. I have rarely seen such wealth and poverty living cheek by jowl in a major world capital. Particularly in one that was formally a superpower. There is little sign of resolution. On top of this we should expect a major financial crisis post the presidential election, whoever wins the contest. The Western press currently spends little time reporting that this will happen – but just wait. More will be explained later.[12] Barter is becoming a way of life for many. They have reverted to an ancient form of trade. Cash is a scarce commodity. A sad reflection on the breakdown of a sound system of product exchange for monetary value. In time I understood, but the lessons were painful and the observations sometimes heartbreaking.

Many of the Russian businessmen one meets believe that politics and economics are on two separate planets and the twain shall never meet. They have heard dire warnings about their economy before. But they believe in the

---

[10]Over the course of these letters, exchange rates drop dramatically.

[11]At the time of writing the state pension is Rbl.52.000 per month per person.

[12]Financial crises occurred with regularity during all my time in Russia. Mostly government induced.

omnipotent continuance of Russia. They ignore the parlous state of their manufacturing industry and public-sector finances. This time may be different. Yet they still do not agree. Many seem to believe that the worst is over. A situation that is unfortunately not true. But the government is cleverly hiding the true statistics prior to the election and Clinton and Kohl are helping Yeltsin to fudge the truth by lending unrepayable loans. The Russian businessmen I know, think they have apparently invented a new form of economics and believe it works. One example is that one of our suppliers of Russian-made machinery[13] uses barter for ninety per cent of sales, as there is little cash in the system to pay for their goods. At the office we have no choice but to barter oil and hoses to buy machines from them. This surely cannot be a long-term solution. A significant proportion of Russian employees, particularly in the regions, live their lives in such a manner. We in the West have forgotten the trauma of returning to basic existence. Thus our superficial judgements of them are based on pontificating from the comfort of a Western armchair.

The current liquidity crisis has been caused by government mismanagement of finances and an archaic tax system is expected to lead to between five hundred and one thousand of the two thousand, five hundred Russian clearing banks going to the wall in the next six months (yes, I said two thousand, five hundred). These are not my words, but those of the chairman of the Inkombank, Mr Vinogradov, published in an open letter this week.[14] The fact is that these banks lend less than five per cent of total lending to industry. It is all to government. No self-respecting Russian puts his hard-earned Roubles into them.

---

[13]Raskat road rollers from Rabinsk.

[14]The *Moscow Times*. Little did he realise then that his bank would join the list of failed banks some two years later.

The beds may be full of cash, well probably dollars. The banks make their profits (and they have been huge) from the trade in Russian treasury bills which currently yield interest rates of two hundred and eighty per cent with six months maturity. This is unsaleable paper in the West. Tax receipts in the last nine months are twenty-five per cent lower than expenditure. The only way the government has temporarily balanced the books is by using IMF loans[15] ($10 billion);[16] sales of treasury bills to Russian banks ($20 billion is due to be repaid over the five months following the election – this equates to the current total tax receipts expected for the same period); and borrowing $3 billion from the Germans all in the last five months. It is reported locally (privately) that the Russian treasury tried for six weeks post-Christmas 1995 to find the latter amount to tide the government over till the June election was over. When Kohl visited Moscow in February 1996, he was told that without the loan they should appoint Zuganov as president tomorrow and not bother with the expense of an election. It is publicly (well here anyway) reported that the German Embassy in Moscow learnt of the loan from the newspapers, and that the Dresdner Bank had three days' notification of the syndication! If this is true, then politics again rules the natural laws of economics.

The truth is that the Russian manufacturing industry is hurting, and hurting bad. For seventy years they had little

---

[15]It is reported that the managing director of the IMF, Michel Camdessus, was vigorously opposed to the loan, but was politically persuaded by Kohl and Clinton.

[16]History has shown us that this is small change compared to the amounts the IMF has lent to struggling Asian economies following the demise of their fortunes in 1998. We should not be surprised at the negative Russian reactions to the massive IMF loans to Korea, Indonesia etc. in view of the resultant self-interest of the West in assisting the Asian economies.

regenerative investment. Those factories that I have visited equate to Third World operations. With up to two hundred and forty per cent interest rates on local Rouble-denominated loans for commercial investment, there is understandably no incentive or ability to improve productivity. It just cannot be paid for today. AvtoVAZ, who make Lada and Volga cars, have not produced a new model for nine years, and are two years behind with their tax payments.[17] The reward is that the general director of the company, Vladimir Kadonikov, was appointed First Deputy Prime Minister primarily responsible for economic policy three months ago.[18]

Some four years ago when my employer began to import construction machinery, the price differential to local machines was ten to one. Today it is three to one. But the imported machines work. Unfortunately most Russian products do not, in our understanding of modern technology. The reason is partly inflation, partly the exchange rate movement but mostly that local manufacturing industry has now to cope with unsubsidised world prices for raw materials for the first time – and has not invested (or has the wherewithal) for this comparative eventuality. Subsidies have ended, with no alternative policies. The barriers with the rest of the world have come down in a cruel way for modern day Russian citizens. Few politicians,

---

[17]It has been estimated by the Kremlin that half of Russian industry's overdue tax payments are due by only six companies. Among them are GazProm, AvtoVAZ and Norilsk-Nickel. Another estimate from the same source says that two thirds of all tax arrears are down to only sixty-seven companies across Russia. AvtoVAZ is believed to owe over $1 billion and GazProm nearly $2.8 billion in past tax. According to a Russian news agency on 1 October 1996 all GazProm bank accounts were frozen with a view to seizing such tax arrears. Tax authorities have such radical statutory powers in Russia for any size of business.

[18]Since sacked from the government post the presidential election. Now back as AvtoVAZ chairman.

other than the 'reformed' Communists under Zuganov, have begun to address the question of the slow death and eventual resurrection of manufacturing industry in the country. In 1988, the exchange rate was parity with the US $. Today US $1 will give you Rbl.4,950.[19] Inflation has been rampant over the last six years.[20] Although chemical, metallurgy, oil and gas producers will benefit from a devaluation, albeit creeping, (certain after the presidential election of up to fifteen per cent), as they are major exporters, the rest of the manufacturing sector will continue to die a slow and painful death without fundamental changes in tax and investment incentives.

Little wonder that some view 'freedom' through the bottom of a vodka bottle. The drink problem associated with Russia's past has worsened. After this letter was originally sent, a competition to choose a new symbol for Russia was held.[21] Among the ideas put forward were 'New Russians' at the wheel of a Mercedes, a skull and crossbones and other such nonsense. The winner of the competition was a Kalashnikov automatic rifle, with second prize going to the Kristall Vodka distillery in Moscow.

Yet the untapped natural wealth of the country is staggering. Thirty per cent of the world's known diamonds, oil, gas, gold, titanium, coal, iron ore, aluminium etc. for starters. In the diamond and precious metal stakes they are ahead of South African riches. However, they cannot bring themselves to 'sell' the soil of Mother Russia to the potentially 'rapist foreigner'. Encouragement to attract foreign investment is slow (less than $3 billion per year, compared to nearly $50 billion into China). This is as true of Yeltsin

---

[19] On 4 December 1996 it was 5,517.

[20] When I arrived, the Moscow Metro cost Rbl.600 per trip, today it is Rbl.1,500. By September 1998 it had risen to Rbl.3 (after re-denomination with the 000 removed).

[21] The *Daily Telegraph,* 1 January 1998.

as it is of Zuganov. Unless these resources are exploited for the full benefit of the local economy (never mind who the investor is), little of substance will change. Foreign investors are understandably wary of such investment without protective legal and tax structures. They have come to realise that the only protection is 'influence' or the rule of the gun. Some estimate that thirty-five per cent of Moscow businesses are 'protected' by the Mafia. Not really a comfort for foreign partners to help release the vast sums required to develop natural resources, or anything else. Yet local politicians continue to believe they are the equal of the G7 nations. Little is further from the truth when one sees what really happens here.

No doubt Thatcher and Reagan will go down in Western history as the destroyers of Communism. I believed this till I came here – our Western media told us so. These two happened to be in power when the money ran out locally to continue the status quo. Nothing as grandiose as a change of system through Western pressure occurred. It was a natural consequence of a defence-related economy that just ran out of money and resources. As simple as that. They had no other choices. One has only to observe daily life here to see that. Quite where the CIA and others were looking to make an assessment of this country for their political masters beats me. When one travels to the provinces, the picture is reinforced. The Soviet tradition, created for security reasons by Stalin, of the solitary town in the middle of nowhere to produce single items was a further witness to economic failure. Take Tutaev, some four hundred kilometres north of Moscow as an example of hundreds of similar communities. This town with three hundred thousand souls has only one major factory producing diesel engines of 1965 design vintage. Today less than twenty-five per cent of pre-*perestroika* production occurs. These manufacturing statistics in single-industry towns are replicated across the country. Rostov-on-Don, the twelve-month home of one hundred and twenty thousand combine harvesters before the curtain fell, now produces a fifth of those glory years – twenty-five thousand annually. Naberezhnyye Chelny has seen production of the KamAZ truck go from one hundred and ten thousand in 1989 to twenty-three thousand per year today. Another truck factory, UralAS, in Miass in the Urals tells the same story.[22] The people just work shorter hours for less money (if they are paid at all) as there is less work to go around. Few have been retrenched. But where is any alternative work in these places? Little new industrial activity is evident. Those industries and towns, previously geared to the military, fare far worse. There are hundreds of similar examples across the country. Unless this decline is reversed, the regional economic and social consequences in due course will be great. It certainly increases the divide between the rich service and banking-related centre and the poor regions.

Tax breaks to resurrect industry of the sort we would expect just do not exist. The tax regime is both incomprehensible and in tatters. When the town of Corby, in the UK, died because of the demise of the steelworks some years ago, there was later economic revival due to, among other things, tax incentives. In a society where both tax avoidance and tax evasion are endemic the alternatives are narrowed. It is easy to reduce a tax burden, or to avoid it altogether. Just bribe a tax official. They may even suggest it. Until incentives (based on an equitable tax regime) exist to spread the influence of the successful Russian or foreign entrepreneur out of Moscow, it will take more than two

---

[22]UralAS stopped paying wages in September 1996, and gave their employees vouchers to exchange for food at local shops. How these shops recouped their reward is unclear.

generations of painful grind to recover some economic dignity for the population. Mind you, stamping out rampant bribery and corruption would help as well. Just to further illustrate the lack of cash in the economy, on the way to Tutaev I came upon rows of stalls selling towels in a long country road. The reason was simple but tragic. The small local towel factory could not afford to pay wages in cash, so payment was in towels. The employees then took to selling them for cash as they had no other alternatives. If you want one, tell me, I can help the locals.

The sheer size of the place compared to smaller former Eastern European territories such as the Czech Republic or Poland and particularly a long and past permanent physical and social divorce from the West, makes attitudes against change so much more entrenched. They have no capitalist or democratic traditions. They – the average citizens – have paid the price in spades of a government, alien to the people, supporting their former sphere of influence. A subservience to national totalitarianism remains.

As indicated earlier, some fifty per cent of all industrial production created by Stalin was based on defence. For them an economic benefit under totalitarianism. A national disaster today as few alternatives have risen from the ashes. One of our suppliers has agreed to produce construction machines with a local assembly content in a former tank and personnel carrier factory in Siberia.[23] This factory, 2,500 miles from Moscow, produced enough tanks and personnel carriers to have one every thirty-five metres from Vladivostock to Moscow! The former generals who run the plant have little else to do today other than to try to find new sources of work. We have been allocated eight hundred square metres among the tanks to assemble asphalt pavers. The idea of turning former armament factories into

---

[23] Rubsovsk in Altai Region.

peaceful production purposes is excellent, but what has been achieved to date is a drop in the ocean of that required to redirect nearly fifty per cent of Russia's productive capacity. I am constantly reminded of the army major who gave us tea, chocolates and biscuits in Rostov-on-Don in the hope we would favour his future existence by using his plant. Former paranoia with security even went so far as to make the production level of buttons a state secret. This in case someone extrapolated the resulting numbers into uniforms, and thus members of the armed forces. What a change today from before.

You can divide the country socially, economically and politically into different territories. The richer areas are Moscow, St Petersburg and the metal, coal, oil and gas producing areas of the Urals and Western Siberia.[24] These cities appear superficially Western in many respects, although the bulk of services we take for granted do not work. The infrastructure in hospitals, schools, universities, roads etc. are all generally in poor (or non-existent) repair and lack the short-term funds to restore matters to as near normal as possible. Our construction-division premises are Federal property and are rented from a local university. We had to assist in paying their telephone bill last year just to keep a creaking communication system going for ourselves. Such is an everyday effect of the illiquidity in Federal funds on public institutions, particularly education, but more of that later.

In 1989, in former East Germany, Kohl said in a rallying unification speech in Dresden, that the task of rebuilding that country to make it economically equal to the West of their land would only take three years. Look what happened there. I dread to think of the real outcome in terms of time

---

[24]Despite some views, Siberia is the generic term for all the territory east of the Urals, north and south.

and human disappointment here till a Russian rebirth is complete. Yet they have an extremely educated population – some would say better than in the UK – who are capable of much innovation and original thought, if led correctly. History also shows the Russian character to be extremely patient till he irrationally blows his top. Living here, one always expects an explosion, but has no idea when and if it will come. I often wonder if the time is ripe for that.

In the UK it took a generation after the war to understand that the nation was no longer 'top dog'. Here the population is expected to assimilate the same message in less than five years. Yet if one were to say that they were really living in an economic 'banana' republic that would be a personal insult. But it is not far from reality. Gorbachev may be loved in the West, but is hated here. His presidential election chances are zero. The reasons are twofold. Firstly, he lost 'the empire' without creating another functioning system. Thus creating a social and economic vacuum filled by rabid self-seeking capitalism of the few and, secondly, that as a teetotal individual he endeavoured to control the production and consumption of alcoholic drinks during his tenure. The latter event is remembered more than the former. Russia, now some one hundred and forty-seven million people, consumes more alcohol today than the former USSR with two hundred and fifty million. My liver protests on occasions during the long and wearisome business meetings one has to attend with drink thrown in. My driver even uses the cheaper sorts of vodka as a form of antifreeze and as a windscreen wash in the winter.

They have a political system that is not democratic in our sense of the word. Communism – that is old style – has been replaced by a tenacious form of patronage. There has been insufficient time to acquaint the population with all the benefits of democracy and public accountability. They, the apparatchik, certainly do not understand, or appear to want, the discomfort of attendant responsibilities of a modern democratic state. The old style Communists in former days had little better wages and salaries than the rest. They compensated by using the 'system' to obtain better housing and other material benefits. The current ordinary Muscovite has to make do with kitchen, bathroom and toilet, plus nine square metres per person. It is up to fifteen in the newer blocks. This means that the average size of flat in Moscow is about forty-one square metres. Tell that to a Western consumer – would he accept that?

Today such 'benefit' for the apparatchik is the bribe. Requests of up to fifteen per cent at the highest levels are normal, particularly in the public sector. Under Brezhnev and before, there was less evident corruption. It was there, but less public. Yeltsin and his henchmen have created an industry in the matter. Just take the cigarette distribution business. The tax stamps on each cigarette packet are US 5 cents each. Some \$4 billion of tax revenue could be raised each year if these were all paid for. It is a condition from the IMF that this should be so. But the Church controls thirty per cent of cigarette tax stamp distribution and the Sports Fund a similar amount. Distribution of alcoholic products is similarly 'controlled'. One of the senior administrators of the Sports Fund is Boris's tennis partner. The former is politically expedient (possibly correctly, to encourage the rebuilding of a lost religious heritage), but the latter is sheer corruption.[25] Some observers estimate that 'slush' and illegal capital flight is worth

---

[25] I never did discover why the Sports Fund needs all this money. Sending athletes to the Olympic Games can surely be achieved with lesser sums than appear to be gathered here. Similar tax breaks are also given to army veteran organisations, the Mafia-style implications of that were evident on my penultimate day of my first sojourn in Moscow. See Chapter XIII, 'Any Conclusions'.

$20 billion per annum into Swiss and other banks. Others rate the figure as high as $80 billion. I can well believe either figure. The latter is not far from total estimated governmental tax revenues in 1996. At least the sort of commissions we have become used to in the Middle East over the years are accompanied by free education, housing and fuel for the locals there. Here nothing is free. The first question is always how we will pay the bill. Everyone is out for themselves and the personal main chance. It is intensely depressing to see this situation while the pensioners[26] near the Duma still beg for a meagre existence.

The black economy is estimated by some to be up to thirty per cent of total economic activity. Add this to the corrupt capital flight, then there is little wonder that the state coffers are empty. This economy is based on the US $ and not the Rouble. Some will tell you that there are more $ notes in circulation here than in the US. During the change of design of the $100 note in 1996, the US embassy in Moscow had to conduct a media campaign reassuring worried Russians that their old notes would be honoured. Their unfortunate memories of a past Rouble reform were short. Yet tax rates are high (real personal rate of sixty-five per cent, and two hundred and eighty per cent on employers) and legislation is totally prohibitive and confusing. We, at the office, had a technical question on VAT (currently at twenty per cent), so, in the hope of resolving this issue, we wrote to the Finance Ministry and to Customs and Excise quoting the same paragraph of the law. One reply came back and said we had to charge VAT on the total, the other said on the margin. Two different sets of accountants including KPMG gave us contradictory advice on the same issue. One ends up by a shrug of the shoulder and says – 'Well… this is Russia' as an excuse for lack of compre-

---

[26]Since joined by unpaid military recruits.

hension. Money talks, and the Mafia is generally in control of real action. I have seen situations where the key element of a proper business deal is damaged because the arguments revolve around who gets paid what commission rather than concentrate on the real business in hand and only then pay the required graft.

If a commercial, or other, dispute is to be settled, the 'legal department', usually consisting of three men with guns, visits. The law is mostly powerless and few use it. I have been visited by such people – from our largest customer to ensure prompt delivery – and telling me... 'You have ten days to perform or you are personally liable', it does not take a genius to work out the meaning of that phrase. Although they were very polite, their firmness gave no doubts they meant it. To say the least it was very disconcerting and almost led me to pack my bags. Russian businesses are more likely to be affected. It is estimated that some thirty-five per cent of commercial enterprises in Moscow are thus controlled. The banking community is the worst, indeed one bank actually syndicated with twenty-six others to fund arms purchases for Dudayev (the assassinated former Chechen leader), and was a bank regularly used by a major governmental organisation. I could be in serious trouble with such information, but it was cheap to obtain as part of a routine credit-rating check. Information gleaned from the same source made me realise how fragile the banking institutions really are. Their reliance on 'influence' and in our parlance – illegal activity – is vast. Too big for any longer-term comfort. In many cases commercial criteria are few, politics and personal gain are paramount. The banks are the Kremlin's paymasters. The KGB now sells such stuff. Part of privatisation I guess. Being a banker in Moscow is definitely a risk profession. Many will tell you, and my credit searches confirm that the Mafia involvement in this particular sector is vast. About two bankers a month are found shot, crimes rarely solved. Maybe there will be more after the elections. Could this have been a solution in the UK recession of the early nineties? (Sorry, sick). Possibly I will be at risk myself for such general comments, but they are known by all to be sadly true.

The election is of course uppermost in our minds today. Now only some one month away, and business activity has ground to a halt. This is not helped by the advent of six holidays in May. From the traditional May Day on the 1 to Victory Day on the 9 May (celebrating the end of the Second World War) when most discerning Muscovites ignore it all and go to their Dachas to plant food for the summer. Some fifty per cent of Muscovites have some sort of Dacha, or at least their family has access to one. The city is now empty at weekends. Certainly the flow of investment is at a standstill. Opinion polls apparently show that Yeltsin is winning. He, however, controls the press at the moment. So I for one have some doubts about their veracity. Who knows the real truth.

Taking account of the geography of the country, we should expect, on the basis of previous elections, the East (Siberia North and South – well most of the territory east of the Urals) to favour Zhirinovsky. The agricultural areas and pensioners are with Zuganov and the cities are for Yeltsin. Expect about ten per cent of the vote to be fiddled. In the Duma elections in December, it was amusing to find a national vote of about twelve per cent for Chernomyrdin's (the prime minister) party, 'Our House is Russia'. Yet the army apparently voted sixty per cent for him. The army vote was announced as a single block – no one believed it. But the words of Stalin still remain, 'It is not the vote that counts, but who counts the vote.' So Yeltsin will probably win by a narrow margin if the actual count is 46/54 against him. That is still within the fiddle factor.

However, private polls within the political parties are now showing a different picture. Zuganov is in the lead, and Yeltsin and Zhirinovsky tie for second place. So the results of the first round on the 17 June will be interesting. The second round with the two top candidates from the first will take place three weeks later. If I were asked to guess, I would bet on Zuganov winning.[27] But it will be a dirty fight to the end.

What is important to us from a business point of view are the expected different fiscal and economic policies that will follow. Zuganov is expected to hammer the banks (this will get rid of much of the repayment problems of treasury bills – the GKOs)[28] and there will be some high profile supporters of Yeltsin in the courts for corruption (great). But wages will only be partially paid (not great). If Yeltsin wins, the reverse will be true. The wages will cease again,[29] some banks will go,[30] but investment may flow again.[31] Even if Zhirinovsky were to get to the second round, he has little chance of winning against either of the other two. A creeping devaluation and a return to inflation is certain whoever wins. The result will, however, determine the commercial policies of remaining investment in the country for many foreign businesses. We await the result with bated breath.

With the above scenario, you might wonder how business is ever done. Every economy has a certain inertia, which continues despite many problems. Food, drink and clothing are essential to all. The privatisation of some fifty

---

[27]Since proved incorrect.

[28]Please remember the abbreviation 'GKO'. Much more comment on these treasury bills and their effects on the crash of 1998 are found in later chapters.

[29]Since proved correct.

[30]Since proved correct.

[31]Since proved incorrect.

per cent of dwellings, certainly in Moscow (flats at an average privatisation cost of $20 each, yes twenty), fuels a rise in the DIY and building industry. Much of this in the 'black economy', and because of the huge distances transport is essential. Those natural resources, such as oil, gas and raw metals that are mined, are mainly exported, so there is a balance of payment surplus, which continues. We, in our supply of construction machinery have built on the renewal phase that does exist. Parts of Moscow and selected regions do look like building sites, and there are some foreign mining houses active. World Bank money is supporting road renewal, so there is plenty for us, in our construction equipment division, to go at. We could fill the Albert Hall with 'potential' orders, but only one seat with people able to pay the final bill. If there were a market, or legal framework, for housing mortgages and a sensible leasing structure we would surge in sales. But we only deal for cash before delivery, and that restricts activity to a great degree. We have managed to nearly treble the size of the business in the last year, but do not expect to do so these coming twelve months.

I find the people rather more relaxed, on the surface, than I was expecting. But not straightforward as to allow immediate understanding. Maybe that will be a subject for a later letter. They do have a hard life and take their troubles with unexplained equanimity. A Westerner would not in the same circumstances. Yet one expects some explosion to come, the signals are there. Although welcoming some foreign involvement, they would rather rebuild their country on their own, and in their own manner and timescale. The signs of a possible rejection of foreign assistance and nationalism are also spreading.

They appear to have little sense of natural beauty as the ugly dehumanising Soviet era tower blocks and other physical surroundings will demonstrate. That, however, may be slightly unfair, and could be a direct result of central planning and little individual choice of ownership. They do have an affinity for intellectual pursuits, the written word and the performing arts. I have to say that the latter is one of my great pleasures in being here. Again more will be reported on that subject later. Were you to come, you will see that the tourist pleasures of Moscow and particularly St Petersburg are faded symbols of a glorious past which they are trying hard to recreate albeit along different lines to those we might wish them to have. But it is their country and we should let them do it their way.

Chapter III
A Return to the Past?
May 1996

Extract from a Fax of 9 May to Home

...What a farce this morning. Today is the day the Russians celebrate the anniversary of victory in the Second World War. The West uses 8 May, but Stalin wanted to be sure of the facts, and have his own ceremony. Thus he delayed signature of the armistice documents on the Russian side by one day. So Red Square was, as usual, the focal point for another set of official celebrations. There was to be a parade. Well there is. All the streets inside the Garden Ring are closed to traffic since 6.30 this morning. We were warned in the local press. In the last few days there have been columns of troops going into the city to practise. I did not expect to get into the square on the assumption that it is invited quests, veterans and diplomats only. But at least it seemed to me to be reasonable to expect that one would see something of the parade assembling or marching into the square.

For those who have not been here, Red Square is not tarmac, but cobbles – and certainly not level. Pretty lousy for marching. After all, this particular celebration should be a communal remembrance of the events fifty-one years ago and be open to all. Aren't we in a free society today? The outcome of those past events affected all the populations of Europe – indeed the whole world. Their citizens should have the ability to participate now. To add to the confusion, the event, traditionally in the afternoon to coincide with the original date and time, has been moved to the morning, so Yeltsin can go to Volgograd for an election rally in the afternoon. Well guess what happened? Apart from the fact that most of Moscow has begun the annual summer weekend trek to Dachaland planting potatoes or whatever, the place is now sealed off like an armed fortress. I had expected these affairs to be less bombastic and more muted these days. But no. Even the red military flag with a single star has been wheeled out in celebration of the army. Tverskaya is closed. I cannot get to Okhotny Ryad Metro Station. The only place I can go is out of the city – and that with difficulty. The area behind the Duma is an armed camp with special forces guarding it. Police have sealed off every entrance around my block. I feel like a virtual prisoner – indeed I am. It is totally daft. Those few other people (mainly foreigners) who were around were as frustrated as myself. I am most disappointed and more than a bit cheesed off with what appears to me to be a return to the habits of the bad old days of ignoring the wishes of the people and over reaction. Nothing could be seen by anyone. The only moment of note was the ice-cream vendor going through the police cordon. He might have been carrying a bomb in his cart, but was not searched by the multitude of security forces. So I went back to watch it on TV. It was meant to last two hours. They only showed the first hour. What is the point of a celebration parade if no one is allowed to see it or take an interest?

Muscovites had better ideas; they went to their Dachas to begin the serious part of summer relaxation. They apparently have had enough of these fanciful official parades to last them a life time. Our 'tame general' in the office (who helps the commercial wheels go around in places of political influence) told me on the following

Monday that he could have produced a ticket to see the parade in the square – influence produced too late, to my increased annoyance.

Chapter IV
A Day in the Country
June 1996

After my last attempts to become a minor 'literary genius' and report via circular letters a little on some of my experiences of the problems and opportunities of modern Russia over the last fourteen months, some of you encouraged me to take the process forward. You wanted to know a little more about the ways of the world here in these strange times. I do not know how many of you received the last fifteen-page tome, and did not use it to light the fire during the current English summer. Local reports tell me that your summer has lasted for at least three days. The last letter was sent via Speedbird 873 (British Airways afternoon flight from Moscow to London to the uninitiated) and one of my business friends who was returning home from a verbal grilling by the KGB[1] in Moscow – really. He and other UK businesses were visited by them recently during the last British spy scandal. Apparently they wanted to find out if he was extracting state secrets. Negative on that front as far as I am aware. Some of his London colleagues were less sanguine on that point, but I understand their problem. Apparently the amount, location and quality of precious metals in the ground is still a state secret. All a bit difficult, as part of his office is involved in the development of gold

---

[1]Now Federal Security Bureau – FSB, but I continue to use the term KGB for ease of understanding.

mining.

A few of you suggested that instead of cramming fifteen pages with impressions that covered the gamut of nearly twenty varied superficial commentaries, just one theme should be developed, a little and often. There are so many themes that could be chosen: politics and the current dramas of the presidential election; the parlous state of the banks and the forthcoming banking and tax collection crisis which will occur after the election; the strange way business is conducted; the appalling level of corruption in governmental circles and how it affects people in my position; or stupidities like having now to produce medical certificates as an additional customs form to import excavators and similar equipment (in case eating them might be injurious to one's health, is the declared reason!); or the social dilemma for the population in determining their existence beyond tomorrow – should a generation be sacrificed for the sake of the younger generation and a more secure future? Or commentary on the local Western press articles that state Americans have a secure bolt hole in their embassy when the shooting starts after the election – since denied by the US embassy.[2]

All of these are heavy themes which do not fit into a sunny Sunday Moscow afternoon with the temperature at 24°C and a gentle breeze calming the strains of Vivaldi and Mozart on the radio. This being regularly interrupted by a Babushka two flats below, shouting to all who want to hear in the courtyard, how much she hates Russia, the world and her husband. This is a regular occurrence, which often starts at 6 a.m. and goes on till the evening. On occasions it happens in the middle of the night. I do not think she is related to the witch who lives next door – twigs and candles on all souls night etc. Lovely neighbours I have!

---

[2] Reported in The *Moscow Times* and *Moscow Tribune*.

So here goes. I am encouraged to attack the word processor after a delightful Saturday out in the country with Russian colleagues at their Dacha. This is the fifth time I have been invited to different country abodes. So much that follows is common to them as well. Let me therefore start the way I left the last but one missive, by talking about the people. How they live part of their everyday lives and how they try to block out the grey and difficult pressures the current situation in the country imposes on their daily toil.

The word Dacha may conjure up different thoughts to different people, so let me describe the concept. It is more than just a summer house, it is a place of true escape. In days gone by, all, workers and apparatchik at whatever hierarchical level, earned at least similar salaries and wages, and in those days they were actually paid. The differences of status were rewarded for the privileged few by the trappings of power. A car and driver, a better flat (mine behind Tverskaya – formerly Gorky Street in the centre – is an example of that), cheaper shops selling Western goods, or a country escape – a Dacha. The harsh winter does not allow too much freedom to visit between November and April. But the snow-free months were, and are, used to the full. As the concept of land ownership did not exist then – and still not now in our legal sense – the gift of a Dacha by the government was among the highest and most sought after honours. Around Moscow the area covered by Dachaland is up to one hundred and fifty kilometres from the centre and starts from the outer ring road some thirty-five kilometres from the Kremlin. Over the years, all families who had 'connections' tried to acquire such a piece of property which could be anything from a shed on a small allotment to a four-bedroom house with an acre of garden. The state of repair of each building gives clues to the economic status of their owners. Such properties, large and small are seen all across the land, many made of wood and highly decorated, particularly around the windows.

Today, smaller plots have been sold and subdivided, to the extent that some fifty per cent of Muscovite families have access to such a bolt hole for the summer months. The sellers have been those who had more land than they required, thus many newer Dachas are found in groups as a result. To develop new Dachas on virgin land is apparently still very difficult, unless you have 'New Russian influence'. Possibly less than half have proper title to their summer residence, but that matters little. The legal process to recover property back to former owners is just not invoked. Only recently has a land registry been started with little power of establishing the rights of ownership we would expect. Possession appears to be nine tenths of the law and it works.

As an aside. While in St Petersburg during last winter I visited one of our sub-distributors and passed a very large group of lorries next to what appeared to be an allotment complex. This turned out to be partly true. They were allotments in the summer, but were being used as the local 'Forte (sorry Granada) Posthouse' for the winter by their enterprising owners. Better described as the allotment owners having created a system of hiring out their individual garden sheds to the lorry drivers as a bed for the night – breakfast was not included in the price. Such is rampant capitalism when the individual is out for himself. But not such a bad idea. I hate to think of the conditions inside the sheds after six months of 'enterprise'. Toilet facilities are a luxury, or at least an optional extra in most Dachas.

There is also no concept in Russian local planning laws that dictate how a building out in the country should be planned or erected – and it shows. This does not apply only to the cities. A strange system. If you have gained possession of a piece of ground and want to build, just do it.

There is no need to ask anyone about drains, building regulations, plumbing etc. Unless, of course, you come from the West, and want to build a factory. Oh dear, how the rules then suddenly change. Here, just find a source of electricity or buy your own generator, plug in and start to build whatever takes your fancy. Some of the results are monstrous, others very pleasant. The burgeoning number of garish Dachas around Moscow belonging to 'New Russians' – usually surrounded by a concrete security fence – are more than evident. Some of these places are reputed to have cost more than one million dollars. My driver Valera always mutters 'Mafia' under his breath when we pass them. That apart, all these are places where the Russians can truly do what they want for the first time in many generations. And they do that in spades.

The owner of the Dacha I visited had spent five years with his family designing and building a very plush abode. His son-in-law described him as a benevolent 'New Russian', slightly tongue in cheek, but certainly he was a self-made man of my age with some twenty-five retail DIY outlets in the suburbs of Moscow, and is apparently the largest private spec builder in Moscow. On top of that he also has a factory producing kits for smaller wooden Dachas. Its success is evident. Having visited on another occasion, his five hundred or so employees were extremely busy supplying a multitude of orders. At least his BMW 5 series was red, not black – the usual New Russian badge. It is rumoured in some circles that know him that he is in fact a member of the 'gang'. Being in the building trade probably meant he was. But who really knows these things. More specifically BMW 5 series are the minor Mafia, and BMW 7 series and Mercedes the heavy-mob symbols. So beware. When I return home, owners of similar machines may be regarded in the same way. A mobile telephone is also a must, to go with the new local image. Unfortunately they have as yet not learnt to turn off these banes of modern society in the Bolshoi. I was disturbed four times in my box at the last visit.

The term Mafia is used by many commentators on Russia, just as these pages make a similar general use of the word. It may therefore be useful to divert for a moment from the theme of this letter to put the term into proper context. Not all references in the West are completely accurate in their definition. The word Mafia has been used mainly to describe the activities of less desirable elements of Sicilian extraction. To many this gives the connotation that Russia has a similar closely-knit criminal organisation. Although I have no detailed contact with such people, observation tells me that this is not true in the Russian context. The general use of the word here refers to the formidable, and all-pervading corruption surrounding everyday existence, and not to a single grouping of organised criminality. I would define 'The Mafia' as used in these pages in five distinct categories.

1. Governmental corruption at the most senior level is vast. The taking of bribes is nothing new in Russian political life. In today's world it is the level and widespread nature that has changed. The insecurity of tenure in political office compared to the past leads to a desire for commercial rape of as much and as quickly as possible.[3] Favours can be, and are, bought at the highest

---

[3]One of the reasons the oligarchs held such sway over Yeltsin and his fellow politicians in the 1998 crash was that these people knew where the political and financial skeletons were buried. Mainly in overseas banks. The oligarchy and their banking organisations are reputed to have been the channels of much political graft. The vastness of this rape of the country's resources and the inside knowledge of the oligarchy were powerful factors in the demise of Kiriyenko and his group of so-called 'reformers'.

level. I have been asked for such favours, and they usually have to be clarified before a major commercial deal can be consummated. Of course a Western organisation has to have its accounts audited, and such payment is simply added to the 'commissions' line.

2. Petty government officials, policemen, or customs and tax inspectors are paid so little, that they regard a little 'grease' as a legitimate way of supplementing a meagre income. These people know full well that every businessman in the country has to try to avoid the punitive corporation taxes to make a success of commercial life. Legal accounting would demand the payment of profit taxes of at least 122 Kopecks in the Rouble. Few unsurprisingly pay, often with a little help from minor officials in governmental institutions. As for the customs authorities, well, they are the most corrupt of all. Probably half the goods entering the country are falsely declared to avoid punitive taxes. Certainly there are many ways around the legal jungle and they are used to the full.

3. The law is currently powerless to protect an individual or organisation in a claim they might have to redress their perceived hurt. Such matters are often solved by the 'legal department'. Most large organisations have appropriate people, none of whom have any training in the law. They have the tactics of the 'heavy mob', guns and hit men. Our own offices which we rent from a bank are 'protected' by similar people. The customer who sent his heavy mob with guns to visit me to obtain delivery of a crane thought such action as a normal method of redress.

4. The industrial privatisation process in Russia was fast and painful for the ordinary man. The vouchers that

each employee (as well as wives, husbands and offspring) were given, soon found their way into the hands of a select few. These few have come to be known as the 'oligarchs'. They have accumulated vast power through building huge business empires based on the acquisition of former state assets at bargain prices. The size, scale and speed of growth of some of the groupings is amazing. Banks, oil companies, media interests et al. This commercial rape of Russia is aided and abetted by the apparatchik. They gain from this development just as much as the oligarchy itself.

5. And lastly there is the accepted criminality of drugs, prostitution and smuggling that is traditionally associated with the word Mafia. That is no different to any other country in the world. The closer to the consumer one gets in the commercial chain with one's product, the higher the risk of protection rackets appearing on the doorstep. Distribution of such products as cigarettes and alcohol are perfect examples.

Gorbachev has much to answer for when the Communist Party fell in 1991. The legal and social vacuum he left was filled by such activities as described above. It remains all around us here. So the word Mafia as used in the Russian context is only a description of the lawless and unregulated capitalism that has taken hold in the absence of proper state and institutional structures. Unfortunately it pervades all walks of life. To date the rulers of this land had appeared helpless in resolving matters. But then they are among the main gainers from such activity.

Enough of that, back to the theme of the letter. On about three quarters of an acre a three-storey house had risen with three bedrooms, more upwards than using the land area sensibly. In the garden, a greenhouse produced cucumbers, tomatoes and herbs. Next to this, they were in the final throes of erecting a banya (Russian sauna – the difference escapes me) and store room. The garden had been carefully tended since the beginning of May with potatoes, fruit trees, gooseberries, currants, herbs and a varied collection of vegetables for harvesting during the summer. Having decided that they wanted to have a tennis court as well, they were in the process of 'possessing' the land next door adjacent to the silver birch forest which stretches across the whole country. As they considered that no one owned the patch for the tennis court, personal added value would be given to the neighbourhood by just taking it. After all, they said it bothered no one else and anyway it was the other side of the communal lake, so no one ever went there. At no stage had anyone either thought of, or asked for permission from any local authority for their actions, and they expected no comeback in the future. It was their property and they were going to keep it.

Water came from two wells about twenty metres deep and fuel for the hot-water boiler, in the winter, spring and autumn, from the forest. I did not discover where the drains went. Possibly just as well. But I saw some pipes pointing in the direction of the lake. They suggested a swim, but I declined. They as a family, parents, two daughters, son-in-law, grandson and excitable dog, had built their own version of paradise with their own efforts over five years and no one was about to disturb their obvious pleasure. Compare this with the forty-five square metre flat the owners had been allocated in the suburbs of Moscow for their life during the working week and in the winter. Life out here in the five months of 'real' spring, summer and autumn enjoyment was special to them. They and their ilk could forget their other difficult existence out here.

As was mentioned in my first letter, Russia had lost the

ability to feed itself. Close examination of the multitude of Dachas outside Moscow shows this to be only partly true for those lucky enough to have a suitable piece of ground, however small. While the world has the impression that the population is seduced by the celebration of May Day processions on Red Square and similar political nonsense, the reality is that the citizens have departed to the country-side to start their annual planting of enough staple vegetables for the immediate family. They ignore all the political rubbish out in Dachaland. The rest of the world (and our Western media) seems more interested in that than they do. On those May Days and the holidays in the following week in early May, the only people in Moscow were the foreign community or those who had no access to Dachas. Self-help is a key to their survival. Good luck to them, shame on us in believing they are, or have been, the madly committed political animals portrayed in the Western press. As usual The *Moscow Times* had an appropriate cartoon for the opening of the Dacha season, which for most starts at the beginning of May.

In honour of my visit, the traditional Sunday lunch for the whole family (similar meals had been served on other occasions) had been moved to Saturday. Family still has a firmer hold on the conscious mind than in the West – certainly here. Maybe this is because in past times there were few who could be confided in about views and opinions without KGB or state interference. That close-knit body survives intact today. Possibly also because the living permit required in the bigger cities does not extend to single parent families. Anyway we were seven people to lunch, although another three joined later on in the day. The roast was the traditional Shashlick. To us, a bar-b-que. I have had such grills in the depths of winter in the snow. The meat, veal, had been marinated overnight in a mixture of home grown herbs in its own juices. At about eleven o'clock the final preparation of the forthcoming feast began. The meat spent about an hour on the embers being carefully tended before being taken off the skewers and placed in an iron pot with onion rings and more herbs in the bottom for a longer cooking period to allow the juices to circulate. This was the key male contribution to the feast and we all helped by turning the skewers while discussing the world's problems. Really hard work that.

Holiday spirit at the Dacha

Inside, the ladies were busy with boiled potatoes, baked aubergines, a salad of whole vegetables, tomatoes, peppers, olives, cut spring onions, and radishes. The table was weighed down by salmon caviar (the red stuff – black caviar is from the sturgeon in the Caspian Sea), salami and a wonderful plate of mixed fresh herbs. The latter being uncut, fresh and delicious consisting of whole spring onions, dill, parsley, basil leaves, two sorts of salad leaves I had never seen or tasted before. The pot of meat was brought from the fire, and the object was to eat the meat with the raw herbs using fingers. Only a fork was required for the potatoes. On other occasions I have had a sort of Russian coleslaw. This was better. No salt was found on the table. They use it sparingly and prefer herbs. To my delight there was no vodka to be seen. They had compromised for me and produced some French white wine. Oh was I mistaken! No vodka, but four sorts of brandy were added to the required tipple. The meal lasted some three hours, and over five bottles of such brandy were consumed. Moldavia, Armenia, Georgia and then finally France were celebrated as producers of inebriation. This interspersed with further bottles of Georgian red and white wine. A London restaurant clientele would kill for such tastes as happened yesterday. So why none of this in central Moscow? At least for the benefit of the foreign community.

The talk was of life in the country today, dominated of course by the election. The consensus was that Yeltsin would win, but they preferred the social reformer Yavlinski. I pointed out that they were privileged and asked whether their opinion was influenced by their desire to keep the hard-earned gains for themselves and their counterparts in Moscow with little thought for the regions. Of course yes, was the answer. But their fear of a return of Communism (defined as that existent prior to 1991) was not far from the heart of most discussion. Such fears are restricted to the city populations of Moscow and St Petersburg. Their conclusion was that their vote was really negative – just like us really. Yeltsin was the worst of a very bad bunch that would in the medium-term future lead to the further break-up of the Russian Federation itself. The regions just had to fend for themselves, was their view. Such opinions are rife in the circle of friends and acquaintances I have made in my time in Moscow. Few expected Yeltsin to last the term of office,[4] and hoped that a deal could be made with Yavlinski (or another true reformer) to be prime minister. He takes over for three months, before new elections, in the event of the demise of the president. We shall just have to wait for the final fiddle factor in the vote – please do not believe any official or unofficial opinion polls. Rumour has it that this factor could have risen to be as high as twenty per cent.

Of course the differences in family life, earnings, costs between themselves and our life in the West were also part of the merry debate. Events of this nature in Russia have reinforced my view that we in the West are digging a grave for our society in the slow decline of the family as a complete unit as a focus for our future. Here, certainly in this part of Dachaland, it is still strong. Let us hope that it remains a force for them in their difficult lives. There are the beginnings of anti-Western feelings in some circles and they commented on this on occasions during the day, more in the manner of the West having failed them in their recent modern hour of need since 1991. As such, they must now work out their problems themselves, and they fear the resulting timescale. We should fear the drawbridge rising.

Lunch over, then the obligatory card game. Three others had joined by then. The game was simple – 21. Pontoon I think we call it. Their card pack had only thirty-six cards. There were no 2s, 3s, 4s or 5s. Jacks counted as 2, Queens as 3, Kings as 4 and Aces as 11. The object just as with us was to play against the banker, with a score of more than 21 busting the game. The final object being to win the accumulated pot of money in the middle of the table. The minimum stake was Rbl.5,000 (just over $1) per player per round. Two of us had the bank for short periods, till one of the new visitors (who were fed from the communal pot of

---

[4]At that time there was no public talk or knowledge of heart surgery.

remaining Shashlick) took over.

What a character. He wore an army uniform but was not a member of the service anymore. One is allowed to keep the uniform after leaving service and many still wear it with pride. He served for over thirty years, including a long stint in former East Germany – which was the top posting in those days. From the way he played cards, he must have owned the gaming rights to the barracks he used to occupy. In about two hours he had accumulated about Rbl.1.5 million (about $300) from our minor stakes. But all losses were made in the best of humour. I discovered later that our new card-playing partner was the head of my host's security organisation. Well he was a very pleasant head of this particular 'legal department'.

Such is a family day in Dachaland and it certainly helps improve my Russian. In my honour they had put their tools away and not tended the garden or continued to build the house, tennis court etc. The Russians I have met change character when out in the country. The harshness goes, and they relax from the tensions of life in the dreary city they inhabit from Monday to Friday. Even I felt a rise in tension as I was driven back to the flat through ugly and decrepit flats in this capital of a former superpower. Long may their escape give them pleasure. Not all is bad in life out here, but such glimpses are not often given to the foreigner. I look forward to many such Saturdays.

Chapter V
The Cost of Existence
July 1996

Hello again, Russia calling. My letters from Russia appear to have gathered a 'following'. So I am encouraged to continue the dialogue. Please remember that it is important to me to have some feedback as to whether I have interested the reader or caught a 'nerve' of conscience. I hope so, but please let me know, it helps spur on the effort. This letter was begun as a result of the Germans spoiling my TV schedule[1] by being their usual arrogant pain at football. Shame about the result.[2] So I had to concentrate on the presidential election instead.

One thing about Russia, love it or hate it, this place is never boring. They seem to want to hold the *Guinness Book of Records* prize in drama of one sort or another. There will be severe internal political ups and downs here over the next nine months or so, to a degree that 'short term' Western journalism probably will misreport or misunderstand if current form is repeated. If our press actually gets round to doing so, then only in sound bites and for

---

[1] The satellite TV programmes available in Moscow are all pretty useless. The Russian ones are little better. However my neighbour cut my satellite cable over Christmas 1995 to gain reception using my subscription. I had to pay fifty dollars to recover usage, even though I was not to blame. Such is minor justice.

[2] Euro '96 and the Germans won.

dramatic purposes. But then news at 30p (or has Murdoch reduced the price again?) in the morning is only for today and not for longer-term digestion, if you see what I mean. Possibly that is unfair in as much as any news away from home that apparently has little impact on one's daily domestic life, is only of superficial interest anyway. When I return home, my mission will be to reform the UK press. Some hope.

Not long after sending you the last letter on impressions of Dachaland, the group of Dachas in that part of the Russian 'Taiga' outside Moscow was raided by a local criminal gang. Aside from the point, the Taiga is the birch and coniferous forest which stretches for 6,000 miles across the country – and is miles larger or more important to the world's oxygen supply than the Brazilian rain forest. For the purists among you, the Taiga properly starts east of the Urals in the wilder parts of the land. Within this vastness are half the world's known coniferous trees, making up twenty per cent of the total world's forests. Anyway, back to the story. At about 3 a.m., the family I had visited and described in my last letter, were woken and asked to open the house to this particular group. Obviously the occupants refused. I would not do so in my flat either. The dramatic results of what followed can be seen on the outside of the house, and in the ceiling of the living room – high calibre Kalashnikov bullet holes! It would appear that the gang, not getting what they wanted – easy money – decided to try to take the house by force. This was the story I was given. Or was it a rival Mafia gang? Anyway, the family defended themselves by returning gun fire. Eventually someone in the Dacha complex managed to call the local police. They then proceeded to take three hours to get there. Upon arrival of the police, the bandits promptly disappeared. They, the police, then stayed for two more days to protect the whole compound of about one hundred and twenty residences, but turned out to be pretty useless. They proceeded to empty the wine and brandy bottles in the cellar and descended into a drunken stupor. Some protection. There is a happy ending to this salutary story. The gang tried to repeat the same tactics a few days later not realising that their next target, a nearby Dacha, belonged to the local district police chief. They had short shrift, were surrounded and are now in one of the 'nicer' jails in Moscow. I am told that one is 'allocated' about half a square metre per person in such places. But such is the every day life for us all out here. Similar stories abound elsewhere. Just to add though, during a further visit to my friends in Dachaland last week, the statutory card game resumed as though nothing had happened and I lost another pile of Roubles to Sergei the card sharp. For some unknown reason Sergei wants me to visit again!

In the final run-up to the presidential election, it became clear from West European and American TV and press that reached us here, that fear remained in your part of the world. Stopping a return to 'Communism' in Russia is apparently stronger than a need to help the desire to see the living standards of the Russian nation rise to something akin to that which the West has achieved over the last one hundred years. Oh well, self-interest at work. Understandable from the comfort of a Western living room, but rather 'head in sand' for the future. The same fears are apparent in the younger (under fifty) population in Moscow and St Petersburg, even though they know that the creation of a Western-style industrial and consumer society for all may take two more generations. Fuelling this fear has led to irrational financial support for Boris and his corrupt regime, and supported by the oligarchs, to remain in power by Western politicians, particularly from Clinton and Kohl. After all the USA and Germany want to perpetuate a weak Russian regime to remain in power for their own security and economic purposes. Unfortunately many of these funds did not go to the intended recipients – the well-being of the population.

Think on the following factual statement.

'The Russian economy, as measured by any international economic standards, has shrunk further, in the last six years, than that of the USA or Germany during the Great Depression of the 1930s.'[3]

This is the real and dreadful legacy of eighty years of totalitarianism, but recognised truth.

Communism old style may have been evil and deserved to die, but please spare a thought for the individual members of the population who have to live their daily lives with the so-called 'capitalist reforms' of recent years preceded by eighty years of totalitarian stagnation. The term 'market or capitalist reform' is often used in relation to the current economic development of Eastern Europe since the fall of the 'Iron Curtain'. In simple terms my definition of this is:

The process of moving control of daily human life from the hands of 'cradle to grave' state protection, into the creation of a society where individuals determine their own fate by their own efforts.

This is a battle of the 'mindset', as the Americans would say, as much as it is with a regeneration of the physical infrastructure of housing, factories, roads, schools, hospitals, single-industry towns etc. The latter needs money – oodles of it (see events in former East Germany), the former needs human determination and a government that

---

[3] IMF and World Bank statistics.

does not see the population as pawns in their power politics, to succeed. They, a very educated population, earnestly want to succeed in their quest to improve their lot, but in the short term the lack of ready money may defeat the total process. Some optimists estimate it will take ten years; sadly, I now believe up to two generations.

Those with few financial opportunities, or access to the benefits of life in Moscow or St Petersburg have found adjustment to new realities difficult in the extreme. They are the unfortunate losers in this modern Russian tragedy. History has shown that lurches from one extreme of political persuasion to another, creates more pain than is welcome and stores up problems for the future (Lady Thatcher please note). Unfortunately the common sense gradual approach never works in practice. Everyone wants instant results, and believes the holy grail is around the corner. We all know it is not. Just remember what has happened to the total German economy in its search to pay for the integration and modernisation of former East Germany into Western ways and the overnight trauma of 'living with the Deutschmark'. The pain for the average Russian citizen is doubly higher, as they have no rich 'sugar daddy' to help pay the astronomic bill. They, however, do have untold mineral wealth, but have a strange inability to use it wisely, or even sometimes at all. In addition, Russian politicians currently play the nationalistic card with vigour. They mistrust the intentions of the foreigners almost as much as they fear each other. This rise in dislike of foreigners is slow, but creepingly evident. That helps little to create rational foreign investment policies of any sort.

Those who have experience of East German economic conditions since 1989 will remember that the older population there (over fifty) had difficulty coping with the new capitalist realities. The younger members of their society came to accept reluctantly that the welfare of a whole generation may have to be sacrificed to achieve 'progress'. Russia has had to come to similar conclusions with a greater degree of pain, as their comparative starting point for future growth is lower and their problems greater.

Some of you will undoubtedly comment on my apparent socialist tendencies. My Russian friends hate this, and find it rather strange in an apparent representative of capitalism. My past voting pattern in the UK has been for the 'middle ground'. Truly I am genuinely trying to be objective in my analysis of life in modern Russia. That said, if I were a Russian voter, I still would have voted for Yavlinski (Liberal) in the first presidential round, and Zuganov (Communist), or nothing, in the second. There is nothing in Yeltsin's manifesto that I can see about helping the regeneration of Russian manufacturing industry. There is in the Communist agenda. They, the Communist Party, should have changed their name just like others in former Eastern European countries did. It would have helped, in Western perception anyway. The reason they did not do so to date, I am told, is that they believe this could alienate the important agricultural and pensioner vote. Yeltsin and his cronies seem more interested in policies that line their already full pockets. This continual corruption in high places has surely got to stop for the future well-being of their land. Why should we comment on the habits of the oligarchy and 'New Russians' when their example comes from the top echelons of power?

Anyway I see no difference between Yeltsin and a former Communist label. They are all, Yeltsin, Chernomyrdin, Zhirinovsky, Zuganov et al, from the same past stable of Communist apparatchik thought and training. As such, there may be some minor difference in political policy, but there is no divergence in method or arrogance toward the common people. They have an extraordinarily close circle of political contacts, unlike the West, where different political groups may tolerate each other but do not habitually fraternise. They all share the view that the 'political elite' of whatever persuasion should not be compromised by the 'peasants', the ordinary man. Some call this 'moral corruption'. The biggest crime in their eyes is to remove political control from the hands of this privileged 'elite'. It will take years to breed another form of politician in this country who has a degree of inherent national 'duty'. Who knows the price the population will have to pay to wait for this event?

Please tell me what happened to these former members of the old system when they 'rediscovered' the dignity of man, went to church each Sunday to impress the voters and pandered to the 'common man' in their search for approval. It is only an outward show for the media. They, however, remain the hard line apparatchik as they ever were despite such public appearances. A deputy mayor of Moscow told me, as an aside, during a joint trip to the UK, that he was now more influential than he ever was in times past. Was he talking about political or financial power? I suspect both. They have learnt to use old Communist alliances to their personal benefit in new circumstances with adept skill.

Well, the presidential election is over, Boris has won, with an unofficial estimated three per cent fiddle factor.[4] Well, he won for the moment, and certainly the fiddle was lower than originally expected. Lebed certainly saved Yeltsin, but there will be little thanks for that now the election is over. The published results showed among other things that in Chechnya (of all places) voters were sixty-seven per cent for Yeltsin. If you really believe that, you will believe anything. The formal dramas of political and economic reality will now become evident, and I earnestly hope that the result will be to the longer-term benefit of the

---

[4] Now finally believed to have been approximately eight per cent.

Russian people or to the West. But fear not. In past letters I have alluded to forthcoming drama; financial crash in the banking and governmental debt sector, economic and tax collection problems etc. It is beginning in earnest – watch this space for developments. The trouble is that continually trying to correct the Western press (and my UK masters) in explaining the reasons behind the true situation becomes rather tedious. To read the sort of rubbish that is printed with you, recycled as 'truth' and sent over here for us to purchase at an exorbitant price[5] is worrying. The fact is, that Yeltsin's economic policies, based on corruption for the privileged few, are unsustainable.[6] These policies are designed to line the pockets of the ruling class – the oligarchs, including factory managers of newly privatised enterprises, but not for the many who have nothing. The first signs of social discontent are beginning to seriously stir. Despite expensive election promises to fully pay back wages, unpaid workers blocked the streets of Samara (six hundred kilometres from Moscow) and Ulyanovsk (Western Siberia) at the end of June for achievement of this goal. As yet nothing has been delivered. Is this a sign of things to come? I suspect it is.

As an aside, the date for the second round of the election had been set for a Wednesday. The powers that be, knew that Sunday voting would be affected by the normal Dacha weekend absence from the voting booths. No chance – the Russians aren't stupid. On Tuesday evening all the roads *out* of Moscow were jammed. It normally takes half an hour to get from my office to my flat. This time it was one and a half hours for the same journey. On Wednesday, voting

---

[5]The London *Times* costs the equivalent of $10 at the National Hotel.

[6]It had not been revealed that Yeltsin had heart problems. When it was, all governmental action went into paralysis while Yeltsin's health was temporarily restored.

day, the city was quiet as the grave. The people again demonstrated their priorities. Escape from political nonsense.

In the first round of voting in the presidential election, had it not been for the strength of the vote in Moscow, St Petersburg and Ekaterinburg (formerly Sverdlovsk, Boris's home town in the Urals) he would have been in second place. The rest of the country rejected him into second place or worse (despite the apparent overall margin of victory). This rejection by many of the regions is as much to do with the known current and future economic prospects, the region's dislike of Moscow politics and central economic mismanagement, as it is to do with the way the population has to deal with the difficult matter of feeding its daily stomach. Despite the fact that the currently poorer regions sit on untold mineral and precious metal riches, it is not developed for their local benefit. Further major gripe with Moscow politicians.

It is a peculiar Russian mystery as to how families continue to exist when wages have not been paid for three or more months, some even dating back one year. I have as yet not been able to rationalise or understand how they manage properly under these circumstances.[7] This tragic phenomenon will increase dramatically over the next few months as a result of the lack of governmental financial options following Boris's extravagant vote-buying promises to gain re-election.

The stark choice facing Russia today is to repay short-term treasury bill (GKO) borrowing[8] to their 'friends' – the

---

[7] Nor did I ever really understand how they managed in all my time here.

[8] With the subsequent crash of August 1998, it is amazing to me that the genius Western financiers did not see this situation coming back in 1996. No, they carried on piling in with speculative zeal and then lost their shirts. I have little sympathy for them. Does the rest of the paragraph sound familiar?

bankers; *or* to pay wages to the public-sector employees, *or even* to pay all other normal public-sector needs. The fact is that current tax income to government coffers is just too small to pay for all three. The unfortunate figures are, that between June and October this year some $20.8 billion is due back in six-month treasury bills to some two thousand, five hundred Russian domestic banks.[9] These banks have reaped huge profits of up to three hundred and fifty per cent interest, based on Western accounting practice (GAPP), in recent times.[10] They cannot even bring themselves to allow Western banks to participate in this market segment – despite the fact that our banks may be more stable and like such treasury profits. The reason is simple, it would destabilise the Russian banks even further, despite being of benefit to the national exchequer. The government's wish to protect their 'friends' is higher than their national duty. The estimated tax income in the same period is estimated to be $18 billion, if it is all collected. These are published figures, not figments of my extravagant imagination. Hence the question – 'What financial sources are to be used to pay wages, investment and rebuilding of the infrastructure in the shorter term?' No one seems to know. There is nothing spare. What is fact, is that many of the banks will fail, or be swallowed by their larger brethren. The twenty-second largest closed this last week, four failed in the last three weeks, hundreds (yes hundreds) are expected to follow. So something has to give. General Alexander Lebed, the new whiz kid on the block, has given few real answers, but protectionism and pulling up the isolationist drawbridge is now back on the agenda via his influence. The West will unfortunately reap these conse-

---

[9]Russian Central Bank Statistics.

[10]During the autumn of 1996, these rates reduced to about sixty per cent. Even so this is still prohibitive.

quences just as the unfortunate local citizens will.

Just to add some more political spice to what you read in the newspapers or see on the TV at home, Boris is not ill – he just had a severe case of the 'vodkaitis'. His doctors have banned him from strenuous activity.[11] Apparently he was so depressed that he did not have a better result in the first round – he apparently believed he would win – and no one dared tell him otherwise.[12] As a result he returned to the bottle. His heart, unsurprisingly, did not like the mixture. The battle for succession has begun in earnest, together with the possibility of a coalition government. There are three main governmental groups of political infighting. These are between Anatoly Chubais, the Kremlin Chief of Staff (formerly head of the privatisation agency, and Yeltsin's election campaign chief), General Lebed and the Prime Minister, Viktor Chernomyrdin. Four critical political matters have to be resolved in the very short term.

- Firstly: the matter of the 1997 governmental expenditure budget against the current shortage of liquidity. Balancing the national books and the attendant political and social fallout in 1997 will be the most critical matter affecting the Russian political scene in the forthcoming months.[13] Even more important than who the next president might be.

- Secondly: how to deal with this liquidity crisis with a Communist-controlled Duma. They can (and would if the conditions were right) bring down the new administration at any time.

---

[11]It has since been revealed that a third heart attack and vodka do not mix.

[12]Source, the Kremlin.

[13]The national budget for 1997 was still not resolved in December 1996.

- Thirdly: the succession battle for president (a real issue, even one month after election).

- Fourthly: what to do with the forthcoming regional governors' elections. Economics say hold them (we can't pay the wages – so get someone who can). Politics say do not (the Communist opposition will win and separate the regions even more from the centre). Clashes between the two thought processes will be evident in the autumn months.

These four are all intertwined into a good traditional 'Russian drama'. The real situation, should Yeltsin die, get too drunk etc. is constitutionally clear. The prime minister takes over for three months, and then new presidential elections must be held. This issue is of course subject to any machiavellian decision of the Russian constitutional court. I hesitate to question their debate if it comes. This is a tricky one. Yeltsin abolished the post of vice president some time ago to stifle any opposition (a post which Lebed wants to re-establish and have for himself). If there were a vice president, there would be no new presidential election. Just as in the USA – the vice president would take over if the president were to die or step down. However, once the liquidity crisis breaks into public view in the next few weeks and months, (which it now has, with forty-six banks failing in July – including the seventeenth largest in Russia by reported asset base – the Tveruniversalbank) with severe repetition of non-payment of wages. Then Yeltsin's popularity will drop like a stone, and the Communist-dominated Duma could very likely bring down the government (or if Boris returns to the bottle – even more likely). Another presidential election could result and he would lose in spades. He will have been seen to lie to the people. If wage payments are further delayed, then the forthcoming regional governors' elections will lead to a further weakening of Yeltsin's central power.[14] So the individual proposed resolutions appear as follows:

- Chubais wants to dissolve the Duma and stifle any opposition. This is an extreme measure which will cause instant social unrest. This option has few supporters, but is being discussed. Chubais was the minister responsible for privatisation – seen by many as a liner of heavyweight pockets – the oligarchs. He is hated in Moscow and the regions alike as a consequences of these policies. He has now been surprisingly rehabilitated and protecting 'New Russian' wealth could end up as the central theme of short-term policy. The Western press report him as a 'reformer'. In reality he is Yeltsin's 'gatekeeper'.

- General Lebed wants to restore the post of vice president, so that there will be no need for a future presidential election – and of course he wants the post for himself. His wings have been clipped in recent days, but one of his strengths (and at the same time a weakness) is that, so far, he is, publicly anyway, untainted by too much corruption and not a Kremlin insider.

- Chernomyrdin wants to bring into the new administration a percentage of additional ministers and officials who are current members of the defeated Communist Party so that he has a 'controlled' Duma that goes along with an orderly management of the liquidity crisis. Of course there will be significant debates about specific

---

[14]By early December 1996, Yeltsin lost the popular support of the regions by losing about half of the governors' elections held to date.

portfolios for these possible additions.[15] Should the Communists allow themselves to be sucked into 'subservience', then it could even damage their credibility and usefulness as an opposition force.

- Cancel the regional governors' elections (due by December 1996). If so, then the Communists have even more evidence that Yeltsin is losing the game at the centre. Current economic policy will lead to political decline, a pragmatic political line will destroy economic recovery. An unhealthy brew.[16]

There is an old Russian proverb: 'Two (or more) bears cannot live in the same cave'. My guess is that Chernomyrdin will win the power play (but he only has about three to four weeks to solve this situation). This process, if successful, will weaken Yeltsin and in the not too distant future the post of vice president may reappear,[17] with the incumbent being Chernomyrdin (but then Lebed has not yet played his final hand). So when the vodka bottle gets too hot for Boris and he drowns in it, then an orderly handover of power will occur. Chernomyrdin has many followers in Western governmental and financial circles. They say he is a 'safe, but boring, pair of hands'. His current proposals will also be (in my opinion) in the best interests of the people. Having said that, he is only the best of poor alternative candidates. If the above actually does happen, then the Russian people may have won longer term in the battle for democracy, however tentative. If my prognosis is correct we still have some real dramas to come. This is a lot better than watching the 'grey Major' versus

---

[15]He succeeded, and Communist officials are now in many middle and junior governmental ranks.

[16]The governors' elections went ahead, some with surprising results.

[17]It did not.

'Bambi the magnificent' (Tony Blair) in the UK election run-up. But at least this demonstrates that democratic power, however tentative, is marginally on the rise here. In days of old, all this would have been fought out behind closed doors and papal 'puffs' of smoke would appear to announce that decisions had been reached. I am not suggesting all the above is fully public as yet – but the drama is beginning to leak to those who keep their ears and eyes open. It is real fun though to have an inside track on some of these dramatic events. On the other hand matters could all get out of hand and become rather nasty.[18]

Before I became totally diverted by the football, Russian election dramas and lack of sleep, the subject of this letter from Russia was meant to have been twofold: firstly to expand on the situation (mainly outside Moscow, St Petersburg and the industrial Urals) regarding unpaid wages; secondly to delve a little into the shopping habits of the privileged city dwellers, compared to the regions, if they actually have any money left. So, if you have any patience to read on, I will continue. It seems to me that one cannot talk about shopping habits, or the search to keep body and soul together, without understanding the factors affecting income and expenditure. Whether official or from the black economy, wage arrears and economic data – within which the Russian consumer behaves on a daily basis. The following may also help to explain in more detail the background, from the perspective of the individual Russian citizen, as to the political dramas yet to come as explained above.

---

[18]And they did. See Chapter VI, 'Kremlin Intrigues', and later chapters on the crash of 1998. As it turned out, I read some of the signals incorrectly in terms of what happened in the period surrounding the 1996 elections. However, as subsequent events turned out, the results were the same. The power brokers played their games for two more years at the inevitable expense of the people.

Therefore my apologies if some of what follows appears to be an essay on economic theory and boring data, but it is important to understand the reality of statistical data to see the true picture of daily life across Russia today. You can then possibly perceive why the weekend retreat to Dachaland reported on in my last letter is so important to the lucky ones who have that opportunity. They have to escape from such fundamental problems or they would go slightly loopy. Some would say that I have 'gone native' and reached that state already. I ask you to draw your own conclusions as to whether such evident inequality, as will become obvious later, is sustainable for the longer-term health of the Russian citizen, their internal stability and their relations with the rest of the Western world. The lucky Russians you see in the centre of Moscow, St Petersburg, Bromsgrove[19] or Millfield Schools[20] (and other such educational establishments in the UK) et al and associated with the 'New Russian' elite are of course excluded from this analysis. They are the winners – but remain only one per cent of the total population (but about ten per cent in Moscow). Anecdotal comment estimates that there are more $ millionaires in Moscow than in Washington – I can believe it.

In the past the privileged political apparatchik were allowed to shop for scarce foreign goods, at cheaper and subsidised prices, in such places as GUM on Red Square. Today a multitude of upmarket Western shops have opened in the centre of Moscow. The prices are horrendous – about double the same cost for similar goods available in every Western high street. Unfortunately only the few can

---

[19]A West Midland fee-paying school that currently has six Russian pupils.
[20]A fee-paying school where Yeltsin has sent his grandson. It was with amusement that I read that Yeltsin's office announced he would be paying the fees from the royalties on his book. I did not know he had written one. But of course where else would the money come from?

afford such pleasures. The gap between haves and have-nots in this country is vast, with little in between. There are signs of an emerging middle class in Moscow, based on the service sector. But is that a bubble waiting to burst? We shall see.

Let me, firstly, give you some statistics, mostly from Moscow's Interfax Agency.[21] Each of the debts mentioned below are individual, and not a collective total.

- On the 20 February 1996 total wage arrears across Russia were a staggering Rbl.20,400 billion ($4.2 billion), and rising.[22]

- Our largest customer in Moscow, a private construction company, is owed for work completed for the city of Moscow in 1995 and part of 1994.[23] Imagine that in the United Kingdom.[24] Despite this situation, the managing director organised election rallies for and paid political contributions to those who had not paid him.

- The total debt to foreign creditors has risen from almost nil in 1988, to $128 billion in 1996, or $870 for every man woman and child in the country, and

---

[21]Federal GOS statistics.

[22]Since the end of September 1996, the issue of wage arrears is becoming a national scandal. This figure had risen to an even worse situation – $10 billion by mid-1998.

[23]He stopped paying his five thousand workers in September 1996.

[24]By 9 September 1996, these wage arrears had risen to a staggering $7.4 billion. This meant that some sixteen to eighteen million people, a quarter of the working population, had neither received wages nor were owed for their labour. The effect was that some thirty per cent of the Russian population were living below the official subsistence level. Source, *Trud* (Labour) newspaper. In August 1998, Russia's Federation of Independent Trade Unions claimed that total outstanding wages stood at an astonishing $13.87 billion at pre-devaluation rates.

rising.[25] The UK credit agency ECGD – has declared the public sector as bankrupt, and does not extend credit support without extremely good reasons.

- The total bad (and probably unrecoverable) debt in the internal economy in early December 1995 was Rbl.244,300 billion ($50 billion). Of this, thirty-four per cent was from newly privatised businesses not paying Federal or local taxes, and suppliers or wages not having been paid. The remainder was due from Federal authorities non-payment to suppliers or employees.

- One in three businesses is currently running at a loss across the country. This situation is particularly bad in Chita, Magadan and Chukotka (all Russian Far East regions – a heartland of support for Zhirinovsky). In Yakutia (again in Eastern Siberia, where one third of the world's diamonds are to be found), some fifty per cent of businesses are losing money.

- In selected national industrial sectors,[26] the percentage of *loss-making* enterprises is as follows:

Agriculture	57%	Total Fuel	36%
Coal Production	50%	Gas Industry	15%
Pulp Paper	38%	Scientific Products	15%
Consumer Goods	36%	Power Engineering	11%
Non-ferrous Metal	36%	Oil Refining	Nil

- The miners are again declaring a strike for payment of

---

[25]When the bubble did burst and the government defaulted, this foreign debt had risen to over $200 billion.

[26]GOS statistics June 1996.

wages – now outstanding for more than five months.

- The Prime Minister (Viktor Chernomyrdin) is alleged to be a large share holder (three per cent) of GazProm (again local anecdotal gossip – but I have no proof – but if true that would rank him among the world's billionaires). GazProm is the world's largest gas producer, indeed possibly the largest company in the world as measured by sales. It certainly has the highest known gas reserves – estimated at forty per cent of all reserves in the world today. GazProm's full profits have not regularly been declared, nor do they apparently pay their full tax requirements. Is there a connection? In addition, what would the UK stock market have to say if the above table of loss-makers was true of the state of British industry?

- The number of strikes for payment of back-wage payments has risen from 514 in 1994 to 8,856 in 1995. In January 1996, there were 2,108 strikes for back wages alone, of which *all but thirty-one*, were in schools, universities and other educational institutes. What for the future of education?

- At the same time, many of the prestige construction projects in Moscow are financed by eager and willing foreign help. Menazhnaya Square, a massive future shopping complex just below the Kremlin walls is being funded by German loans. American companies use cheap (on occasion at apparently four per cent) money from their Exim Bank. As usual Britain lags at the end of the lending and support queue – on this occasion I cannot but agree with their stance. One wonders if the money will ever be repaid. The signs for that prospect seem more hope than reality. If not, then who pays? We in the West I suppose.

As an aside, I met a young couple recently. He was an engineer teaching at a Moscow Technical University, she was a newly qualified doctor. She now practised psychiatry at a local hospital. Their charm and intelligence belied the manner of raising money for their uncertain future. Having decided that their joint earnings were too low for them to reach, in their opinion, a decent standard of living they had both agreed that the only course for them both to reach some financial future was for her to work as a 'high class' prostitute in one of Moscow's premier night spots. There, her husband told me she could earn up to $500 per evening. Although they had decided this would only happen once a week, it shows the depths some are prepared to sink to, to enable them to secure a 'better' future. They were both sanguine about the path they had embarked upon. Another couple I met, and later came to respect greatly, lived in two rooms consisting of twenty-four square metres at a local army base. They felt that their joint earnings of $72 per month for them and their twelve-year-old son were just sufficient to allow them not to sink into such lowly existence. They were the ones with guts and determination to succeed. Not the pseudo intellectuals.

- Pension arrears in January 1996 amounted to Rbl.4,600 billion ($944 million).[27]

- The average worker across the *whole of Russian industry*, education and commerce was owed on the 20 January 1996, Rbl.717,000 ($147). This had risen from Rbl.529,000 ($109) one month earlier. Some do get paid on time, but an increasingly few. This figure will rise dramatically over the next few weeks and months. Watch this space.

---

[27]Unofficial reports said that payment of pensions may be suspended for August 1996. Source, the Kremlin. And they were.

- Debt per employee, per industry and company defined as total debt of the company, including unpaid wages was as follows on the 20 January 1996[28]:

	Rbl. $		Rbl. $
Gas Industry	4,297,000 (880)	Farming	455,000 (93)
Coal Industry	2,390,000 (490)	Transport	446,000 (91)
Oil Industry	1,991,000 (408)	Education	255,000 (53)
Steel Industry	1,539,000 (315)	Health Care	212,000 (43)
Construction	771,000 (158)	Culture & Arts	70,000 (35)

- The above figures of debt have risen by thirty per cent in just one month from 20 December 1995. They have risen further since. In themselves the figures above do not seem high, but the average official monthly wage is only $154 per month. When reading the above statistics it should be remembered that all Russian businesses are totally overmanned – a historical phenomenon. Retrenching them without tax or other incentives to create new businesses, particularly in the regions will only increase the current regional agony.

- The drive to productivity needs huge amounts of capital and the cost of borrowing from commercial banks is between one hundred and eighty per cent and two hundred and fifty per cent on Rouble-denominated loans which is a major deterrent to the best run of companies anywhere in the world. Investment levels in Russian manufacturing industry to bring them to inter-national standards are dire. The factories I have seen are reminiscent of the 1930s.

---

[28]Please note Mr Chernomyrdin, particularly for the gas industry.

- Under former Communism, there was no declared unemployment, but the true figure today is at least twelve per cent, probably much more, across the country. In Moscow it is about five per cent.

- The mortality rate has risen by thirty-three per cent in the last six years. The total population is declining today by some one million persons per year, some of this from emigration. The birth rate is half of the death rate for the latter part of 1995.

- Gross Domestic Product has dropped by three per cent in the first quarter of 1996, and is now *fifty-one per cent of what it was in 1989*. In some industrial sectors the decline has been even more severe. Hence my previous comparison of the Russian economy with the Great Depression of the 1930s in the USA and Germany.

- It is unofficially estimated that between $20 and $80 billion of 'black money' flows into illegal foreign bank accounts each year from the earnings of the 'New Russian'. It could be more.

The above is a horrifying tally of statistics. If taken in context from the perspective of the average voter, who has been given the fateful choice to decide between 'so-called 'reforms' (Yeltsin) and perceived former apparent stability – or the bad old days, for some – and control of crime (Zuganov) there is no choice at all. There should therefore be some understanding (if the West is actually listening) for the views of the average Russian citizen. An accident of conception for those born in rural Siberia rather than comfortable British suburbia therefore results in attitudes being more than a little aggrieved with his or her lot today.

The resolution of the above internal debt mountain has been Boris's target in the election campaign (for personal power rather than national motives). He has tried to buy, bribe and borrow his way into power again in the most blatant misuse of office of recent political times. He has succeeded temporarily, by making promises which we should expect to be broken after his election. However, every sensible housewife, even in Russia, knows you cannot spend more than you earn for long. So Boris's, and unfortunately Russia's, day of reckoning is at hand – but the price will be paid, as usual by the ordinary people. Let me make one further key statement of reality in today's Russia:

- *The life expectancy of an average Russian male has fallen by ten years since 1988, to fifty-seven years in 1996.* In addition, nearly twice as many deaths (66,586) as births (34,356) were recorded in the first six months of 1996.[29] These are dreadful statistics that say much which will determine the future thinking of all intelligent beings in this sorry country. These statistics will affect the heart and soul of every Russian family that believes in humanity. They also fuel my personal belief that their patience with their rulers and their economic lot will run out sooner rather than later.

It is against this background that the local population tries to feed its daily need for survival. In all previous communications, I have tried to stress the differences in reality between what happens in the key centres of Moscow, St Petersburg, the Urals (particularly Ekaterinburg) and the rest of the country. This statement cannot be repeated too often, but the Western press appears to ignore this reality. It erroneously worries about Zhirinovsky and resurgent Communism, but spends little time pondering about the plight of the vast population of the average rural Russian,

---

[29]Source, Moscow State Statistical Committee.

whose circumstances understandably fuel the rise of people like Zhirinovsky. Is this not the tale of potential revolution?

- We should also expect the prophesy of the chairman of the Inkombank (regarding the demise of some five hundred to one thousand banks in the autumn of 1996) to become a reality.[30] If fulfilled, it will help create uncertain conditions that will exacerbate a sharp decline in Yeltsin's popularity and further distrust of the political establishment by the population. Indeed his words are coming to fruition by the day.[31]

None of you should be surprised about the resulting rise of 'Russian extremism' when they cannot feed their national belly, when the few have more than enough and the many have little or nothing. Try to place yourselves in the desperate position – especially in the regions – of the unfortunate many. Let me add some additional comment that applies to Moscow alone to underline the message.

- Of total food consumption forty per cent is now imported. In Moscow (ten per cent of the population) and St Petersburg (five per cent of the population) this import figure is sixty per cent of usage.

- One third of all Russian citizens live below the 'official' poverty line. In Moscow and St Petersburg this is less than five per cent.

- Special measures have apparently been taken (before

---

[30]Little did he (Mr Vinogradov – chairman of the Inkombank) realise that only two years later his own bank would be one of the victims of the crash of August 1998.

[31]The demise of the banks has been spread over into 1997 due to Kremlin support of some of them in 1996 and by mid-1998 Yeltsin had a popularity rating of only one per cent for performing his function.

the presidential election) to ensure that Moscow has sufficient basic food (butter, oil, dairy products, eggs, sugar and other staple food) for 1996. This includes special tax incentives (Rbl.600 billion–$123 million) for the national railway network to deliver the Russian part of this food to the capital. Is someone expecting trouble?

COST OF A RUSSIAN FOOD BASKET OF NINETEEN STAPLE ITEMS, RENT & METRO (RBL PER MONTH)[32]

	Basic Cost	Metro pass per month	Month's Rent Moscow/ St P	Total Cost
Yakutsk (Eastern Siberia)	544,300			544,300
Petropavlovsk -Kamchatsky (Siberia)	514,100			514,100
Magadan (North Pacific Coast)	501,200			501,200
Ulyanovsk (Western Siberia)	148,400			148,400
Moscow	287,100	65,000	42,000	394,100
St Petersburg	237,300	52,000	35,000	324,300

Sorry, but one further set of statistics helps to complete the picture. That is the income for the 'average' against the cost of a basic food basket of nineteen standard items of food. I

---

[32]Source, GOS statistics, January 1996.

have to say that it is not quite clear what these nineteen items are – but they are regularly quoted here. I have added into the figures some other key data such as the monthly cost of a Metro pass in Moscow and St Petersburg. Other information on the cost of clothing, flat refurbishment and other normal living costs is not to hand. Telephone, electricity and gas are still free for the majority of citizens. That is still paid by the state, but how long for, one wonders.

The variations are clear. It is vastly more expensive to live in far eastern rural regions than it is in key more westerly capital cities. Some remote places did attract higher incomes and subsidised food in past days, to encourage people to move and work there. Unfortunately today those benefits fade, as the non-payment cycle increases, and the product of their labour reduces. I show below the statistics (the last set – honestly) for income. These are national averages. This again demonstrates the regional differences. Do not be surprised at the resulting social tensions – but: the cost of living is lowest in the cities, yet that is where the highest incomes are earned. Those are the places you see on your TV screens. You see little of the poorer, remoter and impoverished parts.

You should spend little time wondering about the rise in nationalistic tendencies or 'Communism', seen by many as a return to a safe, stable and understandable past. The figures speak for themselves. It shows dramatically why Boris came first in those few cities of St Petersburg, Moscow and Ekaterinburg, but *not* in many of the regions, certainly not in the southern populous industrial belt. The people in the depressed regions are not satisfied with their lot that the fall of totalitarianism had given them in the short term, on the other hand *nor have they* seen the benefit of so-called capitalist market reforms. By the way, what are we in the West doing to help? Nothing of substance, other than to try to support a corrupt regime. Some of you will say it is not our affair. Keep out. So be it. I hope you are right, but I fear for our joint future, not.

MONTHLY INCOME AS PER OFFICIAL GOS STATISTICS IN RBL[33]

	Official	Black Economy[34]	Total
Average Official Wage	745,000	300,000	1,045,000
Official Individual Pension	52,000	n/a	52,000

Just to add some spice to the comparisons.

Average ex-pat apartment rent per month (well mine at least)	15,000,000
Average monthly cost of my shopping basket, because I am stupid	5,000,000
Average ex-pat salary per month (I shan't tell you mine)	58,000,000
Average (an inspired guess) 'New Russian' earnings per month.	100,000,000

It is said (by my staff) that an average Muscovite can live, without pain on Rbl.1,000,000 (about $200) per month. I am not sure if this was a mistake by them. It could have led me to reduce their wages? People whom I have met in the regions scoff at these high figures which they believe are figments of someone's exaggerated imagination. It can't be true they say.

---

[33]The denomination of the rouble was changed in January 1998. The '000's were removed.

[34]The black economy may actually be higher, some estimate up to forty per cent of GDP. No taxes are, however, recycled from this source for the benefit of all.

$1 equals Rbl.4,800 (it was Rbl.1 to $1 in 1988). £1 equals Rbl.7,800 (it was Rbl.1.5 to £1 in 1988). These figures apply as at end June 1996.

Well there you are. Here endeth the economic lecture. However, I hope it has put some of the recent political and social events into a broader perspective. Hopefully also you will appreciate the origin of grass-root tension between the centre and the regions a little more. There are many informed local commentators who believe that the process described above will lead to a further break-up of the Russian Federation in the not too distant future. Many believe this to be an inevitable process anyway. The truth is that today Russia is at best an 'economic banana republic' that still tries to believe it remains a cohesive superpower. How can they believe such myths with such a tally of statistics? But then old beliefs always die hard. I said in my first letter, the fall of the former USSR was simply down to a lack of funds and not to Thatcher or Reagan banging an anti-Communist drum. That situation continues in spades. Unfortunately the coming months will see the situation become worse.

At last to the subject of the weekly shop. That is for those of you who got this far. It is Saturday, and some of you (well your wives at least) will have spent part of the day at Tesco, Asda, Sainsbury or similar wonderful British institutions conserving your pennies while trying to satisfy the latent hunger of the gourmets resident in your homes for the forthcoming week. Spare a moment of thought for the souls that do not have the benefits of such marketing institutions. Rather they have places that try to rob hard-won Roubles from the pockets of a despondent population.

Those of you who have been to Moscow (a cocoon for us foreigners) and marvelled at the modern supermarkets that sell products to the stupid Western community at exorbitant prices, and assuming that these institutions are replicated across the land, should think again. Here, in Moscow, we can buy anything we want – at a price. I can go to the various supermarkets serving the Western community twenty-four hours in the day, seven days per week, and then pay by credit card. Eat your heart out Germany – they have not heard of silly restrictive labour laws here yet – well not in this sector. Less than one hundred kilometres from the centre of the capital, shelves remain poorly stocked, and on occasion empty apart from bare necessities. The regional situation is far worse.

But at what price for the weekly shop for us pampered ex-pats? My experience in these (for Russians) palaces of delight in the capital is entirely abnormal. Firstly, for Moscow, I have to accept that I, and others like me, are regularly being ripped off. Try $5 for three apples, $22 for a small jar of Nescafé, $14 for the cheapest bottle of French plonk or $35 for a 750 ml bottle of Bells whisky[35] – never mind the cost of meat and veg.[36] Even things we regard as normal are not always available. Last week it was tonic water, bacon and washing-up liquid that was off the shelves of my local supermarket.[37] Maybe the lack of the latter had something to do with the annual shut down of the central heating stations. So no hot water for a month – now back on thank goodness. That certainly starts the day with a real shock. It removes yesterday's vodka from the system with the utmost speed.

The way it works for the Russians is different. You will see a multitude of shops around the place with signs in

---

[35]Despite creeping Rouble devaluation, these $ prices never went down during my shopping experience.

[36]This was written before I discovered the joy of Russian markets. They turned out to have fresher and cheaper produce. On top of which, the service was far better.

[37]For those who know Moscow, just behind the Lubianka – KGB headquarters.

Cyrillic saying ПРОДУКТы (to the uninitiated called *PRODUKTI).* This is the standard Russian general store serving the majority of the population. In the key cities, there is a beginning of wider product differentiation. Specialist shops selling a specific variety of goods, as we have known for years, begin to abound. Food supermarkets, sports shops, shoe shops, chemists, jewellers etc. (very marked in the centre of Moscow and St Petersburg – but not, as yet in the suburbs).[38] In the regions, that is in its infancy. There you have a general store, which sells whatever happens to be in stock. There is no guarantee of regular supply and multiple visits are inevitable to obtain what you want. Despite the comments made above, food queues are rarely seen today, but there is the likelihood they could return – certainly in the regions. My friends in Moscow (well they are usually the ones who have been paid) tell me things are much better now than they ever were – wow! These Russian shops employ the 'ticket system'. That is, you choose your goods, go to the cash desk, collect your payment receipt and go back to the first counter to collect your product in the hope that someone else hasn't beaten you to the draw. Understand that – good – go to the top of the class. I have to say that I have never mastered this system, partly because my Russian is not yet up to the competitive nature of the Russian housewife, and partly because it takes so long. I am part of the daft local Western population and 'New rich Russians' who take the easy way out in the various expensive Western-style supermarkets in Moscow. My excuse is that my wife is not here to master such important matters. What is theirs? In these institutions, the prices are vastly higher than in the *PRODUKTI* shops, but one gets most things quickly. The differences in cost are demonstrated above.

---

[38]That did change for the better during 1997.

Those who have been to Moscow, in my time, here will have seen the Western shops. Those of an earlier vintage will have experience of the *PRODUKTI* regime. On Novi Arbat, a now plush shopping street, a BHS franchise has opened there this month. What luxury, for underpants and socks for those of us denied Marks & Spencer. Littlewoods apparently opens its store in Moscow shortly – after three franchise operations in St Petersburg. Between the White House and the Kremlin there is the original 'Irish House'. Downstairs is possibly the best Russian food supermarket in town, about four thousand square metres of prime selling space. Even for the average Russian it is expensive – but good. The products are behind counters and only sold by the ticket system. Upstairs in about five hundred square metres, you can shop self-service style for products with only Western labels. This is the place where my ilk are usually found and we pay through the nose for the pleasure.

I recently met the former Russian managing director of this four-year-old venture. He reported that in its first year of existence the sales from these few five hundred square metres were £38 million at net margins of eighty per cent. Unsurprisingly the Mafia 'protection' system got involved. Sainsbury try to obtain net margins of 6.5% with a competitive struggle and no Mafia. One of my development projects involved investigations into a product line that might have retail implications. Some of my ex-pat colleagues informed me that 'protection' was approximately $10,000 per month for a city centre store with about fifteen hundred square metres. Unsurprisingly we went no further with this proposed venture.

The foreign community has become a little smarter in its buying habits in more recent years, but not by much. The 'New Russians' now think this shopping habitat is smart, and one is more likely to bump shopping trolleys with a Russian than a foreigner. So far there have been no local reports of 'trolley rage'. While all this happens in Moscow, the average Russian in the regions thinks only of his daily struggle to survive on meagre wages that may not have been paid for months (and worse in the forthcoming months). The conclusion is fundamental. A divided population. The very rich and very poor, with little in between. We should understandably expect trouble in the future.

Anyone have any thoughts for a lighter subject for the next letter? Suggestions welcome. How about – 'Why are Russian graveyards always situated inside woodlands? I don't know, but it is true. Well I am off to see Spartak and Torpedo play football later today, and back to Dachaland on Sunday. Have a good one.

The living room of my first Moscow pad

The steel front door

The courtyard of the flat

I am on the sixth floor

Me in Red Square

Laura, Gemma and me in Arbat Metro Station

The Bolshoi theatre

Novodevichy Convent in Moscow

Mary in Palace Square in St Petersburg

Catherine the Great's Palace at Tsarskoe Salo, now called Pushkin

Alexander's Column

Mary outside the Hermitage

Golden domes within the Kremlin

Spires in Suzdal

The Summer Palace outside St
Petersburg

The domes at Sergei Possad

Wooden churches in Suzdal

The walled Petrovsky Monastery in Suzdal

The Monastery at Sergei Possad

Proud Tajik and Uzbek, men with their boots and medals

Outside school in Samarkand

Chapter VI

Kremlin Intrigues
July 1996

Extracts from *Zavtra* Newspaper
July 1996 Issue No. 29

No view on Russia would be complete without a peep behind the curtain that surrounds the Kremlin. There is so much material, or so many examples to choose from. I have decided that a more murky incident might give a clue to the Byzantine methods that are used. The following was part of the series of letters home, and is a translation of an article appearing in the *Zavtra* (Tomorrow) Newspaper in the 29th issue in July 1996 and reprinted here with their permission. My Russian is not good enough to vouch for the translation, nor did I read the original Russian, but have done since. However, it comes from a tested and very reliable source who knows most of the players, and who did read the original article and passed me the translated text (since checked). *Zavtra* has apparently a startling record of accuracy in revealing what is going on behind the scenes at the centre. The transcript is included in this compendium of letters with the sole purpose of showing the Byzantine intrigues that the Kremlin continues to play to elect a president and dupe the people, while the reality of normal life outside the Kremlin walls passes them by. It also gives better inside information on some of my own broader observations of political conduct contained in these pages.

If true, this article confirms my worst suspicions that democracy in high places is but a long distant dream in Russia, despite expressing some earlier hope.

As the KGB (the new proper name FSB is used in the article) apparently continues to monitor most events, including presidential telephone calls, it is alleged what follows is reasonably accurate, and therefore most of the information possibly emanates from them. The content of the article was, however, not privileged information. It could have been purchased by any Muscovite at a newspaper kiosk, as I did later. I do not personally vouch for the accuracy, or otherwise, of this article, nor its contents, however, many of the press 'leaks', some of which were quoted in the Western media, would appear to come from this source. Other Moscow papers also carried much of the same material in later editions. My experience here tells me, however, that it is probably a fair account of what chronologically happened. History will decide if what is stated is true. The translation has been reproduced verbatim as handed to me, therefore I cannot be responsible for the use of English, or the explosive content. The translator involved is, however, extremely competent. The article was headed:

Showdown Items. Beginning of Quotes from *Zavtra*

February. First Deputy Premier O Soskovets is appointed the head of Boris Yeltsin's campaign staff The directors of special services and television companies are brought on to the staff. Yeltsin nominates A Chubais for the position of deputy staff director responsible for the collection of funds for his presidential campaign. Then Chubais proposes that Yeltsin's daughter, Tatyana Dyachenko, who, it is planned, was to take on the illustration of the life of the Yeltsin family, be brought on to the staff. Her real role, however, which was rapidly secured for T Dyachenko with Chubais's help, was the coordination of the interaction between Yeltsin and the group of American experts in the field of political commercials, chiefly from the Republican Party; they had been recommended to Chubais by representatives of Goldman Sachs, the US financial group closest to him. In addition, Chubais creates for himself also a direct outlet channel to Yeltsin via his daughter. Confidential relations between Chubais and T Dyachenko had taken shape even earlier, in the period 1992–1994, when he repeatedly carried out the commercial requests of Naina Yeltsina[1] and Tatyana Dyachenko connected with the transfer of public property to various domestic and overseas firms.

March. An advance group of American analysts arrives in Moscow; their analysis establishes the hopelessness of Soskovets's tactics for re-electing Yeltsin. Material on these analyses was handed to Yeltsin by his daughter at Chubais's request. As a result, Soskovets and A Korzhakov, chief of the Presidential Security Service, and FSB Director M Barsukov, who back him, are shoved aside. Promoted in their place is Chernomyrdin, who transfers his entire authority to Chubais and V Ilyushin, first presidential assistant. Although Korzhakov and Barsukov recede into the background, they work actively for the president's campaign along parallel lines (insurance options). An attempt to break up the State Duma, which failed in connection with the refusal of the MVD and the Ministry of Defence of the Russian Federation, was made on the 17 March.[2] Simultaneously the special services prepare via

---

[1] Yeltsin's wife.

[2] This refers to an apparent plan to control and possibly close the Duma by armed force.

LogoVAZ[3] Director B Berezovsky a manoeuvre to enlist A
Lebed on Yeltsin's side and introduce a patriotic element
into Yeltsin's campaign programme as a counterweight to
the purely Westernised ideology of Chubais. Compromising documents in the Dniester region are collected on
Lebed. The collection of funds proceeds under the aegis of
Chubais and Sh Tarpishchev (Minister of Sport and
Yeltsin's personal trainer), who squeeze funds from the
structures close to them. Contradictions between the two
groupings – of Chubais and Korzhakov – intensify, which
has to do primarily with the state of Yeltsin's health and
struggle for control over the No. 2 position – the office of
the prime minister, who automatically succeeds the
president. Berezovsky – the owner of the ORT [TV]
channel, which is oriented toward the political interests of
Korzhakov and the 'national-patriotic idea' – is intended to
balance the influence of the NTV television company,
which is backed by a Moscow group hostile toward
Korzhakov, and also for backstage political manoeuvres
(work with A Lebed and the transfer to him of funds from
Korzhakov and pro-Korzhakov banks). I Malashenko
(president of NTV[4]) is brought on to the election campaign
staff on Chubais's side. Coalitions take shape: Chubais,
who is linked with Yeltsin's daughter T Dyachenko, and
Yuri Luzhkov (Gusinsky and NTV) and also Chernomyrdin and GazProm, who are opposed to the power
grouping (Korzhakov, Grachev, Barsukov, Soskovets,
Tarpishchev, Berezovsky).

April. The letter of '13 bankers', who are headed by

---

[3]A commercial vehicle distribution company with a collection of
prestigious foreign agencies.

[4]NTV have been given permission since the middle of October to go on
air from 6°a.m. And thus claim a higher advertising revenue. The
collection of dues for supporting Yeltsin has already apparently begun.

Berezovsky, but who include Gusinsky [Most Banking Group] and a representative of the Alfa-bank, which had always expressed the interests of Chubais and his American masters, appears. Yeltsin partially accepts the idea of national peace and decides for the 9 May to 'rehabilitate' the Victory Red Banner and also make a lightning trip to Volgograd. He refuses here to meet with opposition leader G Zuganov.

May. At the parade on the 9 May Yeltsin appears at the Mausoleum and also addresses the inhabitants of Volgograd – 'people of Stalingrad'. Despite this, the press and the electronic media crank up a total anti-Communist brain-washing. The contradictions between the two groupings intensify even more in the soil of the collection of slush fund money, fifty per cent of which gets stolen. Tarpish-chev tries to squeeze as much in the way of funds as possible from the National Sports Fund, which in the past two years has imported $5 billion of liquor and tobacco products duty-free. In charge of the Sports Fund is Boris Fedorov, who refuses to increase the transfer of slush fund money to Tarpishchev for Yeltsin's election campaign. This conflict is well known to Berezovsky, who by the middle of May was fully informed also as to the strained relations between Yeltsin's family and Korzhakov. The latter had restricted the commercial activity of the president's children and relatives. Berezovsky decides for himself to play a double game and via T Dyachenko makes contact with Chubais, who pulls into this bunch Malashenko (NTV) and Gusinsky. The new alliance that is now shaping up decides to play the NFS [National Sports Fund] and B Fedorov card. It is decided to take advantage of the unfold-ing conflict between Fedorov and Tarpishchev and have the head of the NFS arrested via the Oblast [region] Special Police Division, which is on the Most-bank's payroll and is under the direct influence of Luzhkov.

16 May. The show arrest of Fedorov, president of the Sports Fund, by forces of the Moscow Oblast Special Police Division. The presence of a small quantity of narcotics, not in an amount large enough for the institution of criminal proceedings, is found in the businessman's car. It was assumed that Fedorov would disclose where the most compromising documents on Korzhakov and Tarpishchev are located. Tarpishchev urgently flies to Moscow from abroad. Korzhakov's people decide to cover the Fund with their own man to prevent a search and the confiscation of documents. Fedorov is released after three days, real evidence not having been obtained. The decision on his removal had already been made by the NFS board of Trustees.

June. Chernomyrdin and Chubais give Yeltsin guarantees of victory in the first round, which he broadcasts publicly. The power ministers consider this impossible and believe that any other result will enable them to dump both Chubais and Chernomyrdin, using compromising material on Chubais from his work with slush fund money. Simultaneously Korzhakov's people are actively engaged in funding Lebed and believe that he could be used not only as an ally of Yeltsin with a patriotic colouring but also as a battering ram against Chubais and Chernomyrdin. Soskovets is planned for the place of premier, as Yeltsin's prospective successor. In this same period prior to the first round, Berezovsky conclusively joins a pact with the Chubais group and the Luzhkov group with the intention of 'chucking' Soskovets and Korzhakov, availing himself of his special relationship with the Yeltsin family. Berezovsky begins to meet with Fedorov, enlists T Dyachenko in this work, and makes special purpose (secret) tape recordings of conversations with Fedorov at his private residence near

Paveletsky Station. Gusinsky is in on this operation. It is impressed upon Fedorov that an attempt will shortly be made on his life on the part of the power officials. Meanwhile, this action is prepared by gang elements of the Moscow group; the intention is a serious, but not fatal, wounding. It is assumed that, after the assassination attempt, Fedorov will fetch up in the hands of the Moscow police and will give evidence against Korzhakov and Tarpishchev.

17 June. The first round of presidential elections with results that are far below those that had been guaranteed by Chubais and Chernomyrdin. Korzhakov and his group commission the 'Lebed factor'. At a meeting of Yeltsin's campaign staff Korzhakov fulminates against Chubais. He and his group decide that at the first opportunity Chubais and Filatov can be cleared out and then, having reported to Yeltsin on the consent to cooperate of 'their guy' Lebed – that they will be able to take over the leadership of the election campaign and on the basis of the results of the second round, in which Lebed delivers a victory for Yeltsin, to bring the government under their control also, having removed Chernomyrdin.

21 June. A secret meeting of Berezovsky and Gusinsky with Chubais. At the recommendations of the Americans, who are informed as to all nuances of the internal clashes, the decision is made to 'deliver a pre-emptive strike' having set as bait the illegal removal of slush-fund money from the government building (this automatically involves Chernomyrdin in the game also). S Lisovsky the 'Vote or Lose' organiser, A Yevstafyev[5] are picked for the 'job'. Upon the arrest it is planned to present Yeltsin with the ultimatum

---

[5]He is deputy director general of ORT, Russian Public Television, and one of Chubais's top aides.

that he clean out the entire Korzhakov grouping. It is decided to keep Lebed 'in the dark' – Berezovsky will undertake this. Meanwhile Tarpishchev contrives with the help of his 'illegal' to take Fedorov to Switzerland and to grease the operation. Berezovsky circulates his tapes, but only A Minkin, who has been connected with Gusinsky since student days and who is supported by the Most-bank, undertakes to play them. The slush-fund manoeuvre takes place at the end of June and produces dazzling results. Lisovsky and Yevstafyev deliberately carry out the box openly. Korzhakov and Barsukov approve their arrest and interrogation. Yeltsin's daughter, Dyachenko, together with Chubais, presents the head of state with an ultimatum. Yeltsin surrenders his power ministers late at night, three days before the second round of the elections. Lebed is used as the main instrument of pressure together with the threat of TV turning its back on Yeltsin on the eve of the second round.

3 July. The second round. As a result, Yeltsin proves to have been insulated by the Chernomyrdin–Chubais and Luzhkov alliance. Yet a danger that the president will bring back the power ministers persists. A Minkin's publication in *Novaya Gazeta* with the transcripts of Berezovsky's conversations with Fedorov intended to completely wipe out the Korzhakov group and to introduce the requisite group of 'democrats' in the power departments, appears. But Tarpishchev obtains a refutation from Fedorov from Germany, which is printed in *Komsomolskaya Pravda* and played on the 'One on One' programme. The news media and the power party demand of the opposition on pain of the break-up of the Duma confirmation of Chernomyrdin as premier. This is to show American financial groups the stability of the regime and the possibility of the buying-up of the domestic Russian debt. It will be hard to obtain the

$10 billion even with Chernomyrdin's confirmation, and without it impossible. There would arise once again the danger of Yeltsin bringing back the ousted generals to exercise power options. These intentions could, most likely, crystallise with Yeltsin at the end of October or in November. Meanwhile Chubais becomes the president's chief of staff. All this is reason for experts to suppose that it was Gusinsky's outfits that organised the incomplete assassination attempt on Fedorov, after which, it was anticipated, he would provide direct evidence against Korzhakov, Tarpishchev, Barsukov, and Soskovets, who would end up in the dock.

Immediately following the first round of the elections, a wave of exposures and charges of corruption came crashing down on Russia. And the initiator, what is more, was not the opposition (its news media have long maintained an unambiguous silence) but certain segments of the power party. What conclusions should be drawn once again by the simple ordinary Russian who learned one fine evening that high-level government officials were attempting to carry out untracked slush-fund money from Government House, but were stopped by the police and then despatched for interrogation to a room of the FSB, and the next morning all this proved to be an 'attempted putsch' aimed at over-turning democracy in the person of Chubais and NTV which culminated no more, no less than in the dismissal of all the power ministers. But even this is not all... Minkin publishes a tape recording with Fedorov, former president of the Sports Fund, which says that the directors of the special services have links with crime bosses. And prior to this, the head of the Sports Fund, Fedorov – a comrade of Korzhakov's, Barsukov's and Sports Minister Tarpishchev's – is arrested in connection with the discovery on him of narcotics. He is urgently replaced in office by another of Korzhakov's men – Steletsky – and suddenly shot, but not fatally, but to precisely the extent necessary to be able subsequently to give evidence against his former partners in crime. The journalist Minkin further circulates to the world an audio tape with Fedorov's appalling monologues about Soskovets, Korzhakov, Barsukov and Tarpishchev. (End of Quotes from *Zavtra*.)

Additional Material (not in this transcript) added as a footnote.[6] Further Footnote.[7]

---

[6]The *Moskovsky Komsomolets* newspaper added much to these events in an article by Alexander Khinshteyn on 15 November 1996. What follows are extracts from his article. I take no responsibility for its contents or implications. The article itself published a transcript of an alleged recording of a secret meeting between Anatoly Chubais, Viktor Ilyushin and Sergei Krasavchenko (the latter two being aides to the president) at the President Hotel in Moscow on the evening of 22 June 1996 at Chubais's office. The article was translated for me by the same people as mentioned above. This article was headed 'Vote or…' The author starts by saying that the recording was made by one of Russia's Special Services and continues that we do not need to guess which one. The transcript talks about many matters, but mainly about the future actions to be taken as a result of the removal of $500,000 from the Kremlin (in a Xerox box) by the people mentioned above. It suggests there may be a need to smuggle people out of the country. This includes using a car driven by the world famous cellist Rostropovich as one alternative. It talks about incriminating documents on murder, stealing which might put Korzhakov and Barsukov behind bars. The article then proceeds to put more flesh on the bones of the *Zavtra* article reproduced here; the comings and goings into Yeltsin's office are given more credence, as are the subsequent sackings of Korzhakov and Barsukov. It continues with the transcript from the tape mentioning among other matters: How to tell Yeltsin the details the following Monday. How to influence the general prosecutor of the Russian Federation. How to get the KGB (FSB) to protect the two men who removed the money by using the main Protectorate GVO Chief Krapivin. Who they had talked to in the FSB, and who was 'trustworthy'. How to transfer unnamed 'documents' to the general prosecutor's office via a Mr Ilyukhin (chairman of the Duma Security Committee, a leader of the Communist Party and a former member of the USSR General Prosecutor's Office Collegium) after Yeltsin had been consulted. A video cassette recording the interrogation of a Mr Lavrov (an officer of the National Reserve Bank)

Author's Note. Many individual parts of the events mentioned above have been separately reported elsewhere, in the newspapers and electronic media. I have seen parts of the puzzle in The *Moscow Times*, The London *Times*, The *Financial Times*, as well as some Russian papers. The above article in *Zavtra* appears to be the first 'exposé' of a combination of all these events. Frederick Forsyth would have been proud to have written a novel on the subject. But often real life appears stranger than fiction. The appalling tragedy is that this appears to be the truth on how this country is really run.

As a further footnote, despite all the above manoeuvres, Fedorov was reappointed to the Sports Fund on the 24 October 1996.

I do not think any further comment is needed, you can draw your own conclusions on the process of government in this land. You may understand why the patience of the people is so sorely tested. I was not made aware of the *Zavtra* article until late October 1996, but include it here as

---

who handed out the $500,000 to Lisovsky. The tape was to be leaked to either the television or the radio stations.

I have no evidence as to whether Yeltsin was actually told the following week. Nor does the article mention that this ever happened. It is not surprising that this article of 15 November and its aftermath caused massive waves in the Russian press. It took the London *Times* seven days to print a commentary on these events. On 22 November it did appear. Within the short article *The Times* said '...Apparently Chubais and Ilyushin are to be questioned by the prosecutors office about a conversation on 19 June (I assume they mean the 22. They later state that the transcript is dated the 22.) They go on '...Chubais says the tape is a forgery.'

[7]*The Times* further speculates that these revelations were made at the instigation of General Korzhakov. Is something about to happen to bring this nonsense to an end? Certainly the fallout from these events is dominating the Moscow political scene in late November and December. We should all watch this space.

part of the logical sequence of events. As a result, many of the comments in my letters appear to have some ring of truth. What a tragedy for the Russian people. They are the losers. It also begins to place the further events of the later Lebed dismissal and his alliance with Korzhakov into better focus.

But worse was to come…

November 1996. In that month further ramifications of the saga described above reached a point of national scandal. Boris Berezovsky gave a Western press interview.[8] Quite why he allowed this interview ever to take place is a puzzle. Certainly some of his colleagues are trying to distance themselves from it.[9] If what he said, and what has been revealed in various other newspapers later, is all true, then he and his 'friends' should expect a heavy backlash.

Its revelations were then taken up in the local Russian and English language press, particularly *Isvestia*.

He is quoted as revealing, that since a secret meeting in January 1996 at the Davos international economic gathering (an event held annually in this Swiss resort) a group of prominent Russian businessmen had been meeting weekly with Anatoly Chubais to plot Russian economic strategy, but apart from him they were not yet in government. These seven people (which included Vladimir Gusinsky, mentioned in the *Zavtra* article) were heads and owners of

---

[8]To the International *Financial Times*. They published the article on 1 November. It was headed 'Russia: Moscow's Group of Seven'. It was by Chrystia Freedland. John Thornhill and Andrew Gowers.

[9]Mikhail Friedman, the president of Alfa Group said that such an interpretation was 'Far from the truth… It was an artistic way of presenting things… It was not the objective reality… Now Mr Berezovsky is taking care of political questions and politics differ from business in that precision is not always needed…' He was referring to the percentage of the Russian economy the group of seven controlled. The *Moscow Times,* 20 November 1996.

major banks, media empires and industrial consortia that, according to Berezovsky, controlled about fifty per cent of the Russian economy.[10] I find this percentage hard to believe, as only a few of the major oil or gas companies were involved. However, looking at the list of names and commercial groupings it is clear that their commercial power is very substantial. Most of these people are powerful, prominent 'New Russians' whose vast wealth has been accumulated in the last five years. This is the inner circle of the grouping known by the common title of 'The Oligarchy'.

They had apparently decided that Chubais was the arch political operator who would help protect their enormous wealth. After all, he had helped them create it as a result of his previous privatisation policies when he had formerly held that government portfolio '...*I am a product of privatisation. That is why I am close to Chubais's mentality.*' Berezovsky is quoted in the *Financial Times* article and adding, '*As such, a Yeltsin re-election was imperative for their future.*' They apparently funded his election campaign to the tune of about $3 million, and were intimately involved in all the murky steps of the campaign. One member, Vladimir Potanin, later became minister responsible for the Economy, and Boris Berezovsky himself, the deputy secretary to the Russian National Security Council with special responsibility for Chechnyan rebuilding.

Berezovsky further revealed, in his interview with the *Financial Times*, how this group had engineered the alliance between Yeltsin and Lebed between the first and second presidential election rounds. By using Yeltsin's daughter as

---

[10]For more details of the accumulated banking, media, trading and industrial holdings of this group, please see Chapter XVI, 'Capitalist Hectic'.

their conduit to the president, they were apparently able to influence more than politics. As some of them were Jewish, they felt that without the status quo remaining, there might be a backlash against them and their newly-founded commercial empires. Most of their enormous fortunes had been created as part of the rise of 'New Russians' in the last few years. Berezovsky is quoted in the article referring to an inevitable nationalist shift in political mood, thus threatening their influence '...*The question is only what price we will pay for it: an ocean of blood or just a cough...*' They obviously knew the real mood of the people, but chose to ignore it in their own self-interest. This group, apart from banks and industry, also controls two of Russia's top TV networks, a popular radio station and a growing number of national newspapers and at least one major oil producer. Imagine seven people controlling fifty per cent of Britain's banking, media, commerce and industry and at the same time having two of their number in the cabinet.

Not surprisingly many critics are coming out of the woodwork. From opposition politicians, human rights' activists and open disgust from ordinary people. The whole procedure smacks of self-interest of the worst sort, and that *within* the ranks of government. Surely this has to be stopped in some way for the credibility of their land and the future benefit of the people. At the same time, Western governments and bankers alike call these people 'reformers'. Really! Whose money are they wasting? Ours!

But even more was yet to be revealed. Berezovsky did not deny to the *Isvestia* newspaper that he had obtained dual nationality, Russian and Jewish. I am not being racist by saying that. But in which other country in the world would a member of a National Security Council be allowed to have any dual nationalities? And in this case with responsibilities of rebuilding a Moslem territory?

Oddly, according to a source near the Kremlin, his

appointment was apparently welcomed by the Chechnyan Rebel Regime. Money could be made out of peace, just as it had apparently been out of war. The intended free economic zone to be located there would vouch for that. At the same time, Berezovsky is reported[11] to have said to Lebed (with regard to his Chechnyan peace agreement) around the time of Lebed's dismissal and just before Berezovsky's appointment (with responsibility for Chechnyan reconstruction), '...*Why should you have ruined such a nice business? Everything was so fine... Well, some people got killed, but that is how it has always been and will remain.*'

Quite amazing. What is really going on in this country's misuse of political power? Do we conclude that the corridors of the Kremlin continually ring with such words and actions? I guess so. What is even more sinister for the independent observer, is that many of the names mentioned above are members of the so-called oligarchy, the unelected yet all-powerful group who appear to pull the Kremlin's strings behind the scenes, and at the same time are the owners of the largest parts of the economy. Words, for once, totally fail me. With revelations like the above, should we wonder at the potential reaction from the people? Unless this soon stops, I fear for the future.

---

[11]An article in *Segodnya* newspaper on 31 October 1996 by Tatyana Malkina headed, 'Another Move in the Consolidation of Power and Money'.

Chapter VII
Where are the Children?
August 1996

Gleb is five years old, a typical boy in anyone's definition. Then there is Stanislav. Stas for short. At three and a half, rather gentler and much more sensitive than Gleb. Like his mother, he spends, in the summer with his five-year-old girlfriend, Katya, much time out at their neighbouring Dachas. They are the lucky ones – born into families with money, prospects and for Russia, a comparatively positive future. They have a 'normal' family life with which we as parents in the West can relate and understand. In their Western-style clothes they ape our children's habits, shown here in the written and electronic media. Their clothes are new, not the usual second-hand cast-offs. The influences on their life are as much dominated by Hollywood as they are by their Russian surroundings. If you want to be bored by reruns of old 'B' movies, just turn on any of the six Moscow TV channels. Fancy coming to Russia to watch Ronald Reagan on the box for the first time.

However, spare a thought for Vladimir and Valera – who spend most of their time without access to Dachas, normality even by Russian standards, or any form of family life. Their unfortunate game of life is to ensure the acquisition of the next crust of bread to feed a hungry stomach and secure another day of existence in a hostile world. Their future is determined by their potential 'street credibility' in their current home – the halls of Belarusskaya Railway

Station, some three kilometres north from the seats of power – the Kremlin and the Duma – in the centre of *Moscow*.

The children in my block, plus in their Moscow environment Stas, Katya and Gleb, play many of the games we recognise. Small groups playing hopscotch, skipping or flicking marbles are to be found on sunny days in the hidden back courtyards of the dreary Moscow blocks of flats. They are not seen unless the weather is kind, hence little sight of them in the colder months. In summer months in the tree-lined central spaces of many housing blocks, you will find dilapidated children's play areas with swings, roundabouts, climbing frames and slides being used by energetic and gleeful groups of youngsters. You have to search for them, they are not immediately evident from a study of a Moscow street map. The old system at least created small havens of pleasure for the younger inhabitants. Unfortunately these playgrounds are in terminal decline as is the housing around them. In the courtyard of my block, the remains of a climbing frame is all that is left of those children's escape of the past. Our Health and Safety Executive would probably close down those left, if they were at home. But be thankful for those that do exist. In the small towns outside Moscow, these play areas are a central focus for community life outside their allocated nine square metres of living space per person.

Mothers gather in the afternoon sunshine, watching

over their toddlers, to discuss the events of the day in these quiet havens of peace among the frenetic life of this crumbling capital city, despite some grandiose projects. A picture of total, but deceptive, normality of mothers and children, just the same all over the world. There are many such small parks behind the grey blocks of Stalin and Kruschev architecture. One glimpses an occasional drunk snoring off his happiness for all to hear, adding true local colour. Another bench may be occupied by a couple of young lovers trying to find solace in each other's company away from the confines of their family's oppressive flat. Such small parks, frequented by the normal citizens of any city are to be found all over Russian towns where people seek some peace from their daily grind. Gleb, Stas and Katya often go with their mothers to such places, but Vladimir and Valera will not be found enjoying themselves there. Their playground is much more serious – the street. Those of you who have been here will not see the children on the main thoroughfares. But then they are rarely found in the central streets of London, New York or Paris. If you do see them, they have other things than normal children's games on their minds. In their homes, the lucky ones play with Barbie dolls® or Action Men® purchased at 'Toys R Us®' or other such Western-type stores. Or at worst watch reruns of older Western films now on regular show on Russian TV.

A particular pleasure, on a summer morning, is to see the chalk marks from the previous evening's games in the small concrete space outside the entrance to my flat. At least these children still have the ability and desire to develop their imagination by disappearing into the special and wonderful creative fantasy of children's games. A skill sadly being lost in the computer-dominated younger generation at home. Do you remember some years ago when school children in South Wales had lost the ability to play hopscotch, in our mindless computer-dominated world, and were re-taught such basic games by their dinner ladies? One thing is, however, missing here. I have not seen a child playing on a bicycle in Moscow's parks or streets. That sight has been restricted to the smaller provincial towns or villages in the regions. A possible reflection of lack of safety and little storage space in Moscow's tiny flats.

Valera and Vladimir and their gang of seven young boys sadly play few innocent games their lucky counterparts have access to. They, at their age, have no choice but to play the serious game of life with attendant social consequences. Like some estimated five hundred thousand other homeless and parentless children across the Russian Federation, they are the victims of the new, selfish, capitalist 'fend for yourself' order. They are unfortunately destined to grow up in the hostile world dominated by drugs, the street and organised crime. They are the natural feeding ground for future membership of the endemic Russian Mafia. Over six years ago such children of the streets did not exist. Or if they did, were hidden and their presence denied. Today, they and their older counterparts have been forced into a different agenda. Drugs, glue-sniffing, child prostitution, theft and worse, are the only solace they can find or are forced to endure.

As seems to be usual in these letters, I start a theme only to divert onto another subject. Sorry, but while gathering my thoughts on impressions of life for the children out here, I was rudely interrupted by 'the shoot-out at the office coral'. I will return to the central theme, but let me explain this deviation.

My office is some thirty-five kilometres outside of the centre of Moscow. For those who have been here, it is just three kilometres north of Sheremetevo 1 (one of the four domestic Moscow airport terminals), just opposite the international terminal. Located in a very large compound of some twenty-five Western and Russian enterprises, it is Federal property. This latter point is important to the story and is central to our commercial security. We thought – paying $30,000 per annum as our share towards physical security – we had a chance of quiet safety. Our construction equipment sales division is five minutes' walk away within the compound. My office is within a three-storey modern office block with a large modern customs terminal next door. The Menatep Bank, our landlords, have spent some $7 million in creating an office and terminal complex of note. The customs department for the neighbouring terminal is on the floor above mine. The entrance and perimeter to the total complex is guarded, as are each of the corridors of the office block by guards with dogs, guns and other weapons of modern Russian 'legal protection departments'.

Tuesday two weeks ago – a quiet, sunny, July Moscow afternoon – the peace was shattered by gunfire and explosions inside our compound. Not knowing what was going on, we hastily went into the corridor to enquire. To be told to go back into our offices fast, lock the doors and hide – there was a bomb in the building. We duly complied and disappeared underneath our desks a little bemused, shaken and worried. If there really were a bomb, we assumed they would evacuate the building. But 'this is Russia'. Don't argue with the man with power, a gun. Logic has no place in this situation here. The gunfire increased, as did the number of explosions. Hindsight would indicate they were stun grenades. Two individuals were seen being taken at gun point into a bus protected by men in masks and black uniforms. On the floor above a group of other hooded and armed individuals were moving from room to room (from the outside – Iran Embassy style) to clear 'suspected terrorists'. Unfortunately the head of the customs department suffered a heart attack and subsequently had to be taken to hospital. Within half an hour the chirpy silence (normally only disturbed by birds – the feathered kind – work and the sound of planes taking off from the nearby airport) of a country afternoon returned and we ventured out to find life returning to Russian normality.

We were given two differing explanations for the disturbance to our office slumbers. The first was that the customs department had been taking bribes, but not delivering the reasons for these payments and a Mafia gang had come to seek revenge or compliance. The second, was that as the offices were on Federal property (with no legal comebacks for such anti-terrorist activity), this building would be an ideal location for the special forces – the OMON (sort of like the SAS) – to practise their skills in anti-terrorist protection. We simply have no clue what the reality was. We do not expect to find out either. An inspection of the outside of the building shows only a couple of bullet holes in the fabric and very few broken window panes. I had expected more damage resulting from the noise. Truth is at a premium in security matters (as with everything else) here, and no one tells the real story. In this respect, nothing has changed out here since the 'bad old days'. In the USA or at home, law suits would be flying if it had been a 'practice'. Certainly if, as with us, no warning had been given. But here? Who knows.

At the time it was not funny, but having lived here for

nearly one and a half years I have come to expect anything being possible. Among such 'events' being possible, previous skirmishes with the KGB, visits from the 'legal department with guns' of a customer and seeing the results of the Dacha shooting, have just re-enforced the tragic lawlessness of this country in these troubled times. A shrug of the shoulders and a determination to get on with daily life is the only real answer to the experience of this unpleasant Moscow afternoon. My Russian colleagues thought the whole thing funny. But then most of them were in a second building, not affected. My UK management declined to comment, other than to indicate, 'Well you wanted to live there'. We can do little other than hope that the customs lady is recovering in her hospital bed. The rest of us just have to get on with our daily lives. What else can we do. If we reacted in any other way we could never live for long in this confusing, frustrating and chaotic country. We would take the first flight out for home. But remember, our Russian staff have no choice but to live here permanently.

The desperate drive by some younger members of the community to find any way to leave the country and start life anew becomes more and more understandable. While sitting reading my newspaper and munching my pizza in a restaurant near the flat last Saturday lunchtime, I was temporarily joined by a lady who asked me to marry her and take her out of the country. No, I did not. But pity the circumstances that lead people to take such action. There are many examples of similar conduct that we would associate with desperation. In recent weeks I feel that such thoughts have become more common to many as the continuing economic chaos continues. I can recall some five approaches, all differently phrased, and not all from ladies, to the same effect in the last month or so. The Russian-born wife of my English financial director has taken such matters a little too far in my opinion. She has managed to 'escape'. She can travel at will, although they have chosen to live in Moscow for the time being. She now has a British passport through marriage. So why take the issue as far as changing her name from Oxana to Roxana? Her explanation is that it sounds more British, and Russia was no longer her 'home'. None of us can surely deny our heritage. I, for one, will not be changing my name. Nor do I deny my heritage.

Another aside from the subject of this letter – the children and their future – I spent much time in a past missive explaining the background to a policy of non-payment of wages and the beginnings of economic chaos. The current problems within the coal fields (another miners' strike is looming after a further five to six months of non-payment of wages in many pits) is small potential beer if the current rumours[1] of potential non-payment of wages to the army until at least the 1 October are true. A Western colleague has reported that soldiers have taken to begging near his local Metro station. I have seen this happen twice. Well, an ill Yeltsin with a new hard-line Kremlin chief of staff – Chubais – whom I thought would not return after his dismissal from the government much earlier this year, has found the will for a new agenda.[2]

Pay nothing, it saves the exchequer, indeed it might even go away if ignored long enough. Not really a new policy, but one forced upon them by the developing banking and liquidity crisis in government coffers predicted in previous letters. It is now in full swing. It would appear that August till December this year are going to be very interesting, if

---

[1]Now confirmed. Non-payment went on well into December. The navy and air force were also affected. BBC TV showed a documentary in November 1996 on the Black Sea Fleet. The sailors were given no more than three meals a week and nettles had become a delicacy.

[2]The *Zavtra* article in the previous chapter shows that one should never take anything for granted here. Particularly in the political sphere.

dangerous, political months. The potential forced dissolution of the Duma (alluded to in my last letter, and the *Zavtra* article – and again reported in the media here – but now thankfully avoided by today's Duma approval of the appointment of Chernomyrdin as prime minister) which if combined with a revolt of an army without wages, will make a very dangerous brew. We await developments with bated breath. Little wonder that parents have less and less desire to bring new children into the world in this troubled land. The birth rate in the first six months of 1996 is half the death rate. Apparently the lowest such recorded statistic in the world today.

Anyway, back to the children who have to live with the dreadful legacy of their parents' former masters and today's social mismanagement. It really is a case of haves and have-nots as with everything else in this society. The two differing seasons – a hot and humid summer contrasting with a cold and crisp winter – determine the way our two differing groups of children react. The lucky ones have homes in the city and in the country and have access to games and stable families. On Dacha weekends, they spend time in the forest with their parents picking mushrooms. A traditional Russian pastime in the late summer that helps improve an otherwise drab diet. The resultant mushrooms, fried, boiled, pickled or in a soup, make a delicious diversion.

The unfortunate ones like our cheeky duo from the railway station suffer from the extremes of climate (as well as politics). Their roof and shelter is a small unheated shed by the railway lines, when they are not being harassed by the police to find another haven. Having talked to them on a number of occasions in recent months, I fell for their engaging smiles and easy manner, but they were understandably wary of me, or my motives. At least they knew the rules of the game and charged me $20 for each interview. They appeared on the surface to be happy with their lot. They had created a world of their own surrounded by artificial barriers of defence from further hurt. Possibly a childlike ability to shut out the serious plight they would have in the future to re-enter any possible prospective mainstream life, was high on their conscious thoughts. To them and the friends in their gang it appeared a wonderful game to 'cheat' the system and cause the occasional disturbance. How long before they fully realise the depth to which their society had sent them and now rejects their very existence.

Gleb, Stas and Katya will go to school at the age of six. An optional kindergarten from three to six is now available at a price. In previous years, pre-school years were part of the total free education process; today it is available only for those who are willing to pay. Life at school finishes for all at sixteen, a rather early age to decide their future educational or career choice. No sixth form as a preparation for university. Entrance to higher education is with the final school exams at the age our offspring take GCSEs. Still, all schools teach intellectual pursuits like chess. Then for the lucky ones, a minimum of five years of university. Medicine takes seven years.

In previous times, the Russian education process produced one of the most literate and accomplished populations in the world. It was their developed technical skills that led them to past technological achievement, not money. Today, the successful ones in the struggle for places to university are those with the ability to find money. It is the only currency of value here today – little else matters. Of course the bright ones still make it, but a little 'oil' along the way brings higher education to many today who would previously have had to remain at the bottom of the education pile, despite high qualifications. The public purse is so stretched that the country is in serious danger of losing its previous educational pre-eminence. A story we appear to have in common with them.[3] One of the technical universities – MADI – is so short of money, that pay cuts of thirty per cent were announced last month. This to add to lack of payment of promised federal funding. Last year we had to pay the telephone bill for the whole university, because of the physical constraints of our mutual premises, just to have our own office phones reconnected after being cut off for three weeks.[4] Now the news is that the Academy of Sciences (including the former prestigious research element) has been added to the 'No money today' list.

In Moscow it is reported that over two thousand five hundred teachers are required this year,[5] that number having left their employment. This, due to low remuneration compared with the lure of potentially higher and secure earnings, that will be regularly paid, as waiters, drivers, translators and general office staff with Western companies – particularly for the language graduates. In the regions, the situation is even more serious, there are few Western employment alternatives. The new school year has been marked by classes not opening. The teachers are still

---

[3] The London *Times* quoted an international survey of comparative mathematics teaching in November 1996. The UK was sixteenth out of twenty-five countries and behind Russia.

[4] This happened again at a higher cost in September 1996.

[5] Russian Ministry of Education.

on strike, trying to obtain past payment for last term's work. In a previous letter I demonstrated that strikes for back pay were highest in the educational sector. School books are at a premium everywhere – formerly free. Now they have to be obtained, often second-hand, by parents. Another drain on scarce personal resources.

If you look carefully outside my bedroom window, you will see a small primary school tucked away between my flat and the Bolshoi theatre. The building is not immediately obvious, as school time is from 9 a.m. till 12 noon for these youngsters between six and nine years of age, five days a week. A time I am usually away at the office. It goes by the romantic definition of School Number 324. It may not open in the new term, the roof has partly collapsed.

Vladimir and Valera are eight and nine respectively. They boast two years at school between them and only Valera can read. Well just. Their ability to juggle with money is, however, very well developed. It has to be. It is a matter of survival. On a good day, begging, stealing or engaging in a bit of 'trading' they can make up to $15 each. Enough to feed them both pretty well for a week. So my contributions were more than welcome. So far, both of them have not sunk to the depths of child prostitution, (openly advertised here in the newspapers) including to their shame, in the Western-owned press) major crime or drugs. They are into the petty stuff. But there is little doubt that in a few years they will be sucked into the worst forms of crime so dominating life in this city. Education will not be one of their future benefits. Their future is limited by a life of crime. Finding drug pushers is easy. Not far from the Lubianka (KGB headquarters) by the nearby Metro station, or most major railway stations, such products are on open supply. My usual supermarket was not far away and I passed the users and pushers with regularity.

For some reason, the railway stations are also the haunt

of the 'vagrants' in Moscow as the mayor, Yuri Luzhkov, calls them. But then where else have they to go? They are often from the regions where desperation has driven them to the 'rich' centre. Luzhkov is trying to throw these people out of Moscow before the 1997 celebrations of eight hundred and fifty years of that city. No help at all. Just head in sand and let someone else deal with the problem. The Federal government does little to help either.

The catalogue of experience with accidents continues. On a trip to the northern city of Vologda last week, I stayed with business colleagues at a nearby country Dacha. The usual amounts of vodka and Moldavian brandy flowed into the evening, followed by the compulsory visit to the Banya and interspersed by five naked males taking refreshing dips in the lake. According to the locals, it is required to perform this feat at least four times before one is judged to be clean. Unfortunately too much alcohol and a steaming Banya do not mix. The loss of sweat increases the level of alcohol in the blood stream. For our business partner Slav, it was all too much. He fainted and fell from the top bunk of the Banya, cut himself badly and had to be taken to the local hospital. Having visited this place the next morning to wish him well, I am thankful that to date I have no need of rural Russian medical treatment. Some say that city hospitals are little better. Hygiene, equipment, sanitation, a building that has plaster on the walls of the ward and basic organisation were not to be found in the establishment I visited. The quality of nursing staff may be high, but that is all. A doctor only visited every third day and Slav has since had to be treated elsewhere for blood poisoning, but not before having his wallet and money stolen while he slept in this rural institution. I shall never complain about NHS conditions again. Compare that with the cost of an X-ray and blood test I recently had in Moscow at the American clinic – $650. The world is really upside down here.

The parents of those children with a future have money, it is visible all over Moscow – the privileged. Who knows where Valera's and Vladimir's parents are to be found. If they were, they would probably have nothing. In most countries in the world, there are two truisms. We will all die and we will all pay taxes till death moves us to another place. In Russia, the former is the only truism. If those who 'had' were to pay their full and legitimate taxes, then there might be a future. But the 'haves' find every way possible not to pay their proper taxes. This ensures that the national state coffers are empty. All this illiquidity leads to a continuation of the desperate problems for the homeless children of the railway station, the vagrants, the state of the infrastructure as found in the local hospital or the play areas for the children. Where and when will this misery for Valera and Vladimir and their ilk end?

Chapter VIII
But the Arts are World Class
September 1996

The leaves are turning brown, their familiar annual crunch has been felt underfoot since late August. Today's gathering evening chill reminds me it is time to dust off the long warm woollen coat and dig out the gloves and fur hat from the chest of drawers for my second Russian winter. The mushroom picking season for the locals is passing, and bright morning sunlight comes late to my bedroom window. I count the days before the oppressive unregulateable heating switches on from the distant central power station. That is assuming that someone has paid for the coming winter fuel, or the miners have called off their current strike for back wages. I hope also that the rust patches on the living-room radiator will not break into floods of hot water during the winter. Life in Dachaland will soon be at an end and the blessed 'escape' from omnipotent drabness for the locals will be over for another season. Expect some flurries of snow before the month is out.[1] By the middle of October it will begin in earnest. The blue skies of the past five months will soon hide the sun for another seven and change the character of the people from their summer relief. There is an unusual abruptness in the

---

[1] The first light snow fell in Moscow on 21 September. The city did not officially recognise this event. The first winter snowfalls are only recognised as 'official' by the city authorities if snow lies for five days.

change of seasons here. Spring and autumn are almost non-events, blink and they have gone. It seems to me that it is either hot or cold in this vast land. Possibly this is one of the few logical events I can explain about being here. It is certainly a true experience of a continental climate.

It is both a time for sadness and joy. Sadness, because the multitudes of buskers have to find hidden warmer spots from their favourite summer stamping grounds denying us the pleasure of their wonderful sounds. Joy, because the three-month summer shut down of the Bolshoi and Conservatoire is at an end (while the artists have been on holidays, regional or international tours). Even more joy that I can hopefully stop being eaten alive by the mosquitoes in the flat. Try as I can with mozzie killers and spray and all sorts of wild animal hunting methods, it would appear that my flat at least (or my body) is part of the better real estate in town!

Where else in the world can you find a jazz band, a Bach concert and a Mozart opera being performed within five hundred metres of each other in the open air? You can here. The local professional artists and music students turned buskers see to that. Of course busking is an art form existing in all parts of the world. Here it is part of the essential cultural life of the city – a must to experience. It is more, it augments the meagre reward that these talented musicians receive from their normal professional duties. That wonderful group of musicians to be found daily in the underpass at the bottom of Ulitsa Tverskaya playing Bach and Mozart are a regular pleasure, but more on them later.

The Russians have a deep love of the written word and the performing arts, and it shows. They have little else, apart from Dachaland to relieve their grey existence. The road outside my flat is full, winter and summer, of a multitude of stalls selling books of all shapes, sizes and political persuasion. Books they have never been able to read in times past and books that are part of their known heritage. The Chekov Theatre is also in the same street outside the flat, although I have not been there yet. My Russian language skills are not yet up to appreciating the finer points of live theatre. A few months ago, I did venture into the Maly Theatre to see a Chekov tragedy, *Uncle Vanya*, but have to admit that only twenty per cent really went in. So I will try to concentrate on the musical side of life here. Having mentioned the Maly, inside it is a beautifully restored architectural gem and worth a peek just to see it. Maly means small, and you should not be surprised to find it next to the Bolshoi – which means big. This fact is another of the few logical explanations found in Russia today, therefore worth recording.

So after an extended preamble, this letter is an attempt to give some impressions of the cultural, artistic and historical heritage that contributes to my enjoyment of the modern scene within Russia. No comment is made on the post-*perestroika* rage for Western pop music, there is enough explanation of that elsewhere.

The abundance of theatres and concert halls in Moscow is equal to London, New York or Paris, but with an entrance fee that is more acceptable. A very good seat in a box costs about $50 at the Bolshoi. That is the price foreigners pay. The price for the Russian customer for the same seat is about $2. The difference being that we have to buy our tickets at designated agencies and thus get booking priority for the best seats. Tickets cannot be purchased more than sixteen days before a performance, so no planning is necessary. Just get hold of each Friday's copy of The *Moscow Times* or Saturday's *Moscow Tribune* and plan the forthcoming week's cultural extravaganza. One of the reasons I live where I do is because the location is fifteen minutes' walk from three concert halls, four theatres and two opera houses, including the Bolshoi. The latter is four hundred metres, as the crow flies, away and magnificently visible from my bedroom window. Every small and medium-sized town all across Russia has at least three theatres, one for opera, one as a concert hall, and one for lighter entertainment. Not everything of the Communists' legacy was bad, and this was one of them.

This love of all things cultural may have come via their mother's milk. It may have been part of the education in Communist times that culture was for all and at an affordable price. Or it may have been the absence in past times of pop music inundating the ear of the young that has kept many of them in tune with international classics. I do not know, possibly a combination of all three. What I do know is that the music I love – the classics – are currently performed here, at an artistic level that can only be described as world class, by unrewarded and unheralded artists.

As my daughters know and regularly tell me – Dad, you are square – if that expression still holds true, or is 'up to date'. Well my dear daughters, I am happy to tell all of you that the 17 September, and the preceding week, will not be appreciated, Michael Jackson will be in town performing 'HIStory' at the Dynamo football stadium on Leningradsky

Prospekt on that night.[2] An additional pain because I have to drive past the preparations each morning and afternoon, to and from the office. According to BBC prime TV here, Oasis is the latest sound affecting the young in the UK – Knebworth or Loch Lomond concerts and all that. Thank goodness I can hide behind old-age stuffiness. Disappearing into the timeless beauty of our universal musical cultural heritage is something that continues to keep my sanity intact during dark and 'black' days in this strange existence of trying to come to grips with a different culture and lifestyle.

Music has played an important part in Western European culture for centuries. Either the nobles of the past sponsored a composer, or the Church demanded new forms of expressing the faith of the gospels. The two were often intertwined. Here that was equally true, until the 1917 Revolution. Russian religious music under Communist oppression, became a distant memory and is still unknown to many, or largely forgotten today. This art form is beginning to return – the minor key half tones and powerful harmonies of a Russian male voice choir is an enormously dramatic event if heard in its intended location – a stone church with appreciative acoustics.

As an aside, these places are surprisingly small inside. Last September, on a visit to the 'Golden Ring' town of Rostov, I had my first such moving experience. The ancient towns of the so-called Golden Ring, a name invented by the Western marketers of trips to Russia, stem back to the early years of Kiev Rus. This was the kingdom which preceded Muscovy in the early 1100s. This group of towns, Rostov, Vladimir, Suzdal, Yaroslav, Sergei Possad (formerly

---

[2]Possibly another sign of the times (or a new attitude to popular music), the tickets start at $20 and are apparently not selling well. Indeed there were many left over on the day.

Zagorsk) etc. is in a 'ring' with each town about one hundred kilometres apart (a day's ride in those days), north east of Moscow. The one thing they all have in common is that they retain the walls of their original Kreml (Kremlins) – the fortress walls – with churches and monasteries inside. One of the most perfectly preserved such ancient fortresses is in Rostov, north of Moscow. Although in a slightly dilapidated state, this walled complex and town centre outside give a glimpse of the former glory belonging to the Russian Orthodox community. While exploring the empty inside and admiring the wall paintings of one of the three onion-domed churches within the walls, quite unannounced we heard the music of male voices. Turning round, four men in black monastic robes were standing there singing. The setting as well as the unexpected nature of the sound made one of my more magical memories of this land. They were raising money for the restoration of the complex, and their performance made giving to this cause so much easier. I still have their tape. What made it doubly enjoyable was that the four singers were all young men clearly intent on regaining a lost tradition to impart to their fellow citizens unused to such sounds.

In the small ancient city of Suzdal, also on the Golden Ring, you find over one hundred churches. Not bad for a town with no industry other than agriculture and a population of less than two thousand. The four main monasteries and multitude of churches are great to visit, though some will say, 'One more onion and I will go bananas'. Others will comment on this extraordinary time capsule and microcosm of past Russian culture with appreciation.

The origin of the place is historically unclear, although the founder of Moscow – Yuri Dolgoruky, whose statue is found near my flat – stemmed from a line of princes who ruled the area. It quickly became, over the centuries, a place for nobles and princes to send unwanted wives into exile as nuns, while new flirtations and liaisons became established. Quite what our Henry VIII would have done with all his discards located in one place all at the same time would have been interesting. Probably the number of churches multiplied as penances for their matrimonial misdeeds grew.

My answer to the ever-present onion dome of the Russian Orthodox church is not religious. It is far more basic. It is the only shape that keeps off the winter snow and lets the brightness, deep blue with gold stars, green, gold or black, announce their ethereal presence to a former penitent congregation. Who knows.[3] There will be an explanation in the architectural annuls of the past. Possibly a theme for later letters. Despite a description of an Easter service to follow in a later letter, few have been able to initiate me, as yet, into the mysteries of the former dominant religion. It is clearly visible that some of the older generation remember their heritage, and re-grasp it with pleasure, but have not, in days past, dared pass this knowledge on to their offspring. How much this younger generation has missed.

Within the sounds of Russian religious or folk music there is an overriding 'melancholy' and pathos that probably unwittingly describes the character of the people better than any words or meagre description from myself. Maybe we should also ask ourselves why all the great works of classical Russian literature are tragedies; is there a connection? A Russian orchestra playing Tchaikovsky produces a myriad of emotions not given to a Western performance, however professional. The folk singer regularly to be found accompanying a meal at the old royalist-style Iar Restaurant, inside the Sovietsky Hotel on Leningradsky Prospekt

---

[3]Since confirmed as the correct reason by a guide at the Kremlin cathedrals.

(where Rasputin is said to have held court when in Moscow); or the group entertaining the diners in the expensive Boyarsky restaurant in the Metropole Hotel; or even the monks in Rostov sent the same tingle down my spine. They all appear to me to have a quality of sound that leaves the listener both exhilarated but saddened at the same time. The same emotions describe with better accuracy my abiding impressions of their country than all these words. Who says that music is not expressive of deeper passions.

After attending a Tchaikovsky concert at the Conservatoire performed by the Russia State Cappella and their conductor Valerie Polyansky, I sought out their administrator, Alexander Shanin. It was rumoured that they were in financial difficulty. This one-hundred-and-thirty-strong orchestra and choir are one of the oldest in town, but had spent too much time concentrating on their music to worry about the 'mundane' things in life – like how to pay the bills. As with all things out here, the only constant is change. The state no longer provides as in the past and Russian industry has little money or interest for such matters anymore. Others had adapted and found the usual big Western corporations to sponsor a performance or two. They had none. So I became (well my employer) their first sponsor with a contribution of $10,000. This paltry sum paid the rent for rehearsal rooms for the entire ensemble for five months over the winter of 1995/96. Rent for my flat would eat up that figure in three months, and there is only one of me.

If you look at the programme for classical events in most Western European countries today, you will find an abundance of Russian artists. They are the only ones to be found performing in town halls in Hereford, Llandudno, Bognor Regis etc. during this summer. The reason is simple, it is the only way to pay the bills for the rest of the season. Polyansky charges $3,000 per performance (including rehearsals of course), the individual members of the orchestra and choir are paid $130 per month. Compare those sums with the vast moneys demanded by Western artists and the rewards of lucrative recording contracts. The result of the sponsorship was free tickets for myself the office staff and the occasional customer, to all concerts at Moscow's two main concert halls. The highlight of the season being a performance of Rachmaninov's Vespers, a work I had never heard before, but quite breathtaking. Money I think, very well spent. Unfortunately, my commercial budgets do not allow me to repeat the sponsorship for the 1996/97 season.

There is still one international institution that does receive some funds from the state. The Bolshoi. Long may this last. This cathedral of culture is justifiably ranked with the great opera houses of the world. The traditions of mixing a season's programme is based on true repertoire. Each night in the nine-month season they present something different, opera, ballet, a concert or a visiting celebrity. No one work is performed more than ten times in the season. Before I came to Russia, I had only been to the ballet once before – in Birmingham at the Hippodrome to see the visiting Kirov company from St Petersburg. My abiding memory was of the Lloyds Bank manager's wife (her husband had invited us) saying very loudly on the appearance of the male lead – 'Look he's brought his lunch'! The artistry at the time left me a little sceptical. Those doubts have dramatically changed since being here.

A performance of Prokofiev's ballet *Romeo and Juliet* – a revival of the 1956 version choreographed by the Bolshoi company and taken to London that year, was the highlight of last winter's visits.[4] It created a sensation there then, and

---

[4]It was repeated in 1998, and a second visit was just as memorable.

made the Bolshoi for ever famous in the West. Here they just thought it was okay. Muscovites are just spoilt for choice. *Swan Lake*, *Copélia*, *Les Sylphides*, *The Nutcracker*, *Giselle*, *Bayadère*, *Spartacus*, were all among ballets on last year's programme. But with *Romeo and Juliet*, the other most delightful was a piece I had never heard of – 'A Legend of Love' by Arif Melikov. My friends Geoffrey and Löis Iley had visited, and of course the Bolshoi was an obligatory part of the programme. Well we went, not knowing what to expect of this piece. The story, as usual in these conceptions, was pretty pathetic but there the complaints end. The superlatives of movement particularly in the second act made this story set in the lands of Samarkand and Oriental beyond, simply stunning. It made the travels of Marco Polo a visual reality. No more thoughts of male ballet dancers being 'queer'. This was not cacophony. This was a stunning spectacle of sound, vision, movement, power and grace that will live with me for a long time. I have become a fan. Geoffrey and Löis have been making their friends jealous ever since their return home.

One slight disappointment is that the operas are mainly very 'Russian' and a little 'heavy'. Not really a complaint, just an observation. *Eugene Onegin* etc. Only one Mozart opera was on last year's agenda – *The Marriage of Figaro*. Let us hope for more this year.[5] There are the occasional upsets during performances, from New Russians bringing in their mobile telephones and not switching them off. As said previously, four disturbances in one performance. Or during one of my wife's visits, a running commentary from an American – at least luckily only during the intervals – to his neighbour on evangelical themes. The bible thumping from this individual started as interest to the others in the

---

[5]Unfortunately, Bolshoi budget constraints mean that the programme is largely similar to last year.

box, turned to amusement but resulted in annoyance. Such American religious crusades have begun to invade this country. I am not being anti-religious, but feel that there is a time and place for such matters. A box at the Bolshoi does not seem to be appropriate. I do have one general complaint about the Bolshoi. When a piece or section of ballet is performed particularly well, the audience, on occasion, begins a slow hand clap. This is a sign of appreciation here, for a job well done, usually started by a paid supporter of the star involved. It does, however, break the flow of the performance and detracts from the overall experience.

The former home of Communist Party Congresses – The Kremlin Palace – the only modern building inside those ancient walls is now the home to more enjoyable entertainment. *The Life and Times of Napoleon* was, however, an avant-garde ballet entirely missable as the few members of the audience will vouch for. The same applies (well from my point of view) to the pop and folk performance at the concert hall in the Rossia Hotel near St Basil's. Our tame 'general' had tickets for a group of nine of us, but then found he had booked the wrong event. We have been told that the lead singer, whose name I have conveniently forgotten, is rated as one of modern Russia's best, but the sexually aroused young girls orgasming in the aisles to his music were better entertainment, for those in my audience old enough to remember memories of our 'swinging sixties'.

In four visits to St Petersburg, I have as yet not managed to be there when either tickets or a performance I wanted to see have been available to the world famous Kirov ballet at the Mariinsky[6] Theatre. One delightful interlude in that

---

[6]At last on my fifth visit, I managed to see an opera, Tchaikovsky's *Queen of Spades*. For those who are interested, the name Mariinsky derives from Maria, the wife of Alexander II who had it built for her.

city was a ballet evening when my wife visited in April, in the private theatre of Catherine the Great inside the Hermitage. This gem of a room, with the exquisite original stage curtain reminded me of the Maly theatre in Moscow. Excluding a rather strange Spanish gentleman who tried to impress us with his Catalonian art of strange gyrations, the rest of the evening was a delightful compendium of parts of many famous ballets.

But back to our buskers, mentioned earlier. Each group has its regular spot and appears at predetermined times for those who follow it to support its efforts. The jazz band is to be found every Saturday and Sunday evening outside the Intourist Hotel at the bottom of Tverskaya. A group of six middle-aged gentlemen spread their instruments across the pavement and play familiar jazz favourites with abandon. These are the intrepid ones, as they are found at the same spot winter or summer. Outside the Moskva Hotel each Saturday afternoon in the summer is another classical group that reveals its prowess in the operatic field – usually Mozart. Those with a preference for this art form can listen while watching the development of the Menazhnaya Square shopping complex. This enormous hole in the ground just outside the Kremlin walls will become another shopping monstrosity four storeys deep. They wanted six, but found the remains of the ancient city walls and stopped as the money ran out. A prestige project yes, and another $400 million, but a misplaced priority in my opinion.

My favourite busking group is to be found in the underpass at the bottom of Tverskaya, at the entrance to Okhotny Ryad Metro Station.[7] They call themselves by the rather odd name – Commercial Chamber Ensemble Classic. Their repertoire is Vivaldi, Bach, Mozart and Haydn. The *Moscow Times* even prints their telephone number so that companies, mainly Western, can hire their services. Consisting of former Conservatoire students, they play for a variety of orchestras in the winter, but make their money delighting their pedestrian customers. They could have chosen a quieter spot, as only ten metres away the pop music from a stall selling CDs and tapes often drowns their wonderful sound.

For those who want to venture into the world of cinema, you have again a big choice. Two[8] cinemas show current Western films in the English language – one with earphones for the Russian customers with no English language skills. This cinema's customers are usually Russian – not their intended market place, because the discerning ex-pats go to the Russian films, with English language headphones. The marketeers have got it wrong again. I still await some of the classic Russian films: *The Battleship Potemkin*, or *Ivan the Terrible*. In addition one has a further choice of French, German, Italian and other specialist films if so inclined. Then of course there is the circus,[9] so far I have unfortunately not ventured there.

To complete the picture of culture available for all to enjoy, I should not forget the museums. Enough has been

---

[7]Now moved to the underpass between Tverskaya and Menazhnaya Square.

[8]Since increased to four.

[9]I finally managed to get there on my penultimate night in 1996 in Moscow. It was stunning and well worth another visit next time around.

written elsewhere about the glories in the Hermitage, Winter Palace, and other palaces of international repute in St Petersburg and surrounding area. My initial comment after my first visit remains after four further ventures north – that this city is not the real Russia. Well, possibly with the exceptions of Catherine's Palace at Tsarskoe Salo (Tsars Village) and now called Pushkin and also Pavlovsk, some thirty kilometres south of St Petersburg. The former will be seen in Mel Gibson's new film – *Anna Karenina* – to be released onto your screens in the winter of this year – don't miss it.[10] This place has one of the most wonderful ballrooms in any European palace. Quite breathtaking (better and bigger than the Hall of Mirrors in Versailles) and the building is the site of the room with the 'lost amber', spirited away by the Germans during the war, never to be seen again. Wandering the 1,103 rooms of the Hermitage (the Winter Palace and Hermitage are part of a complex of four adjoining buildings on the same site) and trying to take in the 2.8 million art objects on show (another 1.2 million are stored in the cellars) in the vast former palace of Catherine the Great, you could mistake your location as France instead of Russia. You certainly suffer from cultural overload and much of the beauty escapes one's attention in one visit. The most poignant part of a visit to St Petersburg for me was to realise that after nine hundred days and one million deaths resulting from the German siege in the Second World War, it was reduced to poverty and ruins. Yet quite amazingly in 1946 the fountains at Peterhof (Petro Dvorets) and a year later all the palatial glories of former tsarist power in St Petersburg were again alive – courtesy of, of all people, Stalin. He clearly had a latent sense of Russian history (or a machia-

---

[10]I did eventually see it in 1997. Apart from the ballroom scene, it was entirely missable. Sorry.

vellian common touch) by rebuilding the very heart of the culture Lenin and the Communist Party set out to destroy thirty years earlier.

On the other hand the Armoury Museum in the Kremlin in Moscow is just as much (but less publicised) of international stature with specifically Russian related art. It justifiably claims its place as a repository of the country's wider and longer-term symbols of history. This in no way denies the critical position of St Petersburg in determining the modern day (since its founding in 1703) Western perception of Russia (certainly West of the Urals) as a probationary part of Europe today. St Petersburg's culture, however, ignores the more fundamental history of the total land with borders 1,500 miles to the north, 9,000 miles to the east and 1,000 miles to the south of Moscow. St Petersburg represents the perceived historical culture of the country west of the Urals. The Armoury in Moscow encompasses the wealth and glory of the whole – Asia, Europe, Siberia and the Oriental regions of the country. Inside, on two floors you will see a collection of treasures which I would describe as being equal to a combination of the Crown Jewels in the Tower of London; the Queen's Mews in Buckingham Palace; and the fabulous collection of the art of the gold and silversmiths throughout the pages of European and Oriental history 'acquired' by the former kings of Saxony at the end of the long 'Silk Road' from the Orient and now shown in the Grüne Gewölbe Museum in Dresden. The Armoury's collection comprises Russian religious art, diplomatic gifts, carriages, costumes, thrones, crowns (including that of Ivan the Terrible) and in an unmarked room in the basement entrance, the incredible collection of imperial regalia including the Tsar's crown. It does have a small sign in Cyrillic saying 'State Diamond Fund'. Diamonds, gold and silver showing the untapped natural wealth of the total land – a microcosm of the 'real potential' Russia – are housed in the vault containing the imperial heritage. Probably seventy per cent of visitors to the Armoury miss this latter collection as it is not well marked, but on its own is worth a trip to Moscow. Having been round this marvellous collection more than once, I still am overawed by the power the former rulers of this country controlled as demonstrated by their creative endowment, propensity and influence. Even the seven Fabergé eggs in a glass case devoted to his artistic genius are transformed into 'ordinary' objects when measured against the whole collection. To show the nonsense some Communist Party members created in the past, of the fifty-six eggs produced by the house of Fabergé, only ten remain in Russia. The rest were sold to Japan, the UK and America in days gone by to raise, a now paltry sum, in foreign currency.

At least they have learned to make money out of 'loot'.[11] The fate of many works of art lost in the chaos of the Second World War has always puzzled art historians. Many guessed that the Soviet Army had spirited much into dark

---

[11]These words may be misplaced. An open letter to Viktor Chernomyrdin, read out to the audience at St Petersburg's Dramatichesky Theatre on behalf of all the cultural institutions in the city, threatened closure of, among other cultural sites, the Hermitage and the Mariinsky. The National Library in Moscow is also suffering severely from thefts, staff shortage and book damage through lack of heating. The reasons being a massive shortage of state funding – The *Moscow Times*, 1 October 1996. The following day the *Moskovsky Komsomolets* newspaper had a headline, 'All Russia is on Strike'. Apparently the Pushkin and Tretyakov galleries in Moscow and the Hermitage in St Petersburg were threatening to close on 4 October 1996 because the staff were going on strike for back wages and funding. Even the return of rare books to foreign owners is fraught with payment difficulties. Aberdeen University had such a problem earlier this year, because the Russian State Library could not afford the $8 to $16 postage to return a rare copy of a book on African flora. The British Council eventually stepped in to rescue the situation.

and secret vaults, but nothing was ever admitted. Slowly the secrets are being revealed. A collection of sixty-five previously unseen (well for at least fifty years) impressionists were shown last autumn at the Hermitage. They of course did not admit it was war booty. Half the treasures discovered by Schliemann in his excavations of ancient Troy, previously on permanent display in Berlin, and conveniently 'nicked' after the war, were placed on show at the Pushkin gallery in Moscow this year. The other half are in the vaults of the Hermitage as yet unseen by us mere mortals, since 1945 in Berlin. The same Pushkin Museum held an exhibition of some one hundred and twenty cartoons by Holbein, Leonardo da Vinci, Michel-angelo, and others of their time, earlier in 1996 – these coming from a collection put together by a Dutch family over many years and again 'filched' after the war. One wonders how much more is stored, yet to be revealed to a public ready to pay real money to enjoy the rare experience. Certainly the queues outside the Pushkin for the 'Treasures of Troy' were up to two hours for a ticket, and another hour to get in once a ticket had been obtained, and were appreciative of these and hopefully more revelations to come. I do not subscribe to the current protests from the German government to return these 'looted' art treasures. Let's face it, their predecessors probably obtained them by dubious methods in the first place, then to have them 'taken' as a penalty for past crimes. Surely what matters more is that ordinary people can take pleasure in their beauty, wherever they are displayed.

There is so much more to this country than seen in the central cities. Moscow within the so-called Garden Ring (a wide central tree-lined ring around the inner city core) is potentially an architectural delight to place alongside Paris or Vienna. The same can be said to be true of the centre of St Petersburg, although the flat plain stretching a thousand miles in any direction around Moscow gets pretty boring after a while and one birch tree starts to look much like the other. Holiday ads in travel sections of Western papers, selling ten-day Volga boat trips from St Petersburg, via the Golden Ring and on to Moscow may seem glamorous, but in truth rather overrated. Certainly people who take such trips cannot claim to have seen the country. The Urals, Lake Baikal and the southern parts of Russia around the Caucasus, however, have much to appreciate – my visits there have been sadly too few to date. The dramatic vision of Lake Baikal was worth every difficulty in getting there last November.

Architecture is not one of Communism's better legacies. If only Stalin and Kruschev had changed their architect, much current visual misery could be spared. The sight of monstrous rows of high-rise flats are a major blot on the landscape. One has the impression that a single man designed all the boring dehumanising blocks of flats seen in all parts of Russia. If this is not true, then later exponents of Russian housing architecture certainly copied the original monotonous plans.

Today, the energetic mayor of Moscow, Yuri Luzhkov (possibly a future presidential hopeful), is preparing his city for a celebration of eight hundred and fifty years of Moscow's existence in September 1997. Many grandiose schemes reminiscent of some of Paris's better ideas litter the city and disturb the daily traffic flow. Possibly the most important of these projects is the rebuilding of the cathedral church of Christ the Saviour not far from the Kremlin. He, and many others, regard it as a symbol of the rebirth of the nation, post Communism. Reviled by some as a waste of nearly $300 million, to others it represents true resurrection for the country, rich and poor having contributed to the adventure. Its golden domes shimmer in the summer sun as a constant reminder of a new spring in this vast and patient land. The original building took forty years to complete, as a national token of thanks for the saving of Moscow from the hands of Napoleon's army after the battle of Borodino. Memories of a celebration of the events of 1812 litter this city and St Petersburg. Stalin, who could see the domes of the original building from his Kremlin office window, took days to demolish it after three attempts with dynamite. As an apparently unusually superstitious man, he was warned by his soothsayer that if not successful at the first attempt his empire would be doomed. Thereafter few further churches were demolished in Russia by him, although the pursuit of religion was rigorously suppressed. Kruschev apparently did not like Stalin's plan to erect a massive 'Palace of the Soviets', topped by a giant statue of Lenin. The whole was to be higher than the then tallest building in the world, the Empire State Building in New York, and dedicated to the power of 'the people' – well his really – on the site. However, some say that marshy ground would be no place for a massive skyscraper. Kruschev finally converted it to an all-year-round open-air swimming pool (still to be found on recent city maps). Today fifteen hundred men toiling around the clock have taken twenty months to replicate the original cathedral. I view it as an act of faith for future generations and applaud their task, despite the cost. Just like medieval artisans who built our great churches which are now a permanent part of our cultural heritage, they too need symbols of a rebirth as a beacon for their future.

There, a letter with no mention of guns, raids on the office, political drama etc. But wait; another pernicious Western fate awaits you in Moscow. Having cause to visit the doctor for some general ailment, being a good citizen I went to the British Embassy clinic. A place which all members of the NHS will know as a GP's chamber – with not a piece of decent equipment about. The consultation fee was a reasonable £50 (yes pounds, and I could pay by cheque) for two visits. On the first occasion after being poked and prodded for an hour – but wait – more examination was due, so off to the American Medical Centre for an X-ray and a blood sample. Nothing like a consultation there, take your 'holiday snap' and we will fax the blood test results to the Embassy for them to assess – *but* as you leave see the cashier with your AMEX card if you want to exit the building! There, I was proffered a bill for $650 for a jab with a needle and a photo of *my* body, both together taking thirty minutes. Just do not leave home without it – the AMEX card – if you want to have medical treatment in this town. What a comparison to the desperate place I had visited the month before in Vologda to see the Russian equivalent for my business colleague, Slav. What sadness that the Americans have imported their pernicious capitalist habits here in this form as well.

A letter from Russia without some comment on continuing political drama would be missing something. You would all think I had gone sick, or brain dead – well maybe. Withdrawal symptoms were beginning to develop after the election, as nothing of substance was apparently happening, well publicly at least. Yes, Lebed was having the occasional fight with Kulikov (the Minister of the Interior) over Chechnya, to remain visible to all and sundry as the new 'clean' boy on the block. He has little other choice, he needs a power base. All that appears on the surface to be happening is that the positions are being staked out by various possible candidates, including Lebed, for the forthcoming presidential election, should Yeltsin die in the shorter term – something gaining greater credence.[12]

There is a more subtle drama yet to come. The news,

---

[12]Yeltsin's true heart condition was not made public at the time of writing this letter.

the import of which is not yet appreciated by the press in the West is the appointment of Vladimir Potanin as the new first deputy prime minister responsible for the economy. In the reports I have seen (*The Times* and *Financial Times*) he is hailed as a 'reformer'. At thirty-five, a whiz-kid banker who grew the Uneximbank from modest beginnings to be one of the five largest banks in Russia in six years. Not a bad record on the surface – but according to some mainly via his government connections.[13] As a source within the Kremlin commented '*...His appointment is to complete the robbery of Russia.*' Let me explain. Last year was marked by a series of banking scandals, well at least in our definition of impropriety.[14] Apart from dubious goings-on with certain banks purchasing shares in some major oil companies at rates reported to be some ten per cent of those demanded from the foreign investors, there was more skulduggery afoot. It has to be noted that the banks involved had apparently acted as the merchant banks responsible to the shareholders for selling the stakes in the first place. Shades of illegality that would raise more than a few eyebrows here. Change the name of Chinese banking walls to Russian.

At about the same time the Uneximbank purchased a large shareholding in Norilsk-Nickel – the producer of among other things fifteen per cent of the world's supply of nickel. Again the eventual purchaser was the bank charged with the sale – apparently under sealed bids. Norilsk are major exporters for hard currency with a turnover of more than $2 billion per annum. Part of the implicit deal for the Uneximbank was a tax break of nearly $1.3 billion to ensure

---

[13]See Chapter VI, 'Kremlin Intrigues'. Potanin is said by some to be a member of Chubais's group of seven, the oligarchy.

[14]This refers to the so-called 'loans for shares auctions' and is a rather complicated story. But one that was to the benefit of a number of financial institutions.

these past due taxes were never paid.[15] Little wonder that the employees of Norilsk-Nickel have now gone on strike for unpaid back wages. The rules the rich use for themselves are different to those they impose on their underlings. Similar deals are apparently underway with ZIL motors in Moscow and the highly profitable Novi-Lipetsk steelworks six hundred kilometres south of Moscow. Do not wonder that there are those here who are beginning to resist such blatant misuse of power. These protests are, unfortunately, as yet too few in the corridors of influence. At a time when the state coffers are empty, the energy sector, among many others, is not paying its taxes and the 'have-nots' are becoming poorer, those with power are usurping their positions to an extent that 'daylight robbery' is being perpetrated on the Russian populace. The reward is an appointment to the cabinet for the chairman of the Uneximbank – Potanin – to be responsible for the Russian economy. You in the West are fed the line that these people are 'reformers'. Maybe they are, but who is the beneficiary of reform? Not the people. If these events occurred in the UK, even the tarnished Serious Fraud Office could probably manage to win a prosecution for such blatant actions in the high courts of justice.

And lastly my arguments with the Western press continue. While munching a quiet bite in my favourite pizza parlour I was reading *The Times* of Saturday, 17 August. It contained an article headed 'Funds look to Russia, with Love';[16] it dealt with investment advice on the growing number of funds on the London stock market specialising in Russian stocks and shares. My investment criteria has always been to do the opposite of what the analysts say – to date it has been reasonably successful. Here

---

[15]According to The *Moscow Times* and *Moscow Tribune*.

[16]An article in the London *Times* by Robert Miller and Bob Cruwys.

was another article designed to mislead the lemming investor at home. Among other inaccuracies, there were comments on the current Russian inflation rate at thirty to forty per cent – my information tells me it is currently under ten per cent.[17] It ignores potential political changes based on the potential demise of Yeltsin. It even states, 'President Yeltsin's health is not an investment issue.' Really? If that is correct, why do Western stock markets move on such information? Further it adds, 'The Rouble is stable and trades in a "corridor" with minimum and maximum limits against the US dollar.' It was announced here in June that this 'corridor' is to be abolished. It was, and the Rouble would be pegged daily by the central bank.[18] Since the election it has fallen nearly ten per cent in real terms. Further it dealt with a new invention – a McDonald's and BP petrol station on the same site – a venture just announced. Really? I have been driving to the office past such a similar 'event' for the last six months.[19] Where do these people get their information from? All pretty boring stuff to the average reader of my teenage scribblings. But another reminder that it is a dangerous pastime to be influenced by an uninformed press and investment bankers.[20] It is almost as life threatening, but not quite, as living in the country they misreport.

So I bid you farewell for another month, subject to the whims of a capricious employer and hope you have appreciated a little of the wide and varied cultural life this country has to offer that is of real sustenance to a humbled ex-pat during his winter evenings. My mother suggested

---

[17]Russian Ministry of Finance.

[18]Russian Central Bank announcement.

[19]McDonald's and AGIP on Leningradsky Prospekt.

[20]The genius of these financial gurus had its comeuppance in the crash of 1998. A pity they duped so many people, including themselves in the process.

the subject, my wife proposed the theme of my next diatribe. A view of the people, who are they? That will be a challenge.

Chapter IX
The 'Russian Soul'. Is There One?
October 1996

My business colleague, Viktor Sokolov, is fifty-seven. After some years as a senior executive in the overseas sales department of Traktorexport (one of the former USSR's state-export organisations for heavy farm and construction machinery) he joined the staff of MADI University. This educational establishment specialises in the technology of road and automobile construction and allied machinery. Today he is pro-rector and a professor of that institution, as well as being responsible for our Construction Equipment Division. The allowance by the former Communist authorities to let Viktor travel outside the confines of the USSR made him one of the privileged few in those days. With his extensive experience of capitalist life abroad (including one year in the UK in the late 1960s), his education and his last five-year association with Western business methods, he should be regarded as a wise, well-rounded, intelligent and rational individual. So he is, to a point. But he is, like most Russians, trapped by their history. He makes no secret of the fact that he is a proud nationalist, who dreams of a return to a royalist autocracy, being able to trace his ancestors to Swedish nobility. He secretly despairs of the continuing gulf between his political masters' policies and the possible future development of a social and legal framework allowing him to achieve his personal and commercial aims. He knows he will not live to see the day. He tries, like many others, to live his private and business life in a separate world away from the harsh economic realities of Russia – but he can't. Like many that I have met, worked with or have experience of in the course of my time here, he is fully conscious of the resultant split-personality and latent ability to self-destruct the Russian persona expresses today.

In writing this letter, I am constantly reminded of the former imperial crest, now returning as an emblem and symbol of the new Russia – the double-headed eagle surmounted by three crowns. The three crowns, legend has it, represent the fusion of the Ukraine, Belarus and Russia itself under Ivan the Terrible.[1] The double-headed eagle looks to the East and the West at the same time. With a normal modern Russian having a forward looking time span of no more than twenty-four hours, the current interpretation of two heads to the eagle may represent more than national vigilance. It is seen by some as a recognition of a fundamental split-personality. After all, few of us are blessed with the ability to do two things at the same time. Or do the Russians know something we do not? Viktor, just like many others I have met, has used this tsarist symbol as an excuse for Russian double standards in more than one recent conversation.

Viktor tells the story of his father, a naval officer who, like many millions, was taken to the camps under Stalin's ruthless regime. The camp concerned had apparently processed nearly three million 'inhabitants'. The horror stories in Solzhenitsyn's books on the Gulags come to tragic life recalled in Viktor's words. His father was one of the lucky ones to return – although a wreck of a former human being. Viktor was then old enough to learn of and consciously understand the inhuman condition. When a prisoner died in the winter, the body was left out in the freezing conditions, but the face was 'smashed', so that no future repetition of Alexandre Dumas story of the *Prisoner in the Mask* could occur. Thus the visual as well as the emotional remembrance was removed. Others have related 'life' in such places better than I ever can. It is said that ten per cent of the town in which the Sokolov family lived, disappeared into the depths of such despair. Some forty million souls in all of the former USSR under Stalin's bestiality. Who knows the real number? Good and enough cause, one would think, for an intelligent thinking indi-

---

[1] It has to be added that the Kremlin Armoury Museum gives no historical credence to this legend.

vidual to despair his past fate, his family's, that of the community in which they lived and of the country that bred such events. The country of my birth has suffered such pains enough.

Yet, Viktor in the same evening, not more than five minutes later, continued '...When Stalin died, and his body lay in state – I and my mother – like millions of others tried to get into the centre of Moscow to grieve.' Indeed, he continued, he hung out of the windows of the flat opposite mine, which faced Tverskaya, and cried his eyes out with grief. Others of that age have told me the same thing. When I asked him, perplexed and bemused, as to how he explained this total contradiction he said he could not then, and does not now. He explains, or rather rationalises, that he cried because the 'father of the nation' had died. 'What were we all going to do without his guidance and leadership?' Yet he knew all along the damage that Stalin and his policies had enacted on his own beloved father. While the perpetrator of oppressive terror was revealed for what he was (and history has since confirmed this), Stalin was, at the same time, worshipped by many of the people who had suffered at his hands. Such is the contradiction of the psyche of the Russian people. There was no pressure to relate these events to me, especially in the timescale of an evening's conversation. I certainly was not expecting both events to be mentioned within almost the same breath. Viktor himself accepts the contradictory nature of the tale. Even some months after the story was first told, I find the explanation an enigma. Such contradictions are evident at every street corner today, though thankfully not always so disturbing.

Many long conversations with others, or experience of life in this place have made me realise that an understanding, or at least acceptance, of this split-personality and the dangerous latent ability to irrationally self-destruct is fundamental to an appreciation of the modern Russian consciousness. This letter is written with little further conclusion on this phenomenon, or how to deal with it, but with a little more understanding as to its origins. It is clearer to me today that the enigma of this split-personality, when in contact with (in our biased opinion) an apparently cooler and more rational (but not necessarily better) Anglo-Saxon mind, will create confusion, misconceptions, misunderstanding and a multitude of communication problems on both sides of an immense cultural and mental divide, without mutual goodwill. If you use our mindset and standards, you will be way off beam in judging them in their current predicament. Unfortunately, few in the West take the time, or have the opportunity to consider the basics of mutual understanding, which leads to continual misrepresentation and misunderstanding. The reverse is also sadly true.

The terrible legacy of so many conflicts, wars and revolutions, both internal and external, have also formed the Russian psyche. They remember the vast number of sad victims. In the twentieth century some sixty million people lost their lives. They want no return to those days. Thus they have an enormous tolerance to pain and life's daily problems. In all my time in Russia, I could never fully understand the almost stoic acceptance of their fate. Perhaps I never experienced, nor did my family, such a long violent history. We only suffered the tragedy of World Wars I and II. They had Stalin and Lenin to cope with as well. The result is an unfortunate head-in-sand attitude to the current pain of transition to the new democratic and capitalist realities. When asked their opinion of economic or political events they just shrug their shoulders and tell you that they will overcome.[2] Often they do not want to face reality. Their favourite diversion is the Dacha. There they can forget and disappear from reality. This is the card their political leaders continually play upon and ignore their opinion to continue their rule of the land with no consideration of the population. Both people and politicians alike appear to accept such behaviour as normal Russian power politics.

It is difficult to properly analyse how they might rise from their current circumstance while latent Bolshevik politicians still manage a tentative move to democracy and capitalism. This is almost guaranteed to create conflict. But we are foreigners. Only their psyche can solve their problems. Some who have read my letters have commented on the apparent negative views on chaos and slide into anarchy that I portray. This is only partially true. I describe what I see through Western-educated eyes and I too regularly fall into the trap of misunderstanding. We, in the West, have years of training in comprehending the limitations of our ideologies and institutional structures. We know how to change them, or influence change. Often with painful sloth. These are lessons that only experience can teach. Not words. They have had insufficient time and exposure to our concepts to fully understand them. They require to move at their speed and in their direction. Being an outpost of the IMF is an insult to the Russian people. It also simplifies a complex theme. But then, few financiers, Western or Russian are skilled in social understanding.

There are two extreme schools of thought about what might happen in the near future. The one is a vision of

---

[2]The events surrounding the crash of August 1998 may begin to change that. Particularly the middle class within Moscow have a rising tide of anger that may not be stopped. But then it was always the intellectuals that created change in any society.

democracy and capitalism in ascendancy which uses the abundant natural resources to rebuild the land and build a new heaven for the people. The other is a drift to economic anarchy resulting from the failure to control the corrupt activities of politicians and oligarchy alike. The latter scenario inevitably ignores the will of the people and continues the historic course of Russian political life. I suspect that somewhere in the middle lies the truth.[3] Hopefully readers will understand the dilemma of trying to report on observed facts, yet at the same time interpret the correct message which the facts may indeed hide. The split-personality divides politicians from the people just as it divided legitimate business from these same politicians dominated by their pals in the oligarchy. Conversations with many Russians over time increased this belief. However, we as outsiders must recognise that it is the indigenous population who must take control of their destiny. It is they who must create a national purpose. It is not our place to impose it. That demands an understanding of their fears, problems and human motivation as well as of the historic constraints within which they now conduct their lives. Unfortunately few in the West take the time, or have the opportunity to consider the basics of mutual understanding. This in turn leads to continual misrepresentation and misunderstanding. The West and its actions in the past seven years have not helped matters. In recent years, history will show that key opportunities were missed. After so many years spent 'dealing with the enemy', there was understandable caution in the years from 1989 to 1993. But in truth, they needed instant friendship to allow them to concentrate on internal development. These opportunities were sadly missed. The complicated Russian

---

[3]These words appeared to be prophetic at the time of the autumn 1998 economic and political crash.

psyche was as much responsible for that, as was our lack of comprehension of their real situation.

With some trepidation I try, therefore, to embark on what can only be a superficial examination and possible explanation of 'Russia's human soul' today as seen with only two eyes. Thus a perfunctory analysis of the people – who are they? Probably an impossible task, but anyway here goes. It is certainly the most challenging and complex of my letters from Russia to date. There are times when this discourse moves sideways into the realms of politics and social behaviour (my apologies), but all populations in any nation state are affected by the policies of their rulers. It was ever thus. On occasion I also philosophise on what has been, or will be in the future. Please excuse my ramblings. My sincere apologies to the very few I have met who do not fit into the pattern described below.

We foreigners, who live here, have to accept that we should never take anything here initially on face value. Those who do, will fail. Things just are not as they seem on the surface, there always appears to be a hidden or parallel agenda. All events or experiences must be examined more closely before any reactions are initiated. This is not a criticism of the people, or an expression of lack of trust in those with whom we come into daily contact, but a reflection of the fact that we are never clear as to which part of the split-personality we are dealing with at any given moment in time. It is an unfortunate fact requiring deep understanding by us, that the peoples inhabiting this land surface have grown up with totally different perspectives to ours – not better, not worse – just different. The populations of other countries in former Eastern Europe have had both historic and recent contact with the West. Hungary or the Czech Republic were former parts of the Hapsburg empire. Therefore there is a basis of common heritage and understanding with ourselves. This society here has been effectively closed in real terms for centuries. The former aristocracy has departed, and many live with us. But the peasant remained chained to the soil of Mother Russia.

Without many years of detailed study, by people better qualified than myself, conclusions can rarely be reached. It is also accepted that pigeonholing groups of people, by untrained amateurs such as myself, is a dangerous pastime. There will be those among you who would not agree that: Englishmen are reserved; Frenchmen make good lovers; Italians have a Latin emotion; or Germans have little sense of humour and are too pedantic! That may be so, but there is, and always has been, an overall definition that differentiates individual national characteristics. It is these idiosyncratic contrasts that this letter from Russia tries to examine. It is more than just a question of breeding, location of birth, a Slav origin and temperament, or divided culture. It is also part of the geographical nature of past self-imposed isolationism. Just as the offshore islanders – the English – have had their national subconscious dominated by 22 miles of water for the past nine hundred and thirty years; and latent isolationism within the USA ('They are there because they do not want to be here.') has created a national mindset in that land. So the historical constraints and modern realities in this country affect the make-up and behaviour of the multi-ethnic Russian population of today. Being geographically part both of Europe and Asia makes some say they are East Asian, but what on earth is that? It is neither one nor the other, but certainly split.

Let me try to explain what appears to be a complex thought process on a split-personality that is trapped in a historical time warp, with further examples. Let me also allude to their habit of self-destruction. In my last letter on the arts, I tried to stress the dichotomy in the Russian musical experience between enjoyment and sadness, both at the same time. The same confusingly competing elements are found in many other events, experiences and actions in daily life, each of which needs a dissertation on its own, but will be only highlighted here to stress the overall message struggling to emerge.

Four key issues appear to me, above all others, to have created this 'contrasting' approach. I will try to analyse each, except the first, in turn.

Firstly: geography and a harsh mother nature on one sixth of the world's land surface. Colin Thubron wrote in 1985 '…Was the Russian submissiveness to God or tyranny, I wondered, the result of a people crushed by the sheer size of their land.'[4] Human life is easily dwarfed by size and the adversity of Mother Nature. We have seen in other lands that climate changes character, and in some cases even cheapens the value of human life. Previous letters have alluded to this fact, and little more is said on that here – the conclusions are obvious.

Secondly: silent acquiescent acceptance by the population that the average citizen's existence is simply an irritant in the wider game played by successive political masters, whether under the tsars, Communist leaders or modern day presidents. Manipulation of the 'peasants' – the total population – is an art form developed over centuries. The only real purpose to this art form, is the art itself. Democratic elections are just aggravations to those in power – get them over with, and then continue to ignore the will of the people. Anyway, the result can always be fixed. Explosions occur only when their everlasting patience runs out.

Thirdly: the national pastime so expertly practised by rulers and apparatchik alike of the custom of 'divide and rule'. Some even call this the 'conspiracy theory'; and…

Fourthly: a deliberate policy of national isolationism.

---

[4] His book, *Among the Russians*.

They claim to be part of the new 'instant global environment'. But are they? Indeed, do they want to be?

Some of the following explanations and examples may appear to be superficial and appear not to be initially relevant, but be patient, try to see the picture emerge as a whole with all the strands of a complex but interdependent thought process developing over the pages. I will endeavour to analyse, possibly in a disconnected manner, before we reach the summary. My apologies for what might initially seem initially turgid. There is little more to be added to the geographical and climatic context of Russian life. It is a huge country. The vastness is often not recognised by those who have no contact. Nor is the effect of seven months of winter always recognised by those who live and work in milder climates. But under no circumstances should these factors be ignored. Let me therefore try to delve into the complexities that the other three contain.

Silent Acquiescence

- Often friends at home have asked me how people live and eat when wages have not been paid for months on end. No idea is the simple reply – possibly potato and cabbage soup suffices. Certainly the needy stick together and help each other. The harvest from the Dacha garden certainly helps. Should this occur in the modern West, we would regard it as a national disaster and react accordingly. On reading a draft of this letter, my mother, with her experiences of the Russians in 1945 in our home town of Torgau, in former East Germany, commented: 'German soldiers during the war observed part of Russian daily life through different eyes. Whenever there was a danger of attack from the foreigner, the locals understandably went into hiding. The older children scurried off by themselves but the women carried the pig in before the baby was placed into safety. At first puzzlement, then realisation – you can always make another baby, but the pig is vital for immediate survival.' Really little has changed, but the dangers of attack today are from inside and not abroad.

Here the realisation (certainly by the country popu-lation) that they are still the same historical cannon fodder for their political masters has not been dispelled. It will take years to remove. They try with vigour to ignore the political realities, plant their summer crops in small, neatly-tended plots and hope tomorrow will be a better day. Living in the eighteenth century – as some thirty per cent of the rural agricultural population does, creates a mindset of subservient patience that rarely cracks. A conservative acceptance of the status quo is rife among these country people. The fact that this part of the population still clings to Communist ideals is not a reflection of their revolutionary ideas. Today it has more to do with an inability to cope with current crime, corruption and social instability. They yearn for the stable and comprehensible past. The 'intellectuals' in Moscow ignore these 'peasants' as mere anarchic aberrations. Yet they too are treated little differently. Extreme hunger and hardship in these country folk is rewarded by amazing patience and composure. But there is a time for all facades to crack.

- They are capable of extreme violence, but incredible patience at the same time. Over centuries, invasion has come from all directions. The scorched-earth policy of defence against Hitler, and in Tsar Alexander II's time in repelling Napoleon was nothing new. The result may have been defeat for the invaders, but the longer-term effect for those in the path of self-imposed destruction was a loss of livelihood in the interests of national preservation. Your papers, and my letters, are full of a new Mafia, a violent street community, a bankrupt economy and the ravaged population trying to learn to live with new realities. With this background, they believe that time will resolve these problems – but have little or no idea how, or a definition of a timescale. But protective scorched earth violence is not far from the surface.

Yet they are fundamentally afraid of the consequences of such violence. They remember that under Lenin, Hitler and Stalin, up to sixty million of their own citizens perished. Some say more. We will never know the real number. They understandably do not seek that again. They are not a gentle people – this is no kindly land. Mother Nature helps see to that. But they are still led by inherently violent leaders steeped in the historic search for a continuance of power for its own sake. Indeed, the population expect their leaders to demonstrate power as a form of leadership – they respect brutal and raw might. The people have little choice but to try to lead a 'sort of normality' within these apparently acceptable constraints. Again violence and equanimity make strange bed fellows. But taken too far, the populace have shown that their history is littered with examples of an intense reaction once extreme patience is exhausted. Sporadic examples of social unrest are stirring mainly as a result of unpaid wages. Thus a fight for basic existence may become endemic.

• On more than one occasion Viktor Sokolov has said '…We have two hundred years to solve this or that problem,' referring to a normal business matter that we in the West would expect to discuss openly and in detail and then find a timely resolution to. At the same time he, and ninety per cent of those I have met, unwittingly accept that the Russian perception of a stable future is a horizon of twenty-four hours.[5] Yet his comment is based on the belief that Russia has always been there and will be in two hundred years, so why hurry. Again one must understand the 'soul' to understand the message the words are trying to portray. Our use of the language totally misses the message. The summary is simple – 'Do it our way or we will wait till you agree.' Again an example of a split timescale and split-personality.

- They seek shelter from their mundane existence in Dachaland in the summer, only to return to a grey city in the winter. My wife pointed out to me that on the Metro they were a sullen introspective lot. True to a degree. They are certainly a rude lot by our standards. This sounds trite, it depends if it is winter or summer. Look again and see the difference when they are allowed to flower in the manner of their own making. The girls look pretty in new dresses, and even the men have an occasional smile. The coming snows will snuff out that small faltering sign of spring for another year. Not their fault. Just a fact dictated by the seasons and the crushing vastness of their land. They even have a word for the dull and dreary winter weather: *Pasmurno*.

Divide and Rule

Stalin was the ultimate master of the policy of divide and rule. Yeltsin is a willing pupil. Whatever his ministers may plot, expect him to have other alternative scenarios to keep them all guessing, particularly while he is preparing for

---

[5] As my time in Russia lengthened, and their own experience of the 'wider world community' increased, that statement lost much veracity.

heart surgery. In simple terms what this means is that only one man knew the master plan – Stalin, Yeltsin, or whoever was, and is, the 'tsar' at the time. Only parts of the puzzle were passed to subordinates for action or implementation. Thus power, true arbitrary control, rested with one man. It created a constant and now endemic level of intrigue and infighting among ministers. It eventually perpetrated to all levels of Russian society, even down to the lowest levels in the community. The industrial structure of the country was built on this principle. Few factories in the multitude of Stalin's single industry towns made a complete product. One made this, another that component – only to be assembled many miles away in another factory dominating a solitary community. Thus national security and the fundamental principle of divide and rule were maintained, but with little relevance to commercial considerations. Such financial demands were irrelevant then, but are critical now in the new anarchic 'market economy'. After generations of such behaviour it became a part of the landscape – and remains today in all walks of life. Understand please that all current Russian political leaders, from all political parties, come from the same school of thought – the Communist Party. They may despise their past, but they still practise a central plank of its doctrine. They are truly trapped within the structures of their past and find little, but hope that tomorrow will be a better day. Little wonder that introspection is high on the agenda. The continuance of such behaviour will speed the day they press the self-destruct button. The new, post-Communist realities demand different policies from forward-looking leaders. Not ones dedicated to continue past political irrationality.

- Think of Chechnya. There is more to the war there than an ethnic Moslem people trying to regain their land. It is more than the Russian search to protect a strategic oil pipeline from the Azerbaijan oilfields in the Caspian Sea across Chechnya on into Russia. It is even more than an assertion by the Kremlin of national sovereignty over perceived former borders. It is a complex combination of these and other historical factors. Those of you old enough to remember the trauma of loss of empire in post-war Britain may sympathise with the effects of a continual demise of a former superpower on the disintegration of national 'face'. The potential loss of Chechnya is another part of that process. A significant portion of the population desires to return to the borders of the former USSR – most of these voted Communist. They believe 'face' has been destroyed. It is unlikely to happen, but their dream remains alive. Those sunset events of empire in the UK in the 1950s and sixties took a generation with attendant national introspection. In Russia similar decline has happened in less than six years. Maybe Yeltsin does not want a solution because he practises 'divide and rule' and it keeps him in power.[6] However one views it, the result is the same, public confusion. Another view is merely that the former political structures of the USSR are still firmly in place, despite outward appearances. If not the ideologies, then certainly the methods used in the past are intact and dominating the scene.

Let me try to explain a little more. The military forces in this country are not a united power. The Russian Army has a single dedicated constitutional role: to protect the national borders, and they report to the Ministry of Defence. A

---

[6]See Chapter VI, 'Kremlin Intrigues'. Chubais, Berezovsky and company appear to have a personal variant on this agenda.

second powerful body exists under the control of the Ministry of the Interior, the interior defence forces, which also include the police. Then there is a third and potentially more sinister group. Those protecting the president – the so-called 'special forces' – there are a multitude of these troops surrounding Moscow, indeed almost a private presidential army. This last group is under the command of the Kremlin. The forty thousand or so soldiers in Chechnya are mainly made up of the former two groups, but with occasional members of the special forces arriving and departing. So who runs the war – or negotiations for peace? The Ministry of Defence? The Interior Ministry? Or the Kremlin? Small wonder that Lebed has a thankless task, and may eventually, unfortunately, fail on the altar of divide and rule.[7] The self-destruct button at work again. But this unfortunate legacy is part of daily life and demonstrates a preoccupation with deliberately creating chaos as a means of political survival. The democratic will, or fate of the people is secondary. Few here, currently believe that Lebed will be allowed to be successful in his negotiations to find a lasting Chechnyan peace. Entrenched positions of self-preservation, or making money out of war, within the Kremlin may dictate a failure, despite current apparent success. The political game is not over by a long way, despite a 'piece of paper'. Were Lebed to be successful and at the same time save national 'face' it would enhance his position, but help weaken the divide and rule policy. Not something the current Kremlin rulers will accept. Later events proved that point with consummate ease. The price of status quo will be paid, as usual by the people. Please understand their paranoia as a result.

---

[7]As we now all know, he did fail at the altar of divide and rule a few days after this letter was completed. Yet the Kremlin accepted his peace plan in November 1996.

- Far be it for me to criticise my Russian working colleagues, but I must. They think they communicate daily activities fully – but – they do not, well in our sense of the word anyway. Information has to be extracted with an excavator. Their inbred habit of hiding key facts in the subconscious is not deliberate or obstructive, it is part of automatic self-protection against a policy of divide and rule that came via mothers' milk. 'If I reveal this or that, it might reduce my power base' is the message. It is second nature to the Russians. The principles of a split-personality emerge again to us, but not to them. They communicate only what they think is relevant, protective of self and necessary, and sometimes not even that. This behaviour, however, pervades all their dealings with us as well as each other. Endeavouring to impose Western-style management discipline on our business here in Russia has been one of the hardest tasks of my thirty-five-year commercial experience. My Western expatriate colleagues from other companies have similar encounters. I do not think I have succeeded. I know I have not. They hardly know or realise they are practising this art of divide and rule at lower levels, but it has been part of their human intercourse for centuries and therefore second nature. Although they despise the power structures of the past, they apparently cannot live without them. Maybe they think they are 'safe', and an unknown future breeds insecurity.

- One of the fundamentals of Western business life is 'management focus'. Share values of companies are even judged by this parameter, hence the slow decline and break-up of the formerly successful conglomerates at home. By 'focus' I mean that a commercial enterprise has to decide what it wants to achieve, and then to concentrate all management and workforce efforts on its attainment. As long as money is made, then 'focus' is of little interest here. Business groups are growing and have no coherent strategy – a muddled approach. For the moment it makes vast money for some. This is just as confusing as the total lack of diary planning. How often are we told to attend a meeting which is 'important' with possibly a maximum of an hour to be there. We get there and find it to be just routine – no drama – the only drama being to drop everything else. No wonder it takes more time to achieve things than anywhere else I know. Saying that, I draw upon experience of commercial dealings in all five continents and more than fifty countries in over twenty-five years of travelling the globe. Their sense of planning ensures that achievement of those plans is delayed. Lack of planning or focus, emphasises a gulf between their and our commercial philosophy.

• The girls in the office are no exception. Ask for a simple thing like: please buy some envelopes, make a plane booking, let me have the stock and forward order statistics every Monday, or find some paper clips. No automatic feedback on success or otherwise occurs – like – here they are, or the job is done. It is up to us to continually try to extract information that would flow as second nature to a good Western secretary. I do get these tasks performed in the end, but what an effort. They all complain of their political masters' misuse of such concepts, but do little to change their own habits in this respect. This national peculiarity is one of the worst aspects of living here. We Westerners have little protection against such unintentional misinformation particularly in a period of such intense political and social instability. This 'communication gap' is the most difficult element for us to cope with. It leads to more 'stress' among the Western business community than anything else.

I call this behaviour sheer indiscipline. They call it self-protection. As a result it takes twice as long, with endless frustration, to complete a simple task. When questioned as to why they do it, they just shrug their shoulders and reply, 'This is Russia,' as though this answer excuses everything. Even we, the foreigners, have begun to use this catch-all phrase as a cop-out. Possibly a sad reflection on our susceptibility to be drawn into their way of life. To live here we have to try to understand. Otherwise we drown.

Stalin created three essential power blocks within the country which still dominate the landscape. Firstly: the so-called military-industrial complex. This was the industrial base that made up all the defence-related industries and, despite the decline in military production, still dictates manufacturing policy today. Secondly: the energy lobby – oil, gas nuclear energy and coal. Russia's natural gas reserves are huge. The largest known in the world today. Thirdly: the Communist Party apparatus. The power block ruling the country in 1996 emanates from a combination of the former two, but originates from the ranks of the latter Communist Party tradition. They have little interest but to keep the status quo to maintain the current power structure. The democratic wishes of the people expressed in the recent presidential election promises were for them an irrelevancy. The new forces of democratic capitalism emerging are in reality an 'irritant'. They are there to ensure that the existing 'old guard' leadership is supplied with sufficient 'graft' to wield this power – little else. Although the Chubais grouping may think differently, they are currently central in this policy.

A newer 'third force' representing true reform as we would describe it has yet to emerge. Yavlinski, Glazyev, or Lebed may be part of that disparate emerging force, but have no credence or political base on which to build as yet. What has this to do with the people? Who are they, you ask? A great deal in my opinion. You are fed the line that 'reformers' rule the country. Not true. What is true is that there have been enormous changes to the pace and structure of the well-being of life in the central cities in the last five years. But this has led to two independent social structures emerging, which do not conform to 'reform' in our definition. The power remains with the energy and military-industrial complex, the social and economic vacuum is being filled by unregulated and rampant capitalism for the few – the oligarchy. The danger signals are that the latter group will eventually be the true power behind the throne. Result, chaos. Another form of divide and rule. The new, but more liberal Communist Party waits on the side lines expecting to return and pick up the pieces. I hope, however, that Zuganov does not succumb to the overtures of national unity from Chernomyrdin and draw him into the current morass of a coalition.[8] Zuganov should, in my opinion, lead his party as one of true democratic opposition, ready for alternative power. If he chooses any other path his traditional agricultural and pensioner power base will forever dismiss him and his party as mere

---

[8]In October 1996, Zuganov was seriously considering an alliance with Chernomyrdin against Lebed and Chubais to ensure Yeltsin's removal from power as a result of his health problems and the instability of Russian social, economic and fiscal structures. This created a serious split in the Communist hierarchy. The private reason given was Zuganov's lack of interest in national social instability with obvious resulting consequences. The irony of this comment on coalition is that just such events took place after the time of the autumn 1998 economic and political crash under Primakov.

pawns in the usual Kremlin game of power at all costs.

Capitalism as we know it – complete with democratic and financial checks and balances has not arrived here, yet, despite the impression you all might be getting via the written and electronic media. Of course they can, and do now freely express a contrary view, but unless the population have the wherewithal (money) to realise their ideas, little or nothing emerges.

Their leaders appear paralysed and may not help them. Think back to the experimental integration of East Germany into life overnight with the almighty Deutschmark. It proved to be a short-term impossibility – and is still not complete. In a social sense it will take more than a generation there. Mikhail Korolev, our Sales Director, hopes fervently that the Russian situation is 'normalised' by the time his five-year-old son has reached maturity. For his sake I hope so. But fear not. In former East Germany they had blood ties to the West, they had closer contact in that direction than here, over the years. Here, none of that occurred. The average man has a simple request – 'Show me the way to improve my daily lot, so that tomorrow I can do it for myself'. Perfectly reasonable and understandable really. But we Westerners ignore the fact that while the existing Russian political powers continue to hold back true reform (to ensure their own survival), the population is straining at the leash to move forward with tiny awkward steps. But without the fiscal, legal and democratic tools to do the job. Am I expecting too much? No. Look at the progress made in other former Communist satellites. Part of that experience might be useful here, albeit within the known constraints of former Russian isolationism. But will they take a lesson in humility and understand the concern of the population? Probably not, modesty and humble pie are not demonstrated national characteristics.

They have quickly learnt to make money, but in an unregulated and uncontrolled manner. Capitalism, as we know it, will not work for the benefit of the whole, while the required political and legal framework of checks and balances remains merely a dream.[9] The result is a population that has higher expectations than reality will allow. It was ever thus. The split-personality continues its unruly path. On this occasion completely understandable. Self-destruction will occur in due course, unless the 'rules' of commercial and social conduct are more clearly established. The 'have-nots' will rebel against the 'haves' as they have elsewhere. We should beware the dangers of 'imposing' our thought process on a population and system that neither fully understands the message, or likes the messenger – the IMF.[10] When using the term 'capitalism' we in the West remember that rewards and responsibilities go hand-in-hand. Here they look forward to the former, but deny the latter. Without both elements working together, success will be elusive. Foreigners are becoming the whipping boy of the Muscovites, just as Moscow is to the regions. Russian logic says we should have brought such discipline with us when we foreigners came in droves. But it is surely up to them to set the 'rules'. It is their country. If we impose, then mutual misunderstanding increases. If we do not, then our investments in their country must be based on higher risk criteria.

Life is easy, when making judgements sitting at a green baize table far away and remote from events. Instant, theoretical experts. We have all been guilty of that. We, living here, call such people seagulls, that is in the Western

---

[9] A view reinforced by Victor Kremenyuk in the lead article in *The Moscow Tribune* of 21 September 1996.

[10] At the end of October, the IMF held back payments on the $10 billion for the second time in three months. A disturbing development.

business community, because: 'They fly in, eat you out of house and home, make a lot of noise, flap around in an uncontrolled fashion, shit on you and fly out'. Think of the multitude of 'seagulls' ready and willing to be barrack-room lawyers and pronounce on a situation they neither know or understand. Although they may not accept it, they are the eventual losers in this process. We, that live here, have problems of local comprehension. Yet we are judged by individuals who have no personal involvement. Take that thought process into the political and social arena of judging the Russians and their current predicament without true cognisance, and danger signals of miscommunication grow stronger.

Boring you say, tell me about some human interest. Well, my apologies, but social, political and economic background is more than important in understanding the minutia of life out in this neck of the woods. It is certainly meaningful, in my opinion, to gain an understanding of the way people act, work and live. To understand the 'Russian soul' it appears to me to be essential. Love it or hate it, this continuing Russian preoccupation with 'drama' affects us foreigners in another way. It gets under your skin. While we are away in the UK or elsewhere, something might happen that denies us being interested bystanders in their drama. It is a sort of contrary 'fun'. Each Saturday morning I eagerly find my copy of The *Moscow Times* in which Jean McKenzie is a regular columnist. She is an American who tells us that she has lived here for some eight or ten years. On the 24 August there was a lovely article describing this fatal Russian attraction to us foreigners who have a 'feel' for the place. She ends up in that piece, describing a raucous Russian dinner party, with a surfeit of good food, flowery toasts, excess of drink and oodles of home-grown philosophy. I know and have experienced this sort of thing. Eventually they ended in a deep debate as to whether

Russia's reforms were irreversible, who was running the country, whether matters had really changed that much, and whether the time had come to leave. The final sentence was, 'Of course you want to live here,' said Lida (a Russian) a wry intelligent woman in her fifties, when we had all worn ourselves out with debate. 'It's so much more interesting. Even *we* don't know what will happen tomorrow...' The trouble is Lida meant it. How does one untie the 'Gordian Knot' of Russian problems today with people sunk deep within a split-personality and who have little clue of what will happen tomorrow? By tomorrow they really do mean 'in the next twenty-four hours'. Our society could not exist without a firm belief in the future. Here tomorrow is a dream, only today represents understandable reality. Unfortunately for her readers, eventually Jean McKenzie succumbed and has now left Russia herself. She found a man she says, and fell in love.

None of us has the luxury of control experiments to find out what a Russian would be like if he had grown up in 'middle England', and then repeat the process with the same individual in 'middle Russia'. 'What would he or she have done, have thought, have become if?' Change the nationality and location and compare with what would have been elsewhere. It is not possible. When I was five years old, I arrived in England from Germany, but today I do not really know the country of my conception – despite my 'Germanic' upbringing, or even my closest friend's belief to the contrary. Nor can I but speculate what my life and thoughts would have been if history had changed. I have no idea what might have been. None of us knows the results of either comparison. We all have to deal with realities as they are.

As mentioned in an earlier paragraph, generalisation and pigeonholing is a dangerous pastime without deep thought. The import of these letters from Russia began as a desire to record an experience granted to few in the Western world and to communicate them home. Now they have become something else. They are an attempt to record more than perceived wisdom. I am endeavouring to transmit a little of the 'feel' of the place to those of you who have so far not been able to share the experience. I hope I have succeeded in a minor way. Firstly: to observe the facts and 'feel' the history; secondly: to understand why things are as they are – not obvious on first glance; thirdly: to see how people react to problems and deal with opportunities; and fourthly: to try to bring another point of view, for them to see the future more clearly. But as Lee Kuan Yew proved in Singapore, only a local man can resolve their problems. Only the ordinary Russian people can react to their own history. At the end of the day we, the foreigners, can only play the part of a minor and possibly inconsequential catalyst to resolve their entrapment with their historic fate.[11]

National Isolationism

I mentioned a fourth element affecting the modern Russian psyche – enforced isolationism. What is the legacy of one thousand years by political masters of ignoring the people both inside and outside their national boundaries? What follows may again be a superficial and in some cases an obvious list, my apologies. The self-evident is often trite, but necessary to relate in making an overall point. As in China, centuries of life under the emperors (or tsars here)

---

[11]During my second stint in Moscow in 1998, my secretary from past days joined me again. We had many debates on the issues of the day as well as the themes in these letters. Often she would disappear into a cocoon of 'don't worry we will muddle through'. But she never truly understood why a foreigner was so interested in her country. She regularly told me that I could escape, so why bother with their problems. Understandable, but they do need time, patient help and understanding to comprehend our world. Just as the reverse is true.

were little different to those under Communist dictator-ship. Among the effects it had on the population were the following, and without touching, seeing and feeling them, words are inadequate in describing the real meaning and truth:

- It removed individual freedom. An easy phrase to use, but do we in the comfort of 'Middle England' really know what it means to have all independent thought processes taken away and for others to determine even the minutia of our future. They had no freedom of where to live, where to work, what to say, what to buy, with whom to communicate. Their thoughts were their own, but nothing else. I remember vividly the first time I returned to East Germany in 1989. After 6 p.m. the streets were empty with no sight of human habitation. The population had hidden indoors as their only true companionship and ability to express themselves were within the family circle. My own extended family who remained in that land demonstrated this trauma of their past existence once they were free at last to express their true selves. Their experience of seventy years of dicta-torship under Hitler and then Communism, has been a parallel and ever-present lesson to me while living in Moscow. Life in Russia was no different then. Has it changed today? Only in outward vision. Today, the external appearance is of a bustling community with social intercourse for all. But generations of stagnant and repressed thought has left its mark. Particularly on the older generation there and here. For some, there is now a longing for the 'comfort' of the days where others took over the problems of tomorrow.

- It failed to invest in the infrastructure. Look more closely at the reality of life here. The images of the

Kremlin are romantic, powerful and dramatic but surrounding it is a state of decay. Little works in our sense of the word. Drains, roads, hospitals, telephones, electricity, lifts, schools, factories, housing, transport et al are all of a standard that resemble a 'Third World' underdeveloped land – not a former superpower. The amount of 'catch up' is staggering. One generation in Russia can neither pay for its refurbishment or even replicate what it has taken us, with our accumulated wealth, more than fifty years of rebuilding since the Second World War to achieve. The picture in the regions is even more depressing. Where one starts the priorities of rebirth is an almost impossible question. Everything needs attention at the same time. The sense of resulting national failure weighs heavy on the conscience of the population as they begin to see what our countries are really like compared with their reality. Hence the desire for many to 'escape' is growing, almost at any price. There are those who cannot easily hide in their individual disillusionment and increasingly cry inwardly.

• Constant invasion from all sides, Swedes, Mongols, French with Napoleon, British in the Crimea, Germans under Hitler, created not only a paranoiac fear of the West, but grew a form of nationalism which is better described as insular protectionism. The resulting internal and external security organisations are part of that process. The people willingly participated in this process. It was not as a result of brainwashing. They believed, and still do, in the inviolate place of the soil of Mother Russia in their hearts. Disillusionment with the new-found realities is changing that rapidly. Now they understandably desire escape, almost at any price. A resurgent national idea would dramatically change those negative thoughts.

- They did (in the past) educate their population to a degree we can only dream of. Here was one area where the former regime passed any international standards with flying colours. Bearing in mind what I see about me here today, leaves me amazed at their past techno-logical achievements in space and military technology. That legacy is unfortunately changing for the worse. At a time when these latent skills should be put to work for the benefit of the whole, underfunding, lack of amenities, class sizes of forty or more as teachers find better pay in the private sector are ensuring that this benefaction from the past is quickly decaying with little sign of resurrection. In Moscow, a teacher shortage (some two thousand five hundred this year) is causing severe problems. In the regions many schools have not reopened, thanks to non-payment of past wages and lack of Federal funding. It is a modern tragedy that strikes for payment of back wages are highest in the education sector. How would our trade unions react if lack of back pay was as high as they are here? I shudder to think of the social and political consequences back home. It would there, as here, begin to affect funda-mental stability.

- It created a people that had no interest in their leaders or their policies, despite the outward images of popular political support. They grew a mantle of self-protection that enabled them to disappear into their own secret world. There they could dream uncensored dreams of a better and untainted world that recent events have not turned out to represent. Conversations with a wide variety of Russians in my time here have re-enforced the total divergence between far-off unapproachable political life and the daily reality of people's conscious toil. The split-personality between the existence they have had to live (and still do today) and the dreams of what might potentially be, are poles apart. I am not sure if they deserve their current political leaders, or if these leaders merely represent the past they despise, but find unable to shake off. Yet somehow one feels a latent desire for fundamental change is stirring. The direction of that change is as yet unknown.

As mentioned in earlier correspondence, my words represent an entirely personal viewpoint with no side or bias. I have tried to record matters as I see them. At this stage of the letter, the philosophising must stop. The analysis must end, conclusions should be drawn. From now on I will endeavour to bring the strands of the discourse together. The pigeonholing may be superficial and dangerous, but the key elements of the idiosyncratic differences between their world and ours, that I see in the Russian persona today and in the majority of the people, may be summarised as follows (my sincere apologies to the few kind and gentle individuals who are demonstrably different):

- They are patient with their heavy lot in the extreme, but are capable of an explosion without warning.

  Beware the day. 1997 may be a dangerous year in this country.[12] The examples of living with hardship are many, but none more evident than in the Russian far eastern province of Primorsky Krai at the moment. Here the cycle of non-payment has reached fever pitch. Some 16,300 workers of the regional electricity company, Dalenergo, stopped work this month. One

---

[12]As it turned out, 1997 was a year when the sheen of superficial order and growth occurred. The day of reckoning was delayed twelve months, until the chaotic events surrounding the 1998 crash.

hundred and eighty of the staff are on hunger strike for a total of $24 million of unpaid back wages. As the military and commercial users of electricity are not paying their bills, little can be achieved without cash from the Federal paymaster – Moscow. As a result, the region has started to suffer chronic power blackouts lasting up to sixteen hours per day some areas as much as twenty. Moscow has pledged $860 million to the energy sector there, 7.3 million tonnes of coal and 900,000 tonnes of fuel oil. So far nothing has arrived. Thousands more unpaid blue and white-collar workers, including public-transport drivers, teachers, doctors and engineers at the local submarine manufacturer have vowed to join this strike to achieve their past dues.

This is no isolated example. In Rabinsk, only five hundred kilometres north of Moscow, the recent increase of twenty-five per cent in energy prices has proved too much. The three main employers have been cut off. Even the one who had paid his bill! There are many similar situations that show little sign of reduction. A colleague, during a discussion on current economic prospects, told me that we will have good sales in November with the energy-producing companies. The reason being that they will suddenly be flush with money, pay up or otherwise there will be no heating in the winter.[13] Well fine, but what a way to run a 'railway' if you see what I mean. Stop and go of this kind leaves its mark, particularly after all the extravagant promises Yeltsin made in the election campaign – and the resulting boom they were promised.

Even the *Financial Times* has begun to realise the

---

[13]Unfortunately he was wrong. Neither the cash for the energy companies or orders for ourselves materialised. But some heating came to the cities.

truth. It reported, before even the local press could do so – the first time in my experience – that matters in the northern city of Vorkutia, within the arctic circle, had reached breaking point.[14] This coal mining community had run out of food as a result of non-payment of wages since May 1996 – this six months ago. Apparently the Russian Federation cabinet met over the weekend of the 21 and 22 September to discuss what to do to resolve this further escalation of national misery. No reports have yet emanated as to their deliberations, and winter is upon us.

• They have an inordinately relaxed attitude to chaos.

A simplified example is demonstrated by check-in procedures at an airport, or experience of internal flights.[15] The practical example that comes to mind is at Sheremetevo 1, on flights to St Petersburg. When you arrive at the terminal, there is no indication as to which part of the building is reserved for domestic check-in. Normally foreigners have to use the separate Intourist gate – not here, and no one tells you otherwise. Once one has found the right departure hall, the magical mystery tour is then to find the correct check-in desk. In this airport there are about fifteen domestic desks, and guess what – not a single sign anywhere for anything other than the booth for payment of excess luggage. While flights are bound for St Petersburg, Irkutsk, Krasnadar, Vladivostock or anywhere else in the Federation, it is up to us intrepid travellers whether Russian or foreign to find our own way about, a little

---

[14]International *Financial Times*, 23 September 1996.

[15]Things have since changed for the better. At least in the major terminals in Moscow and St Petersburg information is now given on screens and the foreigner is treated the same way as everyone else.

difficult for those who do not always speak the language well. Once you have found the correct desk, stay put. You will then find that seat allocations are an unknown concept. If you are willing enough to let your luggage disappear into the bowels of Aeroflot's bottomless pit – pray that you will find it again. I have never dared to be so bold, and joined the multitude that piles its possessions in luggage racks in the aircraft designed with a toothbrush in mind. Don't sit under a heavy piece, it will fall off on take-off, and don't even try to claim compensation. Yet rarely a cross word from the patient queue, certainly not from the Russians. The foreign community is much more vociferous, but achieve little other than an ulcer for themselves.

On another occasion, I flew to Irkutsk from Moscow. I was amused and a little perplexed that the plane, a Tupolev 154, which (according to the rare example of an Aeroflot magazine found in the seat pocket) had a range of 4,500 miles. Yet I knew that the actual distance between the two cities was 5,500 miles. Clearly another miracle of Russian ingenuity at work? I never did explain this mystery, nor did we reach Irkutsk that day. We landed at an unknown place (later we found out it was some two hundred kilometres beyond our proper destination, and called Ulan Ude). Even my Russian colleagues took two hours to find out where we had arrived. The city had changed its name, and was not on any map we had. After five hours, with the temperature inside the terminal not far above 0°C, we discovered the time of our departure to the place we had longed to reach. No explanation, and no complaints from anyone except the foreign travellers. For the Russian traveller this is regarded as normal. All this accepted with undying patience.

One of the biggest perpetrators of chaos are the

customs authorities. Being involved in selling foreign equipment brings my colleagues and myself into close contact with their archaic practices. The new requirement for medical certificates for construction machines was mentioned in a previous letter (injurious to health etc.). The latest gem is that last week we were informed (we still have no reason for this edict) that transport companies from Germany, Denmark, Poland, Latvia and Estonia can only use one of the many customs terminals in Moscow – and it is not the one within our office building. All goods already delivered, and not cleared by customs were affected. The problem for us is that we have been trying to clear nearly $1 million of machinery from five trucks in our terminal.

- Their long years of isolationism, even from each other, has bred both nationalism and a more virulent form of racism.

  Internal security controls meant that travel inside the USSR was restricted for Russians as well as foreigners. The resulting contact with each other was sparse. Lack of contact breeds lack of knowledge, which in turn develops prejudice. Although many see the one hundred and fifty diverse ethnic groups as part of former 'empire', they show little respect for among others the Georgians and other Caucasians, the Jews or the Moslems, all of whom are part of their varied and intriguing cultural history. I was asked some months ago, by a young lady in the office, 'What do you think of Arabs and Blacks?' Not wishing to fall into an obvious trap, I replied, 'Well Arabs live in the Middle East, and dark-skinned people live mostly in Africa.' No she retorted, 'Don't you think they are dirty?' Unfortunately she meant what she said, based on insufficient knowledge and a multitude of prejudice. She is far from alone in this dreadful misconception among the Russians.

- They have created a strange and disparate class structure.

  Because flats were, and still are, allocated through receipt of living permits, there is little separation of strata in society. There is no way of knowing who within a social group will be one's neighbour. Only the most senior members of the government will live in segregated housing. The rest are mixed, yet they seek no contact with their neighbours. We in the West voluntarily segregate into living areas depending on a perceived social hierarchy. For the intrepid Western marketer we, at home, have all been pigeonholed into A, B, C1, C2 and Ds. To create similar situations here is an impossibility. My housing block is no different, there are poor pensioners, middle-class professionals and one very rich New Russian family in the flat above. The added security is a clue to that. The last eighty years of trying to create a classless society has achieved nothing of lasting value in this regard.

- Thinking and planning for tomorrow is a dangerous pastime.

  Whether it be my former Russian teacher who purports to be an intellectual, my business colleagues or acquaintances met over time, this characteristic is common to all. Their past experience did not encourage individuals to make decisions, nor were they trained on how to live in a world now dominated by the US $, or the full responsibilities of a market economy. We should wonder little as to the resulting confusion. But then tomorrow is another day and another challenge.

- Arrogance is a familiar trait.

I well remember an initial business discussion with a potentially large customer. A Federal department. The opening words from the senior negotiator on the other side (bearing in mind that they had already had our draft proposals) were: 'We have no money. Yeltsin has taken it to pay for his election promises. We don't like your prices. Your interest rates are too high, and your deliveries are too long. What are you going to lend us so we can continue this discussion?' In the West I would have stopped the conversation and thrown him out on his ear. Here one has to accept that this is a standard opening gambit, and go on from there. After some imaginative financial proposals were debated, we obtained the contract and have been paid, but their belief, that our only contribution to life here is finance, (for them to take an enormous personal cut) remains strong. We are merely a means to an end. Unfortunately they have not defined this goal other than they believe they are still 'top dog'. Unfortunately for them, on current evidence, if their economy returned to isolationism, it would affect the major Western markets by not one jot or iota.[16] Their sad historic legacy is that currently they need us more than we need them. Well economically at least.

- They have little social conscience.

But can they afford to have? While their leaders are raping the country, and they accept that the price to pay for national resurrection may be a whole generation, who can blame them for looking after number one before any other consideration. There is little national

---

[16] Still true, despite the Western overreaction to the 1998 economic crash. Russia in 1998 only represented one per cent of world GDP.

unity. Each and everyone looks to his own. Their only solace is their immediate family. Although divorce is easy, they mostly remain within those close confines. The corruption of their masters leaves them with few choices but to try to emulate their example. Who could blame them for that. The price is paid by the pensioner, the weak, the children and the 'have-nots'. There is no place in this land at this moment, or for some time to come, for the frail and dispossessed. They are unfortunately dispensable.

They believe, particularly in Moscow, to have invented a new form of economic existence. Ignore the rules of capitalism, keep your head in the sand. Barter, commissions, trade in anything that moves and rewards will flow. Politics have nothing to do with economics, so let's ignore the Kremlin and their incestuous archaic games. Individual and collective responsibility towards their fellow citizens is a far-off concept. As the law does not protect their enterprise, they take security into their own hands, and anyone who they are not sure is trustworthy is under constant suspicion. I discovered today that a Federal agency mentioned earlier had run a security check on me to find out if I or my family had ever been on any KGB lists. I am pleased to say that they told me that the results of the search were negative.

- They are incredibly hospitable.

    Particularly in the regions. Wherever travel and invitation have taken me, I have always been received with grace and style. Their pride and national stubbornness would not allow for anything else. Even if it means having fish, followed by fish soup with potatoes, accompanied by vodka for breakfast in Naberezhnyye Chelny – not a prospect I relish again. If one refuses, one risks rejection. This hospitality is, however, not accompanied by any humility. They are, and remain a proud and arrogant nation. In all the time spent here, I have never heard the words from a Russian 'I am sorry' – or – 'I apologise'. That would be seen as a sign of weakness. That is not a trait that any Russian will accept, he will go for the jugular in anyone exuding that characteristic. A pity, because they are at times capable of gentleness. But not often.

- They are intensely loyal to their friends.

Once one has made close and lasting contact with them they reward that with long-standing loyalty through thick or thin. Having understood the hardship of daily life, they do not wish that on the people who have given them moral, emotional or monetary support. But do not cross them. Their enmity is as deep as is their bond of mutual support. Beware though their dual ability to play both approaches if they seek personal gain. At the same time, they are able to appear 'friends' with consummate ease, but in parallel play the devious card. Once one's usefulness to them is over, one becomes a discard. Again the politics of divide and rule, with a dose of split-personality, created this behaviour, but this factor does not help endear them to your bosom.

- They are incredibly quick and willing pupils.

Search no further than here for the best computer hackers in the world. Having had little or nothing in the past, they have become expert at mend and make do. If a computer buff can defraud an American bank of $10 million from an on-line personal computer in St Petersburg and get away with it, I have no sympathy for the lack of controls within the US institution. One of the few amusing stories I heard about the tragedy of the nuclear accident at Chernobyl, then in the USSR, is the following: There was a desperate requirement then for remote-controlled excavators and bulldozers. So the engineers were allowed to scour the world to find modern technical solutions. Nothing they purchased worked. The most modern electronic gadgets from all parts of the globe were used to no avail. Eventually they had a brainwave – try old technology, valves, transistors and relays. Hey presto it worked. They had found that radiation affected the new and all-powerful micro technology the West had perfected. They beat the 'system' and revelled in their glory.[17]

- Despite all their complex nature, they are hungry for acceptance.

  They secretly search for symbols of recognition by us in the West and from each other, but try to hide their quest. They do realise the cocoon of isolationism is not for ever, but they fear its return. The young have learnt they have a part to play in economic, social and religious life. Politics continue to be a world apart that still intrudes on and pervades their daily existence. Like in former East Germany, quite where the older generation will find their future solace is a mystery. They reluctantly understand the gulf between life in Moscow and the deprived regions, but they still conduct themselves with the legacy of their past as blocks to their future progress.

- Some say, and observation confirms, that they are apparently lazy.

---

[17]MADI University in Moscow was the agent for this solution.

I could give countless examples from the office, the construction workers on a multitude of building sites and in the factories I have visited. This perception is, however, only true to a point. Of course they are able to drop everything and find an excuse for a party. We are all capable of that. Possibly our parties are less laced with booze, inebriation and raucous behaviour. Well anyway, those I have attended at home at my time of life. Some even say they don't want individual responsibility – let someone else carry the can. Again only true to a point. But centuries of centralised oppression, particularly in Stalin's time dulled the grey cells designed for individual thought.

- They do have an amazing ability to replicate bureaucracy.

In the course of my work I have to sign endless pieces of useless official paper. Employment statistics, customs formalities, police registrations for cars, tax documentation, permits for this and that or a multitude of details that have little to do with real life. The amount is so large, that I cannot imagine who could possibly read or action these useless documents, particularly if one assumes that every business in Russia has to do the same. However, I see this as an unfortunate continuation of former habits of control on personal freedom. No one fills in these forms willingly, yet their very existence creates two very Russian characteristics. Firstly, to create a continuing industry in misinformation; and secondly, to actively find more and more ingenious ways round the 'system'. The result is to establish a set of statistics that may not describe the true nature of the social and economic framework in Russia today. In this sense individual decision-making is actually at work. Its object being to confuse the masters who are trying to manipulate the 'peasants' and keep their individual freedoms no better than past regimes.

They are not inherently lazy, or lack personal accountability. They are prepared to carry individual and collective responsibility if there is a goal in sight. After the Second World War amazing progress was achieved in a short time span to rebuild a shattered land. Then the task of reconstruction was clear to all. Even those who did not like Stalin's oppressive regime, joined in the duty of national resurrection. Like all of us, wherever we are, when there is an individual or collective purpose, we are industrious. They are no different even for little reward. While, however, they see the rape of their heritage by their leaders, and have no real solution to untie their particular national 'Gordian Knot', their search for sovereign purpose is individual and not collective. The result is that all see self as the most important factor in their lives. Today there is, unfortunately, no national collective purpose that the thinking modern Russian can call his own. Until that day arrives the disillusionment, individual despair, drift and chaos will continue.

I cannot recall the exact words Churchill used to describe this place, it was something akin to: 'Russia is an enigma contained within a riddle and surrounded by mystery'. His perception in 1945 remains true today. In 1839 the Marquise de Custine remarked, 'Russia is a country where everyone is part of a conspiracy to mystify the foreigner'. Sometimes I wonder if anything has changed.

We can talk, in our Anglo-Saxon opinion, of logical solutions to their current predicament. Reform of: the tax regime to fill the state coffers; land ownership to encourage agricultural development; the banking system to increase industrial investment; the legal system to ensure proper protection for all; the commercial rules to revive the flagging recovery of immense mineral wealth for the benefit of the population; the education, health and social security system to allow a return of national funding for the young, needy and dispossessed; the proper redirection of the former vast military-industrial complex for peaceful productive purposes; the development of regional structures that allow the single-industry towns to widen their financial and manufacturing horizons. The list of tasks at hand are endless. Just as the potential solutions are. The one thing we cannot do is to impose our jaundiced thoughts on a people who must, at the end of the day, find their own salvation.

The many pages of this letter have left me rather exhausted. At no stage in this letter have I mentioned a sense of humour – not a national trait that I have met in abundance to date. Nor have I mentioned religion. That is the subject of my next letter – a complex topic on its own. I have alluded to the cheapness of individual life to the rulers of this land and the vast territory that dominates their thought... But... have I met the Russian in summer or winter? Have I found the truth? Whom have I described? Have I been unfair in my possibly jaundiced descriptions? Which part of the split-personality and self-destruct ability is the reality of life in Russia in 1996? My Russian friends have told me that I have described their national traits with a degree of accuracy. I hope so. Complexity is never given to easy descriptions. I think I have felt a little of the elusive 'Russian soul', but have not yet experienced the full extent of any partnership of human contact and I am still not completely sure that I have explained who the people really are. But then, they cannot define themselves and their complex nature either.

Chapter X
A Return to Religion?
November 1996

Some of you who have stayed the course of the past letters may have seen my developing fascination, frustration and love-hate relationship that has grown over time with the people and events in Russia today. That is what I have tried to record. Others of you have said that the contents of my writings have been heavy or 'dense'. Understandable to a degree. But such is the nature and condition of its people, their current tragic lot and the subject matter I have chosen to report upon. After all I am of German heritage, and humour and light-hearted comment come in small doses to them!

With a degree of sadness I report that my employer had decided it was soon time for me to return home in the not too distant future. Rather earlier than I expected. However, my commercial task here was coming to a natural conclusion. Local managers are cheaper than expatriates, so my costs were to be reviewed. This trend is gathering pace. He also had understandable concerns about the nature of his capital, credit, security and legal risk within Russia today. What is true, is that current governmental budget constraints have had a serious effect on any new business for us. Few orders for cash were forthcoming in our field. I fear from conversations with others in the Moscow expatriate business community that this will not be an isolated experience. As governmental paralysis resulting from five months of Yeltsin's illness, presidential succession dramas and non-payment of wages grow into an epidemic, then commercial life inevitably suffers, despite the alternative views of my Russian colleagues. Unfortunately they will learn that hard lesson for themselves. Other foreign companies are assessing their tenure in this land at this moment in time. I know of five such occurrences. Although fortune favours the brave and the stayers on the longer course of life, I have commercial sympathy for the position.

My Russian friends and acquaintances, who have been an essential part of my learning process, have asked me to publish the completed letters as a total volume. They believe my writings express their persona and problems with no side or bias. It appears important to them to let the world know of their personal plight. They too have felt that much misrepresentation of their daily lives exists in the West, and any step to rectify that may assist their individual and collective future. I am more than a little humbled at their request. They, the ordinary people, fear for their future without our current support. I will miss them and at the same time also fear for their condition in the next fateful twelve months.[1] One of my readers has commented that my target audience back home may not want anymore bad news. But after much thought, that is exactly what I will record, however few copies may be sold. Someone needs to know the truth seen from a grass-roots perspective. Coincidentally as it happens, I have reached a point where little further unresearched material will add to the fundamental message that I have tried to convey. So the interests of my employers and my 'teenage scribblings' have

---

[1]As it turned out, I did return. A number of flying visits in 1997 and permanent life during 1998 and early 1999. Further letters home were written during this time. Later chapters record those new experiences.

met a convenient conclusive point in time. However, all the above, however, is incidental to the main purpose of this letter which was prepared before these opening comments were added. So enough of this. Into the subject theme.

Some seven months back I was bored on a Saturday evening. Well, not really at a loose end, but there was an urgent need to kill some hours before the object of my perambulation was accomplished. The event I wanted to witness and experience began around midnight, or so information indicated, therefore in the meantime off to the cinema to see *Nixon*. Oliver Stone's presentation was showing at the Raddison Slavanskaya Hotel at the time. Not a memorable two hours. The film was more than heavy. Indeed I thought rather tedious. That event was, however, secondary to the main theme of a letter on religious matters and current attitudes in modern Russia. The object of my patience that evening was to attend a Russian Orthodox Easter service, but more on that shortly.

A point made many times in previous letters has been the difference between what happens in privileged Moscow to that in the regions. The same applies to the subject of these pages. Much of social and economic life has been demonstrated to be underdeveloped and deprived in the more isolated areas of this vast land, and even to a large extent in the larger regional cities. However, on this occasion the roles are reversed. Moscow, is for once, behind the regional resurgence of rediscovering ancient religious belief. I have no intention of delving into what constitutes belief or religious conviction. I can only observe what appears to be a tentative but growing desire to regain a need to associate with pious symbols lost in the tyranny of previous oppression. Moscow and its multitude of endemic 'New Russians' appear to have discovered a new God – the dollar. Others in the land have a freshly-found solace in the spiritual representations of their almost forgotten past.

Although our own Western, increasingly secular society appears currently to have lost the will to openly embrace religious activity, its traditions and historic significance have hardly left the environment in which we live our daily lives. I do wonder if that would have been the case for us, after eighty years of similar suppression.

Having been brought up as a 'WASP' – White Anglo-Saxon Protestant – as the usual American disease for shorthand calls us, and pigeonholing me with millions of others in Western Europe and America, as such I had little knowledge or understanding of other people's traditions in my younger days. Few of us have read the religious teachings of other beliefs. I am no different, although a past glimpse at the pages of the Koran opened my eyes a little. Many years travelling the world in the course of past employment gave me a modicum of insight into the rich and diverse traditions that other religions have given to the varied populations of this planet.

What became clear to me then, and has been re-enforced during my time here, is that the suppression of personal and spiritual belief in a higher being is one of the funda-mental touchstones of backlash against those who create the repression in the first place. It might take many years to regain an outward expression. In the meantime it inevitably drives human godly conduct underground in the expec-tation of later revival. Here, in Russia, the experience was no different. One of the mysteries as to how the former treasures of church panoply have reappeared in those religious places, now resurgent, was explained in a recent conversation. The gold and silver ornaments, vestments, writings and icons of Russian Orthodox churches were just hidden by the faithful few, where prying state eyes could not reach, in the patient hope of future useful reuse. The size and geography of the country allows for secret deposits to remain undisturbed for many years, while their patient guardians guarantee the custody of ancient traditions being protected for future believers. Many such objects have returned to their rightful place. Others, unfortunately 'filched', can be found for sale at such flea markets as Ismailovsky Park in Moscow. Stories abound about a secret continuance of religious practices away from prying KGB eyes. But I have no direct or indirect knowledge of such occurrences.

The traditional Western-stylised image of a Russian rural country scene is inevitably accompanied by an onion-domed church. The European part of Russia may have been historically associated with the traditions of the Russian Orthodox Church, but in a vast land such as this, we have to accept that diverse peoples attract different religious beliefs. So it is here. The mainly Moslem faith of the southern Caucasus and the mysterious lands of central Asia, as well as the Buddhist belief on the border with Mongolia are just as important in examining religious attitudes in this country. However, to place adherence to the main beliefs into perspective, in the former USSR probably less than twenty per cent were historically of Moslem or other faiths. Today, it is estimated that the Russian Federation has less than five per cent – with respect to the Caucasian republics. The bulk of citizens expressed adherence to Orthodoxy. Unfortunately I have spent too little time in the central Asian republics, but I can well believe Colin Thubron's comment on those lands.[2] 'There is a mild cultural resurgence – rather than a doctrinal revolution'. What I observe in European Russia is equally described by that portrayal. The tentative steps of such revival are, however, more than evident. Please forgive me if I spend most of these pages on Russian Orthodoxy, rather than other religious persuasions. Insufficient time,

---

[2]In his book, *The Lost Heart of Asia*.

scholarship and knowledge prevents a comprehensive coverage of all that one hundred and fifty diverse ethnic groups believe in and practise.

Lenin and his more dedicated followers erroneously believed that the 'Communism' expressed by Karl Marx in his 'bible' – *Das Kapital* – was a true alternative religion. We all know that pure Communism has never worked outside the confines of a monastic existence. Stalin redefined the Christian commandment: 'Thou shall have no other gods but me'. He was to be the object of his subservient subject's veneration. History has shown that fundamental spiritual beliefs remain latent in those unable to openly demonstrate their inner convictions. Once again we should not be surprised at the beginnings of a resurgence of reverent activity in this land now that open expression is again an acceptable, albeit tentative, practice. Freedom is a relative concept. Compared to their past, they are 'free'. In comparison to the same philosophy as practised by ourselves, they are only just at liberty. At least the authorities of the USSR allowed preparations to commence for the celebration of the millennium of Russia's conversion to Christianity in 988. Gorbachev, who presided over these events even met the Pope in Rome in that year of 1988. At last the state began to show a heart. The die was cast for change. Unfortunately this loosening of suppression also brought with it an urgent requirement to rebuild decaying churches. This need for cash is viewed by some to be the origin of the Church's involvement in tax-free alcohol and cigarette distribution mentioned before. Unfortunately, even they have begun to be involved in comment on corruption in high places as a result.

Most of us can only listen to, but not fully, or probably ever, comprehend, the message and practice of Stalin's repression of religious activity. In truth Kruschev was more active in reducing such practices than the former tyrant; his legacy was worst of all. The all-seeing eye of the state pervaded every corner of independent thought to an extent that few of us in the West can ever comprehend – it reached every individual nook and cranny of daily life, except the grey cells of the resilient. Any scintilla of obvious religious adherence sent an individual into loss of education, status, job, privileges and future for him, her or their family. Having other gods than the message of a twisted ideology of tyranny determined the fate of many. Such individual thoughts understandably went underground as a result, never to be spoken aloud.

At the beginning of the twentieth century Moscow counted 769 churches and 77 chapels within its city borders. Today only half are still standing. Only one hundred are in operation now as consecrated places of worship. But change is on its way. Some statistics may give us a clue.[3] Throughout the former USSR the number of Russian Orthodox Church societies had fallen from 14,100 in 1945 to 6,740 in 1988, most of them with no clergy. Yet some six years later in 1994 nearly 12,800 communities were again active. In 1914 there were approximately 1,025 convents (and monasteries) in the land with over 95,000 monks or nuns in cloisters. By 1945 the working convent population was only about 105 (yes 105 – no typographical error), with little more than 4,600 monks and nuns. The low point of closed religious institutions was reached between 1961 and 1981, when no more than eighteen (yes, eighteen) such places, with only about one thousand inhabitants, continued their work across the total land. Kruschev's influence was truly evident. By 1989 such establishments were beginning to slowly reopen and nearly one hundred and twenty were active with an attendant rise in religious teachers. The figures today are not known to

---

[3] *A Long Walk to Church* by Nathaniel Davis.

me, but are evidently increasing rapidly. Certainly the steep rise in students at seminaries and academies illustrates the point – from virtually nil in 1943, by 1991 over three thousand individuals were again learning the teachings of the Russian Orthodox community. Two of the most important seminaries are in St Petersburg and at the Trinity Sergius Monastery in Sergei Possad (formally Zagorsk), seventy kilometres north of Moscow. In 1917, before the revolution, there were some fifty thousand ordained priests adhering to Orthodoxy. By 1939 only four bishops and between three and four hundred clergy openly practising their faith. Today, over eight thousand priests are registered with the Patriarch's office in Moscow. However, with a population of two hundred and fifty million in the former USSR (and one hundred and forty-seven million within the boundaries of the current Russian Federation) a low point bordering on death of former religious traditions was clearly not far off.

In recent years, the latent desire of a spiritually and mentally-starved population were beginning to resurrect a new-found spirit of self-expression, albeit from a base, where knowledge of past traditions was almost non-existent. Many of us might believe that this new religious spring was confined to the old, the babushkas and the weak. No, not true. Enough of statistics. I have, on occasion, heard my Russian friends express concern at their sense of religious emptiness. Let me return to the experience of the Easter service and give a real demonstration of current events.

On my way to the cinema on the previously mentioned Saturday evening, I had chosen to pass the church destined for the later visit. This consecrated place was to be found some one hundred metres from MosSoviet, the mayoral office of the rulers of the city of Moscow, not far from the flat. Having walked past on many occasions, this time puzzlement ensued. The building was surrounded by barriers and some seven or eight policemen were evident. Was this a return to old suppression? Or was something else afoot? At 10.30 in the late evening I returned and entered the church. It was packed to overflowing. Apart from one chandelier, only candles lit the night. Monotonous and at the same time evocative bass half-tone chants from a variety of lay and ordained individuals continued for an hour. There was little comprehension by myself of the night's events to date. What to do? I decided to squeeze myself out of the crush within and seek some fresh air. Imagine my astonishment when I returned to face a dark and frosty Moscow night. The square outside, previously empty an hour ago save for the few policemen, was packed to overflowing with some five thousand eager faces directed at the church. They were patiently waiting, half with unlit candles in their hands. But waiting for what? Of immediate significance was that a majority of those I saw were young – at least under forty, and both sexes were represented in equal number. The policemen's attention was equally focused toward the church, and all were outside the barriers. All was to be revealed in time.

Clearly something of significance was about to happen, so no returning to the flat, but wait with a patient and anticipative crowd. At the witching hour the gathering went expectantly silent. The bells began to ring with monotonous urgency and the clergy, some six in all, in their full regalia emerged. The bearded elder among them began to urgently chant and sprinkled those at the front of the throng with holy incense. With staves and crosses carried high, they began to sing in wonderful bass semitones – and a high proportion of the outside congregation joined in. Many of those present, including the young, stutteringly knew the words. Then the relevance of the barriers became clear. The clergy, followed reverently by the congregation from inside the church began slowly to perambulate around the building inside the barriers with no let or hindrance. Observe closely and you will find that all Russian Orthodox churches have a path around them. You must ignore the normally locked rear gates. They appear to lead to nowhere. On this important occasion they were opened.

Three times the clergy slowly processed, and on the final occasion the cry went up from all: *Christus Voskrecen* – Christ is Risen. In their search they had not been able to find the body. So He must have risen. Having seen the sign of these words in Cyrillic in a number of churches in the previous weeks, including on a banner across Tverskaya Ulitsa, I had not fully realised the significance, because the Russian word for Sunday is *Voskrecenye*. You will understand I thought the message was simply Christ's Sunday, with some vague significance for the forthcoming Easter celebration. By this time all in the square who had one, lit their candles and with reverence observed the pious event. All having established that Christ's body was not to be found and all was well with the world, the clergy returned to further celebrations inside the church, which would continue for a further three or so hours. The throng proceeded to kiss their neighbours, albeit total strangers, including three for me – and wished each other a happy and joyous Easter, then proceeded to open the barriers, to place their candles before the painted icons outside the building and drifted contented and enlightened on their way. I have to say that in the greyness of a cold and frosty spring Moscow night this touching and genuine expression of faith in a superior being was more than unexpected. Particularly with so many young people wishing to enjoin themselves in their rich traditions. The symbolism was not lost on me.

The following day I returned to the church, and found that the service continued unabated. In the courtyard, stalls had been set up and Easter regalia was to be seen. Cakes, fruits, and a multitude of painted eggs. Decorated eggs are an important part of the Easter ritual. The story goes thus. The Orthodox tradition originally ordered believers to paint eggs red. Apparently the Bible tells us that Mary Magdalene came to the Roman Emperor Tiberius with an egg to tell him that Christ had risen. The emperor responded that when the white egg turned red then indeed Christ would have risen. Immediately afterwards the egg turned red. I am not sure in which part of the Bible this story appears, but such is the basis of traditional belief. Presumably our Western use of Easter eggs has a similar heritage. Resulting from this Orthodox belief, painting eggs has become an art form here.

Symbols of historical religious devotion of another sort were experienced on another occasion and in another place. In November of 1995, I visited Irkutsk and the nearby dramatic encounter with Lake Baikal. They say three hundred and sixty-five rivers and streams run into this massive site of geography, into which you can squeeze the land surface of England. Yet only one river – the Angara – takes the pure fresh water to far off northward places more than a thousand kilometres away. By the way, it tastes delicious. Half way on the road between the ancient city of Irkutsk and the lake is a hidden lay-by. The vast secret, mysterious and undulating forest would not reveal this magical place if one were a stranger to their land. Our hosts stopped the car and led us to a tree festooned with a multitude of ribbons – hundreds, possibly thousands of them. The branches were barely visible from their burden. It was said that the gods would not let us pass in peace to visit the wonder of the lake if we did not add to the vast collection of past reverence and make a wish for posterity. While we were there, a wedding party from the city arrived to pay their homage to past legends and gods of the present.

The few citizens of this empty quarter of Russia, two hundred and fifty kilometres from the borders of Mongolia and in an administrative area four times the size of France, could not have placed so many memories on that tree in the years since Communism became a secular memory. They seemed to me to have found another form of symbolism to a higher being while apparently adhering to the strictures of their oppression. In a country devoid of signals of another presence, again the sign of longing for a higher being, however pagan, was not to be ignored.

In the early afternoon of the Saturday the Easter service took place, I had been around town to observe other traditions and practices in the churches in the centre. All was well with the world, but anticipation for the forth-coming feast was evident. One of the quainter customs I witnessed that afternoon was a 'conveyer belt' of middle-aged and older ladies clutching parcels and plastic bags in the newly rebuilt church on the north-east corner of Red Square. The ladies' receptacles turned out to contain a variety of cakes, pastries, puddings and sweets. All clearly home made. I use the expression conveyor belt deliberately. These fifty or so ladies were patiently waiting to take their turn for the priest to bless their creations with prayers and holy water so that they could take them back to an expectant family. About seven or eight ladies at a time would open their bags, empty the contents on a makeshift altar laid out for the occasion, await the ministration of the priest, and then depart into the afternoon sun, only for the next group to ask for a repeat performance. As I left the building, the queue had grown to over one hundred metres.

One of the Christian ceremonies many of us in the West attempt to cherish is the wedding service, with its attendant vows for the future. Here, for obvious reasons, only the civil ceremony was in past times the formal outward recognition of a state of marriage. Having had the pleasure to be invited to such an event not long after arriving in Russia, some of the symbolic characteristics are relevant to a letter on religious attitudes and practice. The reception was mostly like any other such event in the West, with an abundance of food, drink, speeches, dancing and general merriment for the happy couple. There were two differences. On arriving at the reception the couple were greeted by the ceremonial gifts of bread and salt which had to be sampled. Then they had to choose one of three carpets on which to walk into the building. Once done, it was revealed from under the carpets which path of life they had chosen. For example – love, honour or obedience. This was my first full introduction to the endless toasts, all accompanied by vodka, that are an integral part of every meal with them. Everyone had to participate. I counted nearly thirty such speeches, including one from me. What is important in the context of these pages are the events prior to the wedding couple's arrival for the family celebrations.

Only the bride, groom, best man and matron of honour take part in these very private symbolic gestures. Strangely no guests or other family members. Three important matters have to be resolved before the celebratory family feast can commence. The bride and groom have by modern tradition to honour: firstly each other; secondly their joint romantic past; and then finally their respects to the motherland. The first of these is achieved by the brief and simple civil marriage ceremony. The second and third have deeper attributes. Because the former Communist world could not accommodate past Christian traditions, new forms of homage to a higher being, then represented by the state, were invented. What happens is simple. The small wedding group, after the civil ceremony, first goes to sites of personal significance to the bride and groom – where they met, their former schools or universities, or other places of mutual importance. In this way they give symbolic reciprocal tokens to each other. Then of key importance, homage to their country is the replication of former Christian allegiance to a higher being. For this reason on a Saturday and Sunday, and on occasion during the week, you will still find a multitude of small wedding groups visiting and laying flowers at shrines of national significance. Despite a newer religious freedom, the Church has, as yet, not reclaimed its full role in these events, notwithstanding figures quoted later. In Moscow, such respect to the motherland is usually at the tomb of the unknown soldier in the gardens of Alexander Sad below the walls of the Kremlin. Other places might be the victory gardens on Kutuzovsky Prospekt, built in 1995 to commemorate fifty years of peace since the end of the Second World War, or even the triumphal arch nearby in celebration of Napoleon's defeat at Borodino in 1812 might be a place of pilgrimage. In Irkutsk the mysterious ribbon tree was clearly one of the sites. Only after these national dues had been paid could the couple return rejuvenated to their family celebrations.

One jarring note has to be added to the celebration of modern Russian marriages. Capitalism is creeping into the process. Nestlé has perceived a marketing loophole to promote its products by handing out packs of instant coffee to the bride and groom in congratulation of their nuptials. Some seventeen thousand gift packs consisting of two red Nescafé mugs and a can of coffee have so far been distributed according to the advertising agency, Momentum, (a part of McCann Erickson). This marketing programme has run in eight cities including Samara, Irkutsk and Vladivostock after successful marketing in Moscow and St Petersburg. Possibly good marketing, but a bit naff I think.

Because there is so little knowledge of past religious tradition, much thought, reading and personal research with books, believers and clergy had to be conducted over time before starting my monthly exercise with the word processor. No one in the office had much knowledge on the subject, or had even been to a church service, so I had to look elsewhere. This research included a lengthy conversation with Father Gennadi of the Church of St Nikolai, and Father Anatoly of the English-speaking Orthodox community, both in Moscow. As part of my further deliberations on this subject, I also went back into the Kremlin grounds to visit the four main cathedrals in the hope of finding a guide who might explain some of the finer points of Orthodoxy, its history and tradition. This included a further visit to the Assumption Cathedral which was the historic site of all major Russian state events over the centuries since its last rebuilding in 1549, as the third church on the same site. I found a knowledgeable lady called Rosa, who had studied art history and was a mine of valuable factual information. Having eventually exhausted her store of scholarship, my final series of questions were to establish from her what she thought of current attitudes to religious belief in the country today. I never got further than the first of these, to which she answered, 'I don't know, my family is Moslem.' As mentioned in the previous letter, never take anything at face value in this country.

The more I learnt of the dogma and rites associated with the Russian Orthodox Church, the more I realised that there were a multitude of connections between hidden, certainly not immediately obvious, former Communist icons; the ecclesiastical strictures of the church and the psyche of the people. While composing the last letter on the elusive Russian 'soul', these interpretations were not immediately clear to me either, but are now beginning to form a pattern. Let me explain a little more. Divide and rule; patient unquestioning subservience to authority; isolationism and totalitarianism were four of the key elements in describing why Russian people conduct their lives as they do. After understanding a little about religious structures in this country, I have come to believe that the immense symbolism associated with the teachings and dogma of the Russian Orthodox Church are closely intertwined with the same four elements which help make up national behaviour. Hence the choice of the three previous examples, the visit to an Easter service, the token tree in Irkutsk and the need for the wedding couple to honour their joint past, each other and their country.

Bear with me while I take you through my possibly complicated thought process. The place I should start is probably the physical manifestation of worship – a Russian Orthodox church. In the faith of my upbringing, a simple pious act of devotion, entering a church to pray silently and then withdraw content, is part of many believers' habit. A moment of quiet contemplation and only an unspoken conversation with a personal god. No need for symbols, or outside help. In Russian Orthodox circles, this might be, and probably is, an impossibility. Here there is a necessity, indeed requirement, to use the formal intercession of an icon, a candle or another symbol which might be part of the architecture of the consecrated building to reach the hearing of one's personal god. The buildings of Russian Orthodox worship are all immensely stylised in character, and have the four key elements mentioned above within their architecture. All are demonstrated by display and use of symbolism which appear to me to reduce any individual thought. Even a much decorated Protestant 'high church' or Catholic building at home bears little comparison.

Divide and Rule is a strange concept to use in terms of a religious community. However, when one enters a church here, the first dramatic vision is of the dominant Iconosta-tis. This is the massive panel of icons facing you, as you enter the main door on the west side of the building and face East. It covers the whole of what initially appears to be the East wall. You will find up to seven levels of icons. It varies according to the size of the structure. In the middle of this setting, at ground level are the 'Royal Doors' leading to the inner sanctum. To the right of these doors is the icon pictorially representing the saint to whom the church is dedicated. Among the other representations, on this huge decorated collage, you will find the four Evangelists, Mary with the baby Jesus, archangels and saintly deacons. The manner in which an Iconostatis is constructed has clear and formal rules applying to all Orthodox churches. I will come to other images in the building later. The Iconostatis may be to some the equivalent of a rood screen in one of our holy places at home. But we can pass through that and go to the altar. Here, on no account, is that possible, not even for a tsar. This barrier in a Russian Orthodox church is the earthly representation of the fundamental *division* between man's sin and God's perfection. Only the ordained clergy can pass through the Royal Doors. The blessing of the bread and wine in communion is performed out of sight of the congregation. The holiest relics are stored here. The high altar is hidden for all. God's sanctity cannot be disturbed by mere uninitiated mortals. The common man cannot pass into God's earthly inner sanctum.

To begin a private conversation with God the worshipper must use the intercession of an icon, by reverently kissing it, or the purchase of a candle and lighting it. Only then does their interpretation mean they have reached a point of communication with their higher being, having invoked and called for the presence of the saints into the congregation. Apparently here even the church does not allow free access, without props or interference, to an individual and personal god. You will understand my conclusion.

Unquestioning subservience to formal authority was my next comparison. All the internal walls of church buildings here are completely covered with frescoes, paintings or representations of one sort or another. Many that I have seen are ancient and quite breathtaking. Having now been in many dozens of such places, this still gave me little evidence as to the explanation of these images or their meaning. What was evident was that they were different on each occasion. My Moslem lady guide in the Kremlin cathedrals explained that the initial clue lies in finding out which saint the building is dedicated to. So each time look first to the right-hand side of the Royal Doors for the church's saint's icon. The frescos then suddenly begin to have meaning. As few of the former congregations could read, particularly in pre-revolutionary days this was a pictorial story for them. So what was depicted, starting from the top left-hand side of the southern wall – round and downwards, west, north and back to the south wall, were the deeds, history and miracles of the church's dedicated saint. This pictorial message, interspersed on the west wall with images of The Last Supper, The Day of Judgement and John the Baptist, was therefore what the Church authorities had deemed that the 'peasants' *needed* to know. Jesus and a dove overseeing the whole will be found in the cupola of the main dome. With the architecture of the building representing a boat journeying to the East (quite how they are meant to look like ships is slightly beyond me), all the believer *needed* to know in religious dogma was laid out for him in pictorial form in the decoration of the building. Little original thought was necessary for the attendant congregation.

Comment has been made in past letters about the glorious sound a Russian choir makes. The development of this form of musical harmony comes in part because the use of instruments of any kind is forbidden in a Russian

Orthodox church. One will look in vain to find an organ. Singing is, however, not restricted to the male voice. You will often hear a female choir hidden behind the screens to the left and right of the Iconostatis.

Isolationism from outside influences under tsarist times meant that little wider contact was encouraged or tolerated for the common man. He was merely a vassal to be dominated by, and subservient to, in particular the state, as well as other secular or religious authorities. Today, there is only grudging acceptance by Russian Orthodoxy that Protestants or Catholics may be brothers in Christ, but that is as far as it apparently goes. Lack of fundamental acceptance of other faiths or minor foreign religious sectarian groups has led to severe tension between the current Church hierarchy and the many visiting evangelical groups who try to bring their individual brands of Western sectarianism to this land. Yury Buyda[4] writes of a past group of three hundred Orthodox believers who were tempted by propagandist brochures and the novelty of being baptised by a Seventh-Day-Adventist missionary in Nizhny Novgorod in Gorbachev's day. He continued,[5] 'The Church was later to disappoint many of those who had put much hope in it. Its first concern was to actively fight against so-called sectarianism, including not only Evangelists and Adventists, who were little known in Russia at the time, but Protestants and Catholics as well, with whom the Orthodox Church had never experienced any love, but whom it at least recognised as brothers in Christ.'

As a result the Moscow patriarch sounded the alarm.

'...We are being bought by foreigners.' The fight against these missionaries was even then taken up by the State

---

[4] A writer on the editorial board of *Novoye Vremya* and *Znamya*.
[5] The *Moscow Times*, 2 October 1996.

Duma at that time. Evangelical visitors, particularly from the American southern 'bible belt' have had much publicity recently, most of it bad, both abroad and within Russia. As mentioned previously, my wife and I experienced one of them in the Bolshoi, with eventual irritating effect to all who were in earshot. Even the American Evangelist, Billy Graham, did not escape criticism. During his crusade, held at Moscow's Luzhniki Stadium (built for the 1980 Olympics), in October 1992 a leading Church newspaper[6] wrote, '...Billy Graham's crusade is a grandiose, self-satisfied, immodest "show" which treated the Russians as if they were natives of New Guinea without religious roots, faith or culture.' With the best motives in the world, an innocent but adult daughter of an old friend who is one of the recipients of these letters faced the same truths while she and her group were recently trying to bring Christianity to the peoples of Uzbekistan. The leader of her party is still unfortunately trying to disentangle her problems as a result with the Islamic state security organisations there.

With the Church here still trying to re-establish its own emerging future mission, subject to dogmatic, ecumenical and property ownership arguments with Estonia and other Episcopal Sees in the former USSR, to the benefit of the people, albeit based on past historical dogmatism, such newfangled ideas are a severe shock to the local system and not really appreciated. Most Russians, well those with some faint interest in religion, find it almost impossible to cope with the foreign message. Those with little interest find such interference irrelevant to their daily lives. These disturbances are thus understandably not welcomed by existing religious or state authorities. The only real acceptable foreign ideas that I have seen to date are those that help the Russian peasant. Intellectual and apparatchik alike make

---

[6]*Moscow Church Herald Weekly.*

money for themselves.

In further comment on the position of the modern Church in Russia today, Yury Buyda continued in an open article[7] that the modern Church authorities had learnt little from past *totalitarianism* and were in effect servants of today's state apparatus. From my own commercial experience here, this rings true. A past example in a previous letter mentioned cigarette distribution from which the church benefited to a large degree by not having to pay the statutory tax stamp. As a result of this (and alcohol tax stamp and distribution involvement) and benefiting from this (and treasury coffers losing), to the tune of possibly $4 billion per annum, was the Church rebuilding programme. Well someone has to pay that bill, and political expediency appeared to be the order of the day. Patriarch Alexis II (the current head of the Russian Orthodox Church) has even managed to move quietly from the Danilov Monastery in Moscow to the former patriarchal Kremlin residence[8] through the efforts of Yeltsin's former all-powerful 'gatekeeper' Alexander Korzhakov,[9] now replaced by Anatoly Chubais. Buyda commented further:

'Until the October (1917) Revolution, Orthodoxy served as an ideological surrogate. Today, politicians are trying to convert Orthodoxy into a new national ideology, not taking into account the consequences of their efforts in a multi-religious country. It is therefore not surprising that the Church is simply lost in conditions of political freedom. It has never had the experience of an independent life and cannot be a

---

[7]The *Moscow Times*, 2 October 1996.
[8]Despite what you might read in Frederick Forsyth's new novel *Icon*.
[9]'Removed' after the presidential election in July 1996. See Chapter VI, 'Kremlin Intrigues'.

support for free people. Until this day, it fears free people who think for themselves. This is why the Church is afraid of an invasion of foreign missionaries, against whom it prefers to struggle not by the force of ideas, but the force of government power.' This September, one of the most influential Church officials, Metropolitan Yuvenaly, said that Orthodoxy needs to be protected, 'if only for a few years.' He criticised a law on the freedom of religion which the Duma adopted this spring (1996) despite its strong pro (Orthodox) Church lobby Buyda concluded, '...Since the Russian Church has never appreciated the democratic values of Christianity, having remained throughout history subordinate to totalitarian regimes, whether Tsarist or Bolshevik.'

These comments by a Russian, on his own country's religious resurgence, appear to be more than profound, and need little further elaboration.[10] These comments, if true – but I would subscribe to them – have social and political consequences in an already troubled land. My observations over the last eighteen months would condone these remarks with the proviso of observing common Muscovites

---

[10]Since this letter was written the relationship between the Orthodox Church and religions without a Russian tradition have been clarified in law. On Friday, 19 September 1997 the Duma passed a law which effectively discriminates against all other religions bar Orthodoxy. Put simplistically, any 'religious organisation' wishing to have the right to practise openly with full rights to preach and worship in modern Russia now has to prove that it has existed in Russia for at least fifteen years. Quite how that will work bearing in mind that Communism only fell in 1991 is not clear. For once the Duma gave little opposition to the bill. It certainly indicates the paranoid views of the modern Church leadership. In reality it will have little impact upon the bulk of people, but it is a sign that democracy or full freedom and tolerance of thought has as yet not fully arrived.

trying to 'feel' something of their simple faith in another god by their penitent and intense participation at the Easter and other services mentioned previously. At the same time, the sight of Boris Yeltsin as the main guest at the consecration of the newly rebuilt Cathedral of Christ the Saviour, in Moscow at Easter 1996, jarred more than a little for many. But clearly, isolationism and totalitarianism have left their indelible mark.

Hopefully my thought process has begun to show that the Russian human psyche was formed not just by an oppressive state over the last thousand years by autocratic princes, tsars and Communist rulers alike, but also by state-influenced Orthodoxy within a vast and closed society. Before I deal with slightly lighter comment on more recent happenings, the stylised symbolism of the remainder of Church ornaments and architecture might add to the picture of feeding formal images, with little room for individual interpretation, to the people.

Icons and onion domes are the Orthodox symbols that immediately spring to mind. Let me take the dome first. I can now confirm that the onion shape had more practical significance. It was thus so that the brightness of the cupola could be seen even in the worst of winter snows, it just fell off more easily. Of larger significance are the number of such domes on an individual building. Look closely and you will see churches with one, three, five or even in some isolated cases thirteen. A building with one is a representation of Christ alone, and usually means that the church is very old. Three denotes the trinity of God, Jesus and the Holy Ghost. When a church has five, then Jesus and the four Evangelists, Matthew, Mark, Luke and John are depicted. The few with thirteen portray Jesus and the twelve disciples. The dome denoting Jesus is always the highest point of the building and constantly contains, on its underside, a pictorial representation of Christ with a dove of peace. All ever-present reminders of the images of their faith, to the uneducated masses of the key Christian persona are thus shown in pictorial form.

The use of an icon – a sign or image – is even more symbolic. There are five types apparently, most have the Virgin Mary as their main theme. They represent: tenderness – Mary with a child kissing her cheek; showing the way – Mary with hand outstretched; the 'Oranta' – Mary blessing the people; an 'Oranta' deviation – the Holy Virgin's sign; and lastly the Trinity. Groups of saintly figures are also occasionally found. Using these different forms of beacon, thus much more importantly, the icon is the main form of intercession with God. The believer enters the church, buys a candle, lights it and then constantly genuflecting, kisses one of many icons around the building, although the Iconostatis itself is out of bounds for that purpose. Only then can communion with God, or involvement in an ongoing service begin. It is common to continue these actions during a service, hence the constant comings and goings, which initially mystified me and appeared to disrupt proceedings. At least with no pews or seating, such movement is unhindered. As services can be lengthy affairs, these individual acts of worship are of prime importance for those who decide to come only part time, and many do.

The rationale for an icon is fourfold, so it is important to know the purpose of the prayer before choosing one to kiss. Firstly it is a source of support; secondly it describes an ideal being, emotion or concept; thirdly it is an object of veneration; and lastly it has spiritual properties. Some of the more famous icons in Russia are: the Smolenskaya Icon which is reputed to have given the tsarist armies strength. That of the Veronica Veil is believed by many to have immense spiritual powers. Legend has it that Christ on the way to the cross had a veil pressed on his face by a follower,

Veronica. When she took the cloth home she found the impression of the face of Christ on the fabric. This image has for evermore been the iconic portrayal of the face of Jesus. Whatever the truth of such legends or traditions, the Orthodox believer apparently cannot engage in his or her worship without such a buttress of comfort.

It all seems far too regimented to me. I would rather have my own image of my personal god rather than that presented to me by earthly authority in a stylistic manner. The Orthodox split from Rome in 1034 has thus developed into not just a spiritual, but a cultural and political gap.

Even different shapes of the cross are used here for different symbolic messages. One rarely sees a simple cross with a simple horizontal and vertical creation. It is either what I can only describe as a Cross of Lorraine, with an additional smaller horizontal beam, which represents the place for the crown of thorns, or more often this variant with a further sloped plank at the bottom. This slope, from the right and rising to the left, is the representation of the direction to either heaven or hell. Having said earlier that the physical building of a church denotes a ship moving to the East, I am also told that other buildings are meant to represent the cross. That description has so far eluded me in any of the architecture I have seen to date.

A strange but interesting sight greets you in Orthodox churches in the spring. The floor is covered by rushes and straw and silver birch twigs surround the inside of the building and are tied to the outside of the doors. All a bit like our harvest festival, but without the offerings, and not in the late summer. What is being celebrated is the end of winter and the joy of forthcoming spring and summer. It does, however, give one a very mediaeval and pagan impression of a form of celebration. I can understand the significance of emerging twigs of birch with new green leaves, but the relevance of the straw escapes me. It has been explained as representing piety in Christ's stable.

With over seventy employees in both our Moscow offices, very few of whom had either been to a service or knew anything of substance about religious matters, it was more than difficult to find out what people really think on religious subjects today. Those to whom I have talked in the office tell me that they are too concerned with the problems of daily life to concern themselves with what some have described as outdated tsarist propaganda. '…We have to look forward, not back,' said one. At the same time they have regularly asked to read my letters so they have a feel for what a visitor thinks of their country. The feedback has been more than helpful and has given me much insight into their thoughts. This also gives me some comfort that the content of my letters is a reasonable representation of life in my world in Russia in 1995 and 1996.

So without months of digging, overall opinions of modern Russian religious attitudes are hard to come by and my observations may be somewhat suspect. Even finding more than one cleric who was willing to talk on the subject was somewhat circuitous. In the end I found two. Therefore I can only on this occasion observe and guess at the background or comment on those attending services and listen closely to the few who have, in Moscow anyway, been of help to me in preparing this letter. The factual content mentioned above has all been confirmed by these knowledgeable individuals, as well as that found in research material and is therefore believed to be accurate.

The numbers evident in the few Orthodox church

services I have sneaked in to observe in the regions were much larger, but appeared to be mainly from the agricultural community that make up some thirty per cent of the population of the Russian Federation. According to some,[11] in the last days of the USSR some thirty million people (or one sixth of the populations of European Soviet Russia including the Ukraine, Belarus, the Baltic republics etc.) attended church at some time or other during a year. Yet in the cities only half a per cent (half a million people) did the same. These figures will have changed, but public religious expression in the regions and agricultural lands is demonstrably higher there than in the cities. But as said before, in respect of the subject of this letter the regions are ahead of the central cities.

For the foreigner who wishes to partake, worship is totally open and free for all. According to the English language press here, Moscow today boasts some twenty places of devotion to diverse faiths. Two mosques, five synagogues and one for the reformed Jews (Hineni), one meeting place for the Baha'i faith, a Mormon church, a Baptist chapel, two Catholic churches, six Protestant meeting places for various denominational groups and a place of worship for the Chabad Lubavitch whose origin or beliefs are not known to me. There may be many more in hidden places. Apart from occasional police and OMON special forces' raids on the mosques, to apparently search for Chechen fighters, and the recent burning of a synagogue, the authorities allow us outsiders to express religious freedom, as long as it does not disturb the locals. Beware, however, the hidden attitude of the European Russian against Judaism and to some extent the Moslem

---

[11]Dimitry Pospielovsky, *Intelligentsia and Religion: Aspects of Religious Revival in the Contemporary Soviet Union* and *The Russian Church under the Soviet Regime 1917–1982*.

community if one of their own were to openly practise these faiths. There is a latent, and on occasion vigorously expressed, bigotry towards them, and particularly anti-Jewish feeling is high. Shades of a darker past, here and elsewhere, returned. The exodus of Russian Jews to Israel is rising rapidly as a result. Both Lebed and Zhirinovsky have added their commentary to that particular subject, in the former case, much to the annoyance of the American White House. Lebed called Mormons and other non-Russian religions 'filth and scum'. Apparently he also compared the Mormons to Aum Shinri Kyo, the Japanese sect who released nerve gas on the Tokyo Underground. And as mentioned before, they are certainly not ready as yet for foreign Evangelical invasions that disturb a fragile religious spring for their former national religion.

On a lighter note, on one of my visits to the small rural city of Suzdal with its multitude of churches, I stayed at the Petrovsky monastery. This ancient walled complex of some six acres contained sixteen Swedish-style log cabins for the tourists. The city has been declared a world heritage site and had been awarded 'La Pomme d'Orée' – Golden Apple – Award for restoration work to date. There were only three brick structures in the monastery. One of these was the refectory. Inside was a large, lovely but simple white-washed vaulted room. The food was very Russian and wholesome. The large elm tables and monastic benches gave it an authentic touch. The second brick building was the church. I had noticed monks attending services as well as young nuns assisting and working in the gardens. What remains a mystery to this day was that both the monks and nuns disappeared into the third brick structure, which looked like living and sleeping accommodation after their religious deliberations and daily work had ended. Orthodox priests are allowed to marry, but was something else afoot? A wicked thought!

Some more recent statistics may give a clue as to the increase in current public religious practice. Metropolitan Vladimir, in his report to the national Church Council in June 1988, stated that thirty million people had been baptised in the USSR between 1971 and 1988, twice the figure admitted by USSR governmental statistics. Christenings were one of the events citizens here had to have recorded in their internal passports. Yet in 1988 (Russian Orthodox millennium year) official state statistics said that thirty per cent of all newborn children had been baptised that year. By June 1990, Patriarch Alexis II said that this figure had risen to fifty per cent. With regard to weddings in church, another reportable matter for internal passports in those days, apparently in 1965 only three per cent were conducted by the church. Yet Alexis II claimed that forty per cent of all weddings occurred in a church by 1990.

Having again been guilty of covering too many pages for an easy read, I guess it is time to draw proceedings to a close. I do, however, wonder if all that I see around me with regard to a new-found religious freedom is merely 'flirting' with Christian faith or a sign of a fundamental revival. Certainly in the regions of the Federation one senses a feeling of more than just token lip service. In the cities it appears to be merely fashionable. It seems to me it has become 'in vogue' in Moscow and St Petersburg to be a superficial Christian. The girls wear crosses around their necks and as earrings – they are even worn by those ladies in the office who have as yet not ever been to a place of worship. But has the former religious vacuum been truly filled? Neither Father Gennadi or Father Anatoly believe it has. They share my sentiments that there is still too much scepticism of an unknown past faith to overcome. What is, however, true is that a larger percentage of Russians, even in the cities, now attend church more regularly than in the

United Kingdom. Colin Thubron's comments on muted doctrinal revolutions in central Asia and his observations on questioning whether they were crushed by tyranny, God or the size of their land seem to me to be appropriate, yet unresolved, thoughts. The citizens of this land certainly need time to deliberate on these complex issues, and we should allow them to take it in their own manner.

I cannot leave this letter without a reflection of sadness. During my last visit to St Petersburg, I again went to visit the glories of Tsarskoe Salo. Near Catherine's palace is a more secret place rarely visited by tourists. Next to the nearby Alexandra Palace is a delightful secluded walled complex built as a monastery and the Feodorovsky Sobor (Cathedral). The totality was built by Tsar Nicholas II for his beloved wife, Alexandra, and their children before their untimely assassination. This place is surrounded by reminders of the history of the last days of the Romanov dynasty. Today the secret garden and church are almost ruins. Even fifty-one years after the end of the brutality of the siege of Leningrad, the inside walls of the church still bear the all-pervading marks of German fire. Nothing of the fabric remains, only a blackened interior. Modest, but touching, attempts were being made to recreate the signs of religious adherence in the building.

This black domed building can be found at the end of a short country path among the lesser remnants of more modern history. An old truck, a shed full of rusting scrap metal and overgrown nettles dominate the initial vision. Behind the building was a recently cleared patch of grass with an unpretentious statue. It is the only image of Russia's last tsar to be found in this place, or indeed the whole of the Russian Federation. The few recent flowers showed some people still cared. Only two years ago through the valiant efforts of Valodin Khromenko, the delightful old gentleman I found tending his dream of restoration, work was begun to rid the remains of decay. But only through private donation. The State was not interested. The underground chapel had been a storage shed, and the main church a cinema in Communist days. When Church and State have been so demonstrably close in recent years, why not remember the key events of contemporary history. If statues of Lenin can be cleaned to commemorate his past association within St Petersburg, then why cannot the same be done for the last memory of three hundred years of church and Romanov state working together? It would seem that there are still Russians who want to return to their heritage, but they have to rely on self-help.

Chapter XI
And What Now?
December 1996

Having had the privilege of finding my heritage in Torgau, in former East Germany in 1989, and the political influence on my split family through my time in Russia in 1995 and 1996, new questions began to surface, some of them disturbing. These questions are an inquiry as a result of my experiences in the last eighteen months on behalf of the people we once thought of as our enemies. Let me try to begin to pull the threads of the totality of my thoughts together with the addition of some further background and then try to look forward. Therefore I call the theme of this letter – 'And What Now?'

Thinking back to the turmoil of impressions gained in the first few weeks in Moscow the overriding thought which remains one and a half years later, was: 'Why had we in the West been fed the line of continuing Russian military, political and industrial omnipotence?' This may have been true in days gone by, but what I experienced must have been the result of many recent years of decline. There was no magical key that opened our, or their, eyes with the glow of *Glasnost* in 1989. Gorbachev's first book[1] is long on rhetoric, but short on answers. Therefore, what had we really to fear from rusting tanks? A demoralised army whose soldiers are not paid today? An industrial base

---
[1] *Perestroika.*

that had little or no modern investment for years? An infrastructure that worked only occasionally? And a nation traumatised by loss of empire and at unease with itself? Where had the Western spies and ambassadorial observers sent by Thatcher, Reagan and others been? Had they seen something I had missed, or not looked in the places I had experienced? Did the CIA have other sources, or were the travel restrictions such that they were simply unable to look, comprehend and report the truth? It is of course true that before 1989 travel was prohibited to all but a select few, including Russians, to the vast number of closed cities throughout the land. Some of them were not even on any published map. Even today the laws on foreigners' travel have not been repealed, they are just ignored and we are free to go where we like, within reason.

But in the mid and late eighties Moscow was a bleaker place than it is today. Where were they looking? Macho cowboy tactics from Ronald Reagan and Margaret Thatcher that spent immeasurable, and in my opinion unnecessary, sums on 'Star Wars' and other such military adventures with our hard-earned Western taxes, could have been saved and redirected to better purposes. America's national debt doubled, as a result of this military spend, in the Reagan years. We all unfortunately await the pain of that legacy. Our politicians just needed to wait a few more years, and the result would have been the same as it is now, but at a cheaper price and less pain for us all. A gradual transition might even have been better for the Russians themselves. The true fact is, this place in recent years was no modern 'superpower' in anything other than lip service to that description. The myth was enhanced by the perception of media and Western political misinformation resulting from years of mutual isolationism. It was certainly not the paradise extolled in the theory of its revolutionary founders.

My Russian friends, certainly in Moscow, tell me that conditions today are vastly better than they were in the late eighties and early nineties. The food queues have gone. Well in the cities anyway. They do not have to travel into the centre of Moscow anymore and wait in empty shops for hours for the few basics of life. They now have choice and the faint possibility of a future for themselves and their children. They no longer look to the threat of a world that will disintegrate from the fear of Western bombs. The only dangers to world peace I have seen are those associated with madmen and lack of money potentially allowing the vast and unstable stockpile of nuclear weapons falling into the wrong hands or not being tended carefully. At least in the days of the Cold War, we all knew the rules of the game: it was not safe, but at least predictable. Today's instability in Russia bodes ill for all but the coolest political heads. Now a political vacuum has been filled by unscrupulous individuals who rage unchecked to the detriment of Russia and ourselves. Our Western pressures, and their national failure, have forced change here, but without any accompanying political or social stability. But few politicians the world over will ever be awarded Nobel prizes for intelligence, interest in their people and perception. They just bask in the glory of short-term votes. It was ever thus.

On a lighter note. While talking of forcing change, instability, wars, unscrupulous individuals and Western bombs, even the makers of James Bond films have changed their tune and see few signs of successfully selling their pictures with a theme of a continuing international Russian threat. They see dangers in other directions. The last film *Goldeneye* was about the St Petersburg Mafia. Our hero 007 was even helped by the KGB – and his old friends at Smersh. Ian Fleming certainly had a sense of humour when he first wrote the books on our handsome smoothie – the international telephone country code for Russia is 007.

Maybe such Western influence affected ten-year-old Yulia Parkhomenko when she was asked at school what she knew about Lenin. 'Lenin?' she repeated a little bemused. 'Well… he's dead.' She paused and then beamed broadly and said '…and he used to play in a rock band called the Beatles.' How the young have a glorious habit to forget the unknown and darker past.

It would of course be folly to blame only the West for current conditions. Ignorance breeds misinformation and poor quality decisions, the Russian psyche, their turbulent history, intransigent leaders and the size of their land has contributed more to their current condition than any other factors. They remain their own worst enemies. Yet I marvel at the patience of the people. We at home could not replicate their composure, we are too pampered with life's luxuries and opportunities. If today's conditions are better than they have experienced in Moscow for years, then the world is truly topsy-turvy. Today's problems are bad enough, it really must have been a dreadful life in past decades. But then the regions have changed little in that time – to their future regret. Acceptance of *Glasnost* and *Perestroika* were therefore more than understandable. Hope was then in the air. In those days people were paid but had nothing to buy. What they had saved was in the bank, only to be later devalued by rampant inflation and painful currency reform in 1993. Today people have choices in the cities but are sometimes not paid. In the regions, they have no choices and are not paid at all. What a paradox. But now the hope is fading.

While composing an earlier letter, I had occasion to travel to the UK on business. At the airport in Moscow I found a delightful book by Conor O'Clery.[2] He was the *Irish Times* correspondent in this city from 1987 to 1991. His compendium of experiences in the heady and expectant days of *Glasnost* and *Perestroika* were a sober comparison to the situation I found four years later. It is the task of a reporter to observe, comment and record accurately what he finds. As a businessman, I have a different function and perspective on life. But his recorded tales and particularly his title – *Melting Snow* – gave rise to my changing the nature of these letters into a wider observation of life in this land today. I thank him for his stimulus. I am no journalist, or have pretensions in that direction, but have seen little in print that records the reality of life here today. That in itself encouraged me to continue my dialogue. The title I have therefore chosen for this compendium of letters alludes to the next phase in the hopefully emerging seasons of their national development. At the same time it stresses concern at the spring not turning easily into summer.

Let me try to summarise the 'big picture' as I have found it to be, and try to bring the varied strands of my discourse together. The analysis summarised below is primarily based on the many questions asked by the recipients of these letters over the course of time, and not answered earlier. Others that bother me personally are also included. I will try to address them as best I can with an eye to what might happen from now on. Pardon please that on occasion my answers appear simplistic. Without more time and research, some of the comment may appear 'off the cuff'. There is sincere hope that real change will come, and these words become more than just hopeful philosophy. But as commented on before, 1997 may be a fateful year for them.

---

[2]*Melting Snow. An Irishman in Moscow.*

Can the innate intransigence of the ruling Russian appa-ratchik face the modern world with true change and they thus mend their ways?

The unfortunate fact for the Russians is that their past and current rulers from whatever political persuasion came from the same school of behaviour. Their ruling inner circle, and opposition, all know and relate to each other in a way that few in the West can ever fathom. They grew up and were educated together in the past Communist Party machine. Can a 'new national idea' emerge from that background?

- The majority are ardent nationalists with an inviolate belief in the omnipotence of Mother Russia. The return to the borders of the former USSR are still within the belief of many.[3] The truth is that the CIS[4] is a Western myth as well as an unrealisable Russian dream. Neither Chernomyrdin or Zuganov or even Zhirinovsky will really achieve its return.[5]

    Yeltsin is not mentioned because he is now regarded by many as 'yesterday's man' despite his apparent

---

[3]In October and November, Yuri Luzhkov (mayor of Moscow) called for a return of the Black Sea Fleet and declared Sevastopol was still a part of Russia. The Ukraine should give them both back, he said. This could, however, be pre new presidential election bluster.

[4]Commonwealth of Independent States. A political grouping that includes most of the former USSR. Among the main exceptions are the three Baltic republics.

[5]Nor will the efforts of President Alexander Lukashenko, the current head of state of the Republic of Belarus. He is trying to push his people back into the fold of the former borders of the USSR. Belarus is the most 'Russified' of the newly independent republics with no markedly separate cultural traditions.

recovery from heart surgery.[6] The play for succession is already well underway, and all the players are staking their positions. His life or possible death will, in time, be seen to be only a blip on the attempt at continuance, by the apparatchik, of the status quo. The former empires of ancient Greece, Rome, China, the Mongols, the Habsburgs, Napoleon, and the British were all witness to decline of former influence once their former subjects had found their own agenda and when the money ran out to pay the bill of being the world's policeman. Russia is experiencing similar pangs. History has an unfortunate habit of repeating itself. When Lebed was booed and called a traitor by the Duma at its first session after the summer election recess[7] for 'giving away the soil of Mother Russia' in his Chechnyan peace plan, the people's national conscience stirred but briefly. Although he has departed[8] the scene (well temporarily), it was not just him the apparatchik were against. It was the potential dismemberment of the remains of empire. I would guess that his removal will do little to ensure a peaceful Caucasus returns. Despite the Yeltsin decree of the 23 November accepting Lebed's peace plan, announcing troop withdrawals and the creation of a free economic zone, I for one am not yet convinced it will end a problem that has run for more than a hundred years.

• They, those in positions of current power or wider political influence, continue to use the people as pawns in their wider game to their own benefit, as has been demonstrated more than once. The alliances currently

---

[6] He appeared for the first time after heart surgery on Russian TV on 20 November 1996.

[7] 2 October 1996.

[8] 17 October 1996.

being formed to ensure continuance of power are Byzantine to say the least.[9] But then, the Kremlin has always acted thus. With Yeltsin recovering on his sickbed, rather than see a true opposition developing policies for the benefit of the people, Chernomyrdin, Zuganov and others club together to try to see off any real change. Anything to get rid of the people's favourite, Lebed. All very 'heavy'. A bit like the Conservative and Labour parties forming a political alliance to get rid of our Liberal Democrats. Their propensity for intrigue of any sort is an integral part of their make-up. Lebed, the apparently untainted, tries to respond with an alliance with, as seen by some, one of the most reputedly corrupt of all, Korzhakov, whose enemies label him a 'Rasputin'.

I was more than amused when reading about the television revelations[10] on Kremlin corruption when figures of a diversion of sums approaching $300 million were mentioned. My only surprise was how few apparently had heard. The amounts mentioned in that evening's TV programme were in my opinion too small, and I was not surprised at the lengths that some would go to discredit Lebed (as a result of rumours of a new-found alliance with Korzhakov, for Lebed to try to make a bid for presidential power). One suspects Chernomyrdin's and Chubais's hand in the matter. One also suspects a significant increase in forthcoming political scandal. Korzhakov is reputed to have taken his 'files' with him when he left the Kremlin in June. If the allegations of massive corruption are actually true, why does not someone in ultimate power place these people under arrest and then convict them for their alleged

---

[9]See Chapter VI, 'Kremlin Intrigues'.
[10]'Itogi'. Russian TV programme, 6 October 1996.

crimes? Or have they all got too much to hide? The fact is that most in power today are at the same game of personal aggrandisement.[11] Power politics and national duty are mutually exclusive in today's Russia.

Lebed's crime that led to his removal was not that he made mistakes, as Yeltsin indicated in his TV address to the nation.[12] It was that he had taken on the Kremlin full frontal – do not believe for a moment he has lost. The allegations on the 16 October by the Minister of the Interior,[13] that Lebed had fifty thousand men ready to stage a coup may not be correct. That he wanted presidential power is. Lebed could, in my opinion, easily ensure the army was behind him if he felt the time was right. This is, however, a typical Russian power play. What I think this is all about is the following: Lebed knew that the 'old guard' would not support him to gain power. He, however, knew he had the support of the population. Firstly, to end the unpopular Chechen war; and secondly, to begin an attack on corruption in high places (after all he now has apparent access to Korzhakov's murky files). Both he and Yeltsin also knew that Yeltsin would not have been elected without his support in July 1996. Therefore he created a situation where Yeltsin had no option but to fire him. He was not winning from the inside. So do it from

---

[11]Apparently the public prosecutor has now begun to formally question Chubais as a result of the published transcript of the tape of the secret meeting of 22 June. See Chapter VI, 'Kremlin Intrigues'.

[12]The *Moscow Times* commenting on Lebed's dismissal in its editorial on 19 October 1996 said: 'Worst of all is a feeling that the current crisis is not a crisis at all, but a return to business as usual – as it was in the dying days of Lenin, Andropov, Chernenko or Brezhnev, when the leader struggled with his health in the background and attention focused on the hungry apparatchiks wrestling for power in his absence.'

[13]Anatoly Kulikov.

outside. He is now in a position to fire political bullets at will at all and sundry and reveal the dirt on the Kremlin. They have now begun to be launched. Just wait for his road show to gather pace. With Korzhakov's reputed millions, (and the fact that Korzhakov[14] was also sacked by Yeltsin) he possibly has a substantial campaign war chest. Yeltsin's decision (or was he helped by Chubais, Chernomyrdin and Zuganov?) may yet backfire on him with venom.

Despite his removal, Lebed's personal popularity with the people is clearly demonstrated by a Public Opinion Fund survey published in October 1996.[15] In the first round of voting in the June 1996 presidential election, Yeltsin received thirty-five per cent of the vote, Zuganov thirty-two per cent and Lebed fifteen per cent. Yeltsin won the final round with Lebed's support. Some four months later, with the news of Yeltsin's health problems, the daily revelations on the true state of the economy and its attendant non-payment problems, debate on government paralysis and Lebed's Chechen peace, the situation is radically different. According to this survey if a first round vote were to take place today, Lebed would get twenty-five per cent, Zuganov twenty-three per cent and Yeltsin only twenty per cent of ballots. Another poll by the VTsIOM Research Group published[16] a view of who was the most trusted current politician. Forty per cent named Lebed, in second place was Zuganov with sixteen per cent, Chernomyrdin – another presidential hopeful – received fourteen per cent and Yeltsin scraped home in

---

[14]And now to be stripped of his military rank. He, however, is reputed to be threatening a counter-suit against Yeltsin.

[15]*Kommersant Daily* newspaper.

[16]*Segodnya* newspaper.

fifth place with only an eleven per cent trust rating. The people have seen the lies of Yeltsin's election promises, and do not like them. Little wonder that Chernomyrdin is trying to transfer power from Yeltsin, with Zuganov's help, without another presidential election. This is unconstitutional, and will add grist to the arguments Lebed will use. The people want their say, but may not get it. We must beware some contradictions of the Russian psyche. They want strong leaders, and they want to trust and follow them. Yet in recent history when they have such an animal, they soon end up neither believing nor trusting him. Power in this country is a corrupting aphrodisiac. Far more so than at home.

On the 21 November 1996, as part of his campaign to woo the West, the *Wall Street Journal* published an interview with Lebed. He was asked about various matters from NATO, his own presidential ambitions, Chubais and the economy. On democracy and the economy some of his words are worth repeating here, because he explains in a nutshell some of the current fundamental problems of current democratic and economic structures.

- '...Well I am not very confident that we have democrats today. It is impossible to go to bed in a totalitarian regime and wake up in a democratic country. It can't be done overnight. But this is exactly the way it was depicted in our case. Totalitarianism is over, now you are living in a free democratic society. Freedom was given to the people, but they don't know how to use it. They haven't learned and no one started teaching them or created conditions for them to learn. Democratisation is a colossal restructuring of the mentality...

- …I'm afraid it may be hard for me to explain it, but the Russian tax policy is making everyone, every single entrepreneur, every single businessman, a criminal. On every Rouble earned out of 100 Kopecks, if you are lucky you pay 90 Kopecks tax… There are forty-three taxes, and even if you are the most honest and decent person, you will be confused. And if you are not lucky or have a good accountant, you will pay 121 Kopecks per Rouble. Given all that, you either have to go bankrupt and stop all business or cross the line and start cheating the state. You can guess that most good Russians are doing exactly that. Everyone is scratching their heads and wrinkling their foreheads and wondering how to cheat the state. And they're doing it pretty well… The first step is to turn everything from head to feet. The average tax should be twenty-five per cent, but it should be differentiated…

- Asked about his economic advisors, he also made comments about the 'old guard'. He said, 'Let them keep their orders, their medals, their diplomas, and let them fish and let them grow strawberries…'

Mr Lebed is beginning to talk sense. As a businessman living in the economic and tax regime he described, I can sympathise with the views he expressed.

A wild card in the continuing game of political skulduggery is of course Yeltsin's future health. Another is the little reported current process of elections of regional governors. Previously these people were presidential political appointees. Now, under the constitution, a majority must be elected before December 1996. As well as being regional governors, they sit on the Federation Council – Russia's upper house. The final result will be fascinating. The anti-Moscow and pro-Lebed factor may begin its work. We shall all see, but so far the Kremlin is not faring as well as it had hoped.

- Even the military is no longer the bastion of national pride, at the altar of tax avoidance and evasion. The nickname for General Grachev (the former Minister of Defence[17]) is 'Pasha Mercedes', due to his apparent preference for this type of vehicle at the expense of the military budget. While he and his cronies lived the life of Riley, his officers and men found their services did not warrant payment. Due to a shortage of cash in the national coffers, the army and civilian defence workers ceased to be paid in mid-1996. I can think of nowhere else in the world where officers are allowed to work for self-gain one week per month to try to relieve the pressures. It is even against the Russian constitution. But when expedient, even these tablets of stone can be ignored by state authority. In October 1996, the Russian military was owed Rbl.7 trillion ($1.3 billion) by the state exchequer. With a salary of $18 per month (if paid) to a junior officer in barracks, this is a vast sum. Where else in the world does a government pay such little attention to its current and future national defence. It is usually a matter of sovereign pride. You can imagine my amusement when I was thoroughly searched at Moscow customs on a recent trip home. A long debate ensued with the customs official because he deduced my computer floppy disks might contain sensitive military secrets. From my observations of life here, including having visited military bases, worked with our tame general, having a married army couple as friends and driven past many other military establish-

---

[17]Ousted by Lebed on his appointment as National Security Advisor.

ments, there is little of value to learn.

• We should however, fear the madmen who may, as a result of lack of cash, sell their own weapons. At the Leipzig Spring Fair in 1990, within the exhibition halls, I was offered a Kalashnikov rifle and officer's uniform by a Russian soldier for DM 100. In September 1996 Lebed predicted[18] that unpaid and poorly equipped soldiers in the remoter regions may mutiny this autumn unless fresh funding was found. With his departure, and lack of wage payments this is more likely to happen. He was the popular hope, and respected as a true leader of men by the troops. General Igor Rodionov (the current Defence Minister) went further; he said[19] '...People will just stop going to work. Instead they will start making money or selling what they guard – things like ammunition depots. I understand the West's alarm when uncontrollable processes begin in a country like Russia with its huge arsenals of strategic weapons...' Yet millions in the country do not pay their taxes, including the apparatchik, 'New Russians' and large companies alike, which should fill state coffers, instead of their own pockets, to alleviate the situation.

• Few are spared this process of shortage of funds. Despite what economists might say, business, particularly investment oriented, finds it hard to cope and no economy can survive for long on only a rampant service sector. Even in our country we know that a strong manufacturing sector is key to economic success. Trading, in Moscow, has been a major growth area, at the expense of real investment. The banks in Moscow

---

[18] In a press conference to mark his one hundred days in ministerial office.

[19] The London *Times*, 9 October 1996.

are of little help. They play at lending each other funny money, at funny interest rates and the people are not amused. Foreign investment is understandably muted. I know and have to deal with the consequences. The prestigious Academy of Sciences, educational institutes, health, roads, industrial investment are all pawns in the game of keeping ultimate power for the 'old guard'. Non-payment of debts keeps the national budget in respectable balance. The cynicism of this statement is not based on any ideological belief by myself. It is simply a fact of life in modern Russia today.

With the IMF declaring in late October that for the second time in three months they would withhold the monthly payments on the $10 billion loan, one wonders if this is a turning point for the worse.[20] Poor tax collection was the declared reason. On the 23 October 1996 it was announced in the Duma that only 71.3% of the required taxes had been collected in the first nine months of 1996. As a result, bankruptcy proceedings against some major concerns, for alleged non-payment of taxes, came on the agenda. Among the first four such targets was the truck maker KamAZ. This company in Tatarstan (West of the Urals and not to be confused with the Tartars in Mongolia) will be a test of power between the regions and Moscow. The president of this republic, Mintimer Shaimiyev, will no

---

[20]On 22 November 1996, The *Moscow Times* reported that Economics Minister Yevgeny Yasin said in relation to the IMF discussions and the 1997 budget debate, '...We won't be able to perform our obligations this year... The situation is difficult... We have problems and there will be certain problems with 1997...' Boris Fyodorov, a 'reformer' and former finance minister was quoted in the same article as saying '...Economics aren't going to get more civilised quickly in Russia.'

doubt make his case, and probably win.[21] But who loses? The ultimate recipients of fewer and fewer tax collections – the people – the employees of such single factory cities.

Until a new generation of political leaders emerges, who are not from the ranks of past Communist apparatchik education, or influenced by the shadowy oligarchy, little will change. That process will take time. The gang of seven bankers and industrialists who claim to control so much of the economy – and are political allies of Chubais are not the answer. Where these potential leaders are is a matter for conjecture. Where indeed is the 'new national idea'? Alexander Lebed may be a possibility, but his biggest strength is also his major weakness, in that as a Kremlin 'outsider' he has no party organisation or power base other than the will of the people. We know that this latter fact has been ignored for centuries, and may continue to be now. He also has no economic or political pedigree that we expect from our leaders, although he is beginning to make the right noises. What is clear, is that the current ruling apparatchik want no competition for power and do all in their capacity to keep it that way.

The patience of the people is sorely tested, and almost at an end. Certainly in the regions. A Western-educated mind concludes that revolt is on its way. Russian equanimity says otherwise. My sources close to the Kremlin do not disagree that revolt may be burgeoning. Our disagreement is only on the timing and whether the people have any organisation through which to act, not whether revolt will happen.[22]

---

[21] The Kremlin has now backed down, with no taxes collected and egg on face.

[22] A national one-day strike for payment of back wages was held on 5 November. Unfortunately this was also US presidential election day and

They believe that they can keep the people subservient a little longer, maybe until 1998. But again that may all change. Lebed could possibly become the focus and leader of organised discontent, earlier rather than later. Particularly in the event they are denied a presidential election on the eventuality of Yeltsin's demise. Today we must recognise a major difference to the past. Then people were fed what the state believed they needed to know. They could be controlled, and their attention channelled. Today, however, the gates of information are open to the West. They can begin to make comparisons of their own. They are not stupid. More than that they are hungry and unpaid. They can see what we have achieved, and they, like the citizens of other Eastern European countries, want it now. On top of that, the humiliation of loss of 'face' in world status sits heavy with many people. We shall see what happens. I suspect that the train will hit the buffers in 1997.[23]

Does the West really want to support true reform in Russia?

There are enough levers that Western governments could use to ensure democratic and economic change, however subtle. Lending money is easy, but real genuine understanding and political partnership is less evident. But do they use such levers to Russia's benefit or their own selfish ends?

- Yeltsin and his henchmen are supported with IMF and other similar funds. Well, since the July presidential election only just. Rumour has it that the managing

---

the date of Yeltsin's surgery, so they did not receive maximum publicity. However, a beginning?

[23] In the event, the timing was delayed by twelve months before the bubble burst.

director[24] of the IMF was unwilling to commit funds, but had his 'arm twisted' by Clinton and Kohl. Now that Clinton does not need to face an election again one wonders if positions will change for the worse. Is it really a fear of resurgent neo-Communism that led them to support Yeltsin rather than Zuganov? I do not think so. If it is, then we should beware of interference in the governmental persuasions of other countries. That never did anyone any good. It is more fundamental. A resurgent, strong and equal Russia would try to reassert its previous place at the world's bargaining table. Lebed, equally does not fit the dream of Western governments in this respect. But as yet few of us really know the man or his policies. A weak, begging and subservient Russia is more 'controllable' to the American White House and the NATO planners. Clinton's announcement on the 22 October 1996 regarding future NATO eastern expansion was in my view part of this process. The posturing toward Russia pandered to the US voter. It also reminded the Kremlin who is currently boss. The timing of the announcement was indicative to both audiences. I would remind them that a weak Russian Bear, suffering from wounded pride, may spin out of control to the future detriment of us all. Misdeeds by unpaid soldiers with strategic nuclear weapons are a perfect example.

- The Cold War may be over, but the legacy of neglect in the infrastructure of Russian industry and cities is evident. Without foreign technical assistance to foster a programme of urgent national renewal, then personal enmity, a sense of national betrayal and a return to isolationism may be characteristics that govern the

---

[24]Michael Camdessus.

thoughts of the Kremlin, the Federation Council, the Duma and the people alike. Certainly, if the role of a 'second class nation' is habitually thrust upon the Russian Federation in coming years. Even though that 'second-class' status may be true. It hurts for many. Lebed was again attacked as a traitor in the Duma and the Russian press when he returned from a visit to NATO headquarters in October 1996. This is not just a fight against him and his bid for power. It is a continuance of a latent belief in their perceived place as a major world power. Anything that disturbs that in the minds of the apparatchik is regarded with suspicion. We should beware the isolationist drawbridge.

It is clear to me that the West misunderstands and misrepresents this country today. Hopefully enough examples of that have been given in these past pages. Western governmental policies demonstrate that enough. They appear to be designed to assist Russia remaining a 'second-class' nation. Our media continues to exacerbate the situation of misinformation. They do report the bare facts, but often too late, and then in small doses. Out of sight means out of mind. But then they give little or no clue as to the background to the events they report. However, when the Russians themselves, both government and people alike, have no clue to their own national direction, they must inevitably face the buffeting from those stronger, richer and more powerful than themselves. Unless they discover a new national purpose with a leadership which has acceptable national and international stature, the 'winds of change' will blow bitter Siberian cold.

And what to the future of their economy?

Much has been said in past pages about the effects of

economic 'reform' since 1989 (more correctly 1991) on the daily life of a Muscovite or an inhabitant of the regions. Reform is a relative process, it depends from which base one starts. I do not subscribe to the view, held by some, that real reform is in place. Equally information is only useful if measured against a known yardstick. Let me therefore try to put the Russian economy into a wider context. A sensible way may be to start with international comparative economic measurements from published data. While reading the figures shown below, please remember that the untapped natural resources of gas, oil, gold, diamonds, coal, nickel, titanium, aluminium, iron ore etc. are among the largest known in the world. Certainly Russian gas reserves are the world's most plentiful, and even the great De Beers company would shudder if Russia began to break their stranglehold on world diamond supply. Yet these resources are largely undeveloped and remain hidden in the ground. Where development has taken place, equipment is old and inefficient so that much benefit is lost. In the past, production of product was often at a higher cost than any selling price received from the customer.

This set of data apparently places the Russian Federation among the larger players in the world economic league. In tenth place out of the twenty-six nations mentioned – with possible apologies to China, Brazil and India. It also partly sets out their claim to be among the rich group of G7 nations to decide the world's economic agenda. Data on such nations as Sweden, Norway, Finland, Turkey Singapore, Indonesia South Africa etc. is not to hand to give a true world ranking list. My local economist friends tell me that in true league-table terms, Russia may actually be in fifteenth place. Of course the figures for the other former constituent parts of the USSR are now excluded.

Country	Population[25] in million	GDP[26] in $ billion	Country	Population in million	GDP in $ billion
USA	249	7,245	Australia	17	349
Japan	126	4,674	Switzerland	7	312
Germany	81	2,413	Argentina (1994)	33	279
France	58	1,566	India (1993)	931	257[27]
Italy	57	1,117	Belgium	10	227
UK	58	1,084	Mexico	94	210
Spain	39	574	Saudi Arabia (1992)	17	121
Canada	29	571	Thailand (1992)	58	110
China (1994)	1,190	508[28]	Poland (1994)	38	86
RUSSIA	147	427	Malaysia (1994)	18	70
Brazil (1993)	147	400 approx.	Chile (1994)	13	52
Holland	15	395	Czech Republic	10	45
S Korea (1994)	45	379	Hungary	10	44

But let me however, change the nature of the data, and simply divide the GDP figures stated above by the population figures shown above. This may of course give rise to slight distortions as these population figures include all men, women and children, including pensioners and

---

[25] These comparisons are rough population estimates; census dates vary.

[26] Gross Domestic Product. This data is for the year 1995 (unless otherwise stated), and is from OECD Quarterly National Accounts. The figures for China, Brazil, South Korea, Argentina, India, Saudi Arabia. Thailand, Malaysia and Chile are from IMF statistics. Current exchange rates have been used rather than purchasing parity.

[27] The current exchange rate greatly understates the real figure.

[28] The current exchange rate greatly understates the real figure.

babies. Also lifespan varies from country to country. With no smoothing for this and the working population, there will be variations. I am by no means a theoretical economist, however, the comparison shown below still makes my overall point and places Russia even further down the same list of nations. Not quite in 'banana republic' territory, but living here and visiting the regions it often feels that way. What is for certain, and shown again, is that they are no longer the superpower they once thought. To reach the top rank again they need to work hard for many years to catch up and regain their previous place in world events. My purist economist friends tell me that I should have quoted the World Bank Tables from a reference library for these following figures. For once I will ignore them, as the principles are demonstrated in simple mathematics.

Country	GDP per[29] Citizen in $	Country	GDP per Citizen in $
Switzerland	44,571	S Korea	8,422
Japan	37,095	Saudi Arabia	7,118
Germany	29,790	Czech Republic	4,500
USA	29,096	Hungary	4,400
France	27,000	Chile	4,000
Holland	26,333	Malaysia	3,888
Belgium	22,700	RUSSIA	2,905
Australia	20,529	Brazil	2,721
Canada	19,690	Poland	2,263
Italy	19,590	Mexico	2,223
UK	18,690	Thailand	1,896
Spain	14,718	China	427
Argentina	8,455	India	276

---

[29]With apologies to the economic purists among you. This simple method of calculation is suspect in the true measurement of an economist.

Again with apologies to China, Brazil and India whose previously mentioned GDP figures may be seriously understated. The above suddenly places Russia in twentieth place on this comparative list, and possibly in reality twenty-first after Brazil. In total world per capita income terms, as calculated by a proper economist, I would guess Russia to be somewhere around fortieth place, with about twice as much per capita income as China. Unfortunately while writing this another trip to the library suddenly became tedious and the correct figure eludes me – sorry. But, more importantly, the individual earnings gap between the rich G7 countries – most of whom have no large natural resources to that of Russia, which has, – is suddenly vast. The true levels of individual living standards of the people are shown to be at levels well below our own. That is my fundamental point. If they want to reach our standards, their catch-up requirements are enormous. Just to feed the people is a struggle. The grain harvest in 1996, at 74.6 million tons is the smallest for nearly thirty years.

Going back from macro to micro economics – or to my simple mind from the big to the little picture, the individual inhabitant of the land knows the real truth. Let me quote the national Russian labour newspaper.[30] '...Wage arrears have risen by 4 trillion Roubles ($740 million) to a total of 40.23 trillion Roubles ($7.4 billion) in the two weeks from the 9 September – by ten per cent The situation has become really tense A vast army of people – sixteen to eighteen million Russians or almost a quarter of the working population – have not received what they are owed for their labour. Poverty is mercilessly taking tens of millions of Russians by the throat.'

'Winter is coming and we do not have boots or coats and

---

[30]*Trud* newspaper, September 1996.

we do not have anything to eat,' said a reader (Maria Kolesnikova from the Volgograd region). She continued, 'It is not easy for me to write this – it is like begging, it is such a disgrace – and I am doing this for the first time in my life, but we are in great trouble, on the very edge.' The newspaper added, '...Those seeking where to borrow money for a piece of bread can only smile bitterly at talk of a "decrease in the number of poor people". In regional elections they will vote for anyone who is not backed by Moscow.' Noting that a Communist took power in the local elections in the Amur region near the border with China, the newspaper said: '...It is not because the Bolshevik spirit is so strong in the region; it is because the people can no longer stand poverty, privation and hardship. They do not vote for the Communists but against the unbelievable cruel social policies of the authorities.'

Figures released in August, and published in the same Labour newspaper, showed that almost thirty million people, or twenty per cent of the total Russian population were now living below the official subsistence level. This is defined by government as $65 per adult person per month. That is the tragic daily truth in the regions of Russia that your television screens and media do not show. But they do know this here. Although the London *Times* did at last report, but briefly on the 12 October 1996, on the tragedy affecting the eleven million people living in the frozen wastes north of the Arctic Circle. With winter now upon them and temperatures likely to reach minus 50°C, fuel and food shortages in among other places Pevek, Dikson and Vorkutia are dire. Seventy per cent of what they need for the winter should have arrived in June. But subsidies have ended. They cannot even 'Get on their bike' (in search of alternative employment) as Norman Tebbit once extolled us to do. To avoid a humanitarian disaster, this situation may even lead to a mass airlifted evacuation, according to some comment. It was further reported[31] that the worst affected regions were Magadan, Chukotka, Kamchatka, Koryasky, Yakutsk and Taymyr. Not only are these among the heartland of support for Zhirinovsky, but are also ironically the regions with most coal, gas, diamonds and gold deposits. That is the paradoxical basis of today from which tomorrow has to be built. There is no economic model I know of that will show the collapse into utter personal despair as a result of mismanaged 'market reforms'.

In a recently published book[32] by Richard Layard[33] and John Parker,[34] predictions are made of great things to come for the economy. The headline in the UK's *Independent* newspaper of the 24 September 1996 extolling the virtues of their academic research and conclusions was, 'Whatever happens, Russia can do no wrong'. The authors give four different political and economic scenarios to Russian economic development over the next years – they take a ten-year view. These are:

- The first, and in their judgement the most likely is: more of the same. That means the current leadership. Yeltsin if still capable, and Chernomyrdin will remain and continue their existing path.

- Their second option is a return to 'neo-Communism'. They say that these policies will be akin to Peron in Argentina of days past. Interesting. I can tell you from inside knowledge and his published speeches, that Zuganov favours the Chinese economic model. Oh

---

[31] *Moskovsky Komsomolets* newspaper.

[32] Entitled, *The Coming Russian Boom*.

[33] Professor at the London School of Economics, and an advisor to Yeltsin on economic affairs.

[34] A former Moscow correspondent for *The Economist*.

well, I sigh, more Western press misinformation.

- Thirdly, they believe an option is a resurgence of right-wing nationalism. Possibly they got that idea from Frederick Forsyth in his recent book, *Icon*, and thus got a hint of real regional despair.

- Finally they say there could be 'reform'. This they say is the least likely outcome, but if it were to happen then there would be a surge of foreign investment which could rise to more than $10 billion per year (still less than that in China today) of outside capital being injected into the economy. This they say will be accompanied by a compound economic growth of more than six per cent per year. Does this mean they agree that 'reform' is not on the agenda today?

Well they are 'theorists' and academics. They are obviously good at playing with complex computer models. Some of the papers my elder daughter brought home from her economic degree course at Leeds University last year had similar theory attached, which seemed to me to have little to do with life's current reality. On top of that, Professor Layard is reputed to be a monetarist, and look where they led Britain. I remind him that Milton Friedman (the arch exponent of monetarism) apparently said at his Nobel Economic Prize acceptance speech in Stockholm in 1979 that he wished Margaret Thatcher well in '…this untried theoretical experiment in economic practice…' Of course there may be a grain of truth in what they say, there always is in such dissertations. However, there is much in their book that fails to describe the Russia that I came to know. I believe their timescale is far too short. They totally under-estimate the scale of reconstruction and their starting point for analysis is too high. But they at least acknowledge that 'reform' is the least likely option. They do appear to accept that 'more of the same' from the current administration is not 'reform' as we know it. At least we agree on something. The heart of their thesis is based on:

- A short-term ability to use and develop the natural wealth of the country. However, this becomes more difficult in times when international commodity prices are falling.

- An educated population wanting to move forward with speed. True. However, moves forward depend on who the leader is and in which direction he can persuade the people to go.

- A willingness for the West to invest short term. However, for this, one has to decide the definition of the word investment. If one means finance to feed the bond markets, then that goal has been achieved. Western bank's investment in treasury and similar markets is high. If one, however, means factory and other productive investments, then this has a poor record. Few real physical investments of number or quality have actually taken place.

- A speedier creation of legal, social and other institutional structures that will benefit the resurgence of public confidence than some observers think possible. However, that has unfortunately not happened.

- And lastly, a period of political stability. That is certainly not given.

They wrote their book before Yeltsin's illness paralysed the government in mid-1996. They also failed to spot the cash crisis that followed.[35] They are correct in many of their

---

[35]They certainly did not foresee the political and economic crash of 1998.

conclusions if one takes a narrow Western perspective and judges life on known, tried and tested economic theories. But few of those theories applied in judging the integration of East with West Germany. Their thesis certainly fails the test of understanding the realities of this land. Not in economic theory, but in methods employed to implement such theory. One comparison in the book did jolt me. They claim that there are more beggars on the streets of London than in Moscow. Really?

Some of you may back the judgement of George Soros, the US financier and a major philanthropic presence in Russia. His charitable Soros Foundation has apparently invested more than $200 million in this country. On the weekly TV programme, *Zerakalo*, he said in October he was very worried about the future of Russia. '…You have now a system of robber capitalism, which is a grotesque distortion of an open society. Unless there is some effort to put things in order, you will have a totalitarian regime, which means all my efforts will have been in vain.' Sorry, Messrs Layard and Parker, but in my opinion George Soros lives in the real world and has backed his words with his own money, despite his endorsement of your work on the back cover of your book.[36]

Thinking back to the observations I make throughout these letters, without the benefit of economic computer models of this or that sector of the economy, I believe there is a fifth more sinister option. I can only report on what I see and experience of the life of the ordinary citizen. Please take a moment and think of the previous quotes from *Trud* magazine on national poverty. Think also of:

---

[36]Soros later changed his tune and invested heavily. But then he too lost a packet – apparently some $2 billion in the events surrounding the 1998 crash.

- Vladimir and Valera at Belarusskaya Railway Station.

- The army officer in the empty former defence factory in Rostov-on-Don.

- The multitude of single-industry towns with factories that produce a quarter of that manufactured eight years ago and of products that were designed between ten and fifteen years ago, on archaic machinery.

- The pensioners patiently lining the underpasses in Moscow Metro stations to eke out a meagre supplement to a paltry pension, and sell a few last possessions.

- The dispossessed in the soup kitchen below my flat and near the Duma.

- The thirty per cent of people living below the official subsistence level.

- The twenty-five per cent of the working population who have not been paid for months.

- The returning food queues in Vorkutia and many other places.

- The power cuts of sixteen to twenty hours per day in the region of Primorsky Krai.

- The cultural institutions of the Hermitage, the Tretyakov and Pushkin galleries which have insufficient funding and may possibly close, despite being an attraction for foreign exchange.

- The army without wages, modern equipment and possibly on the brink of mutiny.

- The crime and Mafia domination of up to thirty-five per cent of business in Moscow and St Petersburg.

- The beggars and dispossessed that the mayor of

Moscow is now throwing out of his city in preparation for the celebrations of Moscow's 850th birthday.

- The rural hospital near Vologda that caused blood poisoning to my colleague Slav through lack of proper hygiene.

- The millions of Russian refugees trying to find 'home'. As a result of the break-up of the USSR some eleven million are 'wandering'. Another thirty million want to move to Russia out of the newly independent parts of the former USSR. For the first time Russians are experiencing persecution by their former subjects.

- Think of…

The list is endless, demoralising and tragic. At the same time think of:

- The swollen bank accounts in foreign places of the apparatchik and the powerful 'New Russians' who gain at the ordinary people's expense.

- The intrigues that the apparatchik play to remain in power for self-aggrandisement.

- The apparent freedoms the people still only dream of and cannot touch or feel.

Is this the 'paradise' that our dear Arthur Scargill, and others of his ilk, have fought all their political lives to achieve? Is this the power that split my family? The bigger tragedy is, that they eventually helped destroy themselves. Thoughts of a capitalist heaven on the one hand, or a corrupt hell on the other may be extremes. But I conclude that matters will get worse before they get better. The problem for all commentators, from Professor Layard to myself, is that none of us has a monopoly on the truth. None of us is privy to the real levers of power in the land. We all look in different places to try to describe the same things in Russia today. I may be totally wrong. The future may indeed be rosy. Few have, however, been able to answer the question of how to get to that holy grail. But then where is this elusive 'national idea'? Will revolt or an economic crash overtake all their dreams?

I have seen all this and more. It is no theoretical economic computer model for me. It is the modern reality in this land I have lived in and tried to record. Of course there will be a tomorrow, even here. It will not be one I would even dare to describe as a boom, as our earlier esteemed economists believe, if the current administration remains in charge. Much more fundamental change is required for that to happen. Yet they have the wherewithal to accomplish their own salvation. Fifty per cent of the world's soft timber; fifty per cent of the planet's known coal reserves; forty per cent of known gas reserves; twenty-five per cent of diamonds and gold, and much more. This with an educated population to boot. Why it cannot be properly harnessed beats me, and most of my Russian friends. Other countries have succeeded in overcoming such problems with far less pain. But then they were not former super-powers. Unless they do, within a short time span, unfortunately I predict the second Russian revolution this century. The people are fed up with their current condition, and winter is upon them. They have no pay, little food or fuel in the regions. I believe the Russian equanimity will break after the coming snows. If not this year, then at some time soon in the nearer future. Some of my economist friends in Moscow take a more narrow theoretical line. I, however, believe it will be a revolution based on achieving the basics of life. Not one that deals with dubious political ideology. It may take two generations to bring their conditions anywhere near ours. It may take longer to erase the trauma of what brought them to this state. It will signal the metamorphosis of a once great and proud nation.

Did I like the place, and would I live there again?

There is a good German expression Jein. Ja is yes, and Nein is No. There is a new-found split-personality in me in answering this question. It certainly gets under your skin. I am both sorry and glad to leave at the same time. However, I will miss some very special people who have been so kind to me in my days in Russia. Their propensity for political drama makes for more than compulsive viewing. Blink or spend a weekend away and you have missed something of interest and importance. One asks for more, just for the contrary fun of being an innocent bystander. At the same time their melancholy, their contrived dramas and intrigues are often more than I can handle. After a while the security worries, a lifestyle of too much vodka, abundant false bonhomie and a poor attitude to self-discipline all create a condition of 'burnout'. Moscow is certainly no place for a pampered Western family for very long. It is not surprising that salaries paid to Western businessmen are higher than most other places. Nor is it surprising that few Western businessmen stay much longer than three years. My tenure sadly, through no fault of my own, has been shorter. In the final analysis, my answer would be yes. I would return with pleasure.[37] Being here I begin to understand the American pioneers in the mid-west a century ago. They portrayed the spirit that is required in modern Russia today. But then, they had a vision, an 'idea'.

---

[37]And I did. On business visits in 1997 and again to live in 1998 and early 1999.

Would I personally invest moneys in their economy?

Well firstly that begs the question of having sufficient sums in the first place. If I did, then again the answer would again be Jein. There is an element of truth in the possibility of a forthcoming 'boom' in the land. In due course. I have said earlier that there will be revolt first, and remain with that view. No investment decision is ever simple. One has to weigh up many of the thoughts in these pages. Although the assassination of Paul Tatum on the 3 October 1996 will not have helped the decision.[38] But on balance I have to see what they have, and measure that against what they do not have.

Here are some examples:

They have	They do not have
Past exceptional education	A current national purpose. An 'idea'
A highly inventive mind	Leaders with national duty and dignity
A desire for progress and stability	Enough ready money
Untold natural resources	Time to regain their short-term future
An infrastructure needing more than repair	A legal, tax and social welfare system that allows progress to the twenty-first century
Huge amounts of land	Equality or a society that equates to the declared vision of Karl Marx and his bible – *Das Kapital*

---

[38]A high profile American investor in the Raddison-Slavanskaya Hotel and Americom Business Centre who tried to 'fight' the system.

A propensity for dramas and melancholy and a complicated and mysterious psyche	International understanding from others or of others
More than enough people	
A long and proud history	

On balance they have more potential positives than negatives for an investment decision. The key word is potential. But the wild card in economic theory is the human mind, and here the reaction of the Russian psyche – unprogrammable in any economic computer model. Here and now, the health and tenacious grip on power from Yeltsin and the existing apparatchik also plays its part. Today's evident problems of cash constraints, non-payment and government paralysis are only within the horizon of twenty-four hours that most Russians can see, as demonstrated in previous letters. How then do we square this circle? How do we cut their Gordian Knot? I have some suggestions, but leave those to the final correspondence. But remember that my solutions are based on inherent Anglo-Saxon attitudes. Even an urgent desire to learn their ways and nature will only allow me to respectfully suggest – no more. They have to succeed on their own.

That of course does not answer the question. So here goes. If I had: time – lots of it; plenty of risk capital – and was prepared to lose the lot; spoke perfect Russian; was prepared to 'use' the system and join in the corrupt tax evasion and avoidance practice so evident to all; was prepared to shift cash around and hide it from the authorities, as so many do – then I would invest for longer-term rewards. But in saying that, the personal risks to carry out this work would be commensurately high. This ignores the fact than many 'New Russians' have made vast fortunes –

many of them illegally. That is the superficial view which would lead a Western company not to invest. Indeed, it has deterred many. The fundamental problem for investors is that most investment criteria have to be based on hope rather than reality. It is entirely a risk. It is entirely based on a long-term view. In the final analysis the decision to invest must be based on very long-term credentials rather than normal medium-term views.

Although there is no legal requirement to have a Russian partner, it is often helpful to open doors closed to us. However, commercial life here is littered with a catalogue of disasters of foreign and Russian partners falling out. Remember please, that our national characteristics and our business methods, rules and ethics are different to theirs. The choice of product is of course important. Anything to do with building, refurbishment and renewal has a chance. Extraction of minerals and natural resources is a longer-term bet, subject to a land-ownership policy and production-sharing agreements. Manufacturing investment may require time. But I would not expect to reap those rewards for the first five years of involvement. By using the criteria that our Western business mind and our stock markets require would lead to immediate rejection. As you can see there is a gulf of business conduct that is as yet unbridged between what we expect and they practise.

A recent survey[39] of one hundred of the largest companies in the UK put the matter into context. In deciding where the most profitable returns could be found through investment abroad in 'emerging' markets, they placed Russia in equal seventeenth place. They considered (in rank order) the following countries to be more attractive: China, Malaysia, Indonesia, India, Brazil, Czech Republic, Thailand, Poland, South Africa, the Gulf States, Chile,

---

[39]By Control Risks Group (CRG) and Industrial Research Bureau (IRB).

Argentina, Mexico, Hungary, Turkey and Saudi Arabia. Russia appeared to have the same attraction as Venezuela.

If, however: a protective legal structure; a sensible land ownership policy; an equitable tax system that worked and did not rely on the 'bung'; a less corrupt public administration; a better profit-sharing framework in oil, gas and mineral investment; and a communication system that functioned regularly, were all in place, then I would say yes with less worries of failure. We may have to wait some time before any of these are available.

What do the people whom I have met think about Yeltsin?

Well do you mean before or after the last presidential election in the middle of 1996? Since being here I have met and talked to bankers, businessmen, politicians, self-described intellectuals, dispossessed children, clerics, housewives, academics, secretaries, clerks and mechanics at the office, government administrators, teachers, economists, ministers in the Moscow City government, diplomats, members of the apparatchik and of course a constant mine of information – my driver Valera. I have only observed the 'have-nots', apart from talking to the cheeky duo at Belarusskaya Station, both in the cities and the regions from a respectful distance. As a foreigner, they would suspect my motives. If this gives the impression that the rest were 'haves', apologies. By 'have-nots' I mean those at poverty level. They, that is apart from the apparatchik among them, all have a common disillusionment with politicians of all persuasions, even rather more than we have at home.

In Moscow, prior to the June and July first and second rounds of the 1996 presidential race, fierce arguments raged from all in the office that my views on Yeltsin were totally wrong: 'How could we even think of a possible return to a

Communist regime led by Zuganov.' Nothing I said made a difference. 'The Gulags will return,' was the cry from some. Others expressed genuine fear of a return to pre-1989 days of oppression. Those who considered themselves as intellectuals wanted Yavlinski. But Moscow, certainly a majority, was for 'more of the same'. They would not heed the warning signals of banking failures, increase in non-payments, problems in the regions etc. from a heathen and 'uninformed' foreigner, though I always found it amusing that our lady translators in the office went reluctantly with us on trips outside Moscow. Five months later, with reality dawning, they are now all more than a little shell shocked. 'How could this be – we have democracy, and now even that does not work. They have lied to us, just like in the old days. We remain the same cannon fodder as before.' The comments I have heard in the regions since the election are almost unprintable.[40] In short, if Yeltsin put himself up for re-election today, he would be hard pressed to get past the first round of voting. He has lied to the people. And they are disgusted. Probably he would end up no higher than fifth place.[41] But until he steps down, or dies, the next four years will replicate the last.

What is their conception of politics, responsibility, freedom and religion?

The subjects of politics and religion have been covered enough in these pages to date, so no more of that. Let me

---

[40] The whole of Russia was aghast at the behaviour of Yeltsin in 1998 in first sacking Chernomyrdin, then appointing Kiriyenko. This was followed swiftly five months later by attempting to reinstate Chernomyrdin. The status of all politicians in August 1998 was at an all-time low.

[41] In October 1998, various opinion polls showed only one per cent of the population supported Yeltsin as president.

deal briefly with the concept of Freedom. Having lived in a free country for most of my life, in my mind, Freedom, Responsibility and Democracy are interlinked. These modes of human behaviour also have to be measured against standards. For example: one's past history.

Other countries' experience and people's needs and desires. Against what standards should we measure their concept and necessity for these matters? Our mindset? Or theirs? They are significantly different.

What you have never seen or understood is always initially alien. So it is here. Since Magna Carta the British have had nearly eight hundred years to come to grips with a current understanding of the rights and responsibilities of the individual and the community. Other countries have taken less time, but many have obtained a broad base of agreement as to how we, or they, should conduct our lives for the good of all. Russia was first properly faced with these major concepts in 1989 – well really 1991. Therefore we do them and ourselves a serious injustice if we believe they are free in our terminology and base our views of them on that. Yes, they can now verbalise their inner thoughts out loud, without fear of past punishment, but due to eighty and more years of inbred subservience; cradle-to-grave state planning of all aspects of their lives; a security presence that still allows my driver to recognise them a mile off; loss of thinking for themselves and basic melancholy: they really have no real idea what these concepts fundamentally mean. Nor should we expect them to. If we had been subject to their history, nor would we.

Without living here it is impossible to fully understand the effect of the legislative, legal and economic vacuum of Gorbachev's legacy. Little wonder he is reviled here by the majority. Destroying Communism was not enough, another system has to be put into place for the wider good of all. It wasn't and hasn't been. It is simply impossible to recreate a basic state law book in less than six years. East Germany had it easier. They just used what West Germany had taken fifty years to create. And look at the state of that land. Their process of reconstruction after ten years is still only part complete. Even they have not fully come to grips with the resulting required collective responsibility. We should therefore not be surprised that this vacuum in this land has been filled by:

- Unscrupulous individuals who have made use of the consequent opportunities for self-gain.

- A state of almost anarchy when wages are not paid to the army and millions of others.

- A situation where legal redress is the 'heavy mob' with a gun or three.

- A self-protective mechanism that puts self before community in a manner I have never experienced to this degree.

- A distrust of politicians that borders on paranoia, particularly after the last presidential election when so many had unfortunately naïve hopes that their 'freedoms' would improve.

- A population that can only turn inward on itself to find its solace.

- And most important of all, a total lack of self-belief resulting in the thought that looking beyond tomorrow will be an unprofitable exercise.

To guess at a timescale of reversal of these thoughts, and the establishment of a concept of freedom that we would recognise, is impossible. However, do not expect it in the near future. It may take a generation, possibly more, given the character of the people and the multitude of problems. If they had a return to a strong but benevolent dictator, they would probably accept him in the shorter term. Their democracy is fledgling and currently misused by the power seeking Kremlin leaders. They may be expectantly ready for freedom but do not fully understand what it really means.

Are education and cultural facilities for all?

The simple answer is yes. In days gone by, no one paid for such fundamental matters, all had equal opportunities. Well not completely true.

Museums, art galleries and the like were always 'cash at entry'. But for them, even today, that is no more than fifty US cents. We foreigners have to pay ten times that for the same privilege. The situation is, however, changing in the educational sphere. Education at primary and secondary level is still free for the majority. But the Ministry of Education reports that there are now over three hundred fee-paying private schools and kindergarten in the country. More worrying is the misuse of academic criteria to obtain places to get into university. Having had close contacts with such an institute and with two Russian teachers who both teach at similar places, they tell me disquieting stories. Even the daughter of the maid who cleaned my flat reported the same. She is currently a language student. They say that today in Moscow, it is more likely that a university place will be obtained if money passes hands first. My secretary tells the same story. Indeed they said that a modern university course in Moscow is as expensive as that in the USA. If that is really true we are indeed in sinister territory for their future.

Which cultural group are they most akin to?

The simple answer is none. Nor is there a single Russian 'nation'. But that is again too simplistic. With over one hundred and fifty ethnic groups that populate the land, who speak some one hundred different languages and dialects, a climate that spans all points of the thermometer and a history that has been carved through northern, eastern, western and southern invasions of culture and military, they have created a different identity. With a land area twice the size of China or the USA there is no single 'Russian' identity. Although the Ural mountains and the river Don are the geographic divide between Europe and Asia, one cannot separate the people into such categories. The vastness of their land creates its own cultural barriers.

Just consider the magnitude of their country. The USA has four time zones, well six if you include the unattached parts of Alaska and Hawaii. Between London and Sydney, in Australia, there are eleven. From London to the tip of the Chukotsky peninsular, inside Russia and opposite Alaska, we have thirteen. Inside the Russian Federation itself there are eleven time zones, including the unattached region of Kaliningrad. From one end of the country it is over three times the distance between London and New York. To fly from Moscow to Petropavlovsk, on the northern Pacific coast would take you longer than London to Los Angeles. It is difficult to see how such a huge landmass can contain a single ethnic or cultural group. The USSR was forged by conflict. Today, the national idea of who and what they are is still a long way off.

You will therefore understand why I hesitate to even attempt to answer this question. What is clear in political terms is that adherence to Moscow as a focal point in a period when state control ruled their lives was reasonably easy. Today, their cultural identification with the political centre in European Russia for an inhabitant of their far eastern regions is no longer so simple. As Moscow abandons the regional subsidies, and continues its current economic course, the previously unifying influence will fade. It may well be that the Federation will divide, in time, into its cultural and geographical constituents. Some believe it to be already happening. The results of the elections of regional governors will give us future clues. The former 'unity' is now for self and not for nationality.

What is the attitude of the Russian to the West and vice versa?

Well you can answer the latter part of the question. The former element is more difficult. Just as we have problems in understanding them, they reverse the process. Neither of us knew each other in days gone by. We are slowly, very slowly, learning and eradicating decades of misinformation. There is no such thing as an average Russian, anymore than there is an average inhabitant of the UK. Their perception of us was moulded, like ours of them, by political and counter-political ideology. We do not expect an American president to resolve or understand the problems of Staffordshire. Nor can they, the many in Russia who have not travelled out of their country, appreciate fully our mindset and lifestyle other than through media dominated by the Hollywood now shown on their TV screens. Or worse, advertising of our daily products now available to those with 'money'. They are no longer interested in the confrontation of the Cold War. The local politicians will tell you they are now a full member of the world community, and they have become a member of the 'G8'. They now do understand that international politics is the art of maintaining national self-interest, while keeping an interested balance with one's neighbours. But the average citizen

I have met is more interested in self. What happens in other lands or even the other regions of Russia is of little consequence. He or she just wants:

- A job that pays regular and good wages.

- An education system that looks after the needs of the children.

- Shops that have the basics of life on regular sale.

- A health system with equipment that elicits comfort and confidence.

- Roads, telephones, utilities and a total infrastructure that works all, not part of, the time.

- An ability to exercise their grey cells to the benefit of intellectual and human stimulation with their peers.

That list could just as well apply to us. They have little real interest what happens in the West. But do we really have similar interests in them? It will all take time to remove barriers and answer such questions in more detail.

Any comments on Human rights?

No, is the short answer. Apart from reading in the newspapers about the Nikin case I have little to add. This gentleman is on trial for treason and espionage. Apparently he revealed the threat of radiation from the Russian northern fleet to an environmental group, of which he is a member. There are many reports on appalling conditions in the country's prisons, but I have no personal wish to check that out. Otherwise I have come across nothing that impinges on this subject.

Well that is apart from my first train journey to Vologda. On all other occasions that I went there the train's final destination was that city. On the first occasion it was travelling on north to Archangel and Murmansk. My Russian companions were not prepared to leave the carriage to go to the dining car. The reason they gave was that they considered most of the passengers to be unsavoury. After all, they said, the main stops for the train were in the areas where the Gulags existed for convicted Russian criminals still held in these places. As such, the train, in their opinion was full of families who were no better than their incarcerated relatives. Well, surely not all who have prisoners as relatives or in their acquaintance are tarred with the same brush. Or are they here?

And lastly: Who will succeed Yeltsin?

This really is taxing my ingenuity. If I knew all the answers to such questions, I would already have won the National Lottery by now, and you would never have had to endure my lengthy discourse. Firstly, we should work on the basis that no one in the current Kremlin administration wants another presidential election in the short term. This time they may suspect they would lose. Chernomyrdin is trying to wrestle control, very gradually, from Yeltsin. At the same time, via a deal with Zuganov, he hopes to organise a seamless transition of power. If there were an election, matters would be substantially different. I see five possible candidates who may have some kind of chance. All of them have appeared in one form or other in these past pages. So only brief comment will be made. Please bear in mind that Russian politics are so complex and archaic that the phrase often used at home that – 'A week in politics is a lifetime' – should be rephrased for them as only twenty-four hours. And anyway, I am not entitled to vote. Those regarded as possible candidates are:

Chernomyrdin. The current prime minister. A bureaucrat, who is respected in Western financial circles. Has the support of the energy lobby, the key industrial cities and to a lesser extent the military-industrial complex. He would keep many of the existing power brokers in place. Moscow's financial community – the banks – would not be pleased to see him go. He is not regarded as a reformer. The regions may have other views, but he is basically acceptable to most that want the status quo. He does, however, lack charisma.

Zhirinovsky. A rabid right-wing nationalist. His power base is in the far eastern and southern regions. If he behaved in a more responsible manner he could be a threat to power. But even the hard-pressed inhabitants of his natural constituency find his 'clowning' a little too much to bear. In their opinion he degrades the political process and standing of Russia in national and international circles even more than it is already.

Luzhkov. The current charismatic mayor of Moscow. Were the election to be held only in Moscow, he would win with some eighty per cent of the vote. When he was re-elected to the post of mayor in July 1996, that was his popularity there. He is a man of action and deeds for his city, and adored by its citizens. But outside Moscow he may lose. There are many in those places who consider that he, more than most, is keeping a larger than normal portion of the Federal budget for the rebuilding of his city at the expense of the regions.

Zuganov. The Communist Party leader. He is slightly 'grey'. But a much more thoughtful man than is presented in the West. They look at the label, rather than the man and his declared policies. His power base is the party machine, the pensioner vote, the agricultural regions in the south of the country and many in the poorer regions. However, his party is split between hard liners and moderates. He has to tread a cautious line within his party.

Lebed. The only outsider in the group. His Chechen peace plan, his gruff but outspoken manner, his 'apparent untainted lack of involvement in corruption', and his ability to take on the Kremlin single-handed has made him the current darling of the voters, certainly outside the major cities. This particularly as a result of his removal from office in October. Among his many enemies are those who still want a return to the borders of the former USSR, and those of the current apparatchik who see him as a serious threat to their cosy way of life. The army will support him. But he is no democrat, despite what he says; his army training does not give him that pedigree. His declared role model is Pinochet, the former dictator in Chile. He may have the elements of a more benevolent dictator about him. He is unproven in political office, but is a quick learner.

A name that is not on that list is Chubais. His name has appeared in past pages and he is a key constituent of current apparatchik control. He and his close group of influential bankers, the oligarchy, mentioned in past chapters, with the apparent help of Yeltsin's daughter, Tatyana, are consolidating immense hidden power. He may not be a candidate for presidential office, but expect him to be a power broker. The people, if given the chance, would oust his grouping, but they currently remain with significant influence behind the scenes. Their final play in any succession battle is by no means exhausted. We should not ignore them, or forget their names. They will play their part in the power struggles to come.

My head says two things if Yeltsin were to depart the scene. Firstly, if there were no election, which is unconstitutional, Chernomyrdin will take over with Zuganov's support. Secondly, if there were an election there will be three clear candidates: Chernomyrdin, Zuganov and Lebed. My heart says that Lebed is so different that he might give the people hope that there could be the beginning of an end to final Kremlin apparatchik control. Am I dreaming? Quite how he might run the economics of the country I have no idea. So far, even he has not fully answered that question. Even if Chernomyrdin or Zuganov were to take control, be sure that we have not heard the last of General Alexander Lebed by a long way. Watch this space. I certainly will be.

Well there you are. And what now?

Having come to their country to take up gainful employment, and through this help find the influences on my former childhood life, it has taken me many pages and words to report on my resulting experiences. I feel fulfilled in the understanding of why my family was split so many years ago, and by whom. But I feel enormously saddened that they have begun the same destruction on themselves. I knew, before I came, that Russia was facing difficulties following the collapse of old-style Communism, as were many of its former satellites. On arrival here, there was hope in my heart that they might have found ingenious ways out of their troubles. But little had prepared me for the depths to which this once great nation had fallen. The more that I learnt, the more it became imperative for me to record my thoughts and impressions. If for no one else, the people, who have been so kind to me deserve, and want, their individual story to be told in its unadulterated form. We have a duty to support their efforts to find their future. Will we?

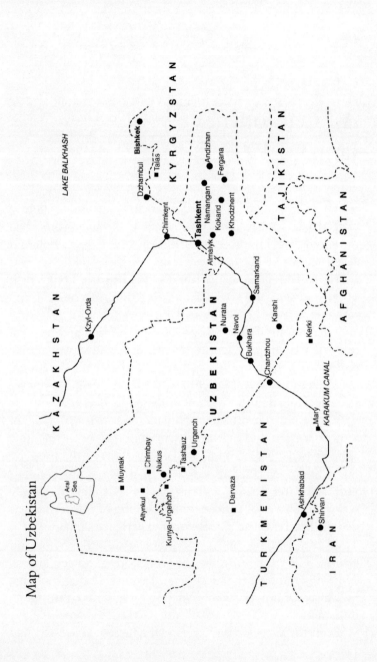

Map of Uzbekistan

Chapter XII
A Final Journey
January 1997

When I looked at a map, Samarkand was not where I expected to find it. This most ancient of cities, some two thousand five hundred years old or was it two thousand seven hundred as the locals later proudly told me, was nearer to Mongolia in my mind's eye. But no. Look north of Afghanistan and 'right a bit'. But then of course I was influenced by a usual abysmal European lack of historical and geographical knowledge of this region and its full importance in past world events. Oh, how we are so ignorant of their history. We replace that with an annual glance at glossy travel brochures. What an appalling way we have developed in the West of judging the world.

With Bukhara and Khiva, Samarkand forms the cradle of a most ancient and cultured civilisation. Now in this new country of Uzbekistan, these places are part of the mysterious Central Asia. Here was my final adventure before I ultimately left Russia and its environs. I did thankfully return. To have some little understanding of this territory, I was glad to have had my Russian experience. Their capital, Tashkent, is long on history, but was rather short on beauty. The influence there of grey, boring, Soviet, artless, concrete architecture is too great. I can see enough of that in Moscow and elsewhere in past places of Communist influence.

Even the Uzbek travel agency in Moscow suggested that

a day in the capital was all that was required to soak in the culture of that place. Maybe I am a little hard on them, as the city suffered greatly during a major earthquake in the mid-sixties. My colleagues in Moscow said: 'Don't drink the water, be careful of the food; be careful of your possessions; they are rather backward; it's very dirty; don't photograph the women – they are Moslem. So really Russian prejudice again emerges, but then they are little different to our habit of pigeon-holing the world. Yet a few years ago it was part of their country. I only heeded their advice once. The water was a problem. How biased they were. How little we all know of such important past influences on our current European culture.

So here I was, basking in 18°C in late November, having left Moscow with snow on the ground at minus 6°C some four hours earlier. Another signal to the vastness of the land, and extremes of climate that continue to so dominate their conscious thoughts. Here was the ancient gateway from the past troubled civilisations of Europe to the cultured East. This was the path of the 'Silk Road' trodden in olden days by Marco Polo that only reluctantly revealed its secret ways. This was the land of the Chaghadai Khanate in the rule of the Mongol Empire. Those lands conquered by them in what is now Russia were then called the Khanate of the Golden Horde. Here was the eastern extent of the Empire created by Alexander the Great who captured Samarkand in 329 BC and destroyed it a year later. Here sadly, was also the north to south path of Russian soldiers in the days of their ill-fated Afghanistan campaign. My excitement to be here was immense. I may never come again.[1]

Travel pictures as usual only tell part of the story. One

---

[1]Well, I did go again. In the summer of 1998 with my wife and two of my daughters, we retraced my previous steps.

thing was certain, it was different that early morning as my recycled Aeroflot plane, now of Uzbek Airways, touched down in Tashkent. Not only did the wrinkled Eastern faces give a clue to that, but they also had an enjoyable general humour. Their crumpled demeanour was a comfort. They appeared to relish their patience. My only aggravation of the trip (well almost only – but I will leave that till later) greeted me before leaving the airport. There were two queues at their untidy immigration control (since much improved). One had a sign indicating the entry for Uzbek nationals, one said nothing. Of course I did the logical thing. With my past Russian experience, I should have known better. Having spent thirty minutes to get to the front, two Dutchmen, one French businessman and I were not too politely told we had to get into the other queue. The one for Uzbek nationals – logical? Oh well. But matters improved immediately. My taxi driver had the usual humour of that ilk and having established my origin immediately launched into '…Ah England – from near Liverpool, Aston Villa or Tottenham Hotspur?' was the question. Sorry Manchester United you were not mentioned. He was probably not a shareholder. Having had similar greetings in the past, in among other places Colombo, Nairobi and Jakarta, it shows there is an international language outside money and politics. He was clearly at peace with the world, despite the early hour. I was less so, having left my flat at 8 p.m. the night before, it now being 6 a.m. local time. So first to bed. At least the Intourist plumbing worked this time and the price was reasonable. But beware of Intourist hotels,[2] the ubiquitous design always leaves out curtains that cover the windows for some

---

[2]On the second visit, we pampered ourselves with the better hotels. The air conditioning was great, but the food was the same rather boring fare of before.

unexplainable reason. So it was here.

How right the Uzbek agency in Moscow was. This capital of a nation with twenty-two million people had few ancient sights my guide could show me that excited my attention. That is apart from proudly pointing out the new stock exchange, the local equivalent of the Bolshoi, the president's boring Soviet-style office block and the central marriage house. The city's three million inhabitants were busy at their work or using their Metro with its twenty-two stations. The only one in Central Asia. Creating traffic jams was not a local habit, the few cars around were not hard to miss as one crossed the road. What however, the Royal Air Force officer in full uniform was doing at the hotel reception was a little beyond me. Was this to become a new outpost of our depleted Empire? I decided that ignorance was the best policy. This also applied to the contents of yesterday's *International Herald Tribune* lying lonely at reception. Finding out about either were not reasons for being here. My wife would be staggered at my latter feat.

What was immediately clear, was the emerging national identity of a newborn nation once more controlling its own destiny since the break-up of the USSR in 1991. My first guide – a cultured Russian lady called Olga, who had decided this was her future country, proudly told me about the two meanings of their flag. The political and the representational. It consisted of horizontal bands of light blue, white and pale green, with a half moon and twelve stars. The crescent obviously represented Islam, and the twelve stars the months of the year. White replicated cotton and good intentions; blue represented the rivers and good hopes for the future; and green denoted the plants and trees of the land as well as being a symbol for Islam. What was even more evident and of current national importance was the use of other past symbols to create a modern identity.

The square outside the hotel had a warrior on horseback

as the central focus. His name was Amur Temir. We, in Europe, know this man as Tamerlane, Temir the Lame – because of his apparent deformity. His image and contemporary influence as a past national hero and modern focus became more visible as days went by.

Wars, occupation, destruction, rape, pillage and genocide had been the order of their lives for centuries from Mongol days to their recent history. They finally became part of the USSR in 1924. Such is the historic price to be paid for immense geographical importance at the crossroads of Asia. The new Moslem government was the first for more than one hundred years. Since the late 1800s they had been occupied by tsarist troops. Before that, countless dynasties had ruled the land. Not all of them benevolent. The modern artificial boundaries of their country hid the mix of Tajik, Turkish, Kazak, Russian, Persian and Uzbek populations who had learnt in modern days to live in relative harmony. Only since 1930 had Tashkent been their capital. A political decision by Stalin. Before that Bukhara and Samarkand had rivalled for pre-eminence. All I spoke to in my short time here appeared proud of the resurgence of the cult of Tamerlane and Ulugh Bek. They had just celebrated the 660th anniversary of the former's birth. Some say Tamerlane was a great man, others say he was a thug and tyrant of the worst pedigree. Today it matters little. To them now he represents a new, independent and Moslem identity. He rose to power some fifty years after the demise of the two hundred and fifty short-lived years of the massive Mongol empire that extended from China to Europe between the twelfth and fourteenth centuries. He then created one of his own that stretched from Samarkand to the Middle East and south to India. But like many autocrats he left little issue and his dynasty lasted only three generations. He said he wanted to rule the world and as such there was no room for more than one potentate across the globe. Yes, *they* knew it was round in those days. To give him comfort in his ideal he named villages and towns surrounding his capital – Samarkand – with names like: Damascus, Cairo, Kiev, Krakow, Madrid and Paris. I later passed through Paris on my bus journey – all six houses and a cow shed.

The name Ulugh Bek may not be familiar to you. It wasn't to me till now. He lived between 1396 and 1449. He was the grandson of Tamerlane and was apparently one of the great men of international scientific culture. His abiding passion was astronomy. With the observatory he built in Samarkand, he measured in those days, the planetary location of over two thousand six hundred stars and the terrestrial position of over five hundred cities in the then known world. All this with only a massive fixed sextant carved out of solid rock and the naked eye. His measurements were apparently so accurate they remain today. His collected calculations, as those of some of his colleagues, are today to be found in the British Museum – pinched in the eighteenth century by the 'benevolent' British. His eminent academic disciples created the first algebraic logarithmic tables in the fifteenth century and these are apparently still relevant today. Guess where they are now? Yes, London. We should really give these treasures back to their rightful owners. But as an Iranian tourist couple (now living in London) explained to me in Samarkand, 'They are safer from future destruction in the stable location where they are today.' Thoughts of current Afghan destruction of their heritage came to the fore.

In a central square in Tashkent a memorial had been erected to Alisher Navoi, a poet from the fifteenth century who had first glorified the Uzbek language – the new national communication medium. Hence the central marriage house being called Navoi. It was at his monument that I received my first detailed lessons in their history. And that from a Russian. She told me that Tashkent stemmed from the first century with the local name of Madinat Ash Shash – Shash for short. It was changed to Binkent in the twelfth century, and only latterly to Tashkent. She was proud of her new-found heritage. Her parents had returned to Russia. But she was staying. It was humbling to find such faith in a very different future. Hers was the language of the place I had left. She told me that when I went to Samarkand and Bukhara some seventy per cent would speak Uzbek or Pharsee. They would also understand Turkish, Uzbek having its roots in that language. She expressed no concern at a possible resurgence of fundamentalist Islam affecting surrounding countries. But then nor were later guides who professed that religion. She, and they, did express some worries, but tinged with hope. The Soviet statue in her town from 1929 of the liberated, emancipated Eastern woman who had thrown off the veil of Islam was a monument she pointed out with continued expectation. Pray five times a day, if you want and only when you have time, was the message she gave of local religious practice. Thoughts of the Afghan fundamentalist Taleban affecting female lives were far from her mind. I was later told that the Uzbek government were much concerned at the Taleban threat to regain the holy Islamic sites of Samarkand and Bukhara. As such they were apparently secretly supplying arms to the opposition fighting around Kabul. But she had heard of Colin Thubron and his travel books of the area and because she had little access to English books I gave her a copy.

And then the bats…

So off to the airport to fly the three hundred kilometres from the capital to Samarkand. A city of some four hundred thousand people, thus equalling the population in Tamerlane's time. From the plane I could see the flat, artificially fertile, irrigated plain that stretched for miles, and mountains were evident on three sides. My first slow realisation of the local importance of that most precious resource – water – became apparent. I had thought only little about that till later reaching Bukhara and then became truly aware of the man-made disaster about to explode – the drying of the Aral Sea some six hundred kilometres north from that place. But more of that later. Here was the real Central Asia, the place of legends, a region with a longer cultured history than ours. The mystery was about to become reality. Samarkand means in some translations – 'exalted town'. It was exactly that. It was here that legend has it the female Moslem veil became reality. Tamerlane's primary wife – Bibi Khanim – apparently succumbed to the request for a kiss from the architect of the Friday Mosque, (they have three kinds: one for the Friday holy day; one for everyday use; and one for ceremonial occasions), Tamerlane had commissioned in that city while he was away somewhere on military campaign. The result on his return was the destruction of the mosque, the slaying of the architect and the introduction of the Islamic veil. I preferred the alternative version, that said the architect had flown off to heaven from a minaret of the mosque he had created. Well it sounded a good story – who knows the truth. The rebuilt structure carries her name to this day.

This oasis was a gentle and beautiful place. The Russian harshness had gone. Few Western faces were evident. The perfect ensemble of the three Madressah surrounding the main Registan Square, the spice market, the moderate patient nature of the people endeared them and this place to me immediately. The sound of their Arabic music interspersed with: proud old bearded men wearing their wartime medals; the ladies in their brightly-coloured dresses; raucous school children in their playground; donkeys carrying their burden to the central market and a cooling breeze, began to seduce my thoughts. While trying to photograph two sweet young girls outside their school, before I could even get the camera at the ready, another seven children had gathered with huge and toothy smiles. Whenever I pointed it, children came running. The people appeared not to have heard of Western frenetic pressure, they were at ease with a proud humility and new sense of national identity.

The guide on my first day in Samarkand was a maturer Russian lady, Ludmilla. She was a mine of information and clearly loved the local history. Unfortunately, as she was the only Italian speaker around and a tour group from there was in town, thus I lost her services later on. But I suppose the pretty young Moslem guide was a visual compensation, but she was less knowledgeable. Samarkand's fame today is based on few real architectural monuments. But what remains is simply stunning. In past days of the conquerors of the region, destruction of all and sundry was the order of the day. Even the precious irrigation system was not spared. There were exceptions, and they were religious buildings. Before the eleventh century, Zoroastrianism was the order of the day. One site of faith was simply replaced or rebuilt for use with another. The key sites of ancient buildings here were: Registan Square from the fifteenth to the seventeenth centuries; the city walls, some from the tenth century; a group of mausolea from the twelfth and thirteenth centuries; Ulugh Bek's observatory, and Tamerlane's Mosque (Bibi Khanim) which was finished in 1404. The towering rectangular portals of the mosques and Madressah in vivid blue, yellow and white majolica tiles were amazing. Most of the buildings are now under

UNESCO protection and had been recently rebuilt with Tamerlane's anniversary in mind. Age, past destruction and earthquakes had taken their toll. Being such a young political entity, they clearly wanted to celebrate as quickly as possible. Apparently it had been a major event. It was a pity that Son et Lumière in Registan Square had been suspended for the coming winter. The tourist season was over.

I had never heard the words Madressah and majolica before, so a word of explanation. They are only connected in the architectural sense. A Madressah is the Moslem name for a place of learning. Usually consisting of dormitories for fifty or so students, a meeting and teaching room and a mosque. Really an Islamic university. It appeared from the dozen or so such buildings I saw in Samarkand and Bukhara that each successive ruler wanted to be seen as a patron of the faith. For some reason, in three locations successive builders placed two such places opposite each other. My only explanation for this is architectural competition. In Samarkand around Registan Square there were three Madressah in one place. This was the crossroads of six major ancient roads and the site of a former market. The adjacent 'Silver Street' was under UNESCO reconstruction. As a visual ensemble it is one of the most perfect places I had ever seen and justifiably takes its place in glossy travel pictures. Majolica is a name for glazed tiles of multiple colours requiring a new firing for each vivid colour. Some buildings had majolica, others had mosaics. The latter was cheaper, even then. It was quickly evident where rebuilding had been completed. The older tiles and bricks showed signs of fading.

I was glad that not all ancient secrets had been revealed. Apparently the new glazing, majolica or single-colour mosaic, might only last between ten and twenty years, against the five hundred and more years of the old.

Although the chemical content of the old tiles and bricks were known, there were other secrets. What temperature was the kiln on firing? How long, or how often, did the glaze stay in the kiln? What wood was used to create the heat? Etc. Past artisans closely guarded such knowledge and only passed this to their sons. Today we cannot apparently replicate the ancient ways. Some past history should remain mysterious.

Two of the structures, one in Registan Square, and one in Bukhara were Islamic oddities. Their religion forbids any use of human, animal or living images. Only floral or regular patterns were allowed. Here though were to be found faces inside a representation of the sun, in Registan Square some tigers, and in Bukhara two phoenix and two pigs. They could have been strange looking horses. But pigs are unclean to the faith, so why had they been allowed and remained for so long? I never did find out. The Zoroastrian influence was evident in most places. This religion worships the elements of: fire, water, air and earth. On the centre of the front of the offending Madressah in Registan Square – which means 'Sandy Place' – was a Swastika design. This Zoroastrian sign meant – Eternity. We should be glad that contemporary history showed that symbol to be misplaced.

One of the more fascinating places in town was the central market and bazaar. Clearly Marks & Spencer or Sainsbury had no role in these cities. The noise, the colour, the bustle, the smells and the abundance of product were amazing. On a three-acre site you could buy most foods we have, and many we do not. Fruit, vegetables, spices, nuts, nails, car parts, clothes, carpets, etc. Each product grouping had its designated place. The local raisins were delicious, but I was a bit wary of the pomegranates. The spices were the centre of my attention. Nutmeg, anis, saffron, oregano, basil, caraway, pepper, salt blocks, cinnamon, paprika, and many dozens more were laid out on rows of stalls in this place for barter. My wife now has years of supply with my purchases. The trader and I eventually agreed half the price he first mentioned, but from the size of his grin as I left, I could not help thinking that I had still been done. Never mind, it was great entertainment for them and for me and I was happy with the result.

So on to Bukhara with a sadder note. The bad Russian habit of non-payment of wages was spreading south to here. Apparently the banks in Samarkand had closed in August, and public-sector employees such as my guide had not been paid since then. Yet they too have oil, gas and gold. On questioning, I was told that their equanimity was better than that further north. There were no thoughts of revolt here.

But before I pass on to a new place, some travel tips for those lucky enough to come in the future. In both Samarkand and Bukhara as everywhere in the former USSR, Intourist is still the main local hotel operator. There are some other newer hotels groups in Tashkent. When booking my trip no choice was offered. In both towns there is a standard old style hotel, and a spanking new one next to each other. I had booked only bed and breakfast and had been allocated the old one twice. One could tell the date of the buildings as the sparse hotel directory in the rooms gave all prices in Kopecks.[3] So a chance to experiment. This particularly after having had greasy chips and meat balls followed by even greasier chips and oblong meat balls (recycled?) on successive nights. The difference between old and new may be price, but there is more. The toilets, showers, food, friendliness in the new hotels was to a higher standard, and the cockroach rating lower. On

---

[3]Please remember that 100 Kopecks to the Rouble, and 5,500 Roubles to the $. Well at the time of writing.

checking in at Bukhara I disturbed the Russian clerk in her concentration on a computer game – she took little notice of me. Although I had seen the occasional Visa sign, I am glad I took sufficient cash – dollars. They appeared to have little idea of how to use such plastic, and don't try adding items to your room bill – it doesn't work. But beware the constant whispered requests from all and sundry to change dollars. The official exchange rate is currently about 55 Summ (new local currency) to the $ and the unofficial rate about 85 Summ, but one needs the exchange receipts on exit.[4] So beware. But everything was cheap compared to Moscow. One could have their wholesome round flat bread, three types of salad, cold roast beef, hot Shashlick and a half bottle of local sweet red wine for about $10. The highest denomination note I saw was for 100 Summ, an indication of local costs I guess.

And then the bats…

So another early start and off to the bus station. Clearly my travel plans and the airline schedule did not mix. Having been told that it would take about four hours to travel the three hundred kilometres to Bukhara I was slightly dismayed that my bus was to take some six. The multitude of stops had been ignored. As a pampered European, I could not remember when I last boarded a commercial bus. Well luxury coaches excluded. National Express would not have been able to pass any safety tests with this machine. Few would have purchased it, even third-hand at home.

---

[4]On the second visit in 1998, the Summ exchanged 'unofficially' at 160 to the $.

Well, I was still game. Our Uzbek driver was clearly pleased to have a 'tourist' aboard and was insistent that I sat in the front seat. I declined, as I wanted to keep an eye out for my luggage. His toothy gold-filled grin increased when the time came to pay – all of $5. Later during the journey it became obvious that I had paid well above the proper fare. I had forgotten to haggle. But compared to the local buses we passed, this was the 'express' service between these two rival cities. You should have seen the slower inter-village transport. That really was archaic. There were forty-one seats in this machine, and on leaving fifteen minutes early, they were only half taken. Oh was that a miscalculation. Within five kilometres and three stops we had taken on more. With constant comings and goings at one stage I counted over seventy-five people aboard, plus huge amounts of carefully bundled personal belongings. Or were they goods to be bartered at the next market? At no stage a cross word. Humour and patience were the order of the day. This was normality for them.

Sitting on the back seat next to me were four Russian mechanics off to find work in the newly-discovered oil fields around Bukhara. They preferred the term engineers. By journey's end they were more than slightly the worse the wear for drink. They stood out from the rest, not only by their European features, but by their loud and raucous behaviour. The remainder of my travel companions were clearly locals. The further we went from civilisation the more the colour of the people's dress increased. Halfway we stopped at a bus station, and were temporarily joined inside by locals selling lunch. The traditional round flat bread, sweet cakes and juice. I did not need any, as all surrounding me had previously shared their few items of food with me. Raisins, biscuits grapes and juice. I responded by distributing two packets of cigarettes and some salami. At one point we were joined by a young couple. She wore the brightly-coloured clothes and hat with gold-coloured tassels indicating they were newly married. It was explained to me that depending on what she thought about the state of her arranged marriage she could wear this apparel from between six months to a year. No one asked this particular lady her timing. At the worst part of the journey's crush there were some fifteen people plus luggage either on the back seat, or in the one and a half by three metre space in front of those seats, and still no word of complaint. With $500 in my pocket I guessed that would be about the total wealth of all the other passengers combined.

At least I was able to see at closer hand the rural nature of their land. We passed through miles of flatness inter-rupted only by an occasional village. The full extent of crop irrigation became clear. Without it we would be in a desert. The ancient habit of conquering armies destroying the culverts when they departed suddenly made sense. Without their water they were dead. Yet now they managed to grow crop after crop. Vines, cabbages, potatoes, grain, and of course miles and miles of cotton fields, the latter being the biggest export earner after the new-found oil, gas and gold. I saw more animals in these six hours than in the last eighteen 'Russian' months put together. Horses, goats, cattle and sheep, all being tended by small groups of children. About an hour before reaching Bukhara, we drove through the desert. Although I did not realise it at the time, we were entering true desert territory. What went by after that was really artificial regeneration of the Kysmil Kum – the red sand desert. Their village houses were no longer brick, but neat and tidy mud and straw houses. Even their graveyards were put to practical use. Among the unmarked Moslem and headstoned Russian graves was the occasional tethered cow contentedly munching the few green shoots

Of course I was the centre of attention for all around me. My fellow travellers asked endless questions. How old was I? Where did I live? Did I have a flat with one or two rooms? What did I pay for this flat in Moscow and did we have them in England? How old were my children and why had I no boys? What was my job? What did a manager do? What did I earn? Was I really a journalist? Why did I use the bus rather than fly? There were no political questions, just genuine interest in another human being from a world they neither knew or understood. Everything was in good humour and with the best of intentions. I was glad to have travelled this way. This journey had been far better than any boring plane. Their contentment with their lot would have humbled many average Europeans who were wealthy beyond these people's dreams. But then not all man's riches are material.

So was Bukhara like Samarkand? At first I was disappointed, because around me at the bus station were many single-storey factories, and one huge cotton processing plant. It had about half the population of the former city and it was a few hours before the ancient centre revealed its presence. But I was sadly back in tourist reality. The taxi driver tried to charge me the same price to travel three kilometres to the hotel as I paid to complete three hundred on the bus. And he wanted dollars to boot. Before I spend a little time describing the ancient old city it may be time to talk about their modern plight – water.

Like Samarkand, Bukhara is an oasis. The former is surrounded by mountains that feed its many springs, the latter has no such outcrops of protection. Bukhara has been located in the true centre of the desert for centuries. In those days the travellers along the Silk Route sought water along the way. Then it was here. Today well? In a north-westerly line from Samarkand are to be found, at about three-hundred-kilometre intervals, Bukhara, Khiva and lastly Nukus near the Aral Sea. Two rivers passed this way and fed this giant inland sea. With the development of industry, but particularly the water-hungry cotton crop, the rivers are virtually dry. For the last fifty years the one million or so people that live in this stretch of territory have consumed their precious future. Multitudinous international experts have pondered the matter with no solutions. At my hotel in Tashkent there had been another such gathering. When this was all Soviet territory, a single government pondered the problem, even considering diverting the path of the Volga in their direction. Now with half of the reducing sea in Kazakhstan and half in Uzbekistan, politics and oil get in the way.

The simple, but tragic problem as explained by a number of people was twofold. Firstly, the water-hungry cotton crop used for foreign exchange and secondly, the increase in population in this part of their country. Today all drinking water in Bukhara is piped from Samarkand; they have insufficient of their own. By the time one passes Nukus and reaches the Aral Sea, there is nothing left. The lake's natural inlets are dry by then. Regional climate, health, living conditions were all being affected. Yet they have discovered vast tracts of oil and gas in recent years. Even that needs water as the inhabitants of the Middle East will tell you. There, they can reprocess sea water. Here they are totally landlocked. North of the Kysmil Kum is the Kara Kum – the black sand desert. The only real solution is to move one million agricultural people from their ancient home. Not a prospect they would relish.

Paradise is a Persian word meaning garden. Their ancient garden, being both beautiful and fragile is about to become a desolate place for the first time in two and a half thousand years. On leaving Bukhara for Moscow I met an

Englishman at the airport. He and his wife had lived here for three years. She taught English at the local university and he ran the blind school. He was clearly in tune with their conditions. His crumpled friendly attire was witness to that. He described the water shortage as catastrophic. He continued with local anecdotal evidence indicating that by the turn of the century, war would return to the region. This time for the return not of land, but water. He further alarmed me by adding, that thanks to the current continuing Afghan civil war, less water was being used. If that stopped, requirements would increase, exacerbating an already dangerous problem. He lived here. I can only assume he has insight into the current political and social mood on the subject. A solution is desperately needed. The reason for being of these ancient cities, an oasis on a trading route, was suddenly no longer there.

The compact centre of Bukhara had none of the spectacular and lavish architectural style of Samarkand, but for that it was more comforting. There were many more relics of days gone by, but less spectacular. A complete small city with a mixture of styles dating from the ninth century were to be found. One tomb was Zoroastrian in origin. The retention of religious buildings during times of conflict appeared more important than keeping the irrigation culverts. The two Dervish hotels were fascinating. One inside the city, one some twenty-five kilometres outside, had catered for these wandering holy men – and one still does. At a central square was a 'café', where the old men spent their days reminiscing on raised carpet-covered 'bunks' and tables. Above them in an ancient tree was an empty storks' nest. Because of lack of running water and growing industrial pollution, the storks had not visited for some ten years. The tenth-century minaret, some forty-five metres high, even captured the awe of Genghis Khan when he first conquered the city. Standing before it and looking up, his cap fell off. He declared that no human had ever managed that, so this tower deserved respect and thus it was saved for posterity from destruction.

On the penultimate day of my travels, the city was suddenly empty. It was a Saturday and the usual bustling central market was a little subdued. My charming Moslem lady guide told me that the president had decreed that all available persons should go out to the cotton fields and assist with the final harvest. The police had ringed the city in an attempt to stop people entering the place. She had paid a 100 Summ bribe to come and show me round. She was not impressed with this annual habit to obtain scarce foreign exchange. Their habits demonstrate that they are both an open and closed society at the same time. How little has changed for them over the centuries.

And then the bats…

This time some explanation is needed. Wherever I went in the day time the multitude of crows and similar birds were self-evident. As the sun dipped below the horizon, they circled to find their nightly rest. The noise of settling birds was deafening for about thirty minutes – and then suddenly silence. Within minutes the hush was replaced by a silent fluttering. Bats were about, not a few, not in tens or twenties, but hundreds. I had never seen such a sight before. There were small, middle-sized and huge-winged creatures. During the day one had to step carefully to avoid their droppings on the pavement. Had Hitchcock been making a film needing such a backdrop he could not have found a better location. Fascinating and very eerie at the same time.

Well the tourist season was at an end, the nights were getting cold and it was time to leave. Having too muchtime, I arrived at Bukhara's dinky little airport far too early. As initially the only foreign passenger in the Intourist lounge, I was given a cup of tea, and promptly asked to assist in translating two government decrees affecting travellers into and out of the country. Well really to improve their English adaptation. The first had to do with prohibiting the import of salacious material that might incite religious tensions. Of particular note in this document were anti-Zionist and pornographic literature, both of which were banned. More amusingly, in the second decree, was that import of aircraft, their parts and lathes to make aircraft and their parts, also prohibited. Quite how I might get any of the latter into my suitcase beats me. But they clearly had time, or had not caught anyone. The decrees were dated some four months earlier – 29 July 1996.

And so back north to Moscow to prepare for my return to the UK. Being an hour late departing seemed no hardship, I would make it to the flat for a late supper. Not to be. No one had said that the aircraft would stop at Nukus on the way back, and no one prepared me for running repairs to an aircraft, Uzbek style. Question. How do you change an aircraft tyre without a hanger? Answer: first, recycle an Aeroflot Tupolev 154 of dubious origin into an Uzbek-coloured plane. Then land at a remote airport at 9 p.m. This place has to have as few lights as possible. I counted all of four around the vast tarmac apron – and none of them would cast much light on a suburban street at home. Then you disembark all the passengers into the airport. It was much too small to have a transit lounge. But at least we were free to wander outside the terminal. Some passengers purchased large dried, smoked fish from the Aral Sea which enterprising traders had brought for sale. They smelt a bit when we re-embarked. After about an hour we were ushered back to the plane. Only once have I been given a seat allocation on an internal[5] 'Aeroflot-type' flight. It was not on this particular journey. So there was the usual crush at the bottom of the aircraft steps.

There we stopped for another forty minutes to witness a most amazing sight. Five men were beavering away at the wheels in front of us. One with a trolley of ancient tools, two with torches and two tinkering. Each undercarriage consisted of six wheels, the back pair had been jacked up on a rickety structure. Possibly a car jack? With many kicks and hammer blows the offending wheel was removed. Putting the 'new' (well maybe) tyre on was more difficult. In the gloom, it looked as worn as the older tyre. A combination of heavy kicks, letting the air out and raising the jack took twenty more minutes. At last it was done. Not a murmur from the observant throng. I was a little more than nervous to say the least, but I appeared to be a minority of one. To them this was an 'event'. At last the signal to get on board. All one hundred and twenty people, but they had not removed the jack. I was still puzzling how an aircraft the size of a Boeing 727 with a full load of passengers could be held by one set of wheels on one side and one third of a wheel and a jack on the other. But it did. The final insult was a loud 'ping' as we taxied away. In the darkness outside, I just saw the 'car-type jack' flying off Our intrepid mechanics had forgotten to extract it after 'the repair'.

You can imagine my relief when three hours later we landed in Moscow. I had returned safe and sound from a

---

[5]I eat my words. Since returning in 1998. I have had this pleasure almost every time.

A mullah teaching the pilgrims outside Bukhara

A coffee shop in Bukhara

Tigers and faces on the Madressah in Registan Square Samarkand

Amur Temir in his capital of Samarkand

Faces on a Samarkand Madressah

Mending majolica tiles in Samarkand

Phoenix and pigs (or horses?) in Bukhara

The market in Samarkand

Spices for sale in Samarkand

Registan Square in Samarkand

Afternoon entertainment in Samarkand

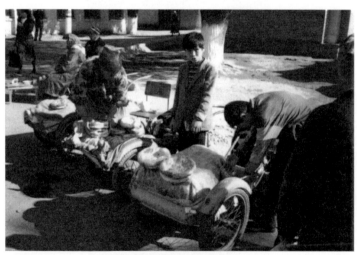

Unleavened bread for sale in Bukhara

The roofs of Bukhara

Chor Minor in Bukhara

Marina and me 'at the office' in 1998

ПАСХАЛЬНОЕ
БОГОСЛУЖЕНИЕ
В ПРЕОБРАЖЕНСКОЙ ЦЕРКВИ
ХРАМА ХРИСТА СПАСИТЕЛЯ

ПАСХА ХРИСТОВА

19 апреля 1998 г.

НАЧАЛО
ПАСХАЛЬНОЙ ЗАУТРЕНИ
в 00.00

Вход в храм с Соймоновского проезда
с 22.30 до 23.45.

Просьба не брать с собой ручные предметы
Проводить кинофотосъемку на богослужении
не разрешается.

The Easter 1998 invitation to Moscow's new Cathedral of Christ the Saviour

The rebuilt Cathedral of Christ the Saviour in Moscow

Ed, myself, Theresa and my daughter Katherine in St Petersburg

rural time warp to the frenetic pace of Moscow life on a wet and cold December day.

But? More importantly… will the storks ever return to the desert city of Bukhara not so far from the ecological disaster of the Aral Sea?

Chapter XIII
Any Conclusions?
February 1997

Well... This was a superpower... But now... 'This is Russia'... This is also the excuse we all glibly use to explain away the status of today, and as a salve to our daily conscience. But why should they, the citizens of the land? Why should we, the foreigners that live and invest here? Having spent many pages trying to give a personal insight into the Russia I came to know in 1995 and 1996, it might be useful to quote another writer who put matters into better context, and more succinctly, than I ever could. On the 19 October 1996, Geoffrey Hosking[1] wrote in the London *Times*, 'To understand the significance of what is going on, one needs to think back not just to the Soviet era, but even before. The tsars used to base their ideology on three cardinal principles: Orthodoxy, Autocracy and Nationality.'

The legacy of that trinity has not been removed today by any stretch of the imagination. It is with us in this land, even as you read these words. After the revolution in 1917, Orthodoxy was replaced by their token adherence to a Communist ideology – an alternative religion. In the time of Gorbachev and Yeltsin, Orthodoxy was allowed to

---

[1] Professor of Russian History at the School of Slavonic and East European Studies at the University of London. He is also author of *The History of the Soviet Union – 1917 to 1991*.

revive, but Autocracy was never lost. The rulers and the apparatchik continued to pay lip service to Democracy, but never truly practised its basic principles. Nor do they today. To do that properly needs time, patience, education and adherence to communal responsibility. The legacy of the tsarist principles has therefore, as yet, not been eradicated from the government of the land or even from the minds of the people. Professor Hosking wrote his article on the 19 October to give background to the aftermath of Yeltsin's sacking of General Alexander Lebed. Hosking continued in that article, 'In his recent autobiography, General Lebed put forward his own holy Russian trinity in a slightly different form: Orthodoxy; Nationality; and the Army.' Even Lebed thus demonstrates that he is no democrat. He too adheres to these basic, worn out, alien, failed and historic principles that still govern the management of the land and its people. It seems a colossal fundamental effort is required to bring the government and the people of Russia into twentieth-century thought and practice. That is if they really want to join a structured world society.

Having said that, it is high time to draw matters to a close and begin to reflect on some conclusions.[2] Most of the previous letters were prepared, researched and written in Russia. This one was begun a few days before I left and prepared in outline. Some of it was also typed there. But with a subject matter as wide-ranging, complex and deep as covered in previous pages, time for reflection would seem appropriate. So the final version has been completed at home. One reader said that they thought the last letter, on my trip to Central Asia was the best to date. 'It was easy to read, flowed well and gave a colourful word picture. There

---

[2]When I wrote these words. I was not to know that a further two years would pass before this work was complete and I would have had further first-hand experience of Russia and its development.

was no talk of doom, gloom, politics, economics or security matters.' Just like many readers, who have found some of the past recording of politics and economics dense and turgid. In describing modern Russia we cannot, unfortunately, take such a singular view as of a pleasure trip. Were it within my grasp, a travel guide would have been preferable to present to you. To do that though, a purpose for travel is required. As you have seen, however, they neither have a current national purpose for their future, nor have they the wherewithal to enjoy matters if they ever reached their individual or collective paradise at this moment in history. 'If you do not know where you are going, you will never get there', as the saying goes. This human void therefore is the unknown path the trinity of unholy principles has led them toward.

Just to bring me back to the reality of this land, a news item on the last afternoon of my first period in Moscow brought me straight back to earth. While stuffing a multitude of possessions gained while living here into various suitcases, before catching my plane home, I had left the television on to catch up with world events on a Russian news programme. It was announced that a bomb had exploded in a churchyard in the southern outskirts of Moscow killing eleven people (three more have since died) while another twenty were seriously injured. Apparently a memorial service was being held for the leader of an Afghan war-veterans' group. Among the economic privileges these ex-servicemen's groups had been granted in the past was access to alcohol and tobacco tax stamps. A rival veterans' group had apparently decided that their share of the loot was not high enough and extracted their perceived dues.

Nor will I easily forget the sight of a man of about my age going through the dustbins below my flat on my last morning in Moscow. I had just cleaned out, in my opinion, unwanted items and thrown the bin-liner into the tip. Five minutes later, on looking out of my window, I saw him carefully going through my rubbish. His expression looked as though Christmas had come early for him. But I saw him and dozens of others like him every morning around our rubbish bins as I left for work.

Poverty, haves and have-nots with nothing in between, dispossessed, revenge, Mafia involvement, tax evasion, personal greed, inter-factional fighting, anarchy, rule by the gun, no legal protection to settle their arguments, lack of respect for the dead and fallen. These were all ingredients of the dreadful crime and the images of the poor man at the rubbish bins. In these two incidents all the current tragedy of their land flashed before me.

Yes. 'This is Russia' as I came to know it in 1995 and 1996. Thus the conclusions that follow below are drawn from the many diverse threads of thought developed in past pages.

'Nothing has Changed'

What has really changed in respect of their attitude to life, politics, social intercourse and concern since tsarist times? I believe, very little indeed. One reader commented a month or so back that not only did their infrastructure, but also their mindset appear 'Third World' from what I had described. Possibly true. Yeltsin and before him Gorbachev may have encouraged some changes to the system, but they have not made any fundamental changes to the trinity of tsarist principles. That is why I have said in the introduction to these completed letters, 'that the existence, or not, of men like him as president will make little difference to the management or future of the land in the short term'. Unless and until any of us in the West can fully appreciate the inbred adherence to their holy trinity of principles, none of us can truly suggest the way forward to solve their modern problems. Most of us fail to understand or to suggest either. As has been demonstrated so many times in these pages, the Russian mindset is as different from ours as chalk is from cheese. Therefore do not judge their failures or resurrection by our principles. It will miss the mark by a mile.

'Boring Reality'

Having had a little time to reflect and gather my concluding thoughts on the time spent here has been difficult. I both loved the place and on occasion hated it at the same time. A new found split-personality. It has been reiterated many times, that this used to be a superpower in days gone by. That was the line we, and they, had been fed for a multitude of years. I found that difficult to reconcile with what I saw. On many occasions I was confused at understanding their 'reality'. So to gain a little distance, I complete this last chapter back home in 'boring reality' as we know it. Before you reach for your pens to complain at this remark, this is not a criticism of life in the West, it is made as a statement of *comforting* fact for us and our lifestyle. Thankfully you don't have to read the phrase 'spin doctor'. I have been away long enough not to know what such stupid English means. But let me explain. All of us at home regularly complain about so many aspects of our daily lives and how 'authority' mismanages our immediate world and misspends our hard-earned taxes. Spare a moment please to compare some of our minutia of daily life with theirs. Spare a thought to put your regular complaints into a comparative balance. Only then decide if 'boring reality' is used in the correct context. Let me pose some questions to make the point.

- Where is your nearest post box? Apart from the central

post and telegraph office opposite my flat, I only saw seven other post boxes. Sorry, I saw a blue one in Samarkand. That was probably why it took six weeks to receive my first letter posted in England.

- At the ex-pat watering holes here, a pint of lager was usually about $4.[3] What do you pay?

- Are you scared of policemen? If lost and you ask a policeman to help find the way in Moscow you usually get a scowl of indifference. If you get the question wrong you may have a gun in your face. The 'legal' department of our customers was little different. Ours at home, usually help, have no guns as yet and even manage a smile. If you stop at the GAI (police who still check travel in and out of cities) you may have to pay a bribe to get the answer to your question. Certainly you will if you want to get past.

- How much do you or your female friends pay for a bra? Well try the equivalent of eight such items as a month's wages. A lingerie factory in Volgograd is so short of money, they pay in kind. On Russian rates that works out at $27 per month.

- Would you pay $10 each day to get your slice of world news as seen by Murdoch? That was the price here for the London *Times*. At home it is slightly cheaper!

- Which of you has steel front doors? My daughters asked me why I had a steel door on the flat, three sliding bolts, each at the top, bottom and side and two locks. Well two locks is just normal, many have three or more. One of our transit flats had five locks. The answer I gave was – 'It is more difficult to copy two or more keys

---

[3]By August 1998 it had reached $8.

and the steel stops the bullets if someone wants to shoot me.' If I had died inside, you would require an acetylene torch to cut it open. I often wondered how many lonely people were hidden thus.

- How many times have you been visited by a plumber unannounced? Three times in six months is the answer here. This because my bath and sink water outlet had apparently been plumbed into the toilet in the flats below with occasional smelly results for me, and worse for my lower neighbours.

- What are the heels of your shoes made from? On my return home, I took all my shoes in for new heels and soles. On collection the assistant asked me where I had been. 'Why?' I asked. 'Well, not only were the heels of different heights, but your rubber heels were made of recycled tyres. I could see the treads.' I had been told that the place I took them to in Moscow was a 'high-class' repairer.

- Can you die from a falling icicle? Yes. About two hundred such deaths are reported each winter in Moscow alone. They don't count the beggars who die of cold in this total.

- How often do you write a cheque per month. When I wanted to cash some money with an exchange cheque at the office, they were always concerned. What if I had no money in the account? What was the value of this piece of paper? We never used such methods to make supplier payments in the office. It was always bank transfer of cleared funds. No one trusted cheques as a method of payment.

- How many times do you need to dial a telephone number and get through? You can usually dial another number on the phone and get through first time.[4] Here it may take two to three goes to reach another number in Moscow. To ring the regions, or even St Petersburg, try about ten times, if you get through at all. On one occasion, to reach a colleague by phone in Yakutia took two days.

- While you read these words whether it be winter or summer, can you regulate the heating to save your comfort as well as your purse? Here it is either on or off And that is a decision made at a far-off power station. To regulate it, open the window and let money burn the Moscow air.

- Would you like your phone or fax tapped? Here expect it as a matter of course. Particularly if you are a foreigner. On one occasion I was reminded by a KGB officer that a fax I had sent to a government official was on the 'computer'. Did I want the internal notes? he asked.

- What would you say to the local council if the heavy drain covers on the inner-city ring road were all taken off for about a mile; the covers were lying in the middle of the road and there were neither workmen or protective barriers in sight? Such events are entirely normal here. No one takes any notice. Certainly not good for your tyres and suspension if driving inattentively.

- How much do you pay for your mobile phone? My standard Finnish model cost $3,500 to buy, and about $1,500 per month to run, although prices are now reducing.

- Would you buy your petrol from an unregistered

---

[4]Now significantly improved.

roadside lorry? You can, and we did here.

- When you last went to Sainsbury or Waitrose did you have to leave your shopping bag at the entrance? Did you have to pass an armed security guard? Did he follow you and reprimand your insolence when you divided twelve eggs into half as you did not need the dozen? Well you do here. And I got a dreadful telling off for splitting the eggs.

- How much is a pizza? A ten-inch pizza and beer at my nearest parlour cost me $20. How much does the same cost you?

- What would you say if on your next trip on an aeroplane the passenger in front of you was smoking as you boarded the plane? Entirely unexceptional here.

- Would you allow your daughter to ring her boyfriend in the same town for two hours without a murmur of complaint about the cost? Little wonder the system works so badly here; calls within the city are free for all. So little money is available for new investment.

- When did you last go through an airport-style metal detector to go to a restaurant? Within three hundred metres of my flat I can think of four such places. Even the nearest McDonald's has armed security at the door.

- How much for a basic feed? My wife's office colleagues arranged a lunch at a local bistro in Wolverhampton for her on her last birthday. As I was home at the time, I went too. It was very good indeed. The bill for fifteen of us cost the same as a meal for two at my local Italian bistro sixty metres from the flat.

- How far do you have to walk to find a destitute beggar? On my last full day in Moscow, I decided to get rid of my remaining Roubles (they are not exchangeable at a Western bank, nor can one take them out of the country) and give them to someone who needed them more than me. The only decision, therefore, was not how far to go, but which of the various directions out of the block. I walked two hundred metres. If the nearby soup kitchen had been open it would have been thirty.

- How long does it take to get your VAT repayment for your company if you have claimed some back? Here the answer is never. The system is the same as in the UK, but claims for repayment are almost never processed.

- What would you do if the council had not mended the fifteen potholes in the road outside your house for more than six months or the water company had left a major leak for four weeks wasting precious resources? You might consider writing or threatening not to pay your taxes or bills. Here they neither pay the bill as a matter of course, nor mend the holes and leaks in that timescale.

- How many times have you had your car stolen? One of our customers had three removed in the space of two months. Two of them at gun point.

- Would you buy a book at Waterstones or Dillons if it were inside a locked glass cabinet and behind a large, fat unfriendly assistant who won't let you scan the contents? That's the way we have to do it here.

- What would you say if your local cottage hospital only saw a doctor every third day? That was the truth in Vologda.

- Would you stand uncomplaining for raids on your office as we have had? Four weeks ago we had the fourth break-in in six months. Do you expect the crime to be solved in due time? We don't here.

- Notwithstanding the dreadful events in Dunblane, do your children have the doors to their school locked as a matter of course to stop vagrants eating the school dinners? They are here in the majority of city schools.

- How many times have you used the words Mafia in the last month? In normal conversation here, about ten times a day. Particularly when we see BMWs with blue lights speeding by in the central lane reserved for 'important' people. There are nearly twenty-five thousand cars registered with such flashing lights in the Moscow region. We have one at the office. Anyone with money or influence can obtain one.

- When you pay your taxes, however reluctantly, do you expect to know how they are spent and have a voice if you are not satisfied? Here they don't pay their taxes nor do they have a say even if they did.

- And what would *you* do if your salary had not been paid for six or more months?

I could go on for hours with such questions and comments about the minor everyday events of life here, compared to home. We do indeed lead a rather sedate and 'boring' life compared to them. Do you prefer their 'exciting' reality or ours? Do you want to swap? Are you going to complain about the poor service for your tax payments again? As commented on before, I find the patience of the people amazing. They complain about their lot so little. To them this is all 'normal'. But if you have lived in a closed society and have known little different (although the armed security and crime has vastly increased in recent times), you would take their daily minutia as 'normal'. Please understand the comfort of using the words 'boring reality'.

'Crime Pays'

Enough has been said in these pages about the frightening nature of this endemic problem. It has to be stopped before anything approaching a quality of normality can return to daily life. Lebed is right when he said that every businessman in Russia is made a criminal as a result of the existing tax system. In Stalin's time, the secret police under Felix Dzerzhinsky was called the CHEKA (a forerunner to the KGB). Today the tax police instituted by Chubais have the same name and apparently similar methods. I simply cannot believe that the vacuum created by Gorbachev was the only reason for current anarchic criminality. Even sturgeon fishing and the caviar trade near the Caspian Sea have now been affected. A recent bomb, that destroyed a housing block was blamed on the Mafia controlling this sector of trade. Is it part of the Russian persona? Is it the social and economic vacuum created in 1991? Is it the circumstances of a land and people in change? Whatever it is, it must be eradicated, or at least reduced for citizens to respect authority in the future. Unless their leaders show a moral example, we cannot expect the people to do other than copy them.

'Open Government. What is that?'

Just as the Russian people have little idea about their responsibilities in a democratic society, nor does the government have any real idea of the checks and balances a parliamentary democracy would, or should, impose on their management of affairs. They still prefer to continue to play their Byzantine games behind closed doors. Chubais and his group of seven are but an example of the control exercised behind closed doors of those who manipulate the levers of power. Chubais was master of that during Yeltsin's illness. Who rules the country, was an often-asked question during Yeltsin's incapacity. Possibly the answer is the mysterious and shadowy oligarchy. But the political games of today are really little better or worse than yesteryear. The 'openness' of the Russian press reported on in the West is merely a gloss. Not much more than skin-deep. Where needed, their loyalty can be 'influenced'. We all saw that during the last presidential election. We can now see it with the lack of media coverage being given to Lebed and his political ambitions.[5]

From The *Moscow Times* of 21 November 1996. The caption said, 'Soon, the real thing'.

---

[5]Lebed has now formally announced on 28 November 1996 that he will be forming a new political party. He is apparently re-thinking his agenda and tactics now that Yeltsin is back in power after surgery.

'Superstition Rules'

An omission in my letter on the Russian soul was not to mention the extraordinary superstitious nature of the Russian people. It occurs in more than a few aspects of daily life. Here are some examples.

- If invited to a Russian family it is polite, just like at home, to bring a small gift. Flowers are the easy option. They love them. However, you must count the number of stems. If the event is a celebration, then there must be an odd number. Even numbers are reserved for funerals or sombre events. Often the flower sellers would remind us foreigners of this custom by asking what purpose the flowers were for to spare any later embarrassment.

- If someone accidentally steps on your foot, you must immediately return the deed. That is to step on the foot that caused the offence, and only then with the foot that had the hurt.

- Never shake hands with someone across the threshold of a doorway. It apparently will bring bad luck to the household.

Even I succumbed before I left to come to Russia. My horoscope in the *London Evening Standard* on the evening before I left the UK to go to Russia was prophetic. 'Current aspects signify that you are about to embark on one of the most exciting and rewarding periods of your life. You are certainly back in control and determined to prove that you have what it takes.' Those who know me personally will understand that both parts of the quote have relevance for me. My experiences in Russia were certainly exciting and rewarding.

Sorry Ivan. This isn't a kids' game.

'Keep Russia Weak'

For some the past confrontation of the 'Cold War' was 'safe'. It represented a known situation. We all knew the rules and how to deal with them. The instability of today breeds enormous internal Russian problems, with a few appalling exports like the Mafia. But the military threat of yesterday has largely gone. Well, only as long as the unstable nuclear stock-piles are better controlled. A weak Russia is 'cheaper' for the West. Military spend can be reduced, and the country thus be largely ignored. The above cartoon, from The *Moscow Times*, needs little extra comment. As long as Russia continues to remain weak in comparative terms, then this situation can be prolonged. Thus it appears to be a deliberate policy of current Western governments to keep today's status quo. But beware the reaction of both the government and the people. It would appear that neither the American White House nor the Kremlin want Lebed to succeed. Both for different reasons, but both with the same result. No more 'strong men' in power in Russia please, they say.

'Revolt is in the Air'

As the economic conditions in the winter of 1996/97 worsen, as the current paralysis of the Yeltsin administration continues, as the fallout from the activities of the Chubais group of seven continues. As the harsh winter chills the bones of the 'have-nots', as the illiquidity of the exchequer becomes worse, as the corruption in high places expands, as the home-grown food production reduces. We should little wonder that the enduring equanimity of the people begins to crack. Alexander Yukish, the president of the Grain Union said in a recent article,[6] 'It will take ten years to produce enough feed grain to restore the harvests of yesteryear... Livestock is being slaughtered because there is not enough food to keep them.' The miners in Vorkutia began another strike on 3 December 1996. These were the people whom Yeltsin visited prior to his election and promised all back wages would be paid. This time there is a new more concerning twist for the Kremlin. The miners have now called for the government to resign. Their perceived 'paradise' of former years has been truly smashed. The mental hurt is as hard to bear as the physical effect of national poverty. The enduring Russian equanimity is one thing, but normal human conduct tells me that something has to give. I believe 1997 will be a bad year for the Russians.

---

[6]The *Moscow Times*, 23 November 1996.

'Endemic Political and Economic Instability'

The former astronomic interest rates on Treasury bills (GKOs) may have come down from over three hundred per cent to the current thirty-eight per cent,[7] but even that is not enough to restore investment in private and public industry in the short term.

Commercial loans are still rarely for longer than one year. Few expect the 1997 fiscal budget to pass through the Duma in 1996. Some Duma members now want to impeach even Yeltsin for accepting the Lebed peace plan in Chechnya. The army, navy and air force remain unpaid. Politics and economics are inextricably intertwined in most countries in the world. So too is it here, despite the protestations to the contrary of some of my former Russian colleagues. The liquidity problems of AvtoVAZ are symp

---

[7]GKO auction on 28 November. But thirty-eight per cent on Rouble-denominated loans is still equivalent to about sixty per cent in GAAP accounting.

tomatic of the whole of Russian economic life today. This company based in Togliatti in the Samara Region, manufactures the Lada. It apparently owes over $2 billion in back taxes, with little hope of finding the money. Their dealers do not pay on time. The workers do not get their wages. The single-industry town produces nearly seven hundred thousand vehicles. Little investment has occurred in plant, machinery or new models in recent years. In short, they are facing public bankruptcy, not only through their trading record, but also by government demands for payment of back taxes. It was even reported[8] that the management are against a possible 'foreign' takeover.

The cartoon on the previous page appeared in The *Moscow Times* on the 28 November 1996. There was no caption. The words simply say: 'AvtoVAZ Bankrupt'. There was no need for any other words. For AvtoVAZ read – Russian manufacturing industry as a whole. The current apparently never-ending cycle of illiquidity, corruption, non-payment of wages and political chicanery has to end somewhere. Otherwise, as the cartoon indicates, the one hundred and fourteen thousand AvtoVAZ workforce will steal their very existence from under the country's nose. Trumpeting a reduction of the 'official' inflation rate down to about twenty-eight per cent is easy when this has been achieved by a monetary policy that represses government expenditure. Well, as the tax income is not there, they cannot spend it. But the newly announced plans[9] to build a Formula 1 race track is surely bordering on economic priorities gone mad.

I have to show some disappointment with the British Embassy. The current ambassador, Sir Andrew Wood, is a

---

[8]The *Moscow Times*, 28 November 1996.

[9]Yuri Luzhkov, The *Moscow Times,* 30 November 1996. And apparently one of the potential investors is Boris Berezovsky.

man who normally demands respect. Having been to a few commercial receptions there, I met and talked to him on a number of occasions and was impressed by his manner. However, in a conversation at such a reception in early October he gave me to understand that he thought that Potanin, the minister responsible for the economy, and his group – which we now all call the oligarchy – were 'good' for the Russian economy. A pity that this appears to be the view possibly passed on to his political masters at the British Foreign Office. If I have misunderstood the ambassador, my apologies.

'Have they the Time?'

Of course Russia will continue to exist, even in a reduced form if the Federation were to split. Of course the vast natural resources will remain at their future disposal. Of course nothing I have described in past letters is a new situation in the history of the world. There is, however, a significant different factor. Few of us have had any experience of such traumatic decline in so short a timescale, of a country that once dominated the lives of every man woman and child on this planet through its superpower confrontation with the West. That fact, in my opinion, will determine the time horizon of their human reaction more than most. The mental hurt of national loss of 'face' that I encountered in the many people I met over my time in Russia is deep. That, even more than lack of money, opportunity, food or employment has been the subject most mentioned in my conversations with Russian friends and acquaintances. The consensus was that they do have time, if:

• A whole generation of the old, weak, dispossessed and have-nots was sacrificed today.

- They accepted that at least two generations would have to pass by before an economic, social, legal and democratic structure as we know in our world were to be created.

- They recognise that the priorities in the task of rebuilding their infrastructure are so great then the ecological problems of their land would have to be ignored in the medium term.

- That what Muscovites have built is not a representation of the Federation as a whole. The wealth at the centre needs to spread to the regions.

If that were accepted by all, then they do have time. But I fear it may not be. The mind heals but slowly, and in some cases never, for those who still believe in their omnipotent place in the world order.

'So "Clever Clogs", if you were President, what would you do?'

A fair question after all that I have pontificated about in these many pages. I could easily say that I have only observed on the here and now, and it is not up to me now to make suggestions. After all, I have also said that only those who understand the Russian psyche can make proposals for their future. More than that, only a local can solve their multitudinous problems. But I do have some views on what might be some of the key political and economic priorities for the leader of their land at this moment in time. By the very nature of the information at my disposal, the following list is clearly superficial, but someone has to make a start of true 'reform'. But I do believe my list contains some of the elements of what might be needed for the start of rebirth in the short and medium term.

- Recognise the true state of the nation, and tell the people officially what they already know. Concentrate on the here and now, and do not look back to a totalitarian past.

- Forget the search for a return to the borders of the former USSR. The CIS as a political body will not work. Concentrate on keeping the current Russian Federation intact. Regain the confidence of the regions by listening to and acting on their individual concerns. That is the land mass that has the mineral resources to finance resurgence. If the mineral-rich regions were to cede, then financing recovery becomes a more difficult path.

- Find a method to remove the power of the oligarchy and its endemic grip on power behind the scenes.

- Update the current distribution and transport system to ensure that the regions and the centre are in close physical contact. This to at least ensure that the food, manufactured goods, and materials for export reach their destinations rather than rot in situ. At the same time give tax incentives to encourage locally grown produce.

- Simplify the tax structure. I had considered thirty per cent as a base tax level, compared to Lebed's suggestion for twenty-five per cent. Certainly reduce the confusion and bureaucracy. Either way the state revenues will increase in leaps and bounds.

- Give an amnesty for past unpaid taxes, but coupled with a new, fair but rigorous and intensive control on a new simplified tax policy.

- Pay all outstanding wages for the military forces. At the same time redirect and retrain an elite corps of the army to be tax inspectors. This group should be paid sufficient reward for their efforts not to be involved in, or tempted by, corruption. Then prosecute a series of high-profile individuals for tax evasion and corruption.

- Use a similar elite corps to begin the fight against the Mafia and all of its tentacles into places of power and influence.

- Pay all other outstanding wages and salaries and give tax breaks to all companies starting new businesses in the multitude of single-industry towns, even if this means printing money.

- Similar tax incentives should be given for longer-term industrial investment, housing renewal and to encourage the return of the multitude of funds held abroad.

- Urgently create a new legal basis to encourage the citizen's respect, foreign investment in infrastructure regeneration and mineral exploitation.

- Allow land ownership to all with a land register that can be challenged in the courts. The current 'lease' arrangements for forty-nine years' tenure are of no interest to local or foreign investors alike.

- Allocate resources away from the military back to three key areas: Education, Health and Agriculture.

- Encourage the Church to create leadership as an independent guardian of the nation's moral as well as religious conscience.

- Reduce official interest rates to say ten per cent, thereby removing many of the 'dubious' banks from the scene. At the same time giving tax-free benefits for savings. This will encourage the international banking community to begin offering proper competition to existing

Russian financial institutions and help weed out the local fringe banks. As in Singapore, create a national recovery fund from say five per cent of current pay.

- Create a new sector in the financial community dealing with personal mortgages and leasing of industrial equipment.

- And critically for the growth of wider wealth for all, move from trading in Western imports to an urgent increase in the manufacture of equally good but cheaper Russian-made products.

Only then begin the long-term task of reform of the constitution into a more democratic and stable environment. Democratic accountability will be a natural consequence of moral leadership. To achieve the above in the short term will not be based on parliamentary democratic actions. It will need a 'benevolent dictator' to start the process. Is that to be Lebed? All the above are well within the wit of Russian thought, but the most difficult will be those associated with a reduction in central control by the existing apparatchik. Whatever the success of the above, it will involve a recognition of the true reality of current national stature, and at the same time help encourage individuals to try to join in national renewal, as they can see, respect and replicate a new moral leadership.

'The Prize'

On the 4 October 1996, John Thornhill wrote a contribution to the *International Financial Times*. The subject was the forthcoming issue of GazProm shares on the New York Stock Exchange. He wrote about the possible current value of GazProm (the world's largest producer of gas) being estimated at about $66 billion. As it turned out the issue was at $15.75 per share, and in his estimation was a little too high. However, more importantly, he continued, 'This is how the markets view Russian risk. If say Exxon's share criteria value were attached, then this one company [GazProm] would be worth more than all the companies listed on the London Stock Exchange put together.' I decided to check what that meant in value terms. I was informed that on the 16 October 1996, if one included all the UK-based companies, overseas companies listed on the London market, the Unlisted (USM) and Alternative (AIM) markets and added them together, their approximate total value on that day was $6,355 billion. If John Thornhill is correct, and the London stock market value is correct it says five fundamental things.

- Russian risk as perceived today by foreign and local investors is truly very high.

- There may be a boom to come if Western criteria were ever reached or replicated. But current analysis indicates that may have to be put on hold for a while.

- The prize to be aimed at for their future is tantalisingly enormous, yet currently elusive.

- A huge amount of national effort and human ingenuity is required to reach this far-off goal.

- To reach Western parity needs at least two generations of patience, hard work, stability and much good fortune.

However hard I have tried to understand them and their ways, it is still their country. Only they can renew and rebuild. As Paulo Xavante said, 'There is one path for all, but each must walk it in his own way.'

Now I have worked, lived or done business in all five

continents. This place was the most personally confusing, stimulating and depressing. I do, however, earnestly hope they reach their individual and national goals of renewal. But sadly I must leave you (only temporarily) with some pertinent recent words from Viktor Chernomyrdin, the current prime minister.

'We wanted it to be better, but it turned out like always.'

Chapter XIV
Reality Revisited
March 1998

Over the last thirteen months it was good fortune to have been able to keep up observance of and involvement in the continually rapid pace of change in Russia today. The one constant for all in that fascinating land is change. They swapped their previous fear of oppression for a fear of poverty, crime and anarchy. Now, in addition, they have to cope with the most rapid changes in their recent history. Changes in a total system – social, economic, political – but most of all, their fundamental attitude to themselves and their desire of modern nationhood.

Past 'Letters from Moscow' have dwelt on themes described by many as gloomy, depressing and often heavy. But they were true. Hopefully this one will cheer you up a little, and it has equal veracity. There appears to be just a chink of light visible at the end of the long tunnel the Russians have to journey down to regain their national dignity and individual self-belief. In the intervening months since last living here, I was able to visit Moscow some five times on behalf of clients whom I was advising on the commercial pitfalls and opportunities which Russia might have to offer. Every time, the journeys revealed more change and thank goodness an increasingly apparent outward appearance of more stable elements within the wider system. I was lucky enough during one of those visits to partake in the lavish celebrations of eight hundred and fifty years since the birth of Moscow. Luzhkov had spruced up his city and all enjoyed a wonderful three-day party. Another visit took me back to my friends out in Dachaland. As usual their hospitality was magnificent. With all the usual group around the lunch table, for once the ladies dominated the conversation. Princess Diana was their theme. All six TV channels in Moscow had carried the funeral live. They were fascinated to watch events. They did admit to a touch of envy at our constitutional structure and its trappings. Secretly the ladies had thoughts of a return to past Russian court life and attendant fashion statements. I could not quite grasp why Diana appeared to mean so much to them. After all she had rarely impinged upon their lives. But then at that time, the whole world was gripped by similar emotions. Tinges of return to former tsarist glory perhaps?

It is entirely possible that some of my past observations were too harsh on them and their perceived plight. Had I been looking in the wrong places? Indeed, many of my Moscow-based friends considered much of what I had previously written as too negative and critical of the land they saw developing. In contrast, my friends in Vologda, five hundred kilometres north of Moscow, felt I had the balance about right. My economist friends and other sources close to the seat of power told me in no uncertain terms how wrong my views of apparent portents of doom were. There will be no revolution. There will just be some occasional shifts, both up and down, which can be managed by sensible politics. Even the ex-pat community was buoyant about the developments in 1997. Certainly all those in that group in the banking community thought Christmas came every day in this land. They in particular were making money, and lots of it. Their later comments on how much they had lost in the crash sounded hollow against the vast sums they had made in recent times. Where was this negative place I had previously written about they said. Nothing bad is going to happen. So life was fine and Russia was at last on the move.[1] So I felt a little lonely in my fundamental views, and decided to go with the flow. It would appear that my previous comments were wrong. Or were they?

After protracted discussions with one client, on the 3 December 1997, I was accompanying them to a presentation in Moscow and I chanced upon the *Daily Mail* for the day. Never believing a word of the horoscope – after all how can one categorise the world's population into twelve equal groups? – but, like all of us, I often read them avidly. Its contents appeared more than prophetic.

Jonathan Cainer wrote on that day: 'Are you feeling you ought to be somewhere else? Have you an urge to travel, to relocate abroad, to be taken anywhere other than where you are? If there's nothing stopping you from taking such an impulse seriously, you may as well consider such a move. For most Taureans, though, this is neither practical nor desirable. But an inner journey can be made. It's time to reconsider an old belief – and to adopt a different philosophy. The change you need is a psychological one.'

---

[1] In those balmy days of 1997 and early 1998, none of us had a real inkling that the house of cards was about to collapse so dramatically. None of us could guess at the speed and vehemence of events from August 1998 onwards. I suppose I could take comfort in saying 'I told you so'. But that is truly cynical. That is not my intent. Having reread all my past words while editing these letters, I am surprised at the veracity of past predictions. Just as I am now surprised at the complete turn about of all those who felt I was too gloomy. Apparently they now feel that I am some sort of guru, with a second sight. Nothing of the sort. Hopefully my past commercial experience has taught me to look into the nooks and crannies to find out the reality of a situation. Hopefully the world will now look more carefully at its instant global reactions and spend more time reflecting on the more strategic view. But again I fear not. We rarely learn the lessons of history.

Well, what was I to make of this. Those of you who remember the last horoscope reference on the day I left to live in Moscow the last time, will wonder with me at these coincidences. The client I was with was in the final stages of offering me a post in Moscow to develop their business here from scratch. After many hours deliberating this opportunity, again with the attendant disruption of family life, I took the plunge. On the 9 February 1998 I returned to live in Moscow for the second time. On this occasion the start to this new life was easier. I knew what to expect, where to live, how to shop, how to use the Metro and most important of all when to sit back and relax at multitudinous daily Russian frustrations. These had not changed one jot or iota.

Having worked with Marina Belenkaya, my secretary at my past employers, and during my time serving clients wanting to examine the commercial realities of Russia over the last fourteen months, she was a blessing, and helped to make my preparations smooth. With her help, a flat was found to move in on arrival. Very nice it is too. Some one hundred and six square metres, compared with a previous seventy-seven, allowed me not only to have more space, but install my initial office there as well. The coincidences continue. On the walls of the flat were some pictures. Guess where they had appeared from? My old Moscow flat of fourteen months ago! Each had an individual memory of purchase in 1995 and 1996. Only a few of those past acquisitions had been taken home. Partly lack of wall space at home, partly excessive luggage. So the ones left behind were rediscovered. But what a delight to return thus to past memories. By chance, Marina had stumbled upon my old landlord who had moved them here as a result of different tastes from the tenant who took over my old pad.

With a fully furnished flat with two bedrooms and the ability to shut off the office from a large kitchen, living area,

I was off to a flying start. Computers and furniture were purchased with speed for the office. Within eight days we had a functioning office only lacking satellite fax and telephone connections to the West. What a difference to the last start in Russia. That took over three months to achieve, the same state I was now in from day one. Then I had two moves and had to purchase furniture. This time, move in, relax and enjoy.

Well, what was new in the Russia of today compared to then? The number of new Western-style supermarkets was top of the list. In the area where I now lived, near to the Russian White House, some five were to be found within a ten-minute walk. Two of them being open twenty-four hours, seven days a week including holidays. People were actually smiling in some! Even the security people, who are certainly not known for any humour at all, smiled and joked with me at a nearby Western-style hotel. That pleasant expression was not an isolated incident. Over the first month here it occurred more than once in various shops and service establishments. So things were apparently changing. Of particular note was the courteous service to be found at Britanski Dom[2] – The British House shopping centre on Novi Arbat. It houses among other goodies BHS and Mothercare. No Marks and Spencer yet. Well I don't need Mothercare, but BHS was necessary after having boiled my underwear at 90°C in my first wash! There is also a branch of NEXT in the centre of town[3]. Prices are understandably higher, but the quality is known. Having said that, the local old-style Russian department store selling office consumables down the road was its usual glum self. Choose what you want, go to the cash desk and

---

[2] Unfortunately this establishment closed in the autumn of 1999. Another victim of the crash of 1998.

[3] Also apparently now pulling out of its Menazhnaya Square location.

pay, then return to pick up your goods and hope someone else has not taken the remaining stock. Take it or leave it 'we don't care if you buy or not'. Even locals were evidently now used to better Western-style service and were making their objections clear. Oh dear what a pain that really is when one is used to better ways of doing things. Even the Muscovites are getting spoilt with our comfortable ways.

The flat itself does have some memories of the more negative media security reports of Moscow life. To get in, first use a key to activate the entrance door. My entrance to the block is number 13. Oh dear. Then past a concierge. Up the lift, another MosOtis of dubious age, and one approaches a steel door with two locks to turn three times each. That gets me into a small lobby with another door facing to my flat and a small neighbouring domicile. This second door has three locks. Two of the keys are so large that they will ruin my pockets, so I have dispensed with them. Then another wooden door with a slider lock. Wow, I'm in. At least the Western renovation is comforting and the German double-glazed windows keep it snug and warm – albeit very dry. Quite how that will work without tilt and turn in the summer, I am not sure. At the moment, despite snow on the ground and a temperature just below zero, I still have the windows open. I still cannot regulate the heating. The wasted energy due to thousands of people opening windows across the city must push the ambient temperature outside up at least 5°C more than it actually is away in the surrounding countryside.

The plumber must have had a similar training to the last one. Hot and cold water on the bath are reversed to that indicated. The electrics also leave a little to be desired, I had to have the spare bedroom, office area and living room earthed; there was none. As the reliability of Moscow power supply is no different from before, power-surge protectors had to be installed to protect the computers, and these devices do not work to specification without earthing. Still that is all done. And how? The electrician concerned did not switch off the mains while changing the wires in the plugs. Everything was live while he carried out the repair. His problem I guess, but it still made me wince. The near neighbours who turn up their TV rather loudly on occasion, and the tuba player upstairs are the only things that disturb my peace in this comforting pad. It would be nice if the tuba exponent had a better variety of tunes, rather than scales all the time. All is currently peace and contentment, well apart from the fire engines that are attending to a fire opposite at the moment. No great shakes, only three tenders and little smoke. I have never quite worked out how the antiquated Moscow fire tenders get their ladders up to the sixteenth or more floors in some of the local buildings.

The weather certainly has its moments. Winter is still upon us, while you at home bask in the onset of spring. For a week in early February the daytime temperature did not rise above minus 15°C, and at night-time, lows of minus 28°C were recorded. Despite four layers of clothes, my fur hat, scarf and boots, it was bitterly cold. When the temperatures rose to around zero it felt almost spring-like, especially with a clear sunny sky. Snow has fallen on five occasions and is still blanketing the park outside my window. Five centimetres fell last night. But even a thaw can be dangerous. The thin layer of melted water then re-freezes overnight and creates an early morning skating rink on pavements. Old habits also die hard, and I always look up when walking past buildings. Falling icicles still kill some two hundred people a year in this city in the winter. But a change here too. Clearing them is, and always was, the responsibility of the individual house caretaker. There have been four cases in recent months where the city council has taken these individuals to court for neglecting their duty and disturbing the safety of Moscow citizens. In all four cases prison sentences were imposed. Individual rights in small things appear to matter now. It would appear from other small signs that the dignity of the individual is now beginning to mean something.

The traffic in Moscow has not improved. It is worse. As we are still in the middle of forming the legal entities, I am unable to purchase a car yet. Establishing company legals, currency transfer and ownership reasons – all legal gobble-degook. So Metro, bus and 'citizen' taxis' are the order of the day. In the past I had mastered enough Russian to use the Metro, but bus travel and negotiating in Russian to take a taxi was a new experience. Actually the bus thing is not so bad. To get to one of the better shopping streets is three bus stops – Nos. 2 or 44, which run every five minutes, and only Rbl.2.50 Well in reality 2,500 but now the 000s have been dropped. Certainly few new parking opportunities exist in Moscow, so public transport appears a better idea for the moment. But of course getting outside of town is difficult. As I have decided not to have a driver, I will brave that experience on my own later on. In the past I had been slightly wary of using the 'citizen' taxis', security and personal safety being uppermost in my mind. But now needs must. As has been said many times before, every one looks for an angle and earning a few Roubles on the side helps them all. Locals just stick their hand out if they want to get a taxi. Then a line of private cars stops for the negotiation process. Of course this is in Russian, and of course we foreigners, even if we speak it, will be charged a higher price. But never mind it is still cheap and gets you to places the Metro cannot reach. At least I remember enough of the language to make myself understood. I have now used this method some twenty or so times and am getting used to negotiating tactics and the correct level of pricing. On one occasion even an official car from the Duma stopped to drive me. I doubt if his employers would ever find out. But a car would still be good for the longer and more complicated journeys.

One notices the many little things that have changed. People appear better dressed, relaxed and more content with life than before. Glum and rude some are, but the spontaneity that was missing previously is more evident in the smiles, the 'thank yous' and the many small positive mannerisms. Despite the negative images still pervading in the Western media, there is much obvious progress. Of course these comments are made only with a current experience of Moscow. Quite what the situation in the regions turns out to be, is something for a later letter.

For the foreigner who had experience of this place in the past there are other new goodies to be discovered. A new bookshop with just English books. This 'Anglia Books' is to be found in a back alley just off Novi Arbat. A gem. None of the take-it-or-leave-it Russian sales tactics. One can actually touch the books and browse among the shelves. And Jean MacKenzie is back. This lady had a hilarious weekly column in The *Moscow Times* in the past before she fell in love and moved to Finland. Presumably she is now out of love and back where she had an eight-year Russian love-hate relationship with all about her, and entertained our Saturdays with her wit, incisive and acerbic observations of life about her in Russia. Her column last week was headed, 'The Willies in New Moscow – Confessions of a Russophile'. And yes she used all the meanings of the word 'Willies' that I can think of. It would appear that she longs for the days of the old 'wilder East' that she so often chastised. She now appears to have difficulty coping with the newer more unregulated Moscow that is emerging. 'Call me a cultural Luddite, but the New Moscow gives me the willies. Just browsing through the club and restaurant pages can induce a fit of depression that only a mega-dose of Dostoevsky can cure. Transvestite bars? Theme dining? Acid Jazz? Help!' she writes.

She appears to long for the old days of the 'Russian experience' in the early nineties. Well for some in this world such matters are progress. For others a disgrace. Whatever one's thoughts on the subject, Moscow now offers all that any world capital can give. Some of it is excessive and garish. Try the wildest bar in the northern hemisphere – The Hungry Duck. What a place. Wow, Stalin and Lenin would certainly turn in their graves. The younger generation here has adapted with vigour to the new realities. But the old unfortunately remain the forgotten generation who paid the ultimate price of radical change. They and their lot are the subject of much Western media comment, not the younger reality I have revisited.

International Women's Day, 8 March.

Yesterday was 'International Women's Day' here in Russia. Not something we at home spend much time celebrating.

Sorry ladies. A three-day holiday has been declared. Does the title of the holiday have shades of past ideological definition? Well yes and no. The cartoon above from last Saturday's *Moscow Times* puts this past Communist ideological celebration into better context in today's Russia. It is now regarded as part Valentine's Day, part Mother's Day. There are no political nuances – apart from the odd extremist. Yesterday all the men were meant to do the cooking, cleaning and generally spoil their womenfolk and employers should have given their female staff flowers and drinks last Friday. Sorry Marina, I forgot. Not a festival we celebrate at home.

Apparently the origin of this past very socialist occasion was in the USA. In 1909 a strike was held by female textile workers in New York. They were protesting over wages and working hours. They won their battle. The symbolism of their victory became historically entwined with the worldwide suffragette movement and the effects found their way to Russia in 1913. After Tsar Nikolas II abdicated in 1917, women here were given the vote. The enfranchisement of Russian women happened on the 8 March 1917 and has been a Communist holiday ever since. Today's realities have changed, and real people celebrate real relationships. Russians have an abiding love of flowers, and the florists of the city have had a field day. The local prices reflected the capitalist gains made on the day. Most flowers came from Kenya and similar sunny climes, via Amsterdam. A single carnation was $2 and a single rose $6. Not bad really if you are a florist.

There are other more real social effects of change to hand. On the 28 April 1997, Yeltsin introduced a decree titled 'On the Reform of Housing and Communal Services in the Russian Federation'. All over the world governments call their parliamentary bills by such boring names. Nothing changes there. Nor is Russia an exception. Before you all turn off and say here goes another boring economic lecture – hold on. I want to make a different point. Apparently Russians have historically been the highest users of the telephone in the world. Conversations go on for hours about nothing at all. The above proposed bill has to do with charging the population at large with the full costs of their utilities. All such services, water, gas, electricity and telephones (inside an individual city) have been free in the past. That is till now. By the year 2003, Russians will have to pay the full cost of such utilities. The increases are in stages, with twenty per cent being levied this year. One of the unforeseen side effects has been an increase in social problems, the biggest of which has been as a result of the telephone charges. Past travel restriction, small flats, small family units result in many people living on their own. The free telephone service inside the city was a lifeline. No longer.

The latter event is even a cause for George Soros, the international financier to change his former tune on Russian capitalism. Not only has he invested some $800 million in the privatisation process within the various telephone networks here, but he is also reported to have funded the government to help pay outstanding wages a month before the privatisation process gave him and his consortium a successful outcome in the bidding. On top of that, his so-called 'Pushkin Project' is donating some one thousand books to each of three and a half thousand provincial libraries across the land. His former comments on the 'Robber Capitalism' of the New Russian business-men appear to have been modified. Well when it comes to making money people change their tune in whatever country they are. Previous protestations of philanthropic involvement in Russia by George Soros may accompany the latter, but not the former action.

Even business related legislation is slowly moving to our

Western models. New laws on the structure and regulation of limited liability companies and the regulation of bankruptcy are evidence of the imposition of a modicum of control over the rampant unregulated private sector. In a past letter, I questioned the validity of some of the thoughts that Professor Layard of the London School of Economics expressed in his book *The Coming Russian Boom*. Maybe I was sucked in by the depressing economic statistics I recorded – despite the fact that the private sector was actually booming in an unrecorded way. Maybe the social plight of the lost generation of pensioners, dispossessed and the parentless children affected my judgement. Maybe I looked and did not see beyond the surface gloss. Maybe I did not fully understand the words I wrote on the patience of the Russian soul. Possibly the thirteen months away from Moscow's hectic matured my thoughts. Whatever it was, there is positive change in the air. It is tangible and evident in all around me. But who knows the reality. Or is it just a bubble about to burst?

Now would we spend a week celebrating pancakes? Not that I know of. Well, two weeks ago, the flags on the two bridges over the Moskva River by the White House and Kievskaya Station were bedecked in different colour flags. The red, white and blue of the Federation flag had been replaced by green, yellow, and other bright colours. What was this I asked the 'citizen' taxi driver. Oh it's pancake week – Maslenitsa – it is called. A mixture of Lent, past pagan traditions on the onset of spring and a good excuse for a party had been revived. So remember if you are in Moscow between the 23 February and the 1 March in future, it's Maslenitsa – Pancake week.

Another significant milestone of change was recorded on the 5 March this year. Exactly forty-five years to the day, after the death of Stalin, the first formal private sales of land were held at an auction in the Saratov region. Yeltsin has been fighting a protracted battle with hard-line socialists and nationalists who regard, among other things, the sale of land as sacrilegious. The soil of Mother Russia cannot be bought and sold they say.

Yet in a cinema in the rural town of Balakova, lots came under the hammer for the first time since tsarist days. The *Moscow Times* recorded the event in its usual humorous way as the cartoon above depicts. Vladimir Zhukov made history by being the first buyer. He acquired 0.035 of a hectare in the centre of town for just Rbl.31,000, or $5,200. He wanted to build a restaurant. Agricultural land was cheaper. Twenty hectares (about forty acres) went for the same sum on the nearby Karl Marx Collective Farm. The day's plum price was another less productive twenty hectare plot. That went to Nikolal Belov for the princely sum of Rbl.20, all of $3.3. Protestors from the 'Hands-off Lenin Party' (whoever they are) were thrown out of the hall just prior to the auction. Apart from that, this historic event passed off peacefully. Each region has its own say as to how, when or if they want to participate in this privatisation process, so all will be watching further developments with interest. Foreigners are currently prohibited from owning land. Apparently we have too much money and would pinch the lot, is the official line. Whatever, change is certainly in the air. Good luck to Messrs Belov, Zhukov and all the other proud owners of land in the new Russia.

Those of you who have been waiting for me to install e-mail will have to wait a little longer. Possibly with the 'pigeon' courier via my employers' head office in London that may be overtaken by events. But I cannot install the e-mail facility till the satellite lines are in. They were ordered over two weeks ago. When the engineers arrived at the flat last Tuesday to complete the task, they found that their colleagues who had laid the cable to the building – $700 installation charge per line (phone and dedicated fax) – had laid it to the wrong entrance to the building. So some things do not change in the new Russia.

My past descriptions in past letters were accurate in factual terms. But with the benefit of thirteen months away – it could be that I was possibly over harsh and hasty in many judgements.[4] Of course the Mafia is ever present. Of course few of the fundamental structural problems have not gone away. Of course the oligarchy still retains its powers. And of course there are a huge number of deprived and destitute citizens with little hope for the future. I then predicted the seeds of another revolution. This time for food, social improvement, modern infrastructure and personal dignity. Not for ideological reasons. My Russian

---

[4] I should have stuck with the courage of my former convictions and not been sucked into an appearance of a false dawn that never really happened.

friends, most of whom live in Moscow, who read my past pages, have since told me that I ignored the inherent determination of their people to overcome their past. They told me I still saw too much through Western eyes. Well maybe. The chink of light at the end of the tunnel they see is bigger in their eyes than that seen through mine. Yet the light is visible. Is it a mirage, or reality? There is still many a mile they have to travel before they and we can say 'they have arrived'. The timescale of two generations for such achievements, which I gave in the past has not changed. But real change is unmistakable in the Moscow of today. The regions have yet to have their say. Anecdotal evidence over the last month tells me that cash and entrepreneurial spirit have not reached them in quantity or quality as yet. I look forward to finding out over the next few months and recording my thoughts.

Chapter XV
Kremlinology '90s Style
May 1998

Having spent Easter at home, with the attendant appalling weather, snow, floods across the Midlands and general disruption of all sensible travel activity, I thought that a return to Moscow would give some respite from the English cold and wet. But no, in the short term. Here in Moscow it was just as bad, possibly worse. In the middle of April it was snowing hard. Some fifteen centimetres of snow fell in two days and caused the mayor of Moscow, Yuri Luzhkov, to suggest the sacking of the weather forecasters who had changed their predictions some seven times in the previous twenty-four hours. Even with seven variations, none of them had apparently forecast snow of an amount that stopped all traffic in this city normally so well used to inclement weather. All a bit reminiscent of Michael Fish and Ian McGaskill and other colleagues on the BBC weather service, and their misplaced predictions before the devastating storms of 1987 which hit the southern part of the UK. As usual we all have scapegoats. This time it is the 1998 version of 'El Niño'. Who knows the course of nature, but winter in Russia has been long and hard this year.

Now, some two weeks later, the change is dramatic. The sun is shining, the city is basking in temperatures around 20°C, with a gentle breeze wafting away the winter blues. The snow and ice from previous months have gone completely and at last the first signs of green on the trees are evident. The blossoming of spring in Moscow is at least a month or more behind Western Europe. The local continental climate has its lasting effects. Outside in the park by the flat, mothers watch their toddlers in the play area with swings and chutes. The older children ride their newly-acquired bikes (at last I have seem some in Moscow), or weave between the strolling couples, on their rollerblades. The sun exudes a brilliant warm glow and heavy winter coats have been discarded. The former grey and muddy morass purporting to be grass, so recently covered in snow, ice and then hidden by resulting water, is beginning to resemble an emerging lawn. New trees have been planted in the expanse of courtyard of my block. We have had the daily arrival of the efficient water tankers, which have cleaned the streets of dust and debris. Seven months of discarded rubbish, previously concealed by the snow, has been efficiently removed by city workmen. And at last the unregulateable heating in the flat has been turned off. An unseen hand, in a distant power station, has done his work. The prolonged stuffiness of winter within Moscow flats is replaced by the freshness of a Russian spring. And what a glorious spring it is. Soon the summer humidity will come. Spring lasts but a week or so here. The extremes of this land are well reflected in the climate and attendant effect on the behaviour of the people.

Since my last missive, many new experiences have kept me busy. A memorable performance of an opera I had never seen before – *Lucia di Lammemoor* – at the Bolshoi rejoined my love of that cathedral of culture. I was hungry for more, and inside a month, three further visits were arranged – *Les Sylphides*, *Romeo and Juliet* and *Bayadère*. They all reacquainted me with the joys and technical brilliance of Russian ballet performances. After all, I must try to ensure my money's worth before the June, July and August shutdown of the Bolshoi. Like the rest of Russia, the

Bolshoi is short of money and has to rely on commercial sponsorship, mostly from Russian banks, in increasing amounts. Despite these shortages, it is still among the best in the world in its offerings to its adoring public.

Then a lovely evening at the only Gothic building in Moscow; St Andrews Church. This hub of the local Anglican community was handed back to the pastoral care of the English church during the Queen's visit to Moscow in 1994. Built between 1882 and 1884, it replaced an earlier English chapel. Under Communism it was confiscated and latterly used as a recording studio. The inside of the church still has the soundproof panelling associated with recording activity. The neglect to the building and fabric is evident and a restoration programme is underway. Cost estimates of $3 million have been mooted. So the church organises regular fund-raising events. The particular evening I much enjoyed was of Russian folk songs. Many of them were familiar from the past. Recordings of this lovely music have more than once sustained me in 'dark' periods of my past Russian life. The bittersweet emotions generated in their folk music is so expressive of their complex character. Many of those traits have been explored and have been amply described in some past letters. They continue to dominate the search for understanding of their current condition.

The discovery of a new chain of Russian restaurants near the flat was also a pleasure. The food and surroundings were clean, wholesome, very reasonably priced and surprising, in as much as it is the only chain of its kind in Moscow to serve national dishes. A Russian equivalent to the quality standardisation of the 'Beefeater' restaurant chain. Further visits enhanced my impression. It has become a regular lunchtime haunt. A pity it has taken some seven years to restore Russian cooking at reasonable prices for the delectation of Muscovites as well as us transient foreigners. In the last year, some five of these restaurants have opened here. With the huge variety of international cuisine now on offer in this city, it is really a surprise that so few traditional Russian restaurants exist. I know of another five, including the wonderfully decorated Boyarsky Zaal in the Metropole Hotel. But they are extremely expensive and not within the budget of the majority. Thus I wish the amusingly named 'Yolki Palki' restaurant group every success. For those foreigners who want to sample their fare, a word of caution. You have to speak Russian to order anything. No ubiquitous English menus here.

Then there was a visit to the Dynamo football stadium on a cold and bitter March evening to see Spartak Moscow beat Ajax of Holland. Having tried to visit a football game in the past and in the search for that contest visited three diverse stadiums without finding the match, this evening's experience was new to me. The atmosphere was electric, as Spartak had never reached the quarter-finals of a European competition before. This was the second leg of the UEFA Cup. Some thirty-two thousand people, plus more than a few glum-looking police were in the stadium. My memory now is more of the period after the match than of the game itself. Having been an RFU steward at Twickenham, crowd safety had been drummed into us there. In the UK, each stadium has to ensure that a sporting ground can be cleared in at least eight minutes, a legacy of the Hillsborough tragedy. Well here it was different. At minus 8°C one forgets the temperature while the excitement of the game distracts. Afterwards when one has to wait one and a half hours to get out of the stadium, attitudes change. A Dutch colleague, new to Moscow, believed that old-style Soviet methods had returned. For older Moscow hands, the explanation was simple. Most people who attend football here have no cars. If they did have them, they would not bring them. There is no parking near the ground. So travel is by Metro. And guess what. For the last three years the second entrance to the Metro at the Dynamo station is still under repair. So thirty-two thousand people had to be channelled into one door of the Metro in the interests of safety. We were shepherded from the stadium in blocks and funnelled down to three abreast. My block was unfortunately the last to be selected. Sour-faced policemen with batons, shields and guns were present in thousands. Well it seemed that way. Their horses, dogs and general armoury were enough to deter the most ardent hooligan. All a bit frightening really. So visits to such matches may be curtailed in the future.

It has been my habit in the past, and remains so today, to brighten the flat with flowers from time to time. A small reminder of my wife's multitudinous plants at home, I guess. Such purchases have been made regularly to brighten a dull winter's day. Russian superstition raised its head again on the last visit to the local flower stall. My purchase consisted of twenty-eight stems of a variety of carnation colours. 'Oh dear,' said the florist. 'Are you sure you want twenty-eight?' The import of her question failed initially to reach my understanding. Suddenly the penny dropped. Russians are superstitious. Even when it comes to buying flowers. I recalled that even numbers of flower stems were for sad events. Funerals etc. Odd numbers for happy occasions. So it was clearly imperative to ensure the continuation of this custom. There was no sadness in this acquisition. Presumably in past purchases the desired even number had not upset local proprieties.

On the subject of Russian beliefs in myths and superstitions, I must spend a little time on the subject of honey. Strange you ask. What has that got to do with a letter from Russia? Well I thought you all might have a little interest in such trivialities to divert from the heavy themes of other letters. Having 'discovered' the local fruit and vegetable market, I found some honeycombs on sale. Apart from that, this wonderful place has fresh meat and vegetables just as good as at home. But with smells and tastes that we do not have. The pickles, the kefir – a sort of yoghurt, the sour cream sold in lumps, the fresh fruits of the Caucasus, and all sorts of foods and spices from parts East. Caviar is found here at $100 per kilo, then exotic varieties of fish by the tonne, salamis and all sorts of other goodies. Prices are half to a third of those at the Western-style supermarkets. So my shopping habits have changed considerably. This is the place to go for all fresh items in the future.

Well back to honey or *Myed* in Russian. It is pronounced just like mead. Is it the same etymological root? Anyway, in Soviet times it was scarce and seen as a luxury. As a result, in this superstitious society, many myths grew up around the use and consumption of the product. Even the academics cannot refrain from such beliefs. Professor Nadezhda Maksimenko of the bee-keeping department at the Moscow Timiryazev Agricultural Academy has listed some of the benefits of honey to the resolution of human medical complaints.[1] I repeat some of her list herewith.

- If honey is consumed every day, it apparently prevents colds as well as tuberculosis and gives much needed vitamin enhancement to the user.

- If one uses *Maisky Myed* (May Honey) it assists in the cure for sleeping disorders, neurosis and improves vision.

- If one mixes honey with black turnips and then feeds oneself with the resulting mixture via nose drops, then this apparently improves one's respiratory condition.

---

[1] The *Moscow Times*, 18 March 1998 in the 'Lifestyle' section.

- Buckwheat honey prevents minor heart disorders and anaemia.

- The Caucasians say that a honeycomb mixed with walnuts is a sure cure for a cold.

- If you are expecting a nervous breakdown, then you should consume a mixture of sweet clover honey and tea. It is apparently a sedative.

- If you are in need of a muscle relaxant then you should rub it into your spine, cover in paper and tie a scarf around it. No explanation was given regarding the scarf.

- Honey mixed with the resin from certain trees is used by some as an antiseptic.

There is no mention of honey as an aphrodisiac in the good professor's article. So honey has no use in that department according to the academics here. I make no claim to either authenticity or experience of any of the above cures. Please write back if you have a need to try out the suggestions and let me know of the success rate!

Visits to the meat, fish and vegetable market spurred me into a Russian first. A dinner party. Well in reality a lunch party for seven Russian friends. The preparations were intense. But without a cookbook to hand, I had to make do with telephone calls home on the best way to prepare the starter, the meat and a selection of vegetables. Those who have tasted my sweets will know that fruit left to slowly mature in the fridge for a day or so, in alcohol, is a little 'dangerous'. Pineapple chunks with half a bottle of vodka are no different, but delicious. The meal was set for 1 p.m. with the guests requested to arrive at 12.30. At about 11 a.m. I received a phone call. 'You know that the clocks have changed last night, so do you want us to arrive at winter time or summer time?' was the question. This appeared to be true Russian logic. 'Please arrive at the time designated,' I replied. The conversation proceeded with the question on winter or summer time repeated. I insisted that winter time was yesterday. Today the clocks had changed. So eventually watches had to be synchronised to the actual time under the new summer season (the proper time) and all was well. Two of the guests failed to arrive till reminded by phone. They blamed that on my poor Russian. A bit spurious really, as all others had properly understood. Unfortunately lunch broke up early as one couple had an appointment elsewhere. In this case early is used in a Russian sense. They departed at 6.30 p.m. Some lunch party! It has spurred me on to repeat the exercise on another occasion.

As was mentioned in the last letter, the plumber in this flat appears to be related to the one who restored my last abode to Western standard. The hot and cold taps in the bathroom are mixed up against reality. Well, I forgot to comment in the past on the other great Russian plumbing secret – 'The Great Russian Sink Plug Mystery'. Those of you who saw Michael Palin's last BBC TV series on his Pacific circumnavigation may remember his time in Magadan in the Russian Far East. He had found a super-market in his search for a bath plug. Those who have stayed in Russian-style hotels here will know about the lack of this amenity, or indeed often any lack of decent plumbing. At least my flat has such a beast in the bath. It was provided with the 'Western' renovation. But my kitchen sink has no such luxury. This is normal in this society where energy was and continues to be wasted in bucketfuls. Having now tried about five hardware shops and a further ten market stalls, I am the proud possessor of four more sink plugs and chains. Unfortunately none of them fits my kitchen sink. So washing up is done under running hot water. It would be helpful if the next visitor to Moscow would please bring me a selection of plugs to see if one fits!

Poor plumbing in Moscow in old apartment blocks has other dangers associated with the passing of time. A week or so back I woke up at my usual early hour and wandered into the bathroom in a sleepy state to find the floor rather wet. No great shakes I thought. That can be cleaned up later. No such luck. Within half an hour, after receiving three telephone calls and a stream of urgent pressing of my doorbell, the truth was out. There were two pinprick water leaks in my hot water pipes which had run all night from my third-floor abode into both the flats below, causing extensive flooding in their bathrooms. After what seemed to have been most of the neighbours examining the damage, the engineers located in the block arrived to replace all the rusty pipes. In the end two sections were removed and the leaks welded shut! Comment must be made about the welding. 'Please do not switch on any computers or other electrical items,' the workmen said as they attached the bare wires of their welding machine into the main fuse box! Not an electrical plug in sight. In addition, to achieve their plumbing feat, two complete blocks of flats, some one thousand apartments, had to have their water turned off, as the mains taps in my block were so old and seized up to render them useless. Such is reality here. Worrying about such matters is useless, it is part of Russia's modern experience for those of us who live here. $150 and four hours later they left with the resulting mess still to be cleared up. To the disgust of my secretary, I left that to her as I had to visit customers in the city. What appeared to be an isolated incident in my abode is common in all Moscow housing blocks. The worst time for such disasters is the approach of winter when the heating is restored and water pressures change. Apparently some thirty per cent of all Moscow flats have such problems at least once a year. As I look at the other rusty parts of my exposed plumbing system, I await the next winter with trepidation.

I cannot leave the lighter part of this letter without a comment on the Russian Orthodox Easter celebration this year. Having experienced this in the past and commented on the appropriate Easter customs in a former letter, my celebration of Orthodox Easter this year was definitely 'different'. I was determined not to miss the midnight service that accompanies this celebration, although a stay until 3 or 4 a.m. was not initially on the agenda. The true faithful attend the whole thing, which starts about 11.30 p.m. and usually finishes at about 4 a.m. There were many options of where to go. So my plan was to go to the new Cathedral of Christ the Saviour in the centre of Moscow. If I could see nothing of interest there, then at about 11 p.m. I would go to another church. Just as I had decided to leave and take up 'Plan B', a young man approached, who handed me a ticket for the cathedral service and suggested I use it. He was not interested. As evidence of this rare privilege, it is reproduced in the pictures in this book. Please note date and time. Even for non-Russian speakers it is evident. Wow, I had a pass into the new cathedral for Easter. Well it was actually only the crypt.

Upstairs in the main building the great and the good of Russian society had gathered. Yeltsin normally leads the cast. But as he was in Japan on some jaunt of a summit, Alexis II, the Patriarch of the Russian Orthodox Church, led that service. Downstairs with the selected plebes it was probably more joyful. The incense, chanting and a wonderfully melodic choir with bass half tones were enough to tingle the spine. At midnight we circled the cathedral in the traditional way – three perambulations – to find the body of Christ. Not having done so, the cry went up *Christus Voskresene*. Christ is risen. All had candles which struggled to stay alight in the late night breeze. To complete matters in the proper manner, just before we returned into the church, as on the last occasion I participated in this event, I was again greeted by kisses from all around me wishing me a happy Easter. At 3 a.m. I finally found my bed, tired but happy.

Having previously given this letter a different title, it was subsequently changed to the current one. Such is the preparation and compilation of these communications. Unfortunately as usual, much illogical wandering from subject to subject inside a few pages. The first part of this epistle appears to have nothing to do with the new title – Kremlinology '90s Style. Sorry. This letter was to be mainly about some more diverse and curious aspects of life in modern Moscow. Most of these subjects fill the part of the brain marked 'useless, but sometimes interesting information'. I was going to concentrate on the above and then among other matters on:

- How Moscow students use modern technology to cheat the system at exam time. A subject confirmed by my secretary's daughter who is studying law at Moscow State University.

- Some further comment on the attitudes of the young in Moscow to current economic and political events.

- The widespread need for Russians to learn English. Without it the young have little chance to obtain employment with Western investors here. Or even to rise within the ranks of forward-looking Russian companies.

- The ceremonial events set to take place on the 17 July in St Petersburg on the occasion of the long-delayed burial of the last Tsar and his family, eighty years to the day after their brutal assassination in Ekaterinburg.

- The understandable growth in protectionism in a society still trying to create an opinion-forming middle class.

- The continuation of the tragedy of unpaid wages, particularly among state employees and in the regions, now at the highest levels ever.

- Or the increase in theft of fossils from museums or nuclear devices from storage depots due to lack of cash for either the army, the security personnel or the museum staff. The problem is the same. But somehow the importance of missing fossils and the removal to places unknown of nuclear devices are a bit different.

Those themes will have to wait. Other matters dominate the current scene. We have had another large dose of Kremlinology to keep us all well occupied in the mean time. It is not clear if Kremlinology is an art or a science. Whatever it is, it has years of well-trodden precedent. This particular event did not grab the immediate attention of the locals. They have up to now largely ignored the issue. The continuing struggle in daily life and enduring disgust at the omnipotent behaviour of their political leaders make them generally ignore such antics. They had enough of that in the past. Only the Western press and the few of us who think these things matter, have followed current events with considerable interest.

I am referring of course to the news that has dominated the minds of 'Russian watchers'. The dismissal of his entire government by Boris Yeltsin on the 23 March and the subsequent power struggles.

However, even those normally apathetic to Kremlin antics, within the Russian population, are now beginning to realise that this latest series of events may have far-reaching consequences. Events as they have now turned out would confirm that they may be correct. So a little time needs to be taken to give the background to this whole situation. As in the past, the Western press and TV comment I have read or seen is as far from the truth of understanding Russian reality as it ever was.

Many have asked, 'Why did he do it?' Others have said, 'Why the whole cabinet?' The latter is easy to answer, the former is a matter of speculation and can only be guessed at. Within the current framework of Russian politics, there are many clues. Commentators in many walks of life have struggled to fathom the true reasons and many sheets of newsprint have been filled with informed comment. I decided to tap my past sources in high places to find out some of the insider rationale. Of course, just as in all things to do with Russian politics, the truth may take years to emerge. One thing is certain though, the series of political twists and turns and their ultimate outcome will have a significant bearing on the medium-term future of Russian economic and social complexion.[2] The appointment of a new prime minister, now complete, is by no means the end of the issue. Rather it is the beginning of a further chapter of political instability. It is, however, very likely that Yeltsin did not intend that events would actually take the turn they now have. His growing irrationality clearly makes him believe in his omnipotence. But no such figures from history ever are.

The first and simple question as to why Yeltsin dismissed his entire government is easy to answer. Yeltsin's primary target for removal was his prime minister, Viktor Chernomyrdin. Under the Russian constitution, the prime minister cannot be sacked as an individual. He is the constitutional person who is meant to pick his own cabinet,

---

[2]Little did I realise the real significance of that statement at the time of writing.

subject to presidential approval, and as such if his removal is demanded by the president then the whole cabinet has to go as well. So a situation was created on the 23 March, that meant that three members of the former government were told – 'Clear your office and don't come back'. They were: Chernomyrdin; Anatoly Chubais, the minister most responsible for Russia's recent drive to rapid privatisation and seen by many as the most hated man in the country; and Kulikov, the Minister of the Interior – a much disliked figure for other reasons which need not concern us here. Chubais's removal was the political price for Chernomyrdin to go. The remainder of the cabinet were told: 'You are sacked, but please turn up for work as usual.' The constitutional procedure for the reappointment of another prime minister is also clear. The president has to select an individual and ask the Duma for his or her ratification. Should the Duma refuse to vote in favour on three separate occasions, then the president has the right to dismiss the Duma and call for new parliamentary elections. That explanation deals with the easy part of the events of the last month. Answering the reasons for the action in the first place needs a little more time and patience to interpret the complexities of modern Russian politics. Many here would tell you little has changed since the 'bad old days'.

But before I give my interpretation of events, a cartoon from a weekly magazine called *The eXile* of the 27 March appears to set the tone of Yeltsin's actions very succinctly. The magazine's perception at the time would appear to be correct some four weeks later.

There are many background reasons for the situation, some logical, some not, some political, others economic. Headlines here have varied from 'Yeltsin is a loose Canon' to 'The Business Oligarchy surrounding Yeltsin runs the Country', or 'Sergei Who?' referring to the new whiz kid on the block – Sergei Kiriyenko, the newly-appointed prime minister designate. There appeared to be no single reason for Yeltsin's actions of the 23 March, but a complex mix of a number of factors coming together. Bear with me while I enumerate some of those diverse issues.

Yeltsin springs a surprise

Yeltsin springs a surprise.

But before I do, please think about the comparisons of Russia's current political and economic situation, in that they have to solve their problems by themselves, to that in former East Germany. In the latter territory the rush, since 1989, to introduce modern capitalist structures from former

Soviet-style management has created a vast number of mainly young unemployed reactionaries possibly erroneously today called by all and sundry Neo Nazis. Are they really such? Or are they in reality the unfortunate victims of our Western 'market-driven' economic principles protesting at the inability of a rich Western constitutional democracy to meet their genuine aspirations for equality with their Western brethren for work, self-respect and self-improvement?

In comparison, the multitude of Russian victims of the newly-established 'market economy' are better behaved. They do not yet riot or take violently to the streets in search of their demands. That may, of course, happen in due time. In Germany, as in other Western countries, the cry goes up 'the government must help us'. Here in Russia, self-help is the only realistic answer. But self-help is difficult in the short term against the overwhelming odds of past and current political creation.

Thus back to the manifold rationale for the current governmental crisis here. Little is simple in Russia. A drama is better than the direct approach, particularly when it comes to political manoeuvring 'in the name of the people'. As these many letters are in no way an attempt at academia, my apologies to those who require an in-depth analysis, and think what follows is simplistic.

• In the UK an electoral race for power usually takes six or seven weeks. In the USA the process to choose the final candidates takes over a year. Here the political temperature is currently dominated by one theme, and has been for some months. Who will stand for and win the presidential elections in the year 2000? All a bit far away for most of us. But not to the power-crazy Russian political establishment. Among the mooted leading candidates are Yeltsin himself, please do not believe any protestations to the contrary; Stroyev, the speaker of the Federation Council; Yuri Luzhkov, the influential and charismatic mayor of Moscow; Alexander Lebed; probably Chernomyrdin; as well as Zuganov the Communist leader. There may be more in time. As far as Yeltsin was concerned, he felt that Chernomyrdin was becoming too powerful and a threat to his own candidacy and as such a potential rival. Like many powerful leaders, Yeltsin does not like influential deputies who may try to step into his shoes. Foreign bankers as well as Western governments were beginning to prefer to do business with the solid, if sober, Viktor than with the increasingly irrational Boris. A rival had to be cleared from the scene, in preparation for the year 2000.

- Despite many economic troubles, one item of continuing good news was ever present. Russia has always had a positive balance of trade, even in Communist times. The natural wealth of the country has produced many years of export excesses over imports. However, 1997 will be the first year that has not been the case. Estimates[3] indicate that 1997 and 1998 will each produce a balance-of-trade deficit of $9 billion, this due mainly to the falling price of oil. Russia, like most oil producers, faces continuing difficult economic times as a result. Yeltsin has publicly complained that his past government had no policies to counter this trend. But then which other government with oil wealth has solutions to such a problem? And why blame them? He is the chief executive.

- The popularity of Yeltsin and his government is declining rapidly among the population. Reforms have

---

[3]Source: Russian Central Bank, RECEP.

stalled.[4] Particularly hard hit are those who continue to suffer from the continuing spiral of unpaid wages. The miners, teachers, pensioners, civil servants in general. Employees of moribund state-owned enterprises being among them. However, the army is also a major sufferer from this problem. It was reported that young conscripts are beginning to take matters into their own hands in increasing numbers. Their access to weapons, and their possible misuse, have apparently caused the government serious concern. I have no direct knowledge of this, only anecdotal. Whatever the truth, a discontented army in a fledgling democracy is always a dangerous animal. Within Russia, the military has historically kept a distance from politics. Hopefully this will remain. But who knows what the future will bring if they are not paid regularly.

• Much has been made in Western media reports about the rich 'New Russians'. Many are indeed mega rich. Commercial and financial groupings have been established here of a size to equal the largest companies in the world. Reference was made in a past letter to the group of seven Russian businessmen who met at the annual Davos Economic Forum in 1996 and then claimed to control fifty per cent of the Russian economy. This oligarchy of financial muscle is indeed rich in the widest possible sense. A few individuals have made their money as much through political influence as through their business acumen. Privatisation in this country has not generally benefited the majority. No shares for all to easily trade as we have in the UK. Here it is winner takes all. *The Sunday Times* in the UK listed[5]

---

[4]Reform is a relative concept. Russian reforms are not in any way akin to a Western definition of progress.

[5]*The Sunday Times,* 19 April 1998.

some of the richest men in Europe in 1998. Two Russians are shown. At number thirty-nine is Boris Berezovsky, who has appeared in these pages before, with an estimated wealth of £1.87 billion and at number forty-nine, Mikhail Kodorkovsky, chairman and majority shareholder of the Menatep Bank with some £1.5 billion. These people are seen by many to have used the political establishment to feather their nests. In Russia, business success at the highest level and political influence are one and the same thing. Others among the mega rich who are not mentioned in *The Sunday Times* list are, Vladimir Potanin, Mikhail Fridman, Vladimir Gusinsky and Alexander Smolensky. Oil, banking, media interests and privatisation influence in such areas as communications, oil and minerals are among the sources of their wealth. More of them and the surrounding capitalist hectic in a later letter. Thus, this oligarchy is seen by many to run Russia and its future economic direction.[6]

• It has been reported here in much depth that Berezovsky, one of the few Russian billionaires with no major visible Western partner was complaining to government about the manner in which the RosNeft privatisation process was being handled. RosNeft is the last large remaining oil giant here to be placed for privatisation tender. The interpretation was emphasised by Russian commentators that Berezovsky used the battle for control of RosNeft to force Yeltsin's hand on the Chernomyrdin removal issue in the first place. After all the Russian papers said, Chernomyrdin is still 'in with GazProm'. Who knows? But, certainly in a Western perception, this business oligarchy appears truly too

---

[6] *The Economist,* 4 April 1998. An article headed 'The Tycoons behind the Politicians'.

close to the government for political or financial comfort.

- Tatyana Dyachenko, Yeltsin's daughter, has in recent years become a hugely influential figure behind the scenes. Since the enforced departure of General Korzhakov, the former presidential gatekeeper, she has apparently taken over the role of controlling access to the presidential office. Some speculate that her former close relationship with Anatoly Chubais came to an end and she has switched her charms to Boris Berezovsky. Thus the 'other Boris' has been able to have considerable but possibly mischievous influence in the corridors of power. Many believe to his own capitalist ends.

- Rich some of these influential businessmen may be. Huge, even in our terms, are their new-found empires. But the government coffers are still empty. The government failure to collect due taxes has continued to result in the non-payment of the state-employed population. The term state employees includes those who work for currently state-owned enterprises, as well as civil servants and public officials. One of Sergei Kiriyenko's first actions as 'acting' prime minister was to announce on the 22 April (two days before his final Duma approval), that poor tax receipts had forced the interim government to reduce state spending by seven per cent in 1998. A saving of \$6 billion from the 1998 budget spend of \$83.32 billion. Yet the 1998 budget had finally been passed only a month or so previously. Big business might be gaining from capitalist hectic, but the population certainly was not. In addition, the past budget debate had failed to take account of the Asian financial crisis and the drop in oil prices on the Russian economy.

- Over the last year or so, the regional, political and economic influence has grown. The natural wealth of the country lies to the east of the Urals, despite the majority of the population living west of them. Regional influence and the privatisation battle over the ownership of Russia's natural resources have increased the attention paid by the business oligarchy to these far-flung places. The major banks have begun an expansion of their activities into the regions. They bring with them the thirst for political influence that goes hand in glove with this process. The elected regional governors who make up the members of the upper house, the Federation Council, have not ignored this development. It has been said that in the past the most powerful institution in the country was that of the office of president. True only to an extent today. Yeltsin has recognised too late that a combination of the Duma and the Federation Council joining forces to exert political influence against his policies is now more powerful than that of the president. Twice in six weeks has a presidential decree been overruled by the Federation Council. An unprecedented situation in this land. During the appointment process for Kiriyenko, the speakers of both the Duma and the Federation Council played important roles behind the scenes. Yeltsin was forced to take note of their joint opposition to the irrationality of the administration. Few previous Russian leaders have had to tread that path.

- Russian politics contains many wild cards. None more intriguing than that of the current role of Alexander Lebed. This bluff former army general who negotiated peace in Chechnya and played such a decisive role in the 1996 presidential victory for Yeltsin, fell out of favour and was dismissed. Many had written him off as a political force. This could still occur, but while Yeltsin was reshuffling his government, Lebed had begun an election campaign in the far-flung region of Krasnoyarsk to become governor. Few people live in this remote place, but among other vast mineral wealth lie some forty per cent of known world reserves of platinum, thirty per cent of known nickel and large reserves of cobalt. Serious potential wealth is to be found under the soil of Krasnoyarsk. In 1996 a bitter battle was fought over privatisation control of a huge employer in the region – Norilsk Nickel. The so-called 'loans for shares scheme' caused waves among the competing business oligarchy at that time. Potanin of Uneximbank won that play. This election was no different. According to the press, the incumbent governor, Valerie Zubov, was being funded in his election campaign by Potanin[7] and possibly other constituent oligarchy member Moscow banks. Some even quoted the Moscow mayor, Yuri Luzhkov, as a prime influence behind the scenes. Lebed, however, had the financial backing of Boris Berezovsky.[8] The place for the election battle may have been remote Western Siberia, but the real tussle is perceived by most observers of the Russian political scene to be the year 2000 presidential race. Lebed was not expected to win the current gubernatorial contest. Some strange bedfellows were recruited to assist in the contest to woo the bemused voters of this far-off place. Even Alain Delon the French singer was recruited to enliven the proceedings. In the Zubov camp, confidence was high. The *Moscow Times* had its usual political cartoon. This is

---

[7] The *Moscow Times,* 25 April 1998, among many other newspapers.

[8] The *Moscow Times,* 25 April 1998 and *Business Week,* 4 May 1998, among many others.

what they showed on the 23 April 1998. How wrong
this turned out to be.

Luzhkov pulls the carpet from under Lebed's feet.

Few here believe the protestations of either side in this
gubernatorial election that it is only about the future course
of what happens in Krasnoyarsk. Such huge sums of money
from either side of the business oligarchy would not be
spent if that were all that was at stake. In the event, shock
waves reverberated around the Kremlin when the result
was declared on the 27 April. With ninety-eight per cent of
the votes counted, Lebed had won forty-five per cent and
Zubov only thirty-five per cent. Zubov was pro-Kremlin. A
second round was required. But the die had been cast. Do
not ignore Lebed in the year 2000 from this performance.
The second round will take place on the 17 May, and we
will see what we will see.[9] Political fun and names are now

---

[9]Lebed duly won the final battle, and secured his platform for an assault
on the presidency in the year 2000.

bubbling nicely for an eighteen-month claim and counter claim from power-hungry politicians. When the London *Times* had its headline in its leader column on the 24 March 'Yeltsin Leaps into the Abyss', they only barely knew the truth of that. Without doubt the unelected and generally uncontrolled Russian business oligarchy will play an important part in the final outcome of both the Krasnoyarsk election and that for presidential office in the year 2000, if not before that date. In the event, Lebed won the second round with ease. As mentioned in past pages, Lebed is not a man to ignore in the future power struggles that will inevitably follow.

The role of the Communist Party in the whole process of confirming Kiriyenko in the Duma has also been questioned and possibly misreported. The final and crucial third vote in the Duma on the 24 April appointed the new prime minister – Sergei Kiriyenko by 251 to 25 votes. The press reported that Zuganov has lost face and the Communist Party had caved in. The truth is that Zuganov knew that should the Duma reject Yeltsin's candidate a third time, he would face two difficult political battles only one of which he might win in the short term. A disillusioned country and a split party. The generally disciplined Communist Party was fighting internal battles between hard-line right wingers and generally more compliant market reformers. Zuganov felt that Yeltsin had weakened his position through 'his irrational dismissal of the government' and enough to eventually lead to Yeltsin's defeat in the presidential elections in the year 2000. Therefore it was not necessary for him to split his own party further, rather to create a humiliation for Yeltsin. Therefore he only needed to ensure such short-term embarrassment for Yeltsin. As the Duma had decided on the Friday of the third vote to make the matter a secret rather than an open ballot,

Zuganov says NO.

Zuganov could ignore his prepared card. An abstention in a secret vote was a vote against Yeltsin and his candidate for prime minister. Had it been an open ballot, his tactic would have been different. Russia has an electoral system akin to Germany where half the parliamentary deputies are directly elected and half are on a party list and are appointed depending on the relevant party's share of the final vote. Therefore Zuganov had secretly arranged that just enough regional Communist Duma deputies on the party list were to vote for Kiriyenko to ensure marginal success for Yeltsin's candidate, and the rest of the Communist Party would vote against. Again The *Moscow Times* had an apt cartoon the day after the vote.

Those of you who are confused about these goings on as a result of the dismissal of the entire government by Yeltsin, should join the club. I have only scratched the surface of the true multitude of nonsense that took place behind closed doors in the last month. Enough to say that not a single Western commentator I have encountered has properly enjoined the events triggered by Yeltsin's action of dismissing his government on the 23 March with the breadth of issues raised above. I was more than amazed at the apparently reliable BBC. On Friday, 24 April, I sat down at 8 p.m. to watch the world news on BBC World TV (their answer to CNN) and heard the BBC Moscow commentator state that the vote for Kiriyenko had now returned Russia to a period of political stability. The same information was passed to listeners in the BBC world service at 9 p.m., Moscow time, that night. I nearly choked on my sandwich. What on earth were they reporting, I thought. This is not what is going on here. At least Richard Beeston, the Moscow correspondent of the London *Times*, who lives near my block of flats, reported matters rather better in an amusing article in his paper in the Saturday's magazine on the 2 May. He equated Yeltsin as being of unsound mind and body and thus being qualified for true tsar quality. He concluded in that article that this nation is headed for some serious short-term turbulence in the potential absence of 'the Tsar'.

Well I cannot leave this letter without some other gossip surrounding this whole issue. It was reported to me by a reliable source, that Yeltsin had to have three takes by the TV crew recording his governmental dismissal statement on the 23 March due to his state of irrationality. Apparently if one watches carefully the joins in the final broadcast tape are clearly visible. Maybe it has something to do with the Stavrapol Distillery that send three truckloads of vodka into the Kremlin each month. In government offices on the night of the 23 March, matters were at pandemonium pitch. Ministers were walking around the White House asking the doormen if they knew what was going on. As I live not far from there, I could observe the multitudinous goings on and arrivals or departures of official cars in their droves.

None of you should think that an irrational Yeltsin is completely finished. He recently appointed Boris Berezovsky to the post of Secretary of the Organisation of the Commonwealth of Independent States, the rather rudderless CIS. This body has few functions. But the head office is in Minsk, in Belarus. Possibly a good place to get rid of him to. Is this Berezovsky's reward for supporting Lebed financially in the gubernatorial election in Krasnoyarsk and being the apparent trigger for the whole governmental crisis in the first place, believed by many to have been about the battle by the oligarchy for control of RosNeft? Well, Berezovsky has recently acquired a new soulmate. It is reported that he has just formed a communications joint venture with Rupert Murdoch in Russia. That will be an interesting partnership.

If you think that this battle for the ultimate prize in the year 2000 is over, think again. It has not even started in earnest. And what of the population? Well what do you think? In Russia's tortuous political process they are hardly important to the political contestants, other than being mere pawns. As Marie Antoinette said to the starving masses at the start of the French revolution – 'Let them eat cake'!

Chapter XVI
Capitalist Hectic
July 1998

Just outside the walls of the Kremlin, on its north-east corner is a place of quiet dignity. To its north is Moscow's new consumer focal point, the Menazhnaya Square underground shopping complex and its distinctive fairy-tale statues. To the east the Soviet architecture of the Moskva Hotel. Within the circle of the Kremlin, new capitalist and old Soviet memories, this simple memorial to Russia's unknown soldier creates a haven of remembrance. This spot is set inside the new-found botanical elegance of the Alexander Sad, and next to the unpretentious, but movingly evocative, marble blocks inscribed with the names of the 'Hero Cities' from the Second World War. For patriotic, not nationalistic, reasons, Russia will always remember the names of Smolensk, Odessa, Leningrad, Volgograd, Minsk, Kiev, Moscow, Novorosirsk, Sevastopol et al, just as we remember the London blitz or events in Coventry, and the Germans, the senseless destruction of Dresden at the end of the last world war. Here has been a solemn focus of Russian political ceremonial for many years. Not more than a hundred metres away is to be found the statue of Marshall Zhukov, Russia's revered military champion in the protection of the motherland during the slaughter of the eastern campaign in the last great conflict among nations. Red Square, and its angular brown marble mausoleum protecting the mortal remains of Lenin, complete the erroneous mental scene for many not familiar with this land, that militarist-dominated political thought is still high on the agenda for some today.

On the 9 May 1945, Stalin signed the armistice documents that finally ceased hostilities on the European continent. Trusting no one, he waited twenty-four hours after the Western powers signalled peace. Ever since 'Victory' Day has been a key focal point in the national celebratory calendar in the USSR, and now Russia. Those of my, and my parents' generation will have seen images of goose-stepping troops parading the uneven, blue-tinged, cobbles of Red Square and being saluted from atop Lenin's mausoleum by an assembled political supremacy. An earlier letter evoked some of these fears. How wrong I was. That is the Russia of the past.

In truth it was never really the Russia of the past for the indigenous majority. Even in the dark former days, the published images of an apparent joyous Communist population bore little resemblance to the truth. With the 1 and 9 May previously being manipulated as holiday highlights of Socialist propaganda, we, in the West, had always been given the impression that such events occurred with the blessing of a compliant population. There were and continue to be, however, other more fundamental practicalities at work. The long hard winter having ended, the many with access to Dachas and allotments in the surrounding countryside used, and do so with increased vigour today, these particular national holidays, and the intervening days, to more fruitful, and less political effect. It is the time when the dwellings in Dachaland have to be aired from the winter melancholy. It is a time to till the soil of the formerly frozen allotment and plant the first seeds for the forthcoming harvest. It is a time to escape the city and think of summer and its multitudinous blessings. Today that portion has remained. But the nature and official content of celebrating these former Soviet holidays has, it appears, changed out of all recognition.

This year, the 9 May fell on a Saturday. Finding Russian business contacts for the last ten days had been difficult. They too had been out in the countryside preparing their rural dwellings for a summer of family relaxation. Not having easy regular access to such a place, I remained in the unusually quiet city to prepare for important business discussions in Nizhny Novgorod the following week. But I did turn on Russian television that morning. Three of the six channels were commemorating the end of hostilities fifty-three years ago. None of the former jingoistic political baggage accompanied any of the programmes. Of course, there were inevitable images of past conflict, but with personal remembrance rather than with political overtones. Red Square did have a parade, but this time only for veterans. Not only to commemorate events of fifty-three years ago, but Afghanistan, Chechnya and other such conflicts. A dignified ceremonial reminiscent of a remembrance parade past London's Whitehall Cenotaph was on display. Official memorial was for the memory of the fallen, not for the victory of one ideology over another.

As I had tickets to see *Swan Lake* with some friends at the nearby Kremlin Palace Congress Hall that evening, a leisurely stroll through the centre of the city to soak up the atmosphere of the day appeared on the agenda. A scene greeted me that could have been found in any city across the globe. Menazhnaya Square, Alexander Sad, Revolution Square in front of the Bolshoi, and Red Square were a throng of smiling faces. People were enjoying themselves. Today was a day for not just remembrance, but also for dignified enjoyment. Respect for the fallen was evident through the sea of flowers placed at all monuments to nationality. The official wreaths at the tomb of the unknown soldier were supplemented by a multitude of single offerings from the reverent visitors. Marx's statue in Ploschad Revolutsini, as well as Lenin's in the entrance to the Metro Station of the same name, had flowers placed at their base. Marshall Zhukov's statue and Lenin's mausoleum were not ignored. These were no offerings to a political past. These were tokens respecting fallen comrades who had died in the protection of the motherland as well as of nationhood.

Muscovites had indeed enjoyed a pageant down Tverskaya Ulitsa earlier in the day. Certainly no militaristic events were on display. The only soldiers on parade were regimental bands. The remaining participants were found on floats of mythical Russian heroes to be discovered in the history books from past centuries and of more inventive depictions of Russian fairy tales. The ceremonial over, in the late afternoon sunshine of a balmy early summer's day the population were enjoying aplenty the celebrations, just as we would in our cities.

Around and within the newly active fountains of Menazhnaya Square, an imaginative hand had created a place for enjoyment. The statues were of Russian fairy tales, bears, foxes, swans, storks and other mythical characters. They captured the imagination of young and old alike. As with us, the young here had to climb the figures, a point of particular enjoyment, because most of them were surrounded by water. The busy ice-cream, hot-dog and Coca-Cola stalls were interspersed with individuals selling flags depicting the emblems of their nation and their city. Queues of hungry individuals stretched out from the fast-food stalls. A string orchestra played classical music for the enjoyment of all. And not more than fifty metres away a pop band was plugging its offering. All around were to be seen proud bemedalled veterans of former conflicts walking slowly among the more boisterous modern young. In one corner, a buxom pensioner held fast to her husband in case his walking stick should falter. Both had their chests adorned with their rewards of past service to their nation. Their pride of remembrance was evident. Even the occasional hippies were to be found among the throng. Such individuals had no place in past Russian society, today's more liberal tolerance has changed that. Occasional earnest groups of debating amateur politicians were to be found dotted among the crowd, some carrying flags of past and present adherence. The occasional red flag, with hammer and sickle, was, however, well outnumbered by the resurgent Russian tricolour. A respectful throng surrounded the tomb of the unknown soldier surveying the floral carpet. Personal tributes outnumbered the official wreaths from earlier in the day. Near the back were wreaths from other nations. The French Cross of Lorraine and a Union Flag were to be seen as tokens of respect. And all around humanity was at peace with itself and its neighbour.

Red Square had been transformed in the gathering dusk from the earlier veteran's parade. Now it was full of singing, dancing and merrymaking. Under St Basil's multi-coloured onion domes was a pop band. By the GUM department store a folk group entertained the crowd. In front of the Historical Museum a swing band energetically displayed their talents. The cacophonous sounds were all competing for the ear of willing listeners. This was no militaristic demonstration. This was the new Moscow and the new Russia showing its benign face to the world. Western media covered former despotic tendencies in full, but was it showing this new enjoyable side of Russia's character? I doubt it.

Later that evening after the ballet at the Kremlin Palace, I wove my way among the swelling crowds to return to the flat. An advertising banner across Tverskaya caught my eye. Older Moscow hands will know that before 1991 this street, formerly Gorky Street, was silent at night. No advertising, other than political slogans were then to be seen. Few lights graced the night air in those now distant days of memory. The then paucity of shops sold only the products of a dying system. Today the transformation is impressive. Today one cannot move around the city without the omnipresent invasion of advertising hoardings, mainly Western. Banners across the streets, neon lights blazing many a multinational company name atop the buildings, posters in the Metro, advertising interrupting TV programmes. In six years the nature of a command economy had been replaced by the urgent messages of a market-driven society. The message that stopped me, and gave rise to the idea of this letter said: REEBOK PUMPS – SALE – 1,000 PAIRS. The address and telephone number were to be found both left and right of the banner. No, this letter is not about running shoes or about the stated manufacturer. It is about some of the capitalist hectic that enhanced the mood of many in the effervescent crowds that assembled that day in May.

Since my return to Russia earlier in the year, I had begun to doubt many of the more negative conclusions drawn in previous pages. My Russian as well as Western friends told me more than once that my earlier more gloomy predictions were out of step with the reality of a recent commercial boom. Of course there are still multitudinous problems inherent within the Russian economy. These letters, your newspapers and electronic media have enough of that. Of course the curse of unpaid wages still dominates the headlines. On the 1 April 1998, they stood at their highest level ever,[1] $9.6 billion. Of course tax receipts are too low to fill government coffers. Of course the Mafia and omnipresent corruption reign supreme in some quarters. There appeared, superficially at least, a rapidly

---

[1]Source, The *Moscow Times*, 1 April 1998.

developing, more positive side to this depressing story. While some sixty-five per cent of the population still lives on less than $100 per month, other statistics gave rise to the hope that matters are truly changing for the better.

- In 1996, some 3.3 million Russians took holidays abroad. The number has significantly increased since.[2] Those of you who have visited the holiday resorts in sunny Mediterranean climes in recent times will have experienced a multitude of Russian visitors. Even the bedroom refrigerators in the most popular tourist hotels have litre, rather than single-portion vodka bottles on supply. In more distant places, the richer Russians also show their presence. Even street traders in far off Kenya had begun to learn the basics of the Russian language to ply their trade.

- In 1997, ownership of colour TV sets had risen from 67% to 82% of the population[3] over the previous year.

- The number of individuals earning less than $100 per month for the whole of 1997 was 39.4% of the population. By December of the same year it had fallen to 34%.[4]

- Those with a monthly income of more than $300, for the whole of 1997 were 12.6% of the Russian population. By December of 1997 this had risen to an impressive 22.3%.[5]

- The private sector of the economy now boasted an

---

[2]Source, GOSKomstat.

[3]Source, VNIKI. All Russia Market Research Institute. Quarterly Review No. 1, February 1998.

[4]Source, GOSKomstat.

[5]Source, GOSKomstat.

impressive 70% of GDP. Twelve months previously this was estimated at only 40%. In 1991 it did not exist.[6] Could we have created such new found structure in a similar period?

- The number of officially registered companies throughout Russia had risen to an impressive 2.71 million by the 1 January 1998. 73.1% of these were private companies of which 844,000 were small, with less than five employees.[7] This explosion to 2.71 million companies has to be compared with only 900,000 registered companies in early 1996.[8] In 1996, 15% of Russia's total labour force was employed by the newly emerging private sector. Today the same statistic shows that 60% of all employees earn their living within the private market place. Not all of this is due to creation of new enterprises, but through the rapid privatisation process.

The message indicated above was clear. Private enterprise was dominant across the land. People had money in their pockets and were spending it on Western imports with gusto. At the same time state-owned industries were still struggling. Yet the balance of the two sectors showed, combined, a modest economic growth. Government and its policies were being overtaken by a population determined on self-help out of their morass. These were the multitude of faces to be seen in the centre of the city on the 9 May, taking a well-earned rest from their labours.

---

[6]Source, VNIKI. All Russia Market Research Institute. Quarterly Review No. 1, February 1998.
[7]Source, VNIKI. All Russia Market Research Institute. Quarterly Review No. 1, February 1998.
[8]Source, VNIKI. All Russia Market Research Institute. Quarterly Review No. 1, February 1998.

But was I witnessing the fruits of real wealth creation? Or was it an outward manifestation of a 'House of Cards'? Was it built on a solid foundation, or on sand? Past letters have expressed much concern about the apparently true state of the land and its people. Previous words have described a country that would take many years to reach what we call economic 'normality'. Yet suddenly I was experiencing a different phenomenon. Contentment of Muscovites with their new-found lot. Pleasure at the fruits of their labours. All around me in the last few months I had seen and felt a new Russia seemingly really emerging. Despite a change of government and apparently despite the emerging talk of another looming financial crisis. According to many commentators the economy was at last on the mend. The optimists even predicted the first growth in GDP since 1991. If true, then I would have to eat many of the negative words I had spent hours compiling in the past. So where is the source of this new-found energy? Who has driven this engine of apparent growth? What was the basis of reality for such confidence on this balmy spring day in the heart of Moscow? Who was correct? The outward joyful expression witnessed on that 9 of May, or my past messages of gloom and despondency? Was occasional talk of devaluation based of the usual Russian ability to make a drama out of nothing? Let me therefore delve a little closer into the 'apparent realities' of the new 'market economy' and describe some aspects of the economic motor of recent months. In past letters I have spoken many times about the 'oligarchy', mostly in negative ways. A better description of them, who they are and what they own, may be a good place to start to understand the commercial frenzy of the last few years.

Quite where their collective title came from is not clear to me. So I sought a definition. The term 'oligarchy' is described in the Oxford English dictionary in three ways.

- Government in the hands of a few.

- Government by the few.

- A form of government in which the power is confined to a few persons or families.

In past days working in the West Midlands in the UK an employee of my then employer said without a trace of envy: 'I see the gaffer has a new Rolls Royce, things must be good for the whole company, including me.' Thus the empires created by the oligarchy and others attracted by Russia's market potential had benefited more than a few in the same vein of thought. Some had estimated that the new financial sectors created in Russia had created more than five hundred thousand new jobs. With these employment opportunities had come restaurants, new shops, new businesses and a wider choice of goods and services across the land. Moscow had the lion's share. But never mind, it was profitable and lucrative employment compared to former days. So how could these oligarchs be all bad?

It would appear that business was not their only concern. Involvement in government to enhance their wealth and power was also on the agenda. Hence the apt title to the group. *The Economist* of the 4 April 1998 described the key players in this powerful group as 'The Tycoons behind the Politicians' in an article about who really runs Russia's new government. This article shows better than I can the extent of their influence in all walks of Russian life. I repeat part of the chart produced in *The Economist* which included the relative political importance of their empires. Please remember that many of their new-found interests either did not exist in 1991, or were then under state control. They had truly been extremely active in six short years.

The Economist also lists another column in that article,

but not repeated here. This is headed 'Political Friends' and shows, among others, the following names: Viktor Chernomyrdin; the Yeltsin family circle, Anatoly Chubais, Yuri Luzhkov and Grigory Yavlinski. The import of the article is totally clear. This group of individuals who control vast slabs of Russia's oil, gas, media and trading sectors are seen by many as the true powers behind the political throne. As mentioned in a past letter, we are talking about big financial numbers here. *The Sunday Times*[9] put Berezovsky with £1.87 billion as the 39th richest man in Europe and Kodorkovsky at 49th with an estimated wealth of £1.5 billion. However one wants to cut the cake of Russian finance, industry and commerce, these people represent true financial power. In a past letter, I had quoted Berezovsky claiming in interview with the *Financial Times* that his 'group of seven who met at the Davos Economic Forum – the oligarchs', those listed as number 2 to 8 in the league of power below controlled some fifty per cent of Russian economic activity. I cannot prove that figure. But their interests are undoubtedly huge. Between them they have created new banking and trading industries which now employ many thousands of middle-class Russians. This new middle class was among the many who are to be found enjoying the fruits of their labours on the 9 May celebrations of earlier description. The influence of employment of their ultimate commercial masters is felt in all corners of Russia, but Moscow is where their true power lies. There too are to be found many of their most ardent fans. These are the many who have reaped personal rewards and the 'benefits' of the new-found consumer society.

---

[9]*The Sunday Times*, 19 April 1998.

Group	Main Man	Financial Vehicle(s)	Industrial and Media Interests	Place in League Table of Power
GazProm	Rem Vyakhirev	Bank Imperial (with Lukoil), GazProm Bank, National Reserve Bank	GazProm (oil & gas). *Trud* magazine. *Rabochaya Tribuna*. NTV (with Most)	1
Berezovsky	Boriz Berezovsky	Obyedienny Bank, LogoVAZ	Sibneft [10] (oil), ORT (TV and two other papers/magazines. Some also say possible interests in Aeroflot.)	2
Uneximbank	Vladimir Potanin	Uneximbank, MFK Renaissance	Sidanko (oil) Norilsk Nickel, Svyazinvest (tel.), *Komsomolskaya Pravda*, *Russky Telegraf*, *Isvestia* with (Lukoil)	3
Lukoil	Vagit Alekperov	Bank Imperial (with GazProm)	Lukoil (oil), *Isvestia* (with Uneximbank)	4
Menatep	Mikhail Kodorkovsky	Bank Menatep	Yukos (oil), some trading firms, independent media	5
Most	Vladimir Gusinsky	Most Bank	*Sevodnya* (paper) Itogi, NTV (with GazProm)	6
SBS-Agro	Alexander Smolensky	SBS-Agro Bank	*Kommersant* (paper)	7
Alfa	Mikhail Fridman	Alfa Bank	Tymen Oil, trading firms	8

What is also abundantly clear to any follower of modern Russia is that thousands of words have been written about these people and their activities. Some of them good, but most of them cautious about how the empires were assembled and what political influence was used to assist the speed of creation of these groupings. I do not want to add more to them here. The chart and its implications say more than enough. Looking more closely at the chart above shows that the empires are made up of five basic components. Oil, gas, minerals, communication, media (mainly press and TV) and trading. Almost no amounts of money appear to have been invested in the stagnant and moribund industrial and manufacturing base of the country. The more the pity for Russia itself. Jobs in trading, media,

---

[10]Sibneft denies Berezovsky has any interest in its shares.

finance etc. may be glamorous, but in other countries these sectors are but froth built upon the real core of wealth creation – manufacturing. Were the crowds in Moscow described earlier just the outward manifestation of that froth?

The oligarchs were not alone in building commercial empires. Others, with a more positive view of investment risks than I, had also participated in the creation of new jobs, building new factories or partaking in the frenzy of making money out of money. Each day in 1997 new commercial entrants into the Russian market were emerging. Russian entrepreneurs were gaining in confidence and reaping due rewards for their hard work and long hours, just as a multitude of foreigners were beginning to examine the potential that rebirth of the Russian market appeared to offer now and into the future. The scenario described by Professor Layard in his book *The Coming Russian Boom,* whose contents and conclusions I had questioned in earlier pages, appeared to have found favour at last. Let me list some of the better news that excited the eager latent Russian capitalist who enjoyed that early spring day in May.

- Fiat, together with ERBD (the European Bank for Reconstruction and Development) signed an agreement with the GAZ motor company in Nizhny Novgorod on the 11 February 1998 to create a new venture to be called Nizhny Novgorod Motors.[11] The target was some 15,000 cars in 1999, 40,000 by the year 2000, and an estimated 100,000 to be assembled by 2005. Over time this was to represent a total spend of $850 million.

- KKR (Kohlberg, Kravis & Roberts) the US buyout specialists who gained international attention in past

---

[11]Source, *New Europe* magazine, 22–28 March 1998.

financial coups[12] reopened negotiations with the KamAZ truck company in Naberezhnyye Chelny to find some $3.5 billion by the year 2000 to revitalise this major Russian market sector.[13]

- Berezovsky's original conception, LogoVAZ, founded in 1989 had by 1997 grown to be Russia's largest car dealership with sales estimated at $500 million. With franchises for General Motors, Volvo, Daewoo, Chrysler, Mercedes, Honda and Russia's AvtoVAZ this company was selling some 40,000 cars per annum.[14]

- The GAZ motor company in Nizhny Novgorod was considered the jewel in Russia's home-grown car industry and had scored a hit with its innovative small van. It had seen a market gap for a small one and a half tonne van for the multitude of new enterprises engaged in trading. Selling at between $8,000 and $15,000, and using Austrian Styer engines made under licence in Nizhny Novgorod, between 1996 and 1997 sales had tripled. Over a two-year period, production had risen from 14,000 to 56,000 units.

- In Russian-made passenger cars, growth was also self-evident. 1997 saw a growth of 13.5% in local production. This helped by the increase in ownership from 90 to 106 cars per 1,000 people in the population in the years 1996 and 1997.[15]

- Market gossip told us that General Motors, Ford, Skoda among others were all considering investing in the new Russia.

---

[12]Made famous in the book *Barbarians at the Gate*.

[13]The *Moscow Times*, 29 October 1997.

[14]The *Moscow Times*, 23 September 1997.

[15]The *Moscow Times*, 28 April 1998.

- Sir Rocco Forte was investing in Russia's hotel industry. From the prestigious Astoria Hotel in St Petersburg to new projects in provincial cities like Nizhny Novgorod he saw major Russian opportunities.

- Oleg Leonov, a dynamic twenty-eight-year-old, represented the aspirations of many young Russian businessmen. In 1992 he had founded the Uniland cash-and-carry chain. From tentative beginnings he had managed to double sales each year from 1994 to 1997. That last year saw a turnover of $500 million. His sales estimate for 1998 was a further doubling of turnover. Through outlets in twenty-two cities stocking some seven thousand, mainly Western, brands, he had truly created a new consumer empire for his estimated two hundred and fifty thousand customers.[16]

- The Turkish-owned Ramstore had opened a 6,000-square-metre supermarket in Moscow in 1998. Plans were underway for a further four in 1999.

- GUM, the former prestigious department store which sold foreign goods to the Communist apparatchik in days gone by had refurbished, grown and in 1997 was seeking a further $100 million investment to increase selling space from 16,500 to 32,000 square metres. They were planning to give room to three hundred franchised stores from the current one hundred and twenty.

- The market for PCs had risen to some $1.5 billion. In 1991 it was virtually nil, as ownership of computers was restricted in former times. Russian assembly accounted for between two thirds and three quarters of this figure. The indigenous Vist company claimed between one fifth and one quarter of total Russian PC sales. A sector

---

[16]The *Moscow Times*, 12 May 1998.

created from nothing seven years ago.

- Moscow's best known mineral water, St Springs had sales approaching $40 million and nearly three hundred new jobs had been created at the factory in Kostrama as well as the sales office in Moscow since its inception in 1994.

- Multinationals from Procter & Gamble to Unilever were investing in margarine, washing powder, cosmetics manufacture in Moscow, Novomoskovsk and St Petersburg. R J Reynolds and BAT were active building cigarette factories. Cadbury had invested $120 million in a new chocolate plant in Chudova. Mars was busy in its new plant in Stupino. Caterpillar was preparing to assemble excavators in St Petersburg.

- The investment bankers were active in droves. Speculative money was pouring into the country and following the supposed holy grail of the GKO (treasury bill) market.

- GazProm, the B-Line mobile phone company, among others, was floating on the New York stock market with spectacular effect.

Examples of rising investment, both Russian and foreign, were endless. Jobs were being created in all sorts of industries in a multitude of places. Moscow alone was not the only beneficiary of the money flowing into the country to feed the capitalist dream. Russians and foreigners alike viewed the future with confidence. The private sector was truly growing with verve and energy. At the same time the shadow economy was keeping pace. Estimates at the low end put this part of wealth creation at twenty-three per cent of GDP.[17] Others told us it was as high as forty per cent. Whatever the truth, the confidence and contentment expressed on the 9 May by the crowds in central Moscow appeared to be well founded. So it seemed that I had been wrong all along in my gloomy predictions. There was to be no revolution. No rejection of a corrupt administration. No hardship for the people. Life was good and was predicted to improve for the regions as well. So why had I been worrying about their future? Clearly Russians and wiser foreigners had seen something that I had not.

But doubt still nagged in my mind. A closer examination of the inward as well as local investments and the flood of money indicated that the bulk was flowing into more and more imports of consumer goods. Trading appeared to be the priority. The bankers were also apparently having a field day. It seemed to me that paper investments took priority over physical investments. But speculative money has rarely fostered real investments. Imports helped little to regenerate the state of Russian manufacturing plants. Bankers lending funny money to each other for speedy gains helped no one but themselves in the short term. I still was unconvinced that the corner had been turned.

But then matters started going wrong… or were they rotten at the core all the time?

Economic bubbles have a nasty habit of bursting. In the process the rush of putrid air from the rotten core of the bubble begin to affect us all. Despite all the efforts described above, it was suddenly beginning to become abundantly apparent that the economic boom of the last few years had been built on sand. The past process of swapping sufficient oil, mineral and other natural resources

---

[17]GOSKomstat.

for consumer goods was stalling. Falling world commodity prices were seeing to that. The generated wealth of the country was flowing into foreign bank accounts and not reaching the people. Wages were still not being paid, with the regions most affected. The flood of good news was suddenly being replaced by an increasing flow of bad.

- Consistent press talk of devaluation was gaining momentum. Few Western observers had observed the Russian banks themselves beginning a slow but certain retrenchment from the start of 1998. It appeared they knew something we had as yet not grasped.

- On the 13 May, the Tokobank, one of Russia's twenty largest banks was placed into administration.

- For parts of June and July the country was cut in half through the blockages caused by hundreds of unpaid miners on the Trans-Siberian railway – a lifeline for the eastern regions.

- In an interview with the *Financial Times* in May, Alexander Lebed was quoted as saying, 'The Russian economy is squeezed between two rocks – the lawless Mafia and the greedy bureaucrats. In Moscow it's a funny thing, the Mafia turns out to be gentler than the state. The Mafia takes just ten per cent, the state takes everything.' The article had a prophetic title – 'Boris the Younger'.

- Tax police started raiding the flats of foreign residents in Moscow in June and July. Their target was not the Western occupant, but the owners who had apparently not registered their income for tax returns. In one way this was good news, as it implied a crackdown on tax evasion. On the other hand it began to scare the Western community to realise that all was not at all well with fundamental economic checks and balances.

- Whole communities were feeling the brunt of the non-payment cycle. In Kostrama two hundred kilometres north of Moscow, the local energy supplier was owed $90 million. Forty per cent of this was due from the city fathers. So all hot water and electricity were cut off. At the same time in Vologda, some three hundred kilometres further north, they were seeking an injection of state funding of some Rbl.89 million to assist in job-creation programmes. The authorities had their priorities reversed. The new prime minister, Kyrienko, was due to visit to discuss the matter. So five kilometres of new road were laid to ensure he had a pleasant journey from the airport.

'...And I will throw in a set of steak knives.'

- On the 27 May the sale of the largest remaining state-owned oil company failed. RosNeft was expected to contribute up to $2 billion to state coffers. In the end there were no takers. Either from the West or from within Russia. Not only had falling world oil prices taken their toll, but the desire to invest within Russia was suddenly stalling. As usual The *Moscow Times* had a humorous comment on the 28 May.

• It was revealed in July that the mammoth United Energy Systems company, which is the largest energy supply company in the whole of the Federation was responsible for one fifth of all non-payments in the economy. Threats were reverberating around the country that if customers did not pay their bills then lights across the land would be extinguished. Computers powering critical machinery, hospitals, factories, homes would all be affected. Little wonder that those selling generating sets were reputed to double sales. The snowball effect of non-payment between gas, coal and electricity suppliers was under severe threat. Barter had been used in the past. You have coal – okay, I will supply you with electricity. But even barter is a sale which attracts taxes under the law. So the state at last stopped talking. It wanted its dues. It started to act. They could just not pay the bills with existing resources. The barter system had started to hit the buffers.

• Yet some continued to fuel the unsustainable bubble. The property developers were pushing the line that Russia only had 0.12 square metres of retail space per inhabitant compared to Germany with 1.2 and the US with 2.3.[18] Possibly true, but was there a comparable level of disposable income? When bubbles burst, it seems to me that property often falls victim first, despite the rhetoric.

---

[18]Source, Nobel Gibbons property consultants in Moscow.

There's a fire to put out! The *Moscow Times*, 4 July 1998

Talk of impending crisis increased. People started to do their mathematics. The short term GKO debt, the tumbling bank assets, increasingly unpaid wages, an increase of the non-payment cycle and the faltering tax collections led to headlines like 'Devaluation will send Banks into Insolvency'.[19] And then just as suddenly reality returned:

1 July: The first crisis bills were placed before the Duma.

3 July: The government launches tax raids to seize GazProm's assets for unpaid back tax.

6 July: The ERBD and the Bank Moscow pulled out of the Tokobank rescue. On the same day the sale of RosNeft is finally abandoned.

---

[19]The *Moscow Times*, 30 June 1998.

9 July: Twelve out of fourteen regions announced default on repayment of agricultural bonds.

More such depressing comment hit the headlines. This was just the tip of another spiral suddenly out of control. After the political crisis and Communist collapse of 1991 and the dramatic events in 1993, this late spring and summer of 1998 would add one more dreary chapter to the woes of modern Russia. The news turned from former capitalist hectic to herald a return to another unfolding crisis that called an abrupt end to thoughts of a new Russian dawn. That was on hold once again despite an injection of significant funds from the International Monetary Fund. How deep the crisis must have been is best demonstrated by the incredibly short timescale, just weeks, between receipt of over $3 billion of IMF funds and the calamitous events about to engulf us all.

It was then revealed later in the month that up to $500 million per day were being used by the Central Bank to prop up a falling Rouble. The precious national currency reserves were depleting fast. This capitalist hectic was truly built on sand. The house of cards came tumbling down around our ears. Suddenly, less than three months from that apparently comforting springtime day in May in central Moscow, the world for the whole Russian population was falling apart once more. It hurt us all, not just in this complex land. The reverberations of collapse began their waltz around far distant lands. Beware the tidings for 1999.

One month before on the 5 June, Yeltsin in his weekly radio address to the nation said: 'The worst of the country's financial crisis is over'. On the same day Alexander Lebed was sworn in as the newly-elected governor of Krasnoyarsk. In a press conference after the ceremonial he said: 'All the blood has flown to the head... I am afraid the country might have a heart attack...'

And so it did.

Chapter XVII
A House of Cards
October 1998

Domestic dramas held part of my attention during the early part of August. As well as having locked myself out of the flat for a whole morning, my eldest daughter showed her virgin skills at the roulette wheel. Let me explain. The bunch of keys to get into my flat is large. Worn trouser pockets dictate that not all six locks on the entrance to the block and the two doors to the flat are in regular use. Despite thoughts of security, two of them were thus rejected. Also in view of the fact that the post box downstairs has no lock, I regularly pried it open with one of my keys. This turned out to be a critical mistake. Not having paid attention to the wear on this key and getting worse, it finally gave up the ghost. But not before I had shut the inside flat door, ruining the tumbler lock in the process. So there I was outside, with no sensible means of return. What to do, having two business visitors from abroad to entertain, and the papers needed being inside as well. As usual my secretary saved the day. A locksmith was called. After repeated attempts that even baffled him, there was only one solution – cut out the recalcitrant lock. Not so easy as it sounds, because that demands a drill or even a saw. Those familiar with the stairwell of a Russian block of flats will know that there are no plugs to garner an electrical supply. So with true ingenuity we managed to find just enough electrical flex, of dubious safety, to reach the nearest plug in a suspicious neighbour's flat and cutting began. It took over thirty strenuous minutes to complete the deed. Four hours after having locked myself out, at last I was back in. We did manage to hold one of the business meetings in the stairwell. So remember that erroneous use of flat keys to pry open broken Russian post boxes can be a dangerous practice.

As for the roulette experience, that was even more illuminating. My eldest daughter, Katherine, was on a flying visit to Moscow before her second climbing trip around the world. By a happy coincidence an old school friend of hers was touring Russia with her boyfriend, a British exchange student at the university in Voronezh. A joint trip to St Petersburg was thus agreed upon. Those with daughters, even those past their teenage days, will all know that Dad has to pay the bills. This trip was no exception. On the last evening in St Petersburg, after, as usual, paying for the evening meal, I rebelled and told them that they now had to feed me with some vodka. Clearly we had all imbibed too much, because later that evening they were introduced to the delights of casino life. It was a first for my three young companions. None of us was suitably dressed for such a place of sin, but never mind. I stupidly let them have the base stake of $100 and off we went. None of them knew the rules, but that made no difference. My daughter, slightly more than tipsy, with a grim determination to succeed, quickly piled up the chips, even though after half an hour she said, 'Am I doing this correctly?' The young man to her left who tried to gain her attention on more than one occasion, got short shrift. On asking the next day why she had not responded to his advances, she replied, 'I never saw him.' She certainly had had too much of the spirit. By 3 a.m. Katherine, and her friend Theresa had amassed the princely sum of $450 between them. I was back to zero. Not bad for amateurs who had never stepped inside a casino before. Theresa and Ed stayed long after my departure to bed. They recounted the next morning that they had protested at their poor treatment when they believed they had just scored the jackpot. The management of the establishment had even taken them into the inner sanctum for argumentative types. A likely story. But at least all three paid for meals for days thereafter.

With more serious events about to break, it seemed upon reflection that these three young people should have been employed by the Russian government to manage national finances. With the luck they showed that August evening in St Petersburg, they could have done better than all the best brains in Russia's financial community put together. But maybe that latter group of people thought their roulette was of the Russian kind. On the 17 August 1998, Russia certainly shot itself in the head. As the nursery rhyme says:

> Humpty Dumpty sat on a wall,
> Humpty Dumpty had a great fall,
> All the king's horses and all the king's men,
> Couldn't put Humpty together again.

The 17 August turned out to be a day when Humpty Dumpty wished he had stayed in bed. Shattered dreams of rebirth were witnessed by all across the Federation from that fateful day forward. Some saw the end of the world, for others it was merely disastrous. Even the exporters of Russian oil, gas and minerals who initially rubbed their hands with glee later had to eat their words. The speed and severity of events that followed caught us all off guard. How could this happen? Why so quickly? Capitalist Hectic had turned to instant melt down. The work of six years to build anew was about to be washed away in weeks.

Dubinin and Kiriyenko: 'We're just going to change the ruble's trajectory.' The *Moscow Times*, 18 August 1998

In subsequent months, resurgent black Russian humour would tell many stories about the crisis. One went like this '…Boris had told us we were standing in front of an economic abyss. Today we took a great step forward.' Well, Dubinin (governor of the Central Bank) and the young Prime Minister Kiriyenko had certainly helped Russia take such steps. Both men will probably remain as no more than footnotes in history. Such is their legacy and that of their political predecessors. Little did they realise in which direction this would all lead. But on that day neither did the rest of us. Russia had solemnly buried the last tsar and his family on the 17 July in St Petersburg. Just one month later they buried all thoughts of foreseeable prosperity.

Questions on many lips were: 'How many more such dramas can the Russian people endure?' 'What had the pain of restructuring and reform brought the Russian people in the last seven years?' Well the second is one that has a simple answer. Not much, apart from a few shiny Western consumer toys. However, it might be prudent to start elsewhere. It might be better to ask what went wrong first. Was the crash the fault of:

- Falling world commodity prices?
- A severe dose of Asian economic flu?
- Incorrect IMF advice?
- Bungled and mismanaged internal reform?
- Greedy 'New Russians' and apparatchik raping the country?
- Botched and hasty privatisation?
- Parasitic banks helping themselves and not the real economy?
- Lack of political leadership with no national and cohesive purpose?
- Unregulated capitalism?
- Trading in imports rather than local manufacturing?
- Russia's national sport of revelling in drama?

Indeed, others might add further reasons. Upon reflection, it seems too simplistic to say it was one or the other. Or even just a combination of some of the above. Of course internal Russian factors played the dominant role in these sad events. Blaming others alone was not always helpful either. Luzhkov told us that the IMF and its policies were at fault in an interview with the *Financial Times* on the 23 September. He repeated his assertion on more than one later occasion. We should delve deeper to find more subtle truths. As usual we learn little from history. More often than not when social or economic catastrophes occur in our fickle world, the hidden reason may better be found in a crisis of ideas.

In this ever-globalising world we often fail to see that clash of ancient, ethnic and nationalistic ideas confronting more modern desires to reduce world economics to a fifteen inch television screen or personal computer. An instant sound bite. The fact is that we are not all the same. Few of us want to be. Indeed, our international community would be a very boring place if we all had to be clones of one or other ideology or system. But the international community expects us all to play by the same rules. Certainly in economic terms. Yet the same community has no institutions of substance and leadership. In that respect Luzhkov was correct in his views about the IMF. In this instant world of the Internet and global stock and money-market gyrations we wake up to news of Tokyo and go to bed with New York. Our life is dominated by one set of rules made up by financiers who seldom look up from a computer screen. The only rules of note are 'Capitalism the way the West demands'. Here in Russia this new demand for immediacy is no different, but in my belief misplaced. Fledgling economies coming to terms with new-found concepts of democracy and capitalism, need time and understanding to emerge. Yet we in the West judge them as having instant adherence to principles and systems it took us years to learn. Professor Gudarov of the Moscow State University may have answered Russia's problems more succinctly in his book *The Paradox of Russian Reform*.

Gudarov argues his case passionately and with some justification. Hopefully my simplistic analysis of his message does not detract from the validity of the thesis. He points the finger of Russia's problems at the fundamental clash of the management of three ideals and systems. For Russians, he says, the new-found democratic freedoms are still but a dream. How can such principles, which had no vigorous roots or history here, be accepted overnight. After all, it took us in our countries in the West, generations to achieve our imperfect interpretation of democratic rule. Even we argue about its management more often than not. The same applies to capitalism as introduced into this land. He criticises neither system. But he concludes that if both these ideas are to take root and flourish in this vast and diverse country, then the methods employed to encourage that process cannot be managed by people still steeped in the methodology of autocratic Bolshevism. He neither criticises the Bolshevik idea, nor supports it. He simply observes three systems in conflict. However, as we all know any pure ideology can fail through mismanagement of its fundamentals. Thus, he argues that the introduction of Western capitalistic market reforms based on democratic principles will fail in Russia if managed by those of adherence to former methods of government. This analysis may not be new, but I for one believe it to be true, having experienced Russian life at first-hand over the last nearly four years.

Democracy and capitalism need checks and balances. They need a safety net. They need time to mature in the minds of a willing populace. They presuppose that restructuring is by example, not by one rule for a few and another for the majority. Democracy is a national idea, as of course is pure Bolshevism. But capitalism as practised here today is based on individual unregulated greed for the fortunate few and not on cohesive teamwork. Methods and cultures thus clash. Who among the modern leaders in this country comes from a democratic stable of our definition? Those who class Gaidar, Chubais, Yeltsin et al as reformers are mistaken. They have fundamentally failed that test, because the framework they used for reform was shock, coercion, the usual Russian political imposition within a legal and constitutional framework that still has roots in Bolshevik thought. Within a mindset still in the comforting and regulated past, only part of the population was willing to accept these new ideas. The majority accepted they were just the usual pawns in a power struggle at the centre. These were the measures of former tsarist and Communist times. Only window dressing was improved for modern consumption. The need for public relations was one lesson they learned well and fast, particularly when it came to borrowing money. Yet we judge them as having instant adherence to our definitions of democracy and capitalism. They do not. But then why should they? Because we say so? What arrogance on our part.

Does this look familiar? MV = PT. No, not a formula of Einstein's creation. It is the creation of a Mr Fisher, an American economist in the 1920s who called it, 'The Quantity Theory of Money'. It is a self-evident truth across the world that there are as many interpretations of economic theory as there are economists. However, even if you are a disciple of theorists as diverse as Adam Smith, Keynes, or Milton Friedman, you will still approve of the formula. M equals the mass of money, V is the velocity it turns over in an economy, P is the price level the economy works at and T represents the number of transactions. Some interpret T as Gross Domestic Product – GDP. Anyway you say this is boring stuff. Well yes and no. What matters in the context of an examination of the problems facing Russia today is how you play with the formula. The difference between the economic view of life is not the formula itself, but the value you place on each component. Thus one should treat each country differently depending upon the individual circumstances or economic cycle in which it finds itself within its curve of development. The globalisation of our individual economies, the daily washing of billions of $s, DM, FF or ¥ around the world, demands we use the same monetarist theories to control diverse situations. According to the IMF we all have to use the same harsh strictures. Did they work in Asia? No. Fisher's formula was now interpreted equally within a developed European or US economy as it was to that in Russia. Because the so-called 'reformers' here danced to the tune of Western voices, money was forthcoming. But what was more important was lost and never used. An understanding of the special and very different circumstances of the Russian mentality, past social and economic structures as well as its turbulent history and most of all endemic corruption. None of that could be placed within an interpretation of economic formula of Western imposition.

Thus I believe that Professor Gudarov has found the true reasons for the economic crash that was to be so painful for us all. The misuse of economic formula adds further food for thought to the conclusions. The West must learn that not all transitions should be managed by their rules. Instant globalisation is no answer. Failure to under-stand what happened and continued Western lecturing will only drive this fledgling country into an old idea in new clothes. Nationalism. New leaders will emerge who preach that message. That could be even more uncomfortable for us and for them.

My friends in Moscow and in the regions were less concerned than I about economic theory or diatribes about ideas. They were in the painful business of learning to live with another daily mess. Lessons from their painful experiences in 1991, past levels of hyperinflation and the currency reform in 1993 helped. But it did not recover their savings they had worked so hard to achieve over the last difficult years. Roger's friend Olga was understandably anxious to obtain her $5,000 from the Rossiskycredit Bank.

Irina and Sasha sought to recoup their accumulated savings of $16,000 from the Alfa Bank. Dima and Svetlana struggled for weeks to extract $3,000 from SBS-Agro Bank. They had worked hard and saved, and all for naught. They had overcome past fears and trusted new-found banking empires to manage their money. Others, with no savings in the banks just faced resulting shortages, lengthening dole queues and rising inflation with faltering confidence in their uncertain future.

Soros tells us that Russia's financial system is at a terminal phase.
The *Moscow Times*, 14 August 1998

History has recorded the headline facts of that time in August 1998 in Russia and beyond. The fallout across the globe will still be felt long after these words are history. Some will tell you this house of cards was triggered by George Soros's letter to the *Financial Times* on the 13

August 1998, telling us that, 'Russia's financial system is at a terminal phase.' As explained above, I believe it had deeper roots. Some have been alluded to above. But enough of that. To more pressing problems. My mother reminded me that she had painful memories of similar events in Germany of the thirties. Were we to return to that? What therefore was life like in Moscow in those darkening autumn days? It certainly got harder. It certainly tested the ingenuity of many. As frustration grew and tempers sometimes frayed, let me therefore return to the reality of life with crisis and record events that either caught my attention, or affected me as well as my friends. No one in this land was spared. We all had stories to tell. Some events mentioned below caught my attention, just because they were bizarre. Few of them were really funny. Just tragic. Your papers and electronic media had most of the headlines – for once correct – but then other happenings began to dominate your news. Among them: Monica Lewinsky and the impeachment process for Clinton; the German parliamentary elections; Kosovo and those dreadful scenes; the crash of Western financial markets following Asia's and Russia's problems and many more.

In early August it became clear to all here that something bad was going on as the Moscow stock exchange crashed and trading had to be suspended on more than a few days. The currency exchange suffered the same fate and some of the major banks such as SBS-Agro and Inkombank each received loans of some $100 million to continue trading. Later it was revealed that the bulk of IMF advances had been used to prop up an ailing Rouble instead of proper use within the economy. So what did daily life bring to us? Here is a flavour of some Milestones of Collapse. The city was a rumour mill; if some comment made below is based on that, my apologies in advance but I experienced most events or heard and read most comments.

Yeltsin and Clinton said they didn't lie…
The *Moscow Times*, 19 August 1998

17 August

- Kiriyenko devalues the Rouble from 6.2 to the $, stating that all he has done is widen the trading band to an expected 9.5 by the year end. At the same time he announces default (he called it a moratorium) of some $40 billion of government GKO debt. Both turned out to be wide of the mark. By mid-September the /$ rate was 21 to 1, and estimates of total debt default rose to $200 billion. The largest ever, by any nation anywhere at any time.

- Rumours began to circulate that Yeltsin did not attend the critical meeting at which the devaluation decision was taken. Indeed some said he knew nothing about devaluation or default until the following morning – an hour or so before the deed was done. Later comment by government officials, including Primakov, appears to confirm that.

- The commercial banking system stalls. Only the state-owned Sberbank continues normal working. Small groups gather outside banks to seek their savings with little success.

- Clinton testifies to the Grand Jury in Washington admitting 'improper conduct'.

- The Rouble falls by 8.7% against the $.

18 August

- Zuganov tells the West not to invest in Yeltsin.[1] 'I want to warn all investors, including Western ones: …If you continue to give money to save a debauched, rotten, immoral person who is incapable even of guiding himself, then you must share the responsibility for the morasmus that now exists in this country.'

- Commercial banks remain 'open' but are 'shut'. The exchange booths in the street start to determine the true exchange rate.

- The government announces that first half-year exports for 1998 have fallen by 13% and imports have risen by 12.8%.[2]

20 August

- All effective banking transactions, private and commercial, are stopped. Commercial cash collections are thus forced to stop.

---

[1] The *Moscow Times*.
[2] Economic Ministry via Interfax.

- Companies begin to wonder how to pay month-end salaries without an effective banking system. What rate to use? How to set sales prices? How to value stock?

- Sales calls start to become difficult. All relevant executives are in crisis meetings.

- The 'official' exchange rate is declared at 6.99 to the $. The street says around 8.

- Having tried five exchange booths, I can't get any Roubles. Even by waving $ bills about. Where have they gone?

- The major hotels are full of Western bankers seeking clarification of their losses. The sums involved are above the decision-making level of local management.

- Yeltsin stays at home.

21 August

- The US bombs alleged terrorist bases in Afghanistan and the Sudan. This in retaliation for the dreadful bombing of US embassies in Nairobi and Dar es Salaam. Clinton did not say if he saw the film *Wag the Dog*. For those who did not see it, it depicts a US president who diverts attention from a sex scandal by creating a 'false war'. Good viewing but a bit scary in concept and execution.

- The Central Bank helpfully says 'hundreds of banks' will collapse and announces insurance of private accounts switched to the state-owned Sberbank. Unsurprisingly the population has little faith. Queues outside banks are longer, angrier and usually unsuccessful in getting money and retrieving savings.

- For those who use them, finding a cash machine that

works becomes a new Moscow pastime. Most stop working.

- Government sets up a 'hot line' for worried private investors. It was just a lightning conductor. Not much point in ringing, it was always engaged.

- World stock markets take fright and begin a downward spiral.

- The Moscow Inter-bank currency exchange closes twice during the day.

- The mood in Moscow's middle class turns 'suicidal' as business grinds to a halt.

- The Duma votes 245 to 32 to 'recommend' Yeltsin's resignation.

- Western bankers are offered only 11% settlement of their total debt holdings. Russian banks are promised 33%. Menatep Bank defaults on a large syndicated loan.

- Olga gets $500 from one account, Sasha and Irina have tried for the fourth time and come away empty handed.

23 August

- The economic crisis becomes political as well. Rumours abound that on Friday, 21, some of the oligarchs meet with Yeltsin and decided that Kiriyenko must go. He was destroying their empires they said, never mind Russia. 'As for you Boris,' they said. 'Resign, or if not then reduce your powers and go and open garden fetes, church bazaars or similar. Our chosen man is Chernomyrdin.' The rest of us remembered that he was the fellow who had presided over the build-up to this mess for the last five years. The bottom line is simple. Yeltsin is humiliated but does not go. Kiriyenko is the scapegoat. The second prime minister and government in 1998 is sacked. We are the victims.

24 August

- Real panic sets in. A stampede to the banks and a rush on staple foods begins.

- Banks fail to pay anybody anything of value.

- Kiriyenko says goodbye to the miners camped out by the White House in search of unpaid wages. He apologises for failing them.

- The oligarchs express public satisfaction for removing Kiriyenko.

- Fighting starts in the bank queues. Dima and Svetlana try for the sixth time to get some of their $3,000.

- The Rouble exchange rate is now 13% lower than devaluation day.

- My supermarket runs out of salt and vegetable oil. Intermittent empty spaces appear on the shelves.

25 August

- Can't get either $s or Roubles. Life starts to get a bit more than frustrating. So I stand at the end of an exchange booth queue and wave my $s about. Very quickly the haggling starts. Succeed in changing $200.

- Uneximbank, Most Bank and Menatep Bank announce a merger plan. Am I getting cynical, or is this one company for assets and three remaining companies for debts, which are then allowed to sink?

- Moscow City Council is seen hiring trucks to drive

around the city to ensure enough $s and Roubles are in the exchange booths in the morning to reduce public tension.

- GKO restructuring announced. Payments are frozen for three to five years, and to be repaid in Roubles at that time. Some say that this works out at 3 US cents in the $.

- Germany[3] said that Russia owed them about $42.2 billion in debt, interest payments and credits.

- Western bankers start to announce a growing list of financial losses in Russian bonds and other local exposure. Barclays Bank among them said it lost £250 million. These pages are too small to list them all.

- The Sverdlovsk region begins to discuss a novel way out of crisis. Print their own bank notes and seal their own economy from the rest of the country.

26 August

- Businesses across the land begin to wonder what to do. Over the next weeks the following begins to happen:

    Physical imports grind to a halt. Indeed, imports (mainly food) fall by 45% in the following month. Russian drivers are left stranded with empty lorries in the West. Wages previously paid in Roubles but tied to the $ are cancelled. Now they are paid as well as denominated only in Roubles; some at between 6 to 8 to the $. Thus devaluation turns into pay cuts as well. A double whammy.

    White and brown goods such as TVs, audio equipment etc. sell out and retailers for such goods close

---

[3]*Handelsblatt* quoted Guenter Rexrodt the Minister of Economics.

their doors.

Some 160,000 finance-related employees in Moscow are made redundant, in the current Russian fashion, without any compensation. Similar heavy cuts follow in the regions.

Associated companies; accountants, restaurants, hairdressers, cleaners, pubs, clubs and other service outlets start to feel the pinch. Job cuts are announced all round.

Western investments begin to halt production. Partly through lack of raw materials; part due to collapse in demand; part due to a wild fluctuation in the Rouble exchange rate; but most of all due to a closure of the commercial banking system. Among the many who shut down production for various periods were: Cadbury, Coca Cola, Pepsi Cola, St Springs Mineral Water and Mars.

Johnson and Johnson and Hershey give signals that they may pull their presence out of Russia.

Marketing budgets are frozen across the board. Costs are trimmed to the bone.

Inchcape plc sells its Coca Cola bottling operations for $87 million, some $100 million below the asking price. Losses of $23 million for the year to date are revealed in Russia.

The big six accounting firms begin to retrench. Figures of 40% job cuts among them emerge. Their consultancy practices are mostly closed.

Western banks close investment departments. Their ex-pat staff begin to leave Russia.

Upmarket shops boom temporarily as 'New Russians' buy the last remaining goodies and suddenly they fail. Those who do remain, have sale signs on prominent display. Increasing reductions from 10% to 20% to 30% and then finally 50% off emerge before final extinction.

Russian business is hit particularly hard. But then slowly re-emerges as it has more experience in dealing with such morass. But they also begin to estimate that only 40% of their particular sector of activity may remain intact.

Re-pricing of goods in supermarkets is a daily event as inflation takes hold.

- My local pub runs out of draught beer. Drinkers tail off considerably.

- Sugar, pasta and crisps disappear from the shelves of my local supermarket.

- Official currency trading is suspended after the morning's trading is declared invalid.

27 August

- Imperial Bank has its trading licence withdrawn.

- Chubais says that the economy is in the most dangerous state since 1991.

- Flour, salt and rice become scarce.

- My secretary's usual pet-supply shop runs out of imported cat food.

- The Central Bank announces it wants to nationalise SBS-Agro, the second largest retail and fourth largest Russian bank (by estimated assets). Millions of depositors fear the danger of losing their savings for ever.

- Rouble rate against the $ is 12 on the street. No one knows the official rate.

- Haggling over the appointment of Chernomyrdin and a

government continues in the Duma as well as in smoke-filled rooms.

- World stock markets fall again. The Dow in New York falls 4%.

- Few private depositors are successful in retrieving savings. Chaotic scenes erupt outside banks across the land.

29 August

- George Soros's Quantum Investment Fund says it has lost $2 billion in Russian investments.

- The Russian stock market index (MT) drops to a low of 49.3 points. It had peaked at 571.66 points just one year earlier on the 6 October 1997. This new low level would mean that most of Russia's largest companies, now privatised, with massive resources of oil, gas, nickel, gold, etc., plus others in telecommunication banking and so forth and added together are now worth less than the current market capitalisation of Sainsbury plc (one of the UK's largest supermarkets). Yet still no one wants to buy Russian shares.

- Yeltsin goes on TV and says he will not resign. Some say that his weekend negotiations were more about his personal safety than national considerations.

- Mikoms, one of Russia's largest sausage producers sacks two thousand employees. Apparently 90% of raw meat used in production is imported. Deliveries have stalled.

- Australian and Canadian currencies fall as fear abounds that Russia will start dumping commodities on world markets to raise revenue.

31 August

- The Duma rejects Chernomyrdin for the first time by 253 to 94. The stumbling block is Yeltsin who will not resign or hand over his considerable constitutional powers.

- Barter for staples among the population begins to rise.

- Tax receipts for August fall by 30%. Bank transmissions continue to fail.

- My local pub has beer again, but at double the previous price. Even less customers.

- Olga gets another $1,000 from her bank, but is sacked by her employer. Dima, Svetlana, Irina and Sasha still have nothing.

1 September

- The *Moscow Times* issues a supplement on how business is coping with the situation.

- Western bankers start to crank up the legal mill to sue any Russian institution that moves, in the search to protect their deposits, investments or financial position. Additional lawyers are recruited by major Western law firms to handle increasing litigation among banks. Moving out of Russia and litigation are the only growth industries in town.

- Advertising agencies report a 50% drop in business. Russian TV cuts its schedules.

- Flat rents for foreigners begin to fall. I am told that I could renegotiate 35% off for mine. That is when the contract runs out next February – but not before.

- *Kommersant Daily* reports that Boris's daughter has purchased a castle for the Yeltsin family in Bavaria. No one is surprised at that.

- Clinton arrives in Moscow for a summit of 'lame ducks'.

- One of the world's more irrelevant economic indicators 'The Big Mac Index' falls from $2 to $1.55 as McDonald's raises prices for the said item from 13 to 15.5 Roubles. This must be the smallest price rise around.

- Chubais says that the IMF loan package should be renegotiated. Great, more money to be thrown down the drain!

2 September

- The British Embassy issues cautious advice to local British investments on how to cope.

- Clinton in town. Russian politics on hold.

- The Kremlin denies it will use force against political opponents.

- The European Union expresses concern about the dramatic drop in food exports to Russia. 44% of EU beef, 32% of pork and 29% of poultry exports worth some $6.1 billion in 1997 are now at risk.

- US chicken farmers start to feel the pinch. Their $750 million of exports to Russia, or 8% of US production, per annum are also under threat. Indeed, most shipments have ceased.

- The Tokobank has its trading licence withdrawn.

- Clinton lectures students at the Moscow Institute of

Foreign Relations on the benefits of 'Market Reform'.

- Draught beer runs out again at my local pub.

- Sasha and Irina get $2,000 of their savings. They are told the rest is frozen.

3 September

- Now a *REAL* crisis emerges. Potato blight has affected this year's harvest. Late rains caused the crop to fail. The annual wheat crop at fifty-five million tonnes is the lowest since 1957. Russians mostly ignore politics, they have a habit of turning a blind eye to crisis. But fewer potatoes and less wheat sounds like the beginning of a really serious problem.

- Yeltsin make a fool of himself at the final press conference of the 'lame-duck' summit. He was asked at the post-summit press conference if he would insist on Chernomyrdin's appointment and if he would dissolve the Duma if it refused his choice three times. Realising that an answer was required he started: 'I must say that,' long pause, '…that rather many events will take place in order for us to achieve those results…' long pause (looking at his aides) '…that's all.' Anyone who can interpret what that all means please tell me. Even Clinton looked bemused, and blushed, before the whole room fell about laughing.

- Menatep Bank fires a third of its staff. In Russia compensation or unemployment pay are a thing of the past.

- The Rouble falls to 17 to the $.

- Alexander Lebed tells Clinton that, 'The situation in Russia is more dangerous than in 1917.'

- Cigarettes in the local market rise from a previous 48 to 85 Roubles per carton of two hundred.

- Did you hear the one about the Russian who went into a Moscow bank and said to the teller: 'I have $10,000 in my pocket. Who do I see about opening a bank account?' The teller looked at the man rather puzzled and replied, 'A psychiatrist?'

7 September

- Chernomyrdin is rejected for a second time by the Duma. This time by 273 to 138. Total political stalemate. No one is running the economy, or the country.

- Central Bank Governor Dubinin resigns.

- The Rouble trades between 24 and 31 to the $ in the street exchange booths. If that were sustained, devaluation would be up to 500%, and inflation at …well?

- European exporters begin to feel the pinch. Job losses start in Germany. Particularly hit are milk, dairy, beef and pork producers.

- Petrol prices rise by 40%. Why? Production costs are in Roubles.

- I was told that Nestlé sent many of its local ex-pats home on paid leave till the crisis was over. They did not say when that would be.

- Default begins on lease payments. Such matters as truck, computer and car leases are affected.

- The Russian ice hockey league cuts its season in half. Lack of sponsorship is one reason mentioned.

- My secretary's husband feels the pinch. He is a free-lance director of photography with his own business.

The film industry stops most activity. He starts the search for work.

10 September

- The British Ambassador addresses members of the local UK commercial community on the crisis and seeks to calm the worried audience.

- The Rouble bounces back to 16 to the $.

- The political crisis reaches a turning point. The Communist Party digs its heels in, forcing Yeltsin into humiliating defeat. Thus Yeltsin gives up with Chernomyrdin as potential prime minister and proposes Yevgeny Primakov as his new choice to the Duma.

- The Association of Russian Bankers say that at least 20% of their employees across the Federation have or will lose their jobs. As they are still shut, none of us knows what they are doing anyway. Most think this figure is totally understated.

- Chubais in an interview with *Kommersant Daily* says that the Kremlin lied to the IMF to get the $22 billion loan negotiated in July. Well, he was chief negotiator for the Russian side. He also said the economy would have collapsed in the spring if no loans were forthcoming. He later retracted both statements. What do you believe the truth to be? One of his legacies in these negotiation is the requirement still to repay some $4 billion in 1998, and another $17 billion in 1999 to the international community. The first sum might be just possible. The second is a pipe dream. More default due to come?

- A Unilever spokesman said that its sales in Russia were plunging 'dozens of percentage points' in the last month.

- The army announces it has no food reserves left and is about to tap the food reserves required by the law to be kept for wartime reserves.

- Politics and economics divide the nation and the Duma and paralyse all commercial activity.

- Butter, available only in small quantities in my super-market. It costs 28 Roubles per 250 gram pack. A month ago this same product was 6 Roubles.

Yeltsin and Zuganov bring Russia in for a landing.
The *Moscow Times*, 10 September 1998

11 September

- The Duma accepts Primakov as prime minister. At last a prime minister. To show his faith in the 'listening ears' in the Kremlin, he has his first meeting of signifi-cance in the FSB (formerly KGB) headquarters. He was head of this national security organisation before he became foreign minister.

- Shuttle traders buying goods from Turkey (these are the multitude of small entrepreneurs who sell on the street from their multi-coloured bags), see business drop by 80%. Indeed, Turkey is affected by some $6 billion in lost sales to Russia overall.

- Central currency exchange closes again for the day.

- Alfa Bank sacks 70% of its employees.

- The Dutch parent company of The *Moscow Times* sues SBS-Agro Bank for $200,000. The claim is that this money was transferred via that bank for August staff salaries, but it apparently never came out the other end.

- Storehouse plc (the UK parent company of Mothercare and BHS) is reported in the UK press[4] to be trying to mount a rescue operation for its Russian franchisee, Mannai Corp. In five locations they apparently owe the UK franchiser some $24.9 million.

- Yogurt sells out at my local supermarket.

- Lebed warns of a potential coup. Morale is at breaking point, he says.

- Some shops begin to accept $s as payment. This is illegal under the law. But what else can they do without sufficient Roubles?

12 September

- Gerashenko appointed as the Central Bank governor. He held this post previously under Gorbachev. Some say he has a reputation for 'printing Roubles'. We await with bated breath. He replaces up to five hundred of the key executives within the Central Bank. A clear-out

---

[4]The *Sunday Telegraph*, 30 August 1998.

of the old. Well okay, but hurry up, we have a problem to solve.

- The oligarchs begin to contemplate their future under Primakov. He does not appear too friendly towards them.

- Luzhkov announces price controls in Moscow. He tries with limited success to restrict retail margins to 20%. Some regional governors follow suit. No one is clear how this will work.

- The government announces that total wage and pension arrears to state employees of Rbl.42.4 billion are to be paid in full by Christmas. These include the army, the health and education sector and the wider defence and scientific community. At the pre-devaluation exchange rate that equals $6.8 billion. These figures do not include unpaid wages to local government, and energy-sector employees. Neither are any private-sector figures included.

- The American Chamber of Commerce in Russia reveals in a survey of crisis effects on corporate members that 39% of companies have emergency evacuation plans. 9% said they had invoked part of their evacuation plans already. These corporate respondents employed twelve thousand people before the crash. 57% revealed significant financial losses for their size. Of those who had reduced their work force, some 55% said this was temporary. The other 45% said it was permanent. Oh dear. The crisis is only one month old.

The British were more phlegmatic. They held a survey at the monthly drinks night at the Commercial Section, a fortnight later. Only one question was asked. 'Those badly affected by the crisis please go to the right of the room, those not, please stay on the left.' Only one person remained on the left. He had just opened a fish and chips restaurant, which was booming because he accepted credit cards!

16 September

- After a month of this, matters begin to become more serious. Humour becomes blacker as nerves become more frayed. Still no economic policy from the government. The shelves get emptier. Business still halted. Banks still closed. Boris still not visible.

- Matters have now turned the 1929 crash in the US into a picnic compared to this.

- Allied Pickfords removal services announce they are having their best trading in Russia ever. Business has doubled in the last few weeks. All moves are out of the country.

17 September

- The Rouble printing presses start. Some commentators say that at least one third of the current money supply needs to be printed to pay off past wages and balance the last 1998 quarter's government budget. Guesses on the inflationary effects abound.

- A job fair in Moscow's central district attracts five thousand job seekers by mid-afternoon.

- Negotiations for payment of the second tranche of IMF funds begin.

- Use of credit cards is turned into a lottery. Those restaurants not taking them are empty, even of foreigners.

- My Italian neighbours move out to return to their

warmer home.

- My employer is still engaged in forming legal entities. Although one is now legal, we have no bank account. The opening procedures are delayed because our Western bank has reduced staff too much and cannot cope with the demand for corporate account moves from Russian banks.

- Our other legal entity formation runs into problems. Due to the fall in requirements for office space in Moscow, the city fathers deem that we have to produce a formal lease when presenting formation applications. Oh dear, more bureaucracy.

21 September

- Companies wonder how to pay September wages, as the commercial banks are still not functioning. Others are still worrying about delayed August payments.

- More Clinton and Lewinsky tapes are released. Did you hear the one about the five hundred women who were interviewed by a polling organisation in Washington? They were asked, 'Would you sleep with the President?' 84% replied, 'Not again.'

- Duma deputies suddenly find that the cash machine in their building ceases to function. Even they now complain, as some cannot get their money out of their accounts.

- Rumours circulate that Yeltsin is terrified as a result of what has happened. According to some, he will sign anything placed before him. Except his resignation. A true lame duck president is at the head of the country. He is rarely seen, and Primakov now takes full command. We still await, however, a comprehensive economic policy.

23 September

- Moscow tax authorities threaten to seize the reserves of one of Europe's largest insurance companies, the Allianz. We all wonder why. Do you know? I don't.

- The liquor department in my local supermarket closes. I have to try four stores to find a bottle of whisky. When I eventually track one down, it costs Rbl.650. In August the same was Rbl.247. Help!

- Re-nationalisation of former state assets now back on the agenda. Luzhkov said that the government should seize any property not used for Russia's good.

- The government introduces more effective exchange controls and starts to stabilise the Rouble temporarily. 50% of all exporters' funds must now immediately be transferred into Roubles, and another 25% must be sold via the control of the Central Bank. Exporters join the queue of complainants.

- Cigarettes are now Rbl.120 per carton of two hundred. A trebling since the 17 August.

24 September

- Lehman Brothers, the US banker persuades a British court to freeze the UK-held assets of Uneximbank and Inkombank to try to recover $113 million.

- The government announces a return to central control of alcohol production and sale of spirits over 28% proof. Well that means all the vodka in the land.

- All talk of 'market reform' on hold.

- Hecketts Multiserve lay off all their workers in Magnitagorst. They have not been paid by the steel works, so they cannot pay their employees.

- The weekly satirical paper called *The eXile* adds a new rating symbol to the list of bars and clubs it regularly features. The previous three were 'Fahkie Factor', or bonkability of female customers, guess for yourself what that means; 'Flathead Factor' which debates customer's thuggery level; and 'Foam Factor', which relates to the alleged quality of beer. Now we have the 'Starving Ivan Factor'. In simple terms, the place has closed.

25 September

- The first flurry of snow reminds us that winter is about to come.

- Leaks from government (later confirmed) say that $2.4 billion of foreign loans are assumed to balance the fourth quarter budget. But from where, and from whom? Most believe that any further IMF money is a dream.

- Uneximbank and Inkombank counter sue Lehman Brothers in Moscow for 'defaulting on obligations'. Anything to do with the London law suit?

- My friend, David, leaves Moscow, as part of Cadbury's retrenchment.

28 September

- By now the international stock markets have really joined in the crash. Currency and share gyrations start to panic investors around the world.

- Realisation of an impending global recession begins to dawn. Talk is of the worst global crash since the last war. Yet the US Congress declares its priorities and continues to play partisan games with impeachment proceedings.

- The Russian oil companies start to argue openly with government about the exchange control procedures. As many are owned by the oligarchs, one wonders why. Have they a problem with control over capital flight?

- The Post Office here stops accepting or transporting mail. The non-payment cycle between Russian railways and the Post Office interrupts the service. Some one thousand rail carriages full of mail are held in sidings. The latter owes the former some $15 million. Cash repayment is demanded.

- Japan's largest post-war bankruptcy occurs. The Long Term Credit Bank falls.

- US based 'hedge funds' reveal financial difficulties and are bailed out by US banks.

- Beer now costs Rbl.130, compared to 32 some five weeks before.

- Dima, Svetlana, Olga, Sasha and Irina give up trying to get their savings from the banks.

- Moscow City Council try out an experimental mortgage scheme to get rid of thousands of unsold flats. There are some takers.

- More beggars are visible on the streets.

- Uneximbank is rumoured to have cut salaries by 70% for those still employed. They did not say if directors were included.

- I find a restaurant that takes AMEX cards.

- Tsarilovsky Myaca Kombinat in Moscow reduces production of its meat products by 25%. Difficulties of obtaining raw materials from abroad are the stated cause. Russia's largest chocolate manufacturer – Red October – faces the same fate.

- Tax collections for the month of September are announced to be 50% of budget. The head of the tax service is fired and replaced by Georgy Boos.

30 September

- Primakov appeals to the regional governors not to engage in moves to cede from the centre.

- The city population is trading down in its search for food. Despite empty shelves in most supermarkets my local meat and vegetable market has sufficient. No, the situation of food supply is not better, just the structure changes. The Mafia grip on supermarket food distribution is loosened. Even they cannot stop the multitude of rural farmers now finding space to sell their country goods. Prices turn out cheaper there for us – we have $s, but not for the Russians who do not.

- All main roads into Moscow are blocked for part of the day. Unpaid scientific workers have begun their protest. A sign of things to come?

- My local supermarket is now half empty. You can hold a party in the empty spaces. I cannot get any Camembert or foreign herbs, but limited supplies of Pepsi and Coke reappear.

- Talk increases that the Primakov administration will not last beyond Christmas. Rumours abound that the political elite are gearing up for early elections: Duma and presidential. Lebed and Luzhkov head the list of favourites. But one poll indicated that 27% of Russians would accept Clinton as their president. Can't the US Congress do a deal?

1 October

- Commercial banks still not functioning. This is day forty-six of this particular scenario. Local comment is that they will remain as such for another month at best. Possibly longer. Most of the Western business community has switched to foreign banks and slowly begins to restart limited activity. However, few of us can understand why the tottering Russian banks remain in business. Is there another agenda?

- Flights into Moscow, although mostly empty, are artificially boosted by business passengers carrying bags full of thousands of dollars in cash for their hard-pressed employers to survive.

- The first proper snowfall of the winter. My flat heating has not been switched on from the distant power station, and it is minus 3°C outside. Temperatures have been at this level for a week to date. A search reveals a shop with heaters.

- Moscow's Company Registration Chamber announces that over thirty thousand businesses in Moscow alone have collapsed since the 17 August.

- The nearest cinema now costs Rbl.150, compared to 40 before the crash. But a good evening of 'swashbuckle' is on the agenda to escape from depressive thoughts. The film was *The Mask of Zorro*. And jolly good it was. But then who could resist the charms of Catherine Zeta-Jones? By the way, has Zorro got a Russian brother? We could do with him to save the situation!

2 October

- Moscow Metro workers strike for unpaid wages.

- The liquor department of my local supermarket reopens. The selection is limited to Bulgarian and Georgian wines plus five bottles of Teachers whisky at $94 each! This is really bad.

- One suggestion emerging from behind 'closed door' government debate is the use of the estimated $40 billion cash held in $s 'under the bed' by the population. Open debate begins about the potential closure of exchange booths on the street and the abolition of the use of $s in the country. Now that is a good solution to create a revolution. It did not get beyond the stage of talk. Well for now anyway.

The *Moscow Times*, 3 October 1998

- Two snow leopards die of starvation in Kazan Zoo. The only one left in that region is on its coat of arms.

- Still no economic policy announced by government. Intelligent suggestions on what to do come from all the best sections of society. Vitaly Chepalyga of the Centre for the Support of Youth Initiatives, and a close ally of Zhirinovsky suggests a novel way out of the crisis. Legalise prostitution is his suggestion. Then make them pay their taxes. In his opinion this would raise at least $1.5 billion. He had obviously not read a later interview in The *Moscow Times* with prostitutes on Tverskaya Ulitsa, who were complaining of a 50% drop in business. The business that was forthcoming was at discounted prices of 40%.

- Estimates abound that some 15% of all ex-pats have now left Moscow. Removal companies are having a field day. In my circle of acquaintances, five have gone. A jolly Friday evening at the pub is a thing of the past.

3 October

- My heating is switched on at last. Then switched off again, because a massive water leak sends gallons into the top four floors of my apartment block. Luckily not on my side.

- Changed $100 at an exchange booth. The only notes available are ten Rouble ones. I get 148 such pieces of paper in exchange. The pile is two centimetres thick. And the exchange rate given is lousy.

- British Embassy sees a rise of 200% of registrations per week by worried local UK citizens who had not bothered about such things before. The spokesman explained the reasons for such action as prudent. 'In case evacuation is considered'. Oh dear, do I get my cases packed?

- Taimuraz Balloyer, the general director of Russia's largest brewing chain, Baltika, announced that sales had fallen by 50%.

- The Central Bank announces that capital flight in September was an estimated $2.5 billion. So that is where all the Roubles and $s went.

- I went dancing. No, not a night club, but a dancing class with some Russian friends. Mazurka, Polonaise, Cha Cha etc. Good fun, must do it again.

- Despite wanting to pay my Russian taxes in full, the tax office will not process my declaration, because they do not believe me that I worked from the UK in 1997, with only occasional Russian visits. An argument ensues as to how I was to prove this fact. All they have to do is to look at the entry and exit stamps in my passport, or consult the immigration service. More stupid bureaucracy.

- Zuganov calls for millions to take to the streets in the forthcoming national strike called to protest at unpaid wages, economic collapse and for Yeltsin's head.

- Having complained to my friend James that he never paid his share of restaurant bills, he delivers ten bottles of vodka.

- Mikhail Shuokov, the leader of Russia's Federation of Independent Trade Unions, claims that wage arrears are actually at $13.87 billion at pre-devaluation exchange rates.

- The Japanese government debate some novel ways to solve their own economic malaise. Firstly, to give every citizen – man, woman and child, some one hundred and twenty-five million in all, a voucher for $130 to kick-start spending. Secondly, to introduce 'Happy Mondays'. This would turn an increasing number of Mondays into holidays, in a bid to persuade consumers to go shopping instead of going to work. Now what would Adam Smith think of that?

- Boris is seen at a government reception. Speculation mounts about his health. Some even go as far as debating the cause of the two plasters on his right hand. Intravenous vodka suggests one. The Kremlin spokesman said he had 'burnt his hand'. Ummm...

7 October

- Nikolai Shamrayev, Deputy Minister of Economics, said that August Gross Domestic Product will probably drop by 8.2%, with a fall of 11.5% in industrial production. September would probably be worse, and inflation would hit 230% by December.

- The US complains at dumping by Russian steel producers. In mid-1997 steel was selling at $480 per tonne in the US. By July 1998 this had dropped to $320 per tonne. Russian manufacturers like Magnitagorst Metals in the Urals, or those factories in Novolipetsk and Cherepovets were spoiling the party by selling at $263. To add to world economic problems we were now to face anti-dumping arguments between governments. Someone see sense. Why not start inter-governmental barter. You need chickens. Okay, I have oil.

- Inkombank places notices in its nationwide branches that there would only be money for corporate customers. Private individuals would have to wait.

- The Golden Casino on Leningradsky has a crisis party. This is the casino that has two distinctive features. Both at the entrance. You walk in on a glass-topped goldfish pond, then to be greeted by a sign: 'Leave your guns here'. By all accounts the party was a great success.

And then on the 7 October came the national day of protest. Some had predicted one in five of the total population would be on the streets of every city and town across the land, to demand justice in wage arrears and the removal of Yeltsin. Depending on whom one believes, the local city police, the Kremlin or the organisers, the Communist Party and the unions, the final figure was far short of that. But the point had still been well made. I decided to join the protest in Moscow. It was due to assemble south of the Moskva river and after a short march gather in the square below St Basil's at 3 p.m. To be there on time, I went into the city centre early for a bite of lunch. It was eerie. Traffic was almost non-existent. It was like 5 a.m. on a quiet Sunday morning. Luzhkov had called up eleven thousand police and four thousand interior ministry troops in case of trouble. In my past regular lunchtime haunt, the pizza parlour outside the Intourist Hotel at the bottom of Tverskaya which normally had queues for tables, only six of the fifty were occupied. The unnatural silence of the streets was only interrupted by the plod of feet. All in the direction of the march. By 2.30 p.m. they began to emerge across the Moskvoresky Bridge into the slope below the ancient cathedral. Flags of red, and blue and yellow. Protest banners by the hundreds. For an hour they marched and then the square was full. But still they came and came and came. I did not witness a damp squib of protest as others had reported. Some two hundred and fifty thousand people had made their point. The message was clear. Enough is enough. We want our dues. And who could blame them.

16 October

- Inkombank is placed under administration by the Central Bank. Oh dear oh dear.

- One of our customers strikes a 'happy' note. Having faced melt down themselves, he tells me that things are 'better'. Sales are only 60% of what they were! This is better?

- Printing money has begun in earnest. Having only obtained ten Rouble notes the last time I exchanged money, this time it is only five hundred Rouble notes. The date thereon is 1997. Who is kidding whom?

- As for the ignominious and senile performance by Yeltsin during his visit to Uzbekistan and Kazakhstan, I leave that episode and its implications to the final letter. That really put the cap on national disgrace.

In less than two short months, six years' rebuilding work had crumbled. Even I had stopped any productive activity for my employer. Appointments were difficult to make. All commercial strategies were for survival, not for development. Even Russian companies with whom I was discussing investment plants were not interested in talking to me. Bad news piled upon bad news. There will undoubtedly be more to come. Was this not the stuff of revolution? I thought so. My Russian friends still said no. 'Remember we survived Leningrad and Stalin.'

'Well, okay, but do you want that all the time?' I asked. But I will stop and leave that to history and others to recall.

By now you may have the picture of life in Moscow in the autumn of 1998. Do you want anymore? No? Even we here were getting fed up with the ever-deteriorating situation. We began to accept such difficult conditions as 'normality'. Emerging news about impeding evacuation of one and a half million inhabitants from the northern regions through lack of food and fuel; or governmental requests to the European Union for humanitarian food aid; or further dire predictions on the level of the Rouble – set to plunge to 30 to the $ or worse – suddenly seemed like no news at all. Even the vast jobs cuts around me in companies I knew well appeared a part of 'normal life'. To protect confidentiality, I cannot give the full extent of job losses that came to my attention within the foreign commercial community. Suffice to say that 30% was a good result. The norm was nearer 50%. I even knew of one Western company that went from 272 employees to 71. If by now you are thoroughly depressed, join the club. The economic news from your neck of the woods was little better. It appeared that all of us were now staring at a bleak winter and a more depressing 1999.

So what to do? The situation we were in did little to enhance the spirit. The leaves were all but gone from the trees and seven months of winter stood before. So just like the Golden Casino, I too, held a crisis dinner party with much hilarity and the usual excess of vodka. Eight merry friends gathered to drown our sorrows. Roger and Olga brought the wine, Paul the vodka and Giles and Oxana the whisky. Ton, from Holland only brought his wife. I did the cooking. We ate and drank our fill from dwindling stocks. But we have money and a foreign home. If it all went sour we can escape. We can still buy from the best of the land and find enough to fill our needs. Caviar – both red and black, roast pork, pineapples drowned in vodka was the fare for evening delight. At least the price of caviar has fallen. Down by more than half in $ terms. But up by one fifth in Rouble value. Obviously the previously rich and famous had decided that such a treat was now too much even for them.

While this letter was in final draft, a *Moscow Times* supplement of the 10 October, dealing with the crisis effects on the art-buying habits of the Russian rich and famous, came to hand. All were suffering it said. Not just impoverished Russians on the streets. Something tells me that when you are down to your last $100 million or so, then life can't be all that bad. On the day of national protest on the 7 October, an exclusive group of art collectors was vying for masterpieces at a London art auction. Sotheby's did not fail to notice that this last sale was a more muted affair. In the past such events disposing of Russian art drew crowds. They were part of the 'must be seen' social calendar. People paid vast prices for trinkets based on sand. Even these 'New Russians' knew the bubble had burst. The 'House of Cards' had gone. The article debated as to 'What was Alexander Smolensky the head of SBS-Agro Bank now going to do with his bank-sponsored art centre, which had in recent years acquired some three thousand works of art'. His days of shopping with his 'New Russian' pals at the world's art auctions may now be all but numbered. You will not be surprised that he and his ilk will have no sympathy from this quarter on that account. Certainly his bank's multitude of private investors who failed to retrieve their deposits in the past eight weeks will not thank him for his 'generosity' in storing these works 'on their behalf'.

Maybe he should talk to Viktor Shenderovich, the creator of a popular satirical show – *Kukly*, and exponent of the new-found black Russian humour. In a recent show at a Moscow supper club the loudest laugh was reserved for his pertinent comment: 'A crisis is nothing special for the Russian people. As long as no one is shooting at us, or sending us to labour camps, as long as we can find food for our children, we just live life as we have always lived it.'

I didn't find that funny. Just very, very sad.

Chapter XVIII
After Yeltsin
January 1999

The title of this, my last letter from Russia, would imply the final passing of Boris Nikolaevitch Yeltsin. Had his heart problems finally given up an uneven contest between apparent excesses of vodka, political intrigue and the multitudinous burdens of state? Possibly the first two matters finally affected the latter. But Yeltsin is not yet dead. He is just no longer a functioning head of state in the service of his country. Some would argue he never served his country, only his all-embracing thirst for personal power. He has not yet resigned his office. He is still president of the Russian Federation. Well, certainly at the time of writing. But by the end of October 1998 he and his surrogates had de facto signalled the end of his presidency. True, but again not true. Another Russian riddle? He has risen from his slumbers in the past to confound us all. But this time, that may not be probable, or politically possible. Despite his incumbency in the Kremlin, his period of influence other than a national disruption appears finally past and the country looks to another leader and without doubt another direction.

Of course, he could confound us all. He could sack Primakov – the third such event in recent times. He could even speed up current discussions with President Luka-shenko of Belarus for a mutual country merger and claim a new presidential office. Rumours on both themes continue to swirl. Either event occurring will only increase discussions on his sanity. I leave that for history to record.

The Russian way of solving power conflicts is usually to find the answer before embarking on the implementation of the solution. Unfortunately, few now seeking presidential office have found the key to a seemly and harmonious transfer of power. Thus a period of nirvana and infighting continues for us all in this confusing land till matters are resolved.

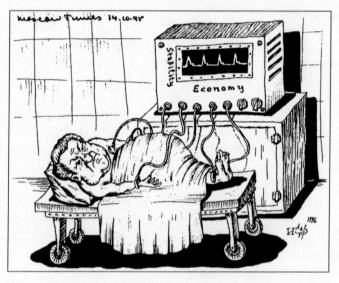

Yeltsin and the economy catch cold again.
The *Moscow Times*, 14 October 1998

Unless a miracle medical cure is found for Yeltsin's apparent condition, we again see a repeat of past days when Soviet leaders were kept in power by wonders of prophylactic science.

Quite who benefits from such deception is unclear. Certainly little good accrues to the Russian people. For Yeltsin and his condition, read also the health and state of the Russian economy and the fragile state of democratic and social development. But then these were always interlinked. Since the demonstrative inability to uphold the dignity of the presidential office during state visits to Uzbekistan and Kazakhstan in October, Yeltsin has become almost an irrelevancy in Russia's political process. Further and persistent bouts of illness forced him to cancel state visits to among other places, Austria and India, as well as visits by foreign heads of state to Russia. Where visits by Keizo Obuchi, the Japanese prime minister, Gerhard Schröder, the new German chancellor or Jiang Zemin, the Chinese leader did take place, his presence was perfunctory. Yeltsin and the Chinese leader met in Boris's hospital suite. The German leader broke the past mould of former Chancellor Kohl, by seeking out opposition and potential future leaders of the land. In public perception Yeltsin now contributes little to national life. He reigns, but his rule is over. On the 5 November 1998, the Russian Constitutional Court declared that Yeltsin could not run for a third term. The debate about his potential candidacy revolved around the central issue that he was first appointed in the days when the Russian Federation had not been formed, thus the question arose: 'Was this first term valid under the current constitution, and could he run again in the year 2000?' As the Russian Federation was deemed the legal successor to the Soviet Union, it was declared that by the year 2000, Yeltsin would have served two terms and could not serve again. Thus in the coming months the process of finding a successor gathers pace. Indeed, increasing comment from leading contenders to the highest office would indicate the race for president has already begun in earnest. In the background an impeachment hearing grinds its poorly publicised course. Few give much hope for its success, but it is an indication of his demise. It might therefore be opportune to dwell a little not only on Yeltsin's legacy, but also what the future holds.

What has been achieved in these last six years since 1993? What have the Russian people gained from their so-called freedom? What is the legacy of six years of so-called market reform? Has a stable foundation been laid for their political, social and economic future? Has the economic bonanza predicted by Professor Layard in his book *The Coming Russian Boom* been initiated? Sadly the consensus I have reached after watching and participating in Russian life for the last four years is essentially negative to all these questions. Of course there are some positives. In any such complex equation in a land of such size and diversity, there will be individual success stories, even in the depths of recession. Moscow as we have seen fares better than most parts of this vast country. But deep in their soul, the bulk of Russian people have hardly progressed from their inertia of past days.

There is one significant matter that has been achieved which does need positive comment. Whoever wins the next presidential contest will probably have power transferred to him or her in a broadly peaceful and essentially constitutional manner. No serious commentators inside or outside Russia expect a revolution or a coup to achieve that. Such potential insurrection may be on hold for a while despite my gloomy predictions in earlier chapters. I still believe that a people's revolution, that will eventually change the status quo, will happen. But now predicted in another form and in another timescale. Bear with me, and I will develop that theme and resulting conclusion.

In the last weekend of October of 1998, I escaped the pressure cooker that is today's post-devaluation normality in Moscow and spent a few days in the Estonian capital – Tallinn. Here I found, despite over sixty years of Communist rule, ordinary people about their business engaged in wonderfully ordinary things. They were rebuilding their charming capital, re-establishing their daily lives, but most important recreating a distinct national identity. The normality of their tasks being conducted with an abundantly evident national purpose and no outward signs of an oppressive or dominating elite. There may be one, but if there is, it was well hidden. How different this all was from Moscow life in the latter part of 1998. Of course any comparison of Russian problems with those in Estonia or other smaller former Communist dominated states will immediately produce a howl of derision by those who will say I am comparing apples with pears. They will tell you that the relative size of the various emerging countries in former Eastern and Central Europe is in proportion to the depth of the problems to be solved. I could in all truth also use the example of Poland, the Czech Republic or Hungary as other comparatives of more rapid progress to meet the aspirations of their citizens. But then we should remember that these places had historic, family and cultural ties to the rest of our part of Western Europe for many a generation. Russia did not. It has chosen the path of isolationism for generations. On that basis, and with the comparable huge geographic size of the Russian Federation itself, critics of my comparison are correct. One could however conclude that the huge physical size of the country and enormous depth of Russian problems equates to a longer timescale of resolution compared to former satellites. Or one could surmise that within that timescale the ever-present patience of the population will eventually snap. But then those thoughts also give rise to some lateral thinking. There could be other ways forward for this formerly great nation. Some will tell you that they have already started. I allude to the gradual break-up of the Federation, and a return to ethnic nationalism. Smaller territories could lead to speedier resolution of pressing fundamental issues. After all with over one hundred ethnic groupings spread across the land and Moscow having lost its moral authority in recent years, these individual peoples may demand their ties to national adherence being severed. That latter thought also raises other relevant and fundamental questions, such as... 'What is national adherence? What is a Russian? Is Russia a land with a single national purpose?' It is not for me to answer these questions. That would be both presumptuous and arrogant in the extreme. I am a foreigner and a transient visitor to their country. It is for the population of this land to do that themselves. The answers are however, to me vital to the understanding of what might happen 'after Yeltsin'. Although I give no answers, please allow some speculation.

In one of many discussions on the future with a diversity of people, I recently asked a well-connected Western friend who understands Russia better than I, a question. He has been in the country for over seven years and is a supporter of both Gerashenko's (governor of the Central Bank) and Primakov's approach to current problems. I asked him, 'What is the purpose of government (in a Russian environment)?' His answer was amazingly unexpected for a person so well versed in the complexity of Russian politics. He replied, 'To create a society for the benefit of the people.' This is what I would have expected to hear in the UK or in the US. But not in Russia, given the traditional political governmental conduct of ignoring the people and using their usual acquiescent behaviour at the altar of political self-interest.

If his answer is correct, then nothing in the air at the moment gives any tangible clue to the resolution of Russia's longer-term problems as far as I am concerned. My friend appears more optimistic. Indeed, he quickly added, probably in mitigation of his earlier answer, 'Russia is in a ten-thousand-metre race, previous governments, since the transition from Communist domination in 1991, have travelled five thousand metres, but in totally the wrong direction with inappropriate policies. At least Primakov has gone back to the starting point and has now moved ten metres on the correct course.' At least we agree that whatever happens, the timescale for rebirth is long and wearisome. There are simply no quick fixes on anyone's horizon.

In the closing days of 1998 and early 1999, I see none of the joy of rebuilding in the faces and demeanour of modern Russians similar to what I found in Estonia in October of last year. Or even a replication of the heady optimism in the earlier part of this year. Past letters written in 1998 described this misplaced expectation. The bubble had burst. Reality had returned. However, a closer look at the consequences of three of the key events of late summer, autumn and early winter of 1998 could give some clues to part of the arduous forward path.

- The economic collapse after the 17 August had brought one fundamental short-term result. It was increasingly evident that a replication of onerous Western capitalist rules and regulations within the corrupt Russian political and business establishment was no longer possible. The benefits of so-called 'market reform' were wanted, but not the attendant Western-style rules and regulations. And certainly not the restrictive continuation of untold pain for the poor and dispossessed living below the official poverty line – now over twenty-five per cent of the total population.[1] At last there were the beginnings of a recognition both inside and outside the country that Russia did not fit the IMF model that had so patently failed in both Russia and in the last year in some countries of South-

---

[1] GOSKomstat.

East Asia. Continual foreign borrowing to pay the bills and feed the indulgences of a select few had done nothing to change the fundamental structure of Russian life for the majority. The nation had begun to tire of the pure unregulated capitalist experiment. It had brought benefits to a few elite, but suffering to the majority. As has been abundantly demonstrated in earlier letters, so-called market reforms as implemented here to date simply were not working. It became clearly evident that another economic direction needed to be sought. Capitalism as we know it was on hold. The ruling elite from former days, and now still in control were not prepared to mend their ways.

• The tragic assassination in late November of Galina Starovoitova, in the stairwell of her St Petersburg apartment block, snuffed out for many the faltering democratic experiment that began with such hope in the days of *Perestroika*. Mrs Starovoitova was recognised by all as a champion of democratic values. Her fight both within and outside the Federal Duma for the cause of individual democratic rights had made her an outspoken, but often a lone voice. She appeared to have gained few friends among her political opponents. Her murder was not a singular event. She was not the first who had suffered thus. But she was a lady of national prominence and that placed extra focus on the sincerity of democratic progress. Her fate was but another sad chapter in the lawless nature of Russian business and politics. Her home city of St Petersburg was worse than most across the land in this respect. Following her death, many voices were heard fearing for the process of democratic reform within Russia itself. Some of these were ordinary members of the public widely quoted in the media, others were prominent politicians of all persuasions. Again it became clear to all that another plank of our Western society – democracy – was seeking a different definition inside the borders of this land.

• As the race for presidential office gathered pace, none of the leading contenders for the post, Alexander Lebed, Yuri Luzhkov, Gennadi Zuganov and Yevgeny Primakov come before the electorate with a classical democratic tradition. Like any Western definitions of capitalism, democracy has a different and only embryonic meaning here. This is no criticism of them. It is simply a statement of their heritage. In their book *Revolution from Above. The Demise of the Soviet System*, the authors,[2] outline in Chapter Seven, with eminent scholarship, the heritage of many of the present political and business leaders. It was the past Soviet system. One paragraph in Chapter Seven caught my eye. It bears repeating here.

> '...The claim that the party-state elite of the Soviet system opted for capitalism seems at first glance implausible. Would the Catholic Church hierarchy suddenly convert to atheism? Would the US Chamber of Commerce call for the nationalisation of private business? Would the Quakers offer a man of the year award to Rambo? Yet the Soviet party-state elite ended up embracing the ideological enemy against which they had always rhetorically battled. When one examines this shift, one finds that it is not only plausible but eminently logical...'

---

[2]David Kotz with Fred Weir.

Thus the past Soviet 'system of privilege' continues today under another name but with the same former players. Again a differing portrait of those in power in both the political and business spheres to that so widely described in the West, or required to manage a Western style of democratic system, emerges. The West continues to describe many of these people as 'reformers'. Those responsible for the management of democracy and capitalism in this modern Russia do not conform to the 'reformee' definition Western commentators have so often given them. They cannot be, they have a completely differing heritage, as have their subjects – the Russian people. Thus transposing our 'ideas' and believing they will work with another mindset is a flawed transaction.

The Russian people are free today. They can and do say what they like, with little fear of persecution. Such past oppressive political burdens are all but gone. But they cannot be given the title or tradition of democrats. They have not as a nation truly demonstrated, to themselves or to others, that they want to be either democrats or capitalists. They have neither had the time or the training to achieve these far-off goals. We call their current economic structure capitalist. But it is not. It takes more than a flick of the switch to achieve such a condition. It requires rules, regulations, checks and balances. They have as yet not achieved a law book to create a framework for this purpose. They have neither had the time, nor the required patience from the West to achieve these goals. But more important, they have rules and an elite society that practises the past pursuit of power and privilege under another guise. I repeat again that if we try to understand the current Russian tragedy with Western definitions we will fail. Thus our judgements based on those definitions are hasty and essentially flawed. It took us many years to arrive at our imperfect systems, yet we deny them the same precious commodity.

At the same time, should we presume that given that time they will accept and embrace the same definition of democracy and capitalism as we do? I do not think so. Certainly not with open arms in the forthcoming generation. Past letters have described an ingrained difference in national and individual behaviour to ours. Little I have seen, even in the younger generation, changes that perception. In late November, I was twice asked to lecture on aspects of British society to second-year students at the Law Faculty at Moscow State University. These young people are the future leaders of their land. Yet they too are fully conversant with the corrupt practices of their elders. They may know the theoretical principles of our Western society, but there were sufficient signs from the question-and-answer session after each of the lectures that they had little clue as to how to gain respect for their state institutions as a basis of their democratic future. Unfortunately I concluded that despite their superficial acceptance of my words, they did not fully understand the democratic message including the resulting individual and collective responsibilities. By those I mean a basic respect for the institutions that manage and govern their system. But why should they, if these institutions do not attract respect by their very behaviour?

Past letters have touched upon many aspects of Russian conduct. Even though those words were written over a four-year period, their validity remains today. The passage of time has not lessened the message. In the context of this letter, some bear repeating again. I am reminded of the words of Professor Gudarov in his book *The Paradox of Russian Reform*. Capitalism, Democracy and Bolshevism are fine ideals in their pure form, but clash when placed into the same brew. Alexander Lebed's words about democracy quoted in a previous letter come to mind. As he said in 1996, going to sleep in a totalitarian system and awaking in a democracy is impossible without time, training, deep understanding and more importantly political desire. My memory is jogged by the split-personality I described in the past letter about the Russian soul. The tsarist trinity of 'Orthodoxy, Autocracy and Nationality' described in a previous chapter and their ever-present use today, came to mind. Like it or not, these people are different to our ideal definition of a modern society. Is it their turbulent history? The inbred nature of a different mindset? The patently distinct system of authority? Or the diverse nature of this vast land? Probably it is all of these and more. Whatever are the divergent themes in their past as well as their future to those we adhere to, we should stop our lecturing and imposition of our ideas. Ever-present Western pomposity ensured an increase of the internal vacuum between 1991 and 1994. Gorbachev and his lack of new ideas did not help either. Major political misjudgement of Russia's intent by the West allowed economic anarchy to gather pace. It continues even today. At the vanguard is the IMF bereft of other ideas than 'Continue to take the Western tablets'. Unfortunately they don't work. The medicine is not accepted by the soul or the system. They at the same time should consider that importation of too many pernicious Western props is just as damaging to their future health. Fast-food restaurants, takeaway pizzas, Hollywood 'culture' and other superficiality do not demonstrate the fundamental mainstays of our culture or civilisation. Living here would give many, who know little better, the impression that they are. Acceptance is fine on both sides. But acceptance must be accompanied by true understanding. The latter is in short supply in Russia of the West and in the West of Russia.

History preaches one important lesson: 'Each must walk their own path of understanding as it suits their circumstances, their heritage and their perception of their own future.' Those who ignore this reality do so at their peril.

That statement applies to individuals, ethnic groupings as well as nations. I am not one who believes in such a thing as a unified global society. Just because our Western financial system tries to bind us together with one set of rules we should not believe it works. It patently does not. Indeed, the difficult financial and economic events of the last year, starting in Japan and Asia and onward through Russia and then on to Brazil has shown that money may be defined in similar ways, but effective solutions to its management are as diverse as the countries affected. Long live cultural, social and ethnic diversity. It is the lifeblood of interest in this fascinating planet. I am no right-wing radical, but it still baffles me how one can place a rural Greek peasant and a Scottish sheep farmer into the same economic and political brew. Yet that is what our European masters think is possible. Economics often fails to understand basic human needs for ethnic identity. At the same time devolution into Scottish, Irish, Welsh and English constituencies is near the top of a British political agenda. Am I missing something? Nothing I have seen in economic models from Adam Smith, Milton Friedman or the IMF acknowledges such human diversity. The same needs for individuality that we in our small part of Europe seek to claim are just as relevant in this vast land. Thus unless we accept the differences in Russia to our world, we fail to understand their diverse past or uncertain future.

With similar thoughts, the central government in Moscow will fail in its quest for national rebirth if it fails to see the same signals within the borders of the current Federation. Reform of sorts may have reached parts of

Moscow, St Petersburg and cities west of the Urals. Democracy, as we understand it may have had a similar journey. But for the millions of citizens in the rural parts of the country, and those east of the Urals, little has changed for them since before the turn of the century. That is except the abundant realisation that they sit upon the true material wealth of the land – the buried minerals, oil and natural gas. They receive nothing of substance from the centre, certainly little from due tax collections. Unfortunately for those far-off citizens, they reside in nearly ninety regions, often sparsely populated. Many are governed as personal fiefdoms, with little regard for national consensus. Their ties to the centre are loosening by the day. Their democratic traditions have even less pedigree than Moscow, St Petersburg or other cities west of the Urals. Although these regional political masters make up the Federation Council, the upper house of Federal government, independent jurisdiction of their future gains ground. They, in those far-flung places, are slowly concluding that self-help from the fruits of the Dacha garden is no longer enough. They too need a framework, a national idea to cling to. It may result in regional adherence and not national. That is itself a conundrum for future resolution. Our cultural, artistic and social history demonstrates that man cannot live from bread alone, he also needs to live with human dignity. He needs more than a basic daily crust. He needs recognition from his peers that he has grown beyond the physical demands of life. It is that which is missing from the current political, social and economic equation in the totality of the Russian Federation today. Unlike other nations, the post Communist national anthem of the Federation has no words. No one can agree what they should be. Possibly for some a minor, but in my opinion a hugely symbolic demonstration of lack of national consensus. It is the failure to search for and find that 'idea' that will drive this land into its component parts. It is that that will be the key to their future 'After Yeltsin'.

The daily purpose of those many Russians I have met over the last forty-five months is today of individual rather than collective survival until the next economic or political crisis. That may not be too far away. The financial mathematics of the Federal budget predicts further national default in 1999 and beyond. But default or no, without a national idea or purpose, continued drift and decline is at hand. It may sound trite and simplistic, but, 'If you do not know in which direction you are going, you will never get to your destination.' How true that is for all who form part of Russia's present troubles. Their horizon still remains survival until the morrow. Next week is an age away. Our Western life has its basic predictability. We live within a well-honed framework. Theirs is one of continual twists and turns. No one in the land knows where tomorrow's surprise is coming from or in what form it will emerge. But one thing is foreseen by all, and that is the unpredictability itself.

Anatoly Chubais is described by many in the West as the arch market reformer. He was the architect of the divisive privatisation of the bulk of Russian industry. In his governmental post he was roundly criticised for selling the 'nation's economic silver' for a song. Many in the land blame him for much of today's economic troubles as a result. It is therefore more than ironic that his elder brother Igor, a distinguished philosopher and sociologist is a sharp critic of the Yeltsin regime. Among his targets for condemnation is the mass privatisation programme conducted by his brother. In a recent interview[3] he said, 'What is reform? It is practically a synonym for a terrible

---

[3]The *Financial Times*, 3 October 1998. This includes extracts from Igor Chubais's recent tract, *Russia in Search of Itself*.

Russian word, anarchy.' He continued, 'The most painful crisis facing society is economic but the most profound, overwhelming all others, is the crisis of ideas... Until Russia has solved the problem of how it looks on itself and the world, it cannot solve any other problem... We understand we are no longer in the Soviet Union. We understand that we are not the Russian empire. We understand that we are not Western Europe. But then who are we? Until we have developed a new identity we cannot conduct serious, reasonable, logical and consistent policies...'

Igor Chubais expressed further fears that if Russian democrats fail in the task of confronting the past then the nation's ideological playing field will be left vacant for the red-brown coalition of Communists and fascists. He argues that fascism arose in post-war Germany in the 1930s precisely because that country lost its sense of identity and grasped an ersatz package of convenient evil national myths. He continued in the interview with the *Financial Times*, 'The same thing is happening with us. Fascism is a reaction to a lack of an identity. It is like a mental asylum where patients think they are Napoleon or Alexander the Great because they do not really know who they are.' Those responsible for the political murder of Igor's philosophical soulmate, Galina Starovoitova, would appear to confirm the pattern he predicts.

Thus I must draw these letters to a close, as once more I am to return earlier than expected to my home. I too am a victim of Russia's economic decline. I too have suffered from the events resulting from the 17 August 1998. At least I can return to a stable home. I have means and a future. Mine is mapped out. What of theirs? Let me therefore not give more economic data or facts but summarise, what I speculate may occur in the next few months and years as a result of my many pages of analysis and comment.

Without the clear development of an accepted national idea, purpose or identity their future journey will be aimless and with no cohesion. Since 1991, they have lurched from one crisis to another because the structure and nature of their future system of government or business has been subject to too many experimental changes. None of those various democratic or often experimental economic models has led to social, political or economic cohesion. None has given a purpose or cohesion to the population. Unless the design appears, the vacuum will be filled, as Igor Chubais predicted, by more sinister forces. In 1917, the vacuum of ideas from tsarist rule allowed Leninist and Marxist ideas to triumph. In 1991, Gorbachev removed the Communist system without replacement. As we have all observed, the result was commercial anarchy. Eight years later, the ideological space has still not been filled. They still fail to find a programme of rebirth built on national consensus. Unfortunately little that I see today gives rise for hope that any of the potential presidential candidates have the moral stature to replicate the position of 'Father to the Nation'. There is no Mandela, Havel or De Gaulle in their leadership. With the complexity of the Russian mindset and some Western help, Yeltsin's unfortunate legacy has left a country bereft of national ideas and with moral, political and economic bankruptcy. Thus:

- The current economics of a weakened Rouble, insufficient tax collection, bank or debt restructuring as well as the printing of money to pay the bills, will only push inherent problems into the future. The complexity of yesterday's legacy is so great and burdensome that today's problems are solved piecemeal. No coherent plan that brings all strands of the equation together has been produced. Again the failure of ideas is evident. Little wonder that the possibly short-term ruling trio of prime minister (Primakov), finance minister (Maslyukov) and Central Bank governor (Gerashenko) ponder the prospects for 1999 and beyond in The *Moscow Times* cartoon of the 6 January. They are not alone, we all seek the same knowledge of what the future holds in this demoralised land.

'For this hangover, let's try a hair of the dog that bit us.'

- Relations with foreign lenders are understandably at an all-time low. Many have withdrawn their participation. In due time some of these overseas institutions will return. But when? One matter our Western financial institutions find impossible to cope with is 'uncertainty'. When high returns dry up they leave. Faster than the time it has taken you to get to this page, they remove their funds to perceived safer havens. The safety they seek is always governed by structures and ideas they claim to understand. Without those ideas being demonstrated here, their investments find other routes to profit.

- A return to partial state control as Primakov appears to advocate, may comfort some. The population needs a goal, not a palliative. They certainly do not need more institutional excuses for state corruption that will inevitably follow. State control will be interpreted by the remaining democratic forces in the country as an assault upon their rights. It will be seen as a return to past days of central planning. That may have been comforting and provided jobs for all. But that was itself a failed experiment.

- With either Lebed or Primakov as potential front runners for presidential office, then a return to a more nationalistic agenda seems assured. Primakov is from the former ruling class. His training would lead one to deduce his adherence to many past political and economic solutions. There may be faint signs that Primakov is different. He does signal some adherence to national duty. That in itself is unusual in past Soviet or Russian leaders. But having just passed his sixty-eighth birthday, he may not have the time. Lebed has openly declared his nationalist credentials. He may rue the day when he declared his political idol as Augusto Pinochet. Neither of these two has yet declared a national idea or purpose. Some may say that Luzhkov has built or restored many symbols in his Moscow fiefdom. The rebuilding of the Cathedral of Christ the Saviour being the most visible on the modern Moscow skyline. If he replicates such vigour on the national stage he may succeed. But who really knows what happens when ultimate power is achieved. All have in one form or other declared 'Russia for the Russians'.

This is code for nationalism in my interpretation.

- Respect for the law starts at the top in any land. Without examples of impeccable behaviour from national leaders, whether implied or actual, then no one should be surprised if those lower down the scale replicate such actions. With forty per cent of the economy being 'black',[4] with politicians, business leaders and all levels of society engaging in what we call corruption, then little will change unless the law shows its teeth. In late November, Primakov began to act by proposing tighter standards for public office. The Duma bills required may take time to pass. But then, the moral pedigree of the Federal Duma itself is subject to more than a little scrutiny. It demands more than a legal framework to succeed. To ensure that happens, the state and its institutions must demonstrate that the 'idea' of integrity benefits all. Privilege must be earned, not purchased. Another problem for future resolution with the concept of national consensus at its heart.

  While Washington convulses with its own impeachment problems and the UK has its minor crisis with the 'Mandelson mortgage affair', it might be useful but ironic to reflect on comparisons of management of these disturbing matters with modern Russian events. I have no intention of commenting on either the US or UK political issues. But what is of importance to our Western understanding of Russia is, that in the West, the 'rule of law' and a desire to maintain constitutional integrity are high on the agenda. It will be a far-off day before such thoughts are spun or practised by the Russian people and politicians alike. Until they do, comparisons between their system and ours are both

---

[4]Vladimir Panskov. State auditor in charge of tax revenues. The *Financial Times*, 27 November 1998.

irrelevant and misplaced and the true latent integrity of the population will not emerge.

- Western talk predicts widespread hunger in the winter of 1998/99. This is well wide of the mark. There is currently enough food for most. But that hides the continuing process of longer-term mismanagement of agriculture. A time bomb is truly ticking. Since 1991, the livestock population in the land has halved as they have been slaughtered for winter food without sufficient progeny. If that continues, and it probably will, the winter of 1999/2000 will be crunch time for food concerns. The fruits of the Dacha garden are no longer sufficient to feed a hungry stomach. While we come to grips with the millennium bug, they will have more humble concerns. This, more than most, stems from a failure of ideas and purpose in the most basic of governmental tasks. The feeding of the daily stomach.

- The Western investment in the Russian Federation (the little that there really is) is based on the hope that a Western financial model is replicated in due time. Post-devaluation pressures have led to a possible theoretical resurgence of Russian manufacturing. The latter neither wants, nor grows within structured rules and regulations. It wants a model that all can manipulate for personal enrichment. The systems clash once more. A national consensus may resolve the issue. Without it, Western investors will collect the shorter straw. Their future in the land is more than uncertain. Economic isolationism thus combines with nationalism.

- As the centre increasingly fails to supply the far-flung regions with either their due returns or a national purpose within which the regions play their part, they will change their allegiance. They will search for their own salvation. They will use their buried treasure – minerals, oil and gas to fund their future. Those regional governors, with less democratic tradition, will seek to protect their personal empires. That will be the source and catalyst for Russia's next revolution. It may not be a bloody affair, but it will be traumatic. But the failure to bring all citizens into a cohesive national framework will inexorably lead to such division.

- In past letters there has been little mention of the rapid growth of tuberculosis and Aids. The collapsing health service has been mentioned, but the crumbling social safety net leaves no place for the suffering, the old, the dispossessed, the pensioner, the abandoned children and the poor. There are more than enough of all of these groups. Their ranks are growing by the day. Will they continue to accept their fate with ever-present equanimity? I doubt it. They will turn to more relevant solutions.

I do not now predict that all these matters will be swift or logical. Their crisis of ideas is truly deep. However, I expect that the Russian Federation we know today will exist in a different form and structure in tomorrow's uncertain world. Of course Russia as a name will survive these many coming traumas. The question for those concerned citizens of the land will be: '...In what form and shape will they emerge from the long dark tunnel of their current existence?'

After nearly four years of close association with this land and its people, what had I learnt about them and their reality? Many pages full of facts, impressions and opinions had attempted to assimilate, analyse and learn about the Russian people and their condition. There is much more I could have written, or examples given. But they would not have added to the message or the trauma. Nor will a single change of leader resolve their current pain in foreseeable time. My personal journey in their land is over. Parts of my grey matter have soaked up a multitude of experiences. I may have described the land and the people in broad-brush accuracy. Daily tribulations may have been observed correctly. Conclusions about their future may have some validity. But did I really know them? Did I truly understand them? Did I comprehend the workings of their complex nature? The simple answer is no. And I probably never will.